AFRICA

World of New Men

ILLUSTRATED

JOHN J. CONSIDINE

DODD, MEAD & COMPANY

NEW YORK   1954

Contents

Illustrations

vii

CENTRAL AND SOUTH AFRICA   FOLLOWING PAGE 150

Costuming is serious business. No Park Avenue matron is prouder of her mink coat than is this Ndekele girl of her colorful triumph in bead work.

Every day through this maternal and child welfare center supported by native funds at Astrida, Ruanda, over 300 mothers pass with their babes.

The goggled ones get ultra-violet rays in Leopoldville.

The traditional ruler in Bantu Africa counts his wealth in wives. The Fon of Bikom in the Cameroons boasted recently more than 600 spouses.

In those two remarkable countries, Ruanda and Urundi, prize long-horned cattle and brilliant group dances are specialties.

Every youngster in new Africa is caught by a fever, the fever to learn.

St. Anne's Cathedral at Brazzaville is described as African Gothic. Its arches are inspired by the prows of the graceful canoes of the Congo.

A little-known side of race-torn South Africa: hundreds of women of good family lead lives of disciplined piety and zeal as Catholic Sisters.

EAST AFRICA   FOLLOWING PAGE 278

Africa counts many fine Christian leaders. Ewald Munseri, of Bukoba, is the able publisher of the first independent newspaper in Tanganyika. Father John Schiff of New York City holds his Luo boys under the spell of his harmonica.

Bishop Laurean Rugambwa talks to Monsignor Grondin the day he ordained Maryknoll's first African priest at Musoma.

Tanganyika's traditionally most valuable crop is sisal, a vegetable fiber important on the world market for making rope and other products.

Section 1

WEST AFRICA

WEST AFRICA

Some 59,000,000 people dwell in West Africa. British West Africa counts over 38,000,000 (Nigeria 31,000,000, Gold Coast 4,300,000, Sierra Leone 2,775,000, Gambia 275,000). The eight divisions of French West Africa plus French Togo count 18,000,000. Little Liberia has 1,700,000. The City of Dakar's Cornish Drive takes us to the westernmost tip of Africa, where the continent is something over a thousand miles from the coast of Brazil.

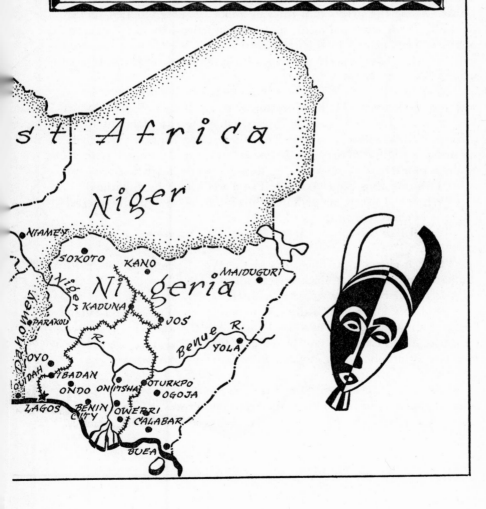

A WOLOF TAKES A WIFE

THE COCKS AND the muezzins vied with each other in waking me up. I watched through the window as the yet unheated sun rose over Dakar. Along the streets thin lines of muffled figures plodded silently to work. Many wore the fez or its local equivalent, for three quarters of the 250,000 people in this capital of French West Africa are Moslem. Small wonder that the Moslem call to prayer, sounded by hoarse-voiced Negro muezzins aloft on many mosques, filled our ears.

After breakfast Father Robert Rummelhardt, my host, took me in tow and we were quickly out into the city. He is a small, wiry White Father, a tried veteran of West Africa, whose words pour out like a torrent. His mountains of ideas and his bulldog courage have made his work as editor of *Afrique Nouvelle,* the weekly of the Catholic Church in French West Africa, a thoroughly dynamic achievement.

"This morning I am taking you to a wedding," he explained.

"Whose?" I asked, immediately intrigued. A wedding is interesting on any continent in the world.

"You'll like the couple—Mark Monet and Angelique Mendy."

"French?"

"French citizens, but members of the Wolof people, a tribe with the handsomest, darkest black skin in all of Africa."

"Is the marriage for richer or poorer?"

"Probably for richer," Father Rummelhardt replied with a laugh. "Mark is the youngest son of a large and successful, and what is known locally as an old Catholic, family. He and his brother have been active in Dakar's Catholic youth movement."

"And Angelique?"

"She is a little dream. She is the next-to-the-youngest child of a similarly outstanding Catholic family. Her father was mayor of Dakar, and Angelique has been a leader in charities and Catholic societies.

4

In her quiet way she can organize not only her fellow Africans, but the local Europeans as well."

"Have you many families like these in Dakar?"

"Not among the Catholics, most of whom are simple workmen. However, a high percentage of Catholics are quite well educated; while few are rich, a considerable number as Government employees or officers in European companies have enough means to live in good homes and follow the ways of cultivated folk of the Western world."

When we reached Dakar's Sacred Heart Church, the building was already filled, and an overflow crowd in the street stood agog at all the finery of the invited guests. I had just found a corner in the sanctuary when there was a burst from the organ, and Angelique with becoming poise walked gracefully down the center aisle. The best of Dakar's African society was on hand. Besides the grownups, there were heavy contingents of teen-agers with the banners of their Catholic youth organizations. These latter gave Angelique their formal salute in loud staccato with much deep feeling. She was their leader; it was evident that they loved her as their little queen.

There were, of course, many of the trappings of European society. Six charming little flower girls in exquisite blue led the procession, and two tiny boy attendants in white brought smiles from everybody, with their unpredictable twists and squirms. As they reached the sanctuary rail, one of the two boys ran quite unceremoniously off to the side to his young mother, a handsome, smartly dressed woman, who with a chuckle gathered him into her arms. Following the bride in her cloud of white, came six bridesmaids, also in blue.

Bishop Guibert celebrated the Nuptial Mass; it was a *missa recitativa*, in which the congregation participated with evidence of long practice. After tying the knot, the bishop delivered a fatherly exhortation, making both bride and groom feel uncomfortable by his reference to their fine leadership. It pleased the congregation immensely.

The Mass at an end, a great concourse of brothers, sisters, fathers, mothers, uncles, aunts, and cousins poured into the sacristy to salute His Excellency and to witness the signing of the record. The men were in morning clothes; the women tastefully dressed in gowns of singular grace and richness. The natural elegance of the Wolof women of Dakar, and their exceptional flair in matters of clothes, make this city the undisputed fashion capital of West Africa. Wolofs are a debonair and versatile people with an unerring sense of color and style.

"You cannot bully these women into buying clothes that don't measure up to their high standards of taste and quality," explained a merchant in Dakar.

"You must come to the wedding reception," insisted one of the young men of the family after the Mass, and I soon found myself in a large hall where great, candied ornaments decorated the long tables. That evening I was a guest of Bishop Guibert at dinner, and one of these huge ornaments was our dessert, a gift of the married couple. Only then did I discover that the ornaments were made of peanut brittle. Dakar is a great center for peanuts, not for eating but for the extraction of oil. I saw huge mountains of peanuts in town; a quarter of a million tons were shipped out of Dakar during the month of my visit. Great areas of West Africa are peanut country.

Among the hundreds of guests present at the reception were some scores of Moslems. Their women folk wore ornate native garb of richly flowing robes, colorful kerchiefs on their heads, their necks and arms heavy with a profusion of hammered gold and silver necklaces and bracelets.

Some of the close friends of the family were very interesting. There were, for instance, Mr. and Mrs. Faye. Mr. Faye, a handsome specimen of Wolof manhood, is a convert from Moslemism. Mrs. Faye, an unassuming but very intelligent member of Dakar's smart set, has two brothers who are Trappist monks—one in the new Trappist monastery in the French Cameroons, and the other in France.

Present also was Martha Kpakpo, a young lady from Dahomey, French West Africa. She was in her third year in medical school in Dakar and due to go to Paris for a doctorate in medicine. Martha is one of the Fon people of Dahomey.

"You'll feel quite alone in Paris," I ventured.

"Oh, no!" replied Martha. "There are five hundred students from West Africa in Paris at present."

I found Mark and Angelique wreathed in smiles when I joined the reception line and offered them my congratulations. I was just one more face at a big party, but this young man and young lady, unknown to me until a few hours previously, loomed very large in my life at that moment. What a wonderful place this so-called Dark Continent would be, I said to myself, if it could be populated with Marks and Angeliques, who might be successful in their home life, faithful in their religious life, happy in their communities, industrious in earning their livelihood, and able in the public affairs of their nation. Was it too much to expect of Africa? More important people than I were asking this question.

The city of Dakar is the hub of France's "Black Africa." At first glance it is as French as Paris. Along the noisy downtown streets jammed with countless French automobiles are luxury shops, sidewalk cafes, splendid new French-style buildings of concrete and glass, with Arabic or African touches in their architecture out of respect for the locale.

Only a tiny fraction of the people in French West Africa are white, but everybody who can read and write is a Frenchman. In the last French elections three million out of a possible eight million West African voters elected 17 African Deputies and 20 African Senators to the French Parliament that sits in Paris.

Dakar has one of the best universities in Africa today and in its entire operation no distinction of race is made. Mark and Angelique when they went to school sat side by side with white children and studied the same textbooks that are used in Paris. Angelique's school, the Institut Sainte-Jeanne d'Arc, conducted by the Sisters of St. Joseph of Cluny, would rank high among the best girls' colleges of France. It was quite charming at the wedding reception to see a little white girl put her arms about Angelique and kiss her lovingly. "She's the daughter of a French school companion of Angelique who married some years ago," a companion told me.

In Dakar restaurants a turbaned Senegalese and his friends will sit at a table next to white businessmen. Angelique goes into any shop in town, chats with white acquaintances as she buys her millinery. Let's not be deceived—there are dislikes and rivalries and some of this is racial, but French Africa has no color bar.

Already a certain amount of self-government has been granted to French African territories (no longer called colonies). After World War II, France saw the hand-writing on the wall and on October 27, 1946, profoundly modified its constitution by providing for the coalescence of all its colonies into a Greater France, to be known as the French Union. Article VIII of the Constitution determines the central organs of the French Union as three: (1) The Presidency, always to be filled by the President of the European French Republic; (2) The High Council, which eventually will possess representatives from France and all the Associated States in Africa and Asia; (3) The Assembly, a purely consultative body with delegates from all of the States—each of which, contrary to the present situation, will possess almost complete local autonomy.

In governing French Africa, the previously effective "Native code" and "Native justice" have been abolished, and now the French penal code is in vogue. Very important was the abolition of forced labor. The original law itself was not severe: it permitted, in place of the payment of a head tax, the requisitioning of an adult male for ten days work a year on public works not more than three miles from the worker's home. However, official records show that, between 1920 and 1930, over 180,000 able-bodied men in the prime of life were transported hundreds of miles from home not only for public works, but for private commercial enterprises. For considerable lengths of time, those men were thus torn from family, marriage, their villages and their fields. When Richard Brunot, as Governor of the Ivory Coast, denounced this forced labor and insisted on voluntary labor, he was recalled to France and disgraced.[1]

One fruit of the new Constitution is the Lamine Gueye Law, which provides equal salaries for French and African employees of the Government in West Africa. I met the tall, exceedingly keen Moslem, Monsieur Lamine Gueye, mayor of Dakar, who was clever enough to secure such an interpretation of this basic law that Moslem members of the Government now receive a special allowance for each wife. Thus we witness the spectacle of Frenchmen officially paying a premium to polygamous employees. Father Rummelhardt in *Afrique Nouvelle,* and the Catholic hierarchy of French Africa in a statement in October, 1952, protested vehemently, but to no avail.

What is the reaction in Africa to these liberation steps by France? Certainly they have improved immensely the relationship between the homeland and Africa. Instead of writing on the walls the inscription

[1] See page 373 for this and following footnote references.

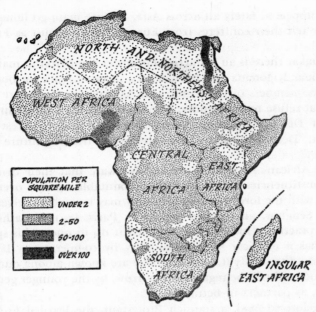

THE DISTRIBUTION OF AFRICA'S PEOPLES

Population statistics for the countries of Africa will be found in Appendix A at the end of the book. By sections the population is as follows:

NORTH AND NORTHEAST AFRICA	70,752,000	34.2%
WEST AFRICA	58,967,369	28.5%
CENTRAL AFRICA	34,302,784	16.5%
SOUTH AFRICA	19,448,700	9.4%
EAST AFRICA	18,317,689	9.0%
INSULAR EAST AFRICA	4,916,800	2.4%
TOTAL POPULATION	206,705,342	100%

Apart from the Egyptian section of the Nile valley, where average density rises to over 500 per square mile, even the most attractive agricultural lands of Africa possess a low density. Only the continent of Australia ranks lower. The more populous areas are: *North and Northeast Africa:* the Mediterranean fringe from Tunisia westwards; the Lower Nile; the Plateau of Ethiopia. *West Africa:* the coastal countries from British Gambia to Nigeria with hinterland density in Nigeria. *Central Africa:* the mouth of the Congo; Ruanda-Urundi; the mining areas. *South Africa:* the mining areas; the Eastern littoral as far as Cape Town. *East Africa:* the Great Lakes region; the Eastern littoral from Mombasa south.

Climatic aridity remains the principal barrier to settlement.

that has appeared lately all across Asia, "White man, go home!" Africans now tell their confreres from Europe, "We are just as French as you are."

In Dakar there is an attractive *Foyer des Eurafricains,* maintained by Monsieur Rigonaux and his wife as a meeting place for both black and white members of the Eurafrican Association. Yet there are elements that refuse to be friendly. A professor at the Lycee Van Vollenhoven of Dakar, largest secondary school in French West Africa, remarked, "Despite all that we do here, we are training future enemies of France!"

The Africans in politics are keenly aware that their demanding Negro constituencies will hold them accountable for any over-concessive pact with the foreigner to which they may make themselves a part. Leopold Senghor, an African deputy in Paris, born a Catholic but now not practicing his religion, summed it up in one of his speeches: "Africa has a mystical faith in equality by co-operation. If you of France refuse to satisfy it, we who today are known among our own as men of goodwill will be regarded tomorrow, by the younger generation of Africa, as partners in betrayal."

Theodore Monod, a staunch Protestant, the learned French Director of the celebrated I.F.A.N. of Dakar (the *Institut Francais d'Afrique Noire,* an admirable project to interest the African in his own culture) recognizes France's grave responsibility in the matter. "The French Union," he states, "will remain a vain phrase if it is not a true 'symbiosis.' I deliberately employ the technical term that designates 'the intimate and constant association of two organisms under conditions which can be considered as assuring them reciprocal benefits,' in opposition to 'commensalism' or to 'parasitism' in which the profit is essentially unilateral." [2]

In the heyday of colonialism, the administrators carried on an unending dispute as to which should be their basic principle in dealing with subject peoples—that of assimilation or that of association, called also indirect rule. In the popular mind, assimilation is linked with France, and association with Great Britain. Robert Delavignette declares that the day of a clearcut pathway leading either to making the African completely a Frenchman, or to leaving him completely a traditional African, is gone forever. "A new fact has come into existence—" says Delavignette, "an African world which has reacted to Europe and which is creating a regime proper to itself, in administration as in everything else. This new African world forces us to be aware of what it wants and to devise laws that will not harm its interests." [3]

The home of the more successful French African evolué is in transition, with much about it that is African but with much that is French if the family has connections with France. On the day after the wedding, Father Rummelhardt took me after dinner to the Medina section of Dakar, which is strongly African and Moslem. On a street lined with neat but modest houses built in European style, we entered a gate, and I found myself the guest of the Faye family, whom we had met the day before at the reception.

"These people are of the same social circle as the Monet and Mendy families," explained Father Rummelhardt. "Mark and Angelique will set up a home something like this."

The house had five rooms. There was a small garden in the rear, and beyond the garden was a cook shed. A maid servant answered our knock, and later I noticed that she enjoyed an easy familiarity in the family, evidently doing a share in raising the children. These were two at the moment: John, aged three, and tiny Marie Regina, six months old.

Husband and wife sat with us in the parlor, Mrs. Faye holding Marie Regina, who was soon engrossed with the huge beads of the missionary's rosary. I quickly discovered that the young couple had a delightful sense of humor. Father Rummelhardt as an editor was very much a man about town in Dakar, and Mr. Faye as an official in the Government was likewise in the main stream of Dakar life. After piquant details on the previous day's wedding, the conversation turned to local politics, to the peanut crop, to Marie Regina's first tooth.

"Are you a soccer fan?" I asked Mr. Faye. We had just passed the field nearby, where thousands watched and from which a roar had gone up worthy of the Yale Bowl as a goal was made.

"Very much so!" replied the young man, with a huge grin. "I played forward on the soccer team at St. Joseph's when I was at school."

The main subject of discussion, however, was Mr. Faye's visit to Europe, from which he had just returned. He had been to Rome, had seen the Holy Father, had stopped at length in Paris, and had gone to Lourdes. On the mantel was a replica of the Grotto of

Lourdes, and on Marie Regina's wrist dangled a tiny bracelet with a Lourdes medal, likewise a souvenir of the journey.

"I dedicated my whole family to Our Lady while at the shrine," the husband explained with engaging simplicity.

After refreshments, Mr. Faye showed us his achievements in the garden. He had built an attractive paved walk and planted several trees. "It will have real charm the next time you call," he promised as we took our leave.

Have people such as these the capacity to build a modern African world for themselves? Currently the enlightened and well-informed men and women on the continent are but a tiny fragment of the whole. What will happen when they become numerous?

"One thing is certain," commented Father Rummelhardt, "they are deeply in earnest in their determination to have an Africa of their own."

Chapter 2

AGOLIAGBO AND THE MEN OF TOMORROW

WITHIN THE HIGH hedge that fenced his little world, Agoliagbo was still a monarch. He advanced toward Bishop Steinmetz and me, smiling and expansive, though doddering and tremulous. He wore a peculiar silver-and-ivory lip rest that kept his lips apart, and thus he breathed through his mouth rather than his nose. Evidently there was no counting of calories in his life: as he dropped his robe from his shoulders, he revealed great fat folds of flesh.

With true royal paternalism he took me by the hand and led me to a chair. About him were gathered some fifty fetishers and dancers, in colorful costumes. An orchestra of ten musicians played with small drums and other instruments and a group of dancers lightly tripped their routines. Then players with heavier drums and instruments appeared, and a larger troupe of dancers with much more complicated movements performed with gravity and decorum and evident pride in their profession.

Bishop Steinmetz had brought me to storied Abomey, ancient capital of the mighty rulers of Dahomey, once one of the most powerful nations of Africa, and now a division of French West Africa a thousand miles from Dakar. The Bishop arrived in Dahomey as a young priest in 1892, the year of the defeat of the mighty Behanzin.

In the summer of 1892 Behanzin said boldly to the French Governor: "When you first came, we were not sure that we could fight your kind of war; now we know we can. I have so many men that they are like the waters that flow to the sea. I am the king of the blacks. The whites will have nothing to say about what I shall do." But between August and November of that year, the boaster was soundly whipped by the French.

In Abomey, the royal palace occupied grounds 130 acres in extent. We saw the remnants of the huge wall and the great moat that surrounded it. For every great ceremony, hundreds of slaves were killed, their blood spilled on the ground, their heads displayed along the wall, their bodies thrown into the dry moat for the vultures. The king's chamber was paved with enemies' skulls; a stool that the bishop pointed out to me had the skull of a chief as foot knob for each of its four legs. Quite categoric treatment was meted out to enemies by all the Dahomean kings and everywhere skulls were employed to express subjugation and disdain.

Dahomey, it will be remembered, was the home of the celebrated female regiments, known as the Amazons, who put fear into every tribe in West Africa. A fourth of the total female population was under arms. These women wore distinctive uniforms and were anything but ladylike; their specialty was to capture the enemy alive and indulge in wild cannibalistic orgies in the course of doing away with him.

This record of cruelties is often used as an argument to prove the inferiority of the African. "But what of the cruelties of the Spanish civil war?" remarked a gentleman with whom I discussed this point. "What of the cruelties of certain regiments of German Nazis and Russian Reds? Do all these indicate an intrinsic character defect, as men argue against the Negro?"

Today Dahomey's mighty past is dead. That morning in Abomey, the Bishop and I visited Behanzin's tomb. A number of his descendants are now Christian, and Bishop Steinmetz asked first for Robert, his son, and then Madeleine, his daughter, but neither was around. Unrecognized by the smaller fry, His Excellency strode unperturbedly through a series of courts toward the tomb, until at one point a mischievous girl, as she saw us approach, locked a passage gate and ran away. With sound and fury the tall, bearded bishop shouted at the little imp to come back and let us through. Finally she relented, lifted the hook, and scampered off again. It was a delightfully disarming little incident to have occur at the shrine of a bloodthirsty African potentate.

Behanzin's tomb is a circular edifice with a great grass roof that reaches down within two feet of the ground. We crawled under this and came to a white-walled hall, in the center of which stood the coffin, draped in green silk. As is customary at such tombs, several former

wives sat about as if on guard. His Excellency had a friendly word
with them and then the two of us said a prayer for the grim warrior's
soul.

Now we were at the unofficial court of Agoliagbo, the rightful successor to Behanzin, whom the French had never permitted to mount
his throne. The entertainment ended and the royal order called for
beer. Three glasses were brought and they were so thick with dust that
the Bishop and I could see the earthy particles mount to the top of
the liquid as it was poured. When we lifted our glasses, the major-
domo, an enormous fellow, opened an umbrella and gave forth a
grunting shout. The king's wives, who squatted nearby, touched the
ground with their foreheads. The umbrella hid His Majesty from us;
the other folk turned their backs. After a moment of theatrical silence,
the king and his glass appeared again—the glass empty, for His Majesty had quaffed.

Conversation ensued. A male attendant on his knees acted as
liaison between the king and the bishop, because direct address would
have been improper. One of the king's wives knelt near him, holding
a silver spit bowl with a little earth in it, into which he expectorated
from time to time.

What did we talk about? Our subjects were all pre-conquest; it
was of the days that had been. The king called up an old man to show
us his costume, with its leather cuirass and ornate bodice, which the
old man's father had worn as a soldier of Behanzin. Then the king
pointed out the costumes of some of the women who, though never
themselves serving as Amazons, wore vestiges of the Amazon regalia.
They carried long daggers in ornate sheaths, and wore rich silver arm
and neck pieces.

"Old Agoliagbo lives with his yesterdays," observed Bishop Steinmetz as we returned home. "How different he is from most of his
countrymen, who have forgotten their king as completely as France
has moved on from Napoleon!"

"The Dahomeans are among the leaders in French West Africa,
are they not?" I observed.

"Yes," replied the bishop. "I see no difference between them and
the whites, except in the color of their skin. The farmers here are
like the farmers of France, hard-working, thrifty, laboring for their
families and fighting for a good price for their crops."

The Bishop's remarks on his people reminded me of one of his distinguished missionaries, Father Aupiais, who was one of the pioneers in the fight for the recognition of the African. His great theses were: Race prejudice is a cancer in the body of Africa and the modern world; We must recognize the good that is to be found in primitive society as well as the bad—the hidden treasures of native culture, morality and spiritual values. His favorite saying to his Africans was, "You are men; you must be governed as men, and you must conduct yourselves as men." [1] Toward the end of his career Father Aupiais was elected by the Dahomeans to represent them in the National Assembly in Paris.

Bishop Steinmetz, my host that day, was one of the great pioneer figures of French West Africa. In 1950, at the age of eighty-three, he celebrated his sixtieth anniversary of ordination and over half a century of service on this West African coast, notorious as the dread "White Man's Grave." Local admirers by thousands turned out with tom-toms and joined the Government officials in honoring him. At each round of a sixty-gun salute, the great crowd roared, "Long live our *daga,* our beloved chief!" A French Government representative said in his address, "You are the true conqueror of Dahomey—you and your missionaries who for over half a century have worked to pacify, civilize, and Christianize this land."

His Excellency passed away in 1952.[2] He had accomplished well his task of Christianizing. Today coastal Dahomey counts one in every eight of its inhabitants a member of the Church. Thus it ranks with the best areas in French West Africa. Catholics in the coastal region of French West Africa total 560,000, which is 6% of the total population. This is not high as averages go in Bantu Africa, but represents a substantial Christian achievement.

The year 1842 witnessed the first effort to organize Catholic missionary forces for West Africa. Then it came through the United States. Catholic Negro-American freed slaves in one of the colonies in Liberia wrote to the Holy Father for a priest. Pope Gregory XVI asked the bishop of New York and the bishop of Philadelphia each to supply a priest. A third volunteer—a layman—came from Baltimore. Thus were enlisted the extraordinary trio who sailed from Baltimore for West Africa on December 21, 1841.[3]

The priest from New York was Father John Kelly, of County

Tyrone, Ireland. The priest from Philadelphia was Father Edward
Barron of a distinguished Anglo-Irish family of County Waterford,
Ireland. The third member of the group was a lay catechist, Dennis
Pindar, born in County Cork, Ireland. He had come to Baltimore in
his early teens and was a young man of nineteen when he volunteered
for West Africa.

On February 6, 1842, the first public Mass was celebrated at Cape
Palmas, at the eastern end of the Liberian coast. Realizing that he
must find laborers, Father Barron sailed in April for the United States
and Europe. In October the Holy See, in order that he might more
effectively fulfill his task, made him a titular bishop. There were still
no missionaries for his field, but soon occurred the dramatic incident
of the shrine of Our Lady of Victories in Paris.

A Jewish convert, Francis Mary Libermann, had founded in
France a little missionary society and had a number of candidates
ready—but had no mission field.[4] Father Libermann made a pilgrimage to Our Lady of Victories and, as he left the altar after Mass, he
met his good friend the pastor, Abbe Desgenettes.

"Mon pere," said Libermann, "we are greatly embarrassed."

"Why, how is that?"

"We have no mission field!"

The good pastor sympathized with his visitor, but Father Libermann could only return to his motherhouse in the country, his problem still unsolved.

Early the next morning, another visitor was announced to Pere
Desgenettes—a Bishop Barron from America.

"I am charged with the Vicariate of the Two Guineas, in West
Africa," the bishop stated, "but I can find no missionaries. May I
celebrate Mass here?"

"Why, of course, Your Excellency."

Bishop Barron was on the altar before the busy Abbe Desgenettes
bethought himself of the visitor's remark. "No missionaries? No missionaries! No missionaries! Then he's the man for Father Libermann!"

So it was that in September, 1843, a mission band of seven members of Father Libermann's community, the Fathers of the Holy Heart
of Mary, sailed for Africa. A year later, five of Father Libermann's
seven missionaries had died, one had returned to France, one remained

in Africa. In addition, Dennis Pindar had died, and Father Kelly, after nursing them all, had returned to New York. Bishop Barron, broken, presented his resignation to the Holy See. He came back to America and died in 1854, serving the sick in a yellow-fever epidemic in Savannah, Georgia.

Libermann's zeal put new missionaries into the field. In 1848, his community was fused into the Congregation of the Holy Ghost, with Father Libermann as superior of the new, joint society. Thus was launched the brilliant career of the first of the three great missionary societies laboring today in West Africa.

The second of these three institutes is the Society of African Missionaries. In 1856, Bishop de Marion Bresillac, after twenty years in India, was permitted by the Holy See to return to France and found a body of priests to serve neglected Africa. With five companions, the bishop sailed for West Africa.

In May, 1859, the ship arrived at Freetown, Sierra Leone. By the end of June—forty-two days later—five of the band of six, including the bishop, were dead. The sixth priest returned home. But the Society of African Missionaries filled the ranks of the fallen. The tradition of Bishop de Marion Bresillac has made courage a commonplace of this community in West Africa.

The third of the three major missionary societies at work in West Africa is that of the White Fathers. They were founded in 1870, in North Africa, by Cardinal Lavigerie, who from the beginning had fixed his vision on the distant Sudan beyond the vast Sahara.[5] In 1876, His Eminence chose three young missionaries—Fathers Paulmier, Bouchard, and Menoret—organized for them a special caravan of camels, and started them on their eight-week journey across the Sahara to far-famed Timbuktu. On the first of April, good news came of their progress. But then on April 13 (Holy Thursday), 1876, news reached His Eminence in Algiers that his three young apostles had been murdered by Tuaregs near Al-Golea. On Easter Monday, the entire community of White Fathers gathered at Algiers to sing, not the "De Profundis," but the "Te Deum." The murdered three were the young society's first martyrs.

The Cardinal was not to be cheated; West Africa was not to be without missionaries. Five years later three new young priests were chosen—Fathers Richard, Morat, and Pouplard—another caravan was organized, and the chosen ones moved toward the desert and mysterious Timbuktu. Beyond the outpost of Rhadames, the travelers were set upon and slain. There was another "Te Deum" in Algiers.

The third mission band for Timbuktu left, not from North Africa but from Dakar, and moved up the Senegal River. It reached Timbuktu, the city of its dreams, on May 21, 1895. The objective was gained; but by today, Timbuktu has lost much of its importance, and the major centers of the White Fathers are elsewhere. Timbuktu, remains, however, a symbol of sacrifice of the apostolic trail makers.

In much of interior French West Africa the main occupation is livestock raising. Mediterranean Africa has influenced this area and the culture is Arabic and Moslem. Here all the large, impressive empires of West Africa have had their day—the Ghana, Mandingo and Songhai regimes, which followed each other from about the year 1000 A.D. to beyond 1500 A.D. Before the white man came, this was the most important part of West Africa.

Thus French West Africa is a land of contrasts. The sharp difference between north and south applies to the fortunes of Christianity as well as all else. While in the south Catholics are six per cent of the population, in the north they are less than one per cent, a little flock of 80,000 scattered from the grim wastes of Mauretania to the shores of Lake Chad, half the distance across the continent.

Unpromising for the Faith though this great area is, its unresponsive millions, its forbidding thorn scrub, its endless sands possess a strong allure. On a previous visit to West Africa, I was companion of three Frenchmen in a journey across the Sahara. It was an unforgettable experience to camp in the desert of deserts, the Tanezrouft, which is the Sahara's classic heart.

I recall an evening when, under a gentle moon, I left our cabin and surveyed the horizon. It was a single line, a perfect circle, everywhere flat, limitless sand meeting the limitless sky. The silence was unearthly. No wind moved the leaves, for there were no leaves. No birds sang, for there were no birds. No water eddied or tapped, for there was no water. No beast took fright and scurried in the darkness, because for hundreds of miles there were no beasts. Only the quintessence of desert: sand under foot, sky overhead. Here was solitude.

For almost a century men have talked of a Trans-Saharan Railroad but as yet the costly financing has not been forthcoming for the

2,500 miles of roadbed. During my recent visit I heard of plans for air-conditioned express trains from the Mediterranean to Dakar in forty-eight hours. Without such a carrier to haul the bulk freight out of the area, all plans for the development of interior Africa remain but idle dreams.

A rail line from Dakar to Bamako is the main entrance to the great northland. The Niger River curls in a huge arc through the area before entering British Nigeria and flowing to the sea. From Bamako to Timbuktu the river has annual floods as heavy as those of the Nile; hence here is a potential Egypt with millions of acres of crops. Beyond Bamako the French have built the great Samsanding Dam that supplies the waters of the Niger to 1,200 miles of canals throughout an area as large as Switzerland. The dead sands have turned green and important crops of rice and cotton are in production. Some forty thousand persons had already moved into the area by 1954. Beyond the Niger in Western Sudan, ranching possibilities are declared to be as great as those of the Argentine and the Australian downs. Better communications are the key to development.

Below the arc of the Niger important developments are in progress in Bobo Dioulasso and Wagadugu, both of which communities are linked by rail with Abidjan, the port of the Ivory Coast. Bobo is now a city of 50,000 and rapidly growing. These two cities hold special interest for us since they represent the two spots in the entire north where Christianity has registered some small victories. Each is the residence of a missionary bishop who directs the work of the White Fathers. In each case the Christian community numbers some 25,000.

"To a modest degree we have succeeded in the Upper Volta," explains Bishop Dupont of Bobo. "True, interior West Africa continues to be a backward area. I have in my vicariate no less than a hundred thousand women whose only clothing is still a few leaves torn from a nearby tree. It is pitiful to watch a file of these women, each with a huge load of wood on her head, attempt to throw themselves in the dust to render the required salute to a passing chief, the while supporting their heavy loads."

Recently the Governor of Upper Volta officially appointed as surgeon of the hospital at Bobo, Mother Anne Elizabeth of the White Sisters. She is an example of the high quality missionary staff that is at work in this area. Mother Anne Elizabeth is a Hollander who was a convert at the age of twenty-nine. At the University of Leyden she was a school companion of Queen Juliana; she spent the war years as a Red Cross doctor in Holland.

At Wagadugu a distinguished male doctor directs the mission clinic that has become celebrated throughout West Africa. In 1924 when this man secured his diploma in medicine he was not satisfied; he wanted also to become a priest and missionary and thus he entered the White Fathers. Today Father Goarnisson is particularly known for his eye work, especially his delicate operations for cataract and other grave afflictions performed for the humble children of the African bush.

At the time of my stay in Wagadugu, Father Goarnisson had the assistance of a highly trained Canadian White Sister, Sister Saint Radegonde, who was likewise a specialist in eye maladies, a particular plague of the region. On the morning of my visit Sister Saint Radegonde had a huge African gentleman on the operating table from whose eye she had just cut a cataract.

Father Goarnisson has had notable success in building a staff of skilled workers among the African Sisters of the Immaculate Conception, who with the White Sisters serve as trained nurses and laboratory technicians. In 1953 this staff under Father Goarnisson cared for some 80,000 patients.

It is interesting to note that from these two relatively remote areas the native personnel in French West Africa has received strong impetus. This is due in great part to the outstanding qualities of the Mossi people, a gifted tribe of fetishist Africa that dwells here in an area under strong Moslem influence. All French West Africa has but 70 African priests. There is one African bishop, His Excellency Prosper Dodds of an old family of St. Louis, above Dakar. He rules the Vicariate of Ziguinchor in Senegal. A third of the priests are in Dahomey, products of the celebrated seminary of Ouidah. A score among the seventy are from the Mossi people. From this area also came a substantial share of the native Sisters of French West Africa— 85 out of the 210 in 1953.

Most remarkable at Wagadugu was the singing of the Mossi schoolboys. Father Edward, a trained musician, had discovered some beautiful voices, had placed them and cultivated them, a thing unheard of in these parts, and the results he had obtained were astounding. His selected schola of twelve rendered *O quam glorificata* for me and it was heavenly.

Then two little youngsters of fifteen, Joseph Bambemba and Gabriel Wemba, came in with the dust of the football field still on them, Joseph with a dirty rag tied over a cut on his leg. With no preliminaries Father Edward launched the pair into a two part rendition of a charming old French song, *"L'Ange et l'Ame"*—"The Angel and the Soul."

"Those youngsters' voices make me weep," said one of the priests with feeling. "Some day our Mossi will play an important role in the new Africa."

"They have already begun to play this role," explained Bishop Dupont. "Only a few years ago Frenchmen at the World's Fair at Paris gazed on the exotic sight of a West African village actually inhabited by authentic 'savages' from the Upper Volta. Now the authentic West Africans in Paris are the parliamentary representatives at the Palais Bourbon! Citizenship, with election of local African representatives, can prove of first importance to our peoples."

Certainly in Bishop Dupont's mind as he spoke was a scene that took place before the faculty of medicine at the University of Paris in December, 1952. Four candidates presented themselves for the doctorate in medicine. Three of the candidates, all of France, received their diplomas. Then the name of the fourth was called: "Monsieur Joseph Conombo, deputy to the National Assembly from the Upper Volta, French West Africa."

A young man with a vivid smile and flashing white teeth stepped forward. He was clad in a natty suit and wore heavy, horn-rimmed glasses. The dean of the faculty, Monsieur Binet, rose and turned, not toward the candidate, but toward a cluster of White Fathers and White Sisters seated among the auditors.

"My first word," the dean said, "must be one of thanks and appreciation to you for all that you have done in forming this candidate, and for all that you are doing for the health of the people of the Upper Volta, a country particularly scourged with disease."

He then turned toward Joseph Conombo and addressed him: "I wish you to know how happy I am today to present you with a State diploma of doctor in medicine, the first to be accorded in Paris to an originaire of the Upper Volta. I read with pleasure in the opening lines of your thesis those words, 'To heal, what a victory, what a conquest!' I am deeply impressed by the spirit of dedication that certainly dwells behind them."

Joseph Conombo, of the Mossi tribe, had been a primary-school lad at the mission in Wagadugu. As a young man, he was elected deputy of the Upper Volta to the National Assembly in Paris and, while serving his term, completed his university studies and thus became a full-fledged doctor of medicine. He had gone first to Dakar and had become what is called an African medical practitioner. During the war he was a medical aid in France and won the Croix de Guerre. Elected to Paris in 1949, he was able to become the first doctor among the Mossi people. Significantly his thesis was titled, "Modern Treatments for Sleeping Sickness." In December of 1953 Joseph was the representative of French West Africa at the African Congress of Catholic Laity held at Kampala in Uganda. His address was one of the notable contributions to the Congress.

Another Mossi, Christopher Kalenzaga, a senator in Paris from Upper Volta, recently made a pilgrimage to the Holy Land. "What struck me most in Palestine," he writes,[6] "is to find that history and tradition have preserved for us such vivid memories of the earthly life of Christ. You would say that the God-Man must have lived there as recently as a century ago. Everything speak of Him. First comes Bethlehem, with the Basilica of the Nativity covering the grotto where He was born. Then there is Galilee, sweet Galilee, where every locality recalls an episode in His life or His miracles. Finally, there is Jerusalem with its holy places of sad renown: the Garden of Gethsemane, the foundations of the palaces of Caiphus and Pilate; above all, the hill of Golgotha, where the Basilica of the Holy Sepulcher encloses Our Lord's tomb. I hope that Christians can organize pilgrimages to Jerusalem as our Moslem friends have done for Mecca."

Those thatched huts of the Upper Volta's savanna country take on for us the allure of Abraham Lincoln's log-cabin birthplace, as we discover even a very few of the sons of West Africa's mud houses who have vaulted the huge culture span and, as good Christians, have won places for themselves in life's mainstream of our day.

What a strange antediluvian figure Agoliagbo cuts alongside of Joseph Conombo and his confreres!

Chapter 3

THE OBSTACLE RACE

THE NIGHT WAS delightfully silent. Father Fischer and I sat on the little porch of his mission in French Togoland and gazed out on the empty, open fields bathed in silver by the huge full moon.

From off in the distance, lightly pulsing along the air waves, came the rhythmic tum-tum! tum-tum! of native drums.

"A perfect night for dancing," remarked the old missionary.

"Is it your biggest problem?" I asked.

"I used to think so," replied Father Fischer. We were both talking in low voices as if we feared to break the charm of the stillness. "Dancing is as old as Africa and it grips these people like a spell. All-night dancing works great havoc. But in the long run, our really formidable enemies lie in the order of ideas."

"What do you regard as the greatest obstacle?"

"Here in West Africa we are all agreed that it is Islamism. Next, I would say, is secularism. Then there is fetishism. A growing problem, though as yet important only as a menace of the future, is communism."

Throughout Africa as I asked this question under many different circumstances it brought forth a similar litany of obstacles that varied from region to region but were impressively similar in the task they created.

In French West Africa, the strongest movement to date with a Red tinge to it has been the R.D.A.—the *Rassemblement democratique Africain*. The founder of the movement was, curiously enough, a wealthy man by local standards, a "capitalist." He was Felix Houghouet-Boigny, a native of the Ivory Coast and an intelligent, popular owner of cocoa plantations. He gave birth to the R.D.A. at a political meeting at Bamako in October of 1946, as "the party of the African masses." Monsieur Felix for years led it along Moscow lines, with

24

great outbursts of fiery oratory, bitter denunciation, violent anger against all established institutions.

Then in 1951, strange phenomenon, our planter-politician completely broke with communism. He disbanded his party of extremists. He himself remained in politics, but is now a rather mild liberal though still an egregious opportunist. Communism with its searing hostility to religion is not today an organized public movement in West Africa. The presence of *agents provocateurs,* professional or amateur, is reported from time to time but no pattern of substantial Red conquest is evident.

The coastal regions of Togo and Dahomey are among the most advanced Christian territories in French West Africa. Yet there is currently in the area a resurgence of time-honored fetishism which would appear to be an anachronism if there were not good reason to suspect that there may be a nationalist motivation behind it. Archbishop Lefebvre, the Papal Delegate for French West Africa, journeyed through the regions in 1953 and called attention to it.

"There is an astonishing fetishism set up here in broad daylight," reported the Delegate. "I took a walk in Abomey, Dahomey: every ten yards I encountered a little fetishist altar. And this fetishism is a redoubtable power. One finds in these areas a curious alliance between educated political leaders and folk chiefs and fetish chiefs. There are rumors that such and such an operator in the Gold Coast or other nearby territory has entered the fetishist corporation and become a fetishist himself in order to maintain stronger authority over the masses. Thus there is a symptomatic of events that reminds us of happenings in Madagascar and among the Mau Mau of Kenya, where native leaders reverted to pagan practices in order to control more completely the rank and file."

While fetishism may still be highly rated for its power over the ignorant, it has lost its prestige among the educated. "The medical students of the Native School of Medicine at Dakar," explains a French administrator, "were indignant when I asked if they still adhered to the fetishism in which they had been reared. They went to a church, or to the temple, or the mosque, or to a masonic lodge, or nowhere at all, but none of them had remained faithful to fetishism, which they regarded as inferior to other religions or philosophies."

Since secularism is but the negation of religion so far as public life is concerned (though the negation easily carries over into the individual), why is it mentioned as a major obstacle of Christianity in Africa? Because it is one of the great destroyers of religion in Africa today.

At the beginning of the modern colonial era, secularism as we know it today was unheard of. Or rather, it was forgotten; for as Arnold Toynbee reminds us, the weak spot in Greek civilization was secularism, the lack of a compelling religion. Now the Western World suffers from this weakness. For two centuries, in the 1500's and 1600's, the West tried to propagate the *whole* of our Western culture, religion included. In the 1700's and 1800's, this effort was dropped.

Toynbee explains our action during the early period: "Our world-storming Western forefathers made a valiant attempt to propagate abroad the whole of our Western cultural heritage, including its religious core as well as its technological rind; and in this they were surely well inspired, for every culture is a whole whose parts are subtly interdependent." [1]

After the Reformation, the religious quarrels in the West became extremely bitter. A tacit agreement was made to end the wars of religion by cutting out religion itself. This was deadly: it was throwing out the baby with the bath water. Thus by cutting out religion, Toynbee reminds us, "the Western civilization that has since run like wildfire around the world has not been the whole of the seamless web; it has been a flare of cotton waste, a technological selvage with the religious centerpiece torn out."

Secularism today has entered into the fabric of world society. In all of the countries of the West, including of course the United States, and in the overseas territories held by these countries, secularist policy in administration is to a greater or less degree the rule. In Africa it has had least influence to date in the Belgian Congo, though there are political elements in Belgium very anxious to introduce it.

It should be emphasized that the great mistake of secularism is not its hostility to Christianity. Naturally, we lament this hostility very keenly. But the great mistake of the West, the irreparable harm done by the Western powers in the period now coming to an end, during which they have exercised real influence over subject peoples, has been their denial of the spiritual as an essential part of life.

Catholic, Protestant, Moslem, Buddhist, Hindu, Animist, all agree on one tremendous tenet, namely, that the spiritual is essential to life. All of these creeds believe that modern governments do harm to the spiritual by ignoring the essential importance of the spiritual in life.

In French possessions overseas, secularism is no mere fuzzy theory but is a well-worked-out administrative science. Apart from the official teaching on the subject, are the attitudes of the individual officers. They represent varying degrees in expressing the negation of religion in the modern state. However, in Africa, all add up to rendering the same gross disservice to the spiritual and to Western culture by convincing the African that religion has no place in the main stream of life in the West.

When an administrative officer deals with an African chief of a district or a village, he enters the sphere of the spiritual. At every contact with native life, he meets the impact of religion. In the political reactions of the native people, in their habits of work and their modes of life, religion is always an invisible factor. The administrator may talk to a native about the prospects of his field of grain, but concealed in the conversation is religion—the prayer the African said before choosing his plot of land, before clearing it, when imploring rain for it, before cultivating it, when gathering its harvest. Yet the administrator is a trained secularist.

"No one will ever catch me boosting anything that has to do with religion!" says one young administrator. He is the completely negative type—just not interested.

"I despise the whole lot of them—Christian, Moslem, pagan! They're unhealthy excrescences on the earth." This is the hostilely negative type—very interested in the direction of destruction.

"The missionaries, even the Moslems and the juju men, are good fellows, but I'll lose my job if I get caught befriending them. So far as the record goes, I ignore them." This is the sympathetically negative type—feeling a friendly interest but careful never to show his hand.

Behind this last category and his official negativeness, may be a private life of active religious practice. But in point of fact, such individuals are exceptional. For most, the official position is also the personal position.

Robert Delavignette, Director of the *Ecole Nationale de la France d'Outre-Mer* in Paris, where colonial officers are trained, has written for his candidates a textbook in which he devotes a chapter to the policy of being secular in religious matters. He recognizes that the spiritual has a place in African life, and then he sets forth the standard French thesis that the French administrator must be secular in his outlook.

"It is absolutely essential," says Delavignette,[2] "though it is difficult, for the administrator to maintain a secular standpoint in dealing with different religions. I am well aware of the first objection that will be raised: that colonial practice will be immoral if it is not inspired by the religion of the colonist. But then, what is to happen to the religion of the colonized? It is the duty of the administrator to see that liberty of conscience is respected, to stand for tolerance, and to hold the balance between the temporal interests of the different religions. . . . I believe that an administrator can preserve his freedom and maintain the secular standpoint in his profession."

"Whether it is the duty of the state to promote the service of God," comments Delavignette, "is a very large question. In fact, since the law is silent on the matter, there will inevitably be a conflict between the missionary who, in the words of L. Barde, 'acts not as the ministrator who also has to give life to a world." [3] practitioner of a cult but as a giver of life to the world,' and the administrator who also has to give life to a world." [3]

Men of experience in French Africa tell me that many individual administrators show themselves understanding in their appreciation of what Christianity can mean for the African. Some are practicing Christians. For the most part, however, the state attitude of cold indifference, of implied hostility toward the religion of its own culture, has devastating effects on the African.

"No one asks that any government engage itself in positive fashion in promoting Christianity," explained one bishop. "It is a matter principally of permitting the West, as a society and as individuals, to stand up and be counted, to be known as spiritual men who acknowledge the overlordship of Almighty God."

Doctor Emory Ross, of New York, a leading Protestant who worked long in Africa, in his book, *African Heritage,* indicates where he believes secularism stands in the hierarchy of obstacles on the continent.

"The division between Roman Catholics and Protestants, the divisions among Protestants, the division between black and white . . . and the even more important division, the generally applied Western

separation of the 'spiritual' from the 'secular': these are the Four Horsemen that ride hardest against Christianity in Africa." [4]

Secularism is not reserved to French Africa. A leading authority on British Africa resident in Mombasa says on the subject, "Secularism is the strong enemy above all others of Christianity in Africa. The philosophy of British administrators in the matter of religion is a river that possesses two streams running in opposite directions; the deep stream underneath, which is secularism, the negation of the spiritual as an element in life, represents the position of many of the upper elements in British administration; the surface stream in the river, recognizing the spiritual as a value in African life, represents the position of many worthy administrators who, however, do not often exercise real authority."

Secularism of another sort, which is in effect aggressive antireligion, is a special product of a powerful minority in France, and its influence is discoverable in French West Africa. In its issue of June 14, 1953, *Documentation Catholique* of Paris published the official text of the proceedings of the General Assembly of the Grand Orient of France, held September 15-18, 1952. These proceedings included an integrated plan for the complete secularization of France and its overseas territories. Monsieur Albert Bayet, one of the architects of this plan, had visited French West Africa shortly before my recent visit there.

Goals outlined in this plan included the following:

1) Abrogation of the Falloux Law (the Falloux Law dates from 1850 and *guarantees freedom of teaching in France* to nongovernmental organizations, which include the Church).

2) Abrogation of the Marie and Barange Laws (these laws accord *subsidies to private teaching institutions*).

3) Strict application of the secularization laws separating Church and the State in France.

4) Application of these same laws throughout the French Union and in all overseas territories.

5) The expulsion of all religious congregations.

An important role in the fight against the right to operate private schools, which of course includes Catholic schools, in French territory, as well as to grant these schools subsidies, is carried on by teaching organizations. *La Ligue Francaise de l'Enseignement* (The French Teaching League) in the April, 1953, issue of *L'Action Laique,* its monthly bulletin, prints a typical lament against the money voted by the French Government to subsidize private teaching in African and other overseas territories—money that thus "has been shunted off from the state teaching program and distributed to the religious missions. . . . In subsidizing the erection and maintenance of mission schools, in place of using these funds to erect and maintain lay schools, the state is in point of fact confiding teaching to the Catholic Church. . . . Where is there any respect for freedom of conscience in this procedure?"

Again, the National Teachers Union, in its 1953 congress at Pau, adopted a motion presented by Monsieur Bayet (of the above-mentioned Masonic plan), which inveighs "against the subsidies accorded in Black Africa to confessional organizations and to religious missions."

In the travelers' camp at Matiacouali on the road to the Niger River, Brother Alexis set up my valise on two gasoline cans, and I said Mass in the round, thatched hut. On finishing, I found, a half dozen yards from our door, two Moslems kneeling toward Mecca, performing their salaams and mumbling their orations. In this fashion we rubbed elbows with the sons of the Prophet throughout our journey to interior French Africa. Deep in the Niger country, the Negro imitates the Arab of North Africa quite as the native of the coast copies the European.

A phenomenon of Africa is the Moslem dividing line that extends completely across the continent at approximately the twelfth parallel of north latitude. It starts in East Africa, at the Red Sea and the northern edge of the Nile swamps in the Anglo-Egyptian Sudan, well to the south of Khartoum, and it proceeds westward along the desertic border on the edge of the greener country that southward becomes the tropical forest. The line passes through the heart of Nigeria and separates fetish West Africa from the Moslem world to the north. Of French West Africa's seventeen million inhabitants, seven million belong to this Moslem world. The majority of the eighty million Moslems in Africa are north of this line though, indeed, many millions are scattered south of it; some 40,000 Moslems are found in the Cape Province of South Africa. Recent Islamic gains in Dahomey and the

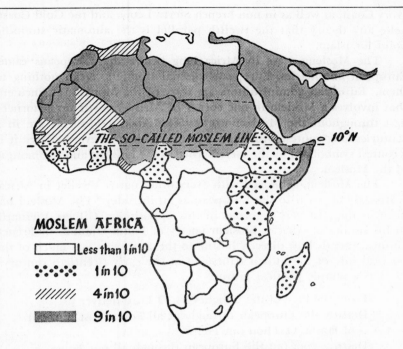

DISTRIBUTION OF MOSLEMISM IN AFRICA

Apart from the Animists, or so-called Fetishists, Islam is the largest religious body in Africa. It counts 85,339,249 adherents, or 41.3% of the total population.

A phenomenon of Africa is the "Moslem Line," traditionally placed at the tenth parallel of north latitude and extending completely across the continent. It is probably more correct to place it higher. It separates fetishist Africa from the almost unbroken Moslem world to the north.

Millions of Moslems, however, are found south of the line; some 40,000 Moslems dwell in the Cape Province of the Union of South Africa. Moslemism is the fastest gaining religious element in fetishist Africa. See Appendix A at the end of the book for distribution according to political divisions.

Ivory Coast, as well as in non-French Sierra Leone and the Gold Coast,
belie any theory that the twelfth parallel is the automatic stopping
point for Islam.

The Moslems were in Africa long before the Europeans came.
European boundaries, European colonial frontiers, mean nothing to
them. European administrators are wary of the Moslem; an incident
that involves a Moslem in one corner of Africa can stir up a hornet's
nest throughout the Moslem world. The African Moslems are in a
centuries-long contest with the African fetishists; in every village it is
a contest symbolized by the sacred grove of the fetishist and the mosque
of the Moslem.

The Moslem, as indeed with every other native dweller in Africa,
is strongly opposed to the European as an intruder. The Moslem has
been in the past very vigorous in this opposition. Gilbert Vieillard,
in his studies of African Moslem poetry of Fouta Djallon, in French
Guinea, reveals how directly hostile to the European was much of the
poetical lore of the Fulani tribesmen of the early twentieth century.[5]
Here is a sample poetical prayer:

> "From the rage of the unbelievers, O Lord deliver us!
> Destroy the European throughout all Fouta; cast him out
>   of Fouta, O Thou our Help.
> Destroy, root out the European through all our Fouta;
>   cast him out of Fouta, O Thou our Help."

So far as Moslemism versus Christianity is concerned, a strong
factor in French West Africa is the consistent policy of the French
Government to encourage Moslemism among the blacks. Maurice
Delafosse, in *Renseignements Coloniaux,* as far back as 1923 noted,
"An opinion unfortunately widely accepted by the French, but based
merely on an a priori concept rather than on observation or logic,
dictated that it was advantageous for the French to encourage Islam
to gain the black peoples and thus to serve as the normal social vesture
within which the Africans should live."

Today one of the civil administrative divisions in Dakar is the
Department of Moslem Affairs. This department, in addition to other
duties, arranges low-price fares for the pilgrimage to Mecca. In 1950,
for instance, 500 Moslems left Dakar by a chartered vessel, each paying
$800 for his round trip to Mecca, while 150 journeyed to Mecca by

plane at $1,200 each. The Government supplied doctors to care for the pilgrims. In 1952, a few moments before the pilgrim vessel sailed, the French High Commissioner went aboard at Dakar and saluted the representatives of all eight territories of French West Africa. "Tell all you meet," the Commissioner said in his address, "that we are citizens of a great nation, the French Republic." We recall no such official godspeed from the High Commissioner when the Catholic pilgrims left Dakar for Rome during the Holy Year of 1950.

A growing segment of French thought, however, pronounces this line of politics detrimental to France. The increasingly frequent contacts with Cairo and the Arab world are giving Islam an anti-European political tinge in West Africa. Arabic, the holy language of Islam, appeals to the African Moslem and draws him away from French. Arabic would make a convenient vehicle for extending the Middle Eastern holy war against France. The more strictly political aspects of this question belong to the realm of the politician. The missionary, however, cannot help indulging in a mirthless chuckle as he sees this pro-Moslem line, which many anticlerical French politicos followed because it gave such evident discomfort to the Church, now backfiring against its authors.

Old hands on the West African scene enumerated for me the factors that currently give Moslemism such great advantage:

1—Easy contact. All the great routes of West Africa are being improved, and the millions of fetishists once isolated from their fellows are now brought close to the centers. These centers, even when they are but secondary posts of one or two thousand inhabitants, have a mosque and Koranic schools, admission to which is regarded as a distinction. By sheer force of numbers, the Moslems are represented at the majority of these centers, and the Christians are not.

2—Secularist civil servants. What the French call *laicisme* and the British term neutrality, and we have just described as secularism, favors Moslemism. These Governments have great numbers of field agents, both European and native, engaged in widespread "protective action" against Christianity because Christianity necessarily strives to change numbers of pagan practices. Government officials tend to ignore the fact that all wise mission action aims to protect all good elements in native culture. Church opposition is focused only on those social and religious customs that unprejudiced observers rate as harmful and false.

3—Moslem brotherhoods and the marabout. "Missionaries tell me," says Archbishop Lefebvre, "that it is only necessary to build a chapel in a village, to start the Moslems building a mosque there."

"On the whole," explains Bishop Guibert, of Dakar, "the Moslem is not very zealous, but our activity for Christianity can stir up new Moslem fervor." An instance occurred among the Holy Ghost Missionaries in Senegal. A Moslem marabout, a so-called holy man, stung by the activity of the Christians, succeeded in rousing the Moslem brotherhood of Casamance to burn the mission church and rectory, on Easter Sunday some years ago.

In West Africa in particular, the Moslem brotherhoods are a source of strength, particularly when led by marabouts. Usually the marabout knows but a few passages from the Koran, but he dispenses *baraka*—which is vaguely comparable to Christian grace—upon all who participate, he directs prayers and religious ceremonies, and he gathers the children.

4—The Moslem trader. In much of West Africa, the Moslem trader is called the *dioula,* or little merchant. "Moslem propaganda is carried on particularly by the *dioula,*" explains Archbishop Lefebvre. "Following the economic trends, these little merchants are establishing themselves everywhere. The missionaries of Nouna and Bobo in the Sudan are establishing buying and selling co-operatives to protect their people against the *dioula.*"

The *dioula* is not an enrolled propagandist for Moslemism, but little by little he makes himself indispensable through his skill and his favors. He marries a local girl, is joined by companions, and soon they establish a Moslem quarter that is more attractive than any other part of the village or town. The *dioula* invites a marabout to come teach the Moslem children; the neighbors' children join in the school circle; neighbors aspire to the Moslems' higher social status; Moslemism grows.

5—The Moslem shepherd. The ambitious young Moslem from among the Fulas or Peuhls of the cattle-raising areas offers his services as a shepherd to a fetishist farmer who owns cattle but has no skill in raising them. The young Moslem patiently insinuates himself into the family, becomes adviser to the farmer, marries one of the farmer's daughters. In some cases, the Moslem ends by hiring the proprietor for whom he first went to work, and then enters local village politics. Again, Moslemism grows.

6—Shame in modern fetishist society. Millions in Africa have conceived a shame for their nakedness, their ignorance, their attachment to fetishism. Many want very much to be Christians, but often if they cannot find a Christian missionary, they will become Moslem. The pagan is fascinated by the prospect of joining a respected social group. He hungers to *belong.*

7—Easy Moslem tenets. Islam makes its own propaganda by the simplicity of its doctrine and by the fact that a convert begins to belong by the mere say-so. The salaam is the outward sign. No teachings need be studied. No great changes in personal life, in family life, or in public life are demanded.

8—Material advantages. Young people who are ambitious come to Moslem centers for jobs, for schooling, for opportunity to rise higher than their humble ancestors. As non-Moslems, they can get nowhere. "Change your name and become a Moslem," someone tells them. They try that, and it works. In the Kong area of the Ivory Coast, Moslems long held a monopoly of the weaving of cotton cloth; pagan peddlers found that, to get cloth to sell, it was necessary to be circumcized and to learn to recite the Koranic prayers.

9—Moslem "missionaries." Until this century, Islam never had a missionary organization in the sense that we understand the concept. But in what is now Pakistan, formerly northern India, the Ahmadiyya movement was born some years ago. This is a modern sect of unorthodox Moslems that sends out organizers. The Ahmadiyya agents first entered Africa through East Coast ports, but now they debark in West Africa as well. A region of the Gold Coast is covered by inspectors of the Ahmadiyya missions—"Moslem bishops," the Africans call them. They are indicative of an accelerated step in the Moslem world.

Shall we Christians overtake our Moslem rivals? Frankly, it would not seem so, given our present pace. French West African statistics, between 1940 and 1946, showed a steady gain of 200,000 new Moslems a year, and the succeeding years provide similarly substantial figures. Today the Catholic Church in West Africa counts three and one-half per cent of the population, while Moslems are 18 per cent. In the remainder of Black Africa, Christianity still holds the lead over Islam.

Although Moslems represent the heaviest threat to Christianity, secularism and communism constitute far graver challenges to basic African society. The Moslem believes in God and in matters touching the common spiritual good of Africa. Catholics, Protestants, Moslems, and even convinced animists, as the fetishists are technically called, have a basis for common action. The first issue of *Afrique Nouvelle* expressed this fact in the name of the Catholic bishops of French West Africa:

"We do not forget that the great bulk of Africans in French West Africa are profoundly religious. Animists, Moslems, Christians, form one great body. All have faith in a better world and practice a morality. We all keep our beliefs and our principles in mind as we face the problems of our family life, our social life, and our civil life."

Chapter 4

DAYBREAK IN THE GOLD COAST

THE GOLD COAST at the time of my visit in 1953 was the land of the great experiment; all Africa was watching it. Cyril L. Sulzberger of *The New York Times* passed through Accra during my stay, and he labeled the Gold Coast "the happiest spot in Africa."

"Everywhere in Africa," remarked a European consular representative, "no matter what people begin talking about, in a few minutes they have switched to what everybody calls 'the problem.' 'The problem' is self-government. But here in the Gold Coast there's no longer any waiting for self-government: here it has arrived. And everybody's astounded at the degree of success it is enjoying."

British West Africa is composed of four units of territory, each separate from the other, and on the map they look as if they were wedged into the coast line of French West Africa. While the French have more land, the British have more people. Nigeria, farthest east, is the largest with some 30,000,000 inhabitants. Next comes the Gold Coast, with more than 4,000,000 people; then Sierra Leone, with 2,000,000; and finally that strange, string-bean segment Gambia, with some 250,000 inhabitants. Thus the British flag in West Africa flies over 36,000,000, and the French flag over 17,000,000 people. The English-language orbit of West Africa also includes Liberia, an independent nation with a population of 2,500,000.

Nigeria is larger, but the Gold Coast, its deadly rival, claims at the moment to lead the procession. Indeed, the Gold Coasters rank high among all the peoples of Africa. Lord Hemingford, who taught for years at Achimota, the Gold Coast University College, and then at Makerere, in Uganda, East Africa, believed that, of the peoples in these two countries, those of the Gold Coast were the more intelligent. Many would place the inhabitants of both Gold Coast and Uganda among the most gifted peoples on the African continent. Father Koster,

American Divine Word missionary, who teaches physics at Achimota, rates his students very high. "I have taught college men both in the United States and in the Gold Coast," Father Koster explains. "I would say that my Gold Coast students are equal in capacity to those I had in the U.S.A."

Gold Coasters are powerful in build and alert in bearing, with a confident air that at times assumes a bit of a swagger. Certainly they give the impression that they are able to take care of themselves. Many wear European clothes; but the African dress, which makes us think of the ancient Romans in their togas, is smart and attractively aflame with bold color.

"How do you like our Gold Coast?" asks the restaurant waiter, the taxi driver, the college boy, the householder. There's an eager pride in the question that makes one think of Texas or Los Angeles.

In 1953, most of this twinkle of excitement stemmed from the doings of a boyish-looking man in his forties—a man with melancholy eyes, a firm, full mouth, an excellent command of English, a resourceful brain, and a passably sure judgment. Three years before my arrival, he was serving a jail sentence for sedition. He is an African, the Right Honorable Kwame Nkrumah (pronounced En-*kroom*-ah), Bachelor of Divinity, Master of Arts, Honorary Doctor of Laws, and Prime Minister of the Gold Coast.

Nkrumah was born in the mud-hut jungle village of Nkroful, where his father, a Twi tribesman, worked as a goldsmith. The boy went to Catholic schools as Francis Nkrumah, and the Lyons missionaries helped him get to Achimota College. He was graduated from college in 1931, and launched enthusiastically into a career of teaching; but suddenly everything changed when his uncle, a gold prospector, offered him the money for a passage to the United States. In the early 1930's, the Catholic missionaries of the Gold Coast did not have in the United States any connections that might give the young student a guiding hand, and thus he drifted away from things Catholic. Protestant friends were more helpful: Nkrumah entered Lincoln University, a college for Negroes, at Oxford, Pennsylvania, where he acquired a divinity degree as a Protestant minister. Later while at the University of Pennsylvania he lived on South 18th Street in Philadelphia. "I have many pleasant memories of Philadelphia," he told a man from the City of Brotherly Love, who called on him recently. "I studied your Philadelphia politics and your labor unions; the way they are organized and the way they operate. I went to Communist meetings and Socialist meetings and Republican meetings and labor meetings. I studied them all—the campaign methods, the way they get out the vote, the way they work with other groups, the way they bring pressure to bear. . . . It was all most useful."

"What was your over-all, big impression of the United States?" his visitor asked him.

"The energy!" the African replied immediately. "And how everybody tries to better his condition."

Nkrumah went to England and spent two years at London University. There he fell in with leftists and, though he failed in his bar examination, he succeeded notably as a radical spellbinder. "Colonial and subject peoples of the world, unite!" was his ringing wind-up to a leftist speech at the Fifth Pan-African Congress in London, in 1945.

From his shabby lodgings in London's East End, Nkrumah returned to the Gold Coast and was immediately made secretary general of the Home-Rule Party. Within ten weeks of his return, on a February day in 1948, a band of demonstrators marched on the British Governor's palace. A nervous guard was frightened into shooting; and from that moment, the Gold Coast was on its way to self-government. The guards killed two Africans, but in the rioting that followed, twenty-nine more were killed and millions of dollars' worth of property was destroyed.

The British shrewdly recognized that the choice was between government by force, a costly and inconclusive procedure, or government by winning over the governed. They immediately offered the Gold Coast a new constitution with free elections. But Nkrumah and the young bloods were feeling their oats. To the astonishment of Doctor James B. Danquah, dignified head of the Home-Rule Party, who had been almost overcome with joy at sight of the constitution, Nkrumah branded the new document as a fraud, and broke with Danquah and the moderates. With the slogan, "Self-government NOW!" Nkrumah led the British such a merry chase that he landed in jail on a sedition charge.

While he was in jail, Father Charles Erb, a Divine Word missionary from Rochester, New York, visited him several times and gave him smokes and some Catholic reading matter. The young man was very cordial and has never forgotten the American's courtesy. It would appear, however, that the faith of his early years has slipped away from him; though he pays lip service to religion, he is not regarded today as a Catholic.

Jail made Nkrumah a martyr in native eyes. When the British-guided elections were over, the Convention People's party, Nkrumah's group, had won eighty per cent of the Gold Coast votes, while Nkrumah had swept Accra. Governor Arden-Clarke of the Gold Coast then swiftly took the gamble of his career: he let Nkrumah out of jail and named him Leader of Government Business—a title that London later changed to Prime Minister. Awed by responsibility, Nkrumah and his followers sobered down, and they have done quite a good job of governing.

"I have no doubt of Nkrumah's ability," a veteran European member of the consular corps in Accra told me. "He is a man with excellent political sense. He has great vision for the Gold Coast. He is not very keen on administration matters, which he leaves to others, but, despite the powerful struggle of the opposition forces to unseat him and get their hands on the spoils, I think he will continue to hold the leadership and to rule well."

An admirable group in Gold Coast life is the body of British career men in the various governmental departments, who are taking pride in guiding and coaching the Gold Coast authorities. The highest British officials are now permanent secretaries of their departments, each with a Gold Coaster over him as minister. Each Britisher addresses his Gold Coast superior as "sir." Despite the impatience that may crop up in the give-and-take of an administration day, the British are fulfilling their tasks faithfully and with the enthusiasm of one of the world's new forms of pioneering. The Africans are keen enough to observe all this and to reveal new respect for their erstwhile overlords.

Unfortunately, the Gold Coast people have a long way to go before they will possess the education and the political principles essential to the establishment of a democracy. At present one suspects that the spirit is rather that of some of the South American republics where political affairs are in the hands of small minority groups ready to go to any lengths to get their hands on the controls and to create a self-perpetuating machine that is anything but democratic. Let us

hope that events give the lie to this dismal prospect. For real greatness, Africa's new leaders must reveal something more substantial than
political cleverness. For evidence of these deeper qualities, we are
still waiting.

"I make reservations on Nkrumah as regards his sense of the
spiritual," commented one gentleman in Accra. "Jungle superstitions
still have a grip on him. Recently when he was threatened with
poisoning, it is quite well established that he went to a juju man for
a protecting spell. He is attached to Communist methods for getting
things done and, I believe, would in a pinch act quite without principle, to serve his own ends."

The British when they arrested Nkrumah found a Communist
Party card in his wallet, but they accepted his statement that he used
it in London merely to get into Communist meetings. "I am not a
Communist," Nkrumah stated to a French journalist, "but I watch
with interest how things are done in the U.S.S.R. I admire Marx,
Engels, Lenin, but not Stalin. I hold a very strong dislike for Stalin-
ism."

I drove through village after village in the Gold Coast and saw
neat, palm-thatched, mud-built bungalows; and in the cities, I noted
the more pretentious homes. Although there is a great deal of poverty
the country as a whole is in good condition economically. It exports
more value proportionately than any other overseas unit in the British
Commonwealth. In the cities, big American cars, driven by chauffeurs,
roll by with African lawyers, traders or politicians on the back seats.
Markets are laden with crimson chilies, golden oranges, green avocado
pears, fat plantains, big purple yams. There is meat to be had, and
there are canned goods in profusion including costly tins of English
biscuits. Sections of Accra, Cape Coast, and Kumasi are like garden
cities with shrubs and blazing flowers—scarlet poinsettias, flame trees,
hibiscus, hydrangeas, purple bougainvillea.

Please do not misunderstand the foregoing statements. There are
not many wealthy persons in the Gold Coast. Most of the inhabitants
possess very little. But—and this is unusual for West Africa—thousands
of farmers in the Gold Coast get a return from a money crop that lifts
them above the miserable level of the householder who barely finds
subsistence. The source of income to the largest number of Gold
Coasters is an industry that the Africans built up themselves.

In 1879, a plantation laborer on the Spanish island of Fernando
Po smuggled in some cocoa pods when he returned to his home in the
Gold Coast. This was the romantic beginning of the industry that
today supplies some 50 per cent of the world's exports of cocoa, or
over 200,000 tons of cocoa per year. This extraordinary achievement
was accomplished in its early stages entirely by African farmers, with
little help from the Government except for transportation. There are
many defects in the operation and, certainly by American standards,
not a high return per family. Nonetheless the Gold Coasters offer an
example for all Africa of large-scale export from small native farms.
Involved are some 300,000 such farms of four or five acres each, with
less than a ton of output per farm family.

Those cocoa growers broke all the rules: they neglected drainage
and forking; they failed to prune, to control disease, to put in shade
trees. Poor management, bad financing including careless dissipation
of money advances for their crops, and chaotic land-tenure conditions,
have prevented most cocoa farmers from becoming rich. Thirteen
European firms exercise a monopoly in buying and shipping the crops.
Despite all these troubles, observers who are genuinely interested in
people insist that these 300,000 farmers are better off as free operators
than they would have been as plantation workers for the great companies, which at one time threatened to gobble up all Africa and
strangle family life as does the mining industry with its herding of
labor. Science is now stepping in to bolster the Gold Coast cocoa
industry by guiding the farmers as regards dangerous plant diseases;
and modern techniques are being taught them, along other lines.

Meanwhile, to many thoughtful men, the cocoa achievement is
proof of the superior gifts of the Gold Coast people. William R.
Bascom, an anthropologist at Northwestern University in Illinois says,
"For the initiative and enterprise which made the Gold Coast a larger
producer than the entire Western Hemisphere, of a crop native to
Mexico, Africans have never received due credit." [1]

The strongest single element in the Gold Coast assortment of
tribes is the Ashanti. When in Kumasi, I duly visited the tombs of the
Ashanti paramount chiefs, structures that evidently borrowed their
architecture from the Moslem north. During the early part of the
twentieth century, an incident occurred in British relations with the
Ashanti that teaches a great lesson to all—including our Catholic

mission leaders—who are truly interested in understanding the peoples of Africa. The incident climaxed and cured a longstanding hostility.

Towards the close of the nineteenth century, when the Ashanti tribes gave the British trouble, the British subdued them by military conquest and in 1896 exiled King Prempeh I. Observing a continued spirit of recalcitrance, and noting that the Ashanti gave great significance to what they called the Golden Stool as a symbol of their nationhood, the British undertook to capture the Golden Stool but did not succeed. Instead, the Ashanti buried that precious possession, and the resentment against the British became more bitter than ever.

In 1905, better opinion prevailed, and the British returned partial authority to the council of chiefs. Then the bitterness diminished. As the years passed, Government authorities advanced so far in their thinking that, after World War I, Captain Robert Rattray, long known as an authority on native languages and customs, was appointed head of a new Anthropology Department in Ashanti. It was only upon receipt of Captain Rattray's detailed investigation of the beliefs and customs of the Ashanti tribes, submitted in a confidential report in 1921, that the British discovered the true cause of the Ashanti rebellions.

The major factor lay, Captain Rattray was able to show, in the Ashanti people's profound conviction, equivalent to a tenet of religion, that the soul of the Ashanti nation truly dwelt in the Golden Stool. In Ashanti eyes, the struggle of the British to capture the Golden Stool had been a grave act of sacrilege.

Oddly enough, in 1921, shortly after these important findings were made known, some Ashanti workmen building a road accidentally uncovered the Golden Stool, grossly ignored its sacredness by stripping it of its gold, and sold the metal. The British caught the workmen and, acting on their new-found knowledge, turned over the stool and the culprits to the Ashanti chiefs for trial. The offenders were condemned to death. The evidence of British respect for the Golden Stool mollified the Ashanti people; and when Princess Mary of England was married, a silver stool was presented to her by the Queen Mother of Mampong, one of the Ashanti states.

A letter accompanying the royal gift read as follows: "It may be that the King's child (Princess Mary) has heard of the Golden Stool of Ashanti. That is the Stool that contains the soul of the Ashanti nation. All we women of Ashanti thank the Governor exceedingly because he has declared to us that the English will never again ask us to hand over that Stool. This stool we give gladly. It does not contain our soul as the Golden Stool does, but it contains all our love, of the Queen Mother and of our women. The spirit of this love we have bound to the stool with silver fetters, just as we are accustomed to bind our own spirits to the base of our stools." [2]

For long, it was the fashion to disdain the folkways of Africa and their significance to Africa's peoples. A few long-haired scientists studied them, but most regarded them as idle trivia. However, as cultural anthropology obtained greater vogue, various trends of new thinking gained ground, including the belief that administrative work must be based on ethnological and psychological knowledge of the people. In my chats with Catholic leaders in different parts of Africa, I found many who have taken steps to systematize knowledge of their peoples for the practical bearing of the information on Catholic life. For a scientific approach to the study of folkways, it is a growing practice to give formal training to select missionaries for this special task. The Church has long had priests who have deeply studied native ways, as for instance the famed Anthropos scholars of the Divine Word Fathers in Vienna.

The viewpoint of such scholars was well expressed years ago by Archbishop Alexander Le Roy, C.S.Sp., in his book, *The Religion of the Primitives:* "If there is one elementary principle to be followed by every man who proposes to bring others to his own faith, it is to know what the others themselves believe."

Africans of truly great stature, as well as their similarly distinguished European confreres, have recognized that intellectual and spiritual growth can come in Africa only if the specially endowed among the Africans, equipped with a good education, will go apart and engage in thought and research. Then will Africa's problems eventually find an answer. Doctor James K. Aggrey, a Gold Coast Methodist of great charm and personal gifts, had this idea very much in mind when during the 1920's he co-operated with the British authorities in the establishment of the University College of Achimota, seven miles outside Accra. A favorite expression of Doctor Aggrey, as regards good relations between European and African, was that it was "necessary to use both black and white keys to produce beautiful music." This idea of the black and white keys was incorporated into the Achimota seal, with the classic Scriptural text, *"Ut omnes unum sint"*—"That all may be one."

"Achimota," Aggrey said, "is destined to influence not only the Gold Coast but, directly and indirectly, the entire African continent."

By the time the college was opened in 1931, some $3,000,000 had gone into it; and generous annual outlays by the state have continued ever since. The college was given an attractive campus, a large administrative block, residential units, hospital, museum, printing press, swimming pool, demonstration farm, model village. Its faculty now ranks with the finest in any comparable institution in Europe or America. Most of its masters have Oxford or Cambridge degrees. I walked the shaded paths of Achimota with Father Koster, physics professor at the University College, and with Father Le Sage, biology-and-botany professor at the Secondary School. Both are American Divine Word Fathers, loaned to the staff. (Father Le Sage has a special claim to fame for the snakes he catches and writes about.)

In the early days of Achimota, two of the staff were English converts: Captain Maxwell-Lawson and his wife. The captain received membership in the Knighthood of Saint Sylvester from Pope Pius XI, for his efforts "to secure due consideration for the Catholic pupils of Achimota College in respect to their religious duties and to insure for them instruction in their faith." I knew the captain and his wife and admired them for their wonderful zeal. The pair met a tragic death in an automobile accident.

"Achimota has a distinct role to fill in building the Gold Coast nation," explained Mr. David M. Balme, native principal of Achimota and a recent convert to the Church. "Without being tools of Government, most of the students will move into Government posts. The student body as a whole is sound and serious and mildly conservative."

Today, of the 450 students enrolled in the University College, 65 are Catholics, and about 50 of these practice their religion. Some are commendably forthright in living according to their Christian Faith.

Chapter 5

MILESTONE AT KUMASI

AT THE HEIGHT of the tension after the fateful elections of 1951, the Catholics of the Gold Coast held the first National Eucharistic Congress ever to be organized in West Africa. British authorities, under strain from the political crisis, were uneasy lest the gathering of great crowds lead to some kind of disturbance. Their fears proved entirely unfounded. The great Eucharistic demonstration took place in an atmosphere of good will displayed by people of every creed. "The Eucharistic Congress turned out to be a milestone for Catholicism in the Gold Coast," said Father Erb, at Accra.

From every corner of the land, thousands of the faithful moved toward the central city of Kumasi, ancient seat of the Ashanti kings. They traveled by hundreds of lorries, by special trains, public busses, private cars, airplanes, and, in the case of great numbers, afoot. Some seventy thousand visitors poured into Kumasi—but the city was ready. Priests and the Catholic laity had worked for weeks preparing for the Congress, with the assistance of all, from the British Governor and the King of Ashanti down.

The full impact of the dramatic plan was first experienced when the Papal Delegate, Archbishop David Mathew, arrived by plane at the Kumasi airport on Monday, February 19. Fifty thousand people were gathered there, and the illustrious visitor was greeted with a truly African roar of drums. Another fifty thousand lined the streets for the procession to St. Peter's Cathedral. Everywhere along the way were colorful Papal emblems. That night and each succeeding night, a huge monstrance, built between the towers of the cathedral by Father Ewers of the Society of African Missions, blazed with electric lights and was visible for miles.

Tuesday was Youth Day. Great crowds gathered at the special Congress Park that had been created at Kumasi Race Course. Then followed a procession of twenty-five thousand children with costumes and tableaux that provided an historical pageant. On Wednesday, Men's Day, besides the great Pontifical High Mass, there were meetings in six different places for the six most important language groups of the Gold Coast. Thursday was Priests' Day, and the celebrant was Bishop Joseph Kiwanuka of Uganda, Africa's first native-born bishop, who had crossed the continent to be present.

Thursday night the most impressive of all the ceremonies was held. It was a torchlight procession, when the pilgrims and the local populace moved out from Kumasi to drum beats and hymn singing, and assembled before the immense altar in Congress Park. There they heard a striking address from the King of Ashanti—Otonfo Sir Nana Osei Agyeman Prempah II, Knight Commander of the Order of the British Empire—a Methodist who had shown his appreciation of Catholicism by visiting Rome during the 1950 Holy Year. The Congress, the King said, would have a vast influence for good, not only on the Gold Coast, but on the whole of West Africa. Such demonstrations of faith, he noted, are important for nations as well as for individuals. It was the King who presented the Congress with its precious monstrance, fashioned by Kumasi artists from local gold, ivory and ebony.

As the week advanced, a remarkable factor in the celebration was its profound effect on the local population. The huge influx of pilgrims from outside the city of Kumasi—a moderate-sized community of eighty thousand—stirred up extraordinary generosity and hospitality among the non-Catholics generally, and gave them unusually close contact with Catholics and Catholic ways. The distinguished non-Christian gentleman who harbored Bishop Kiwanuka found it a thrilling experience to have that scholarly yet simple and gracious prelate in his house. Daily Mass, because priests were so numerous, was celebrated in homes and gardens throughout Kumasi, and every neighborhood saw groups of from one to two hundred fervent faithful kneel in worship at the Divine Sacrifice.

"I did not know that Catholics prayed like that," was a frequent comment of non-Catholic observers.

On the last day of the Congress, the entire population of Kumasi, including Protestants, Moslems, and pagans, turned out for the Living Rosary Pageant in which the fifteen mysteries were portrayed by living tableaux. "We have read of Christ's life and sufferings in the Bible," said one Protestant, "but now here we have seen them before our eyes."

A climactic Pontifical High Mass was celebrated, at which each of the score and more of bishops and ordinaries was seated under a huge multi-colored umbrella such as is reserved for Gold Coast kings and chiefs in their public appearances. The seats were covered with rich Ashanti cloth, and designs of the celebrated Ashanti golden stools, symbol of authority, adorned the pillars supporting the altar canopy. At this ceremony the Gold Coast was consecrated to the Immaculate Heart of Mary. The most solemn moment of the Congress occurred in the evening when, while a great silence gripped the awe-struck throng, the voice of the Holy Father came by wireless directly from the Vatican to his children in the heart of West Africa. The Pontiff praised them, stirred them to still greater deeds for God, and blessed them tenderly.

"Wonderful!" commented a local dignitary in Kumasi, a non-Christian. "The Catholics alone are able to organize something big like this."

The initiators of the Kumasi Congress wrought greater good than they know. At this critical period in Gold Coast history, the Catholics, who total some 400,000 and thus are ten per cent of the total population, shed the inferiority complex that had marked their humble beginnings and their undistinguished years of lowly, hidden loyalty to God in a milieu that, although seldom hostile, usually ignored them or held them in slight regard. Suddenly the Catholics felt themselves a well-disciplined, united whole. Suddenly they found that many thoughtful people outside their ranks had discovered them and admired what they were.

"The Catholic Church," declared Quarshie Idun, a Nigerian official and a Methodist, at one of the Congress public dinners, "is the greatest Christian body and knows how to organize men for good. It has done much to promote the advancement of this country."

It thus happens that, following the Kumasi Eucharistic Congress, the Catholic Church took a new look at itself. There were wide satisfaction and prideful joy in many Catholic neighborhoods, whether along city streets or in jungle villages. But happily, most of the

Catholics' attention was given to sober stock taking and to courageous recognition of the Church's local weaknesses.

"It may well be that in the Gold Coast within the next few years," states Father Patrick O'Neill of the African Missions Society, editor of the *Cape Coast Standard,* "a pattern of Church-and-State relations will emerge which will have wide influence on Catholic missionary effort everywhere in Africa."

Two of the three major missionary societies at work in West Africa are represented in Gold Coast work. The Society of African Missions is responsible for three of the five divisions—Cape Coast, Kumasi, and Keta; while the White Fathers care for Tamale in the less developed Northern Territory. The fifth division, Accra, is assigned to the Fathers of the Divine Word, a large and strong society that has returned to this part of the continent after an absence since World War I. Oddly enough, Accra, though capital of the Gold Coast, is the youngest division. The area was long the ugly duckling among the missions. When the American Divine Word Fathers arrived in 1939, there were only three priests here to care for 12,000 Catholics. Today Catholics there number some 45,000, served by over 50 priests and Brothers.

Father O'Neill, the *Standard* editor, was asked recently, "What is the greatest obstacle holding back the Church in this bright, new day in the Gold Coast?"

"Insufficiency of personnel," he replied. "Let us take by way of illustration the parish and district of Dunkwa, in the Archdiocese of Cape Coast. This place has 9,068 Catholics, 49 outstations, and only two priests. The parish priest has to take care of the town of Dunkwa, so the poor curate gets the 49 outstations, each occupying an area of 30 to 50 square miles. Where roads are good, the priest can travel by motor-truck, but often he must go on foot. Every large village will have 100 or more Catholics; each smaller one, 20 or less. The larger spots may get Mass once a month; the others less frequently, and seldom on Sunday. Catechists or lay instructors systematically cover every district, but they are no real substitutes for the priest.

"In Cape Coast Archdiocese alone we have 19 such parishes and 625 outstations. But that is not all. In Dunkwa—and every other parish has the same difficulty—there are 19 Catholic schools with all their problems. The Gold Coast today has over 1,100 Catholic primary schools.

"But besides these woes at the parochial level, there are the personnel needs at diocesan level. These fall into three categories: first, the administrative staff, which, happily, in mission lands is small; secondly, the specialized works such as Catholic Action, Catholic charities, and the like; thirdly, the staff requirements for secondary schools and teacher-training colleges. In the Gold Coast at present, we have eight secondary schools for boys, all demanding priests, plus seven Catholic teacher-training colleges, a preparatory seminary and two major seminaries. With but a little more than 200 priests in all the Gold Coast, how to profit from our opportunities is a conundrum."

The source of greatest strength to the Church in the Gold Coast is its system of Catholic schools, which employs some 4,000 teachers and cares for 115,000 pupils. Over a third of all the educational institutions in the Gold Coast are Catholic. The Kumasi Eucharistic Congress did good work for the Church's schools. The Congress stiffened the backbone of the Catholics throughout the country, just in time to save the Church from losing its precious schools.

The coming of self-government to the Gold Coast has paralleled the new educational trend in British Africa which can, if care is not taken, bring with it a policy of secularism in education. Recently it looked as if this trend would destroy the Catholic school system, along with practically all other private schools, before proper substitute safeguards could be provided. Ironically, Kojo Botsio, the Minister of Education, is a Catholic, but by his training and his teaching experience in England, as well as through the influence of his British educational advisers, he is frankly anti-private school.

Victory thus far for the Catholic schools has come through wise measures on the part of the bishops, and courageous support by the Catholic laity, who are zealous for all that pertains to the protection of religion. Both clergy and laity work to make both the Government and the people of the Gold Coast appreciate the two great principles that Catholics fight for everywhere in the world: (1) that education cannot be completely separated from religious control without a doctrinal and moral collapse; and (2) that Catholics (and all citizens) have the right to religious education within the framework of the nation's general system of education, and therefore such religious education should be financed from those public resources to which all citizens contribute by taxation.

"Because these principles have not been understood or acknowledged," explains a Catholic leader in the Gold Coast, "we may expect a constant recurrence of educational crises, at governmental levels, both central and local."

The fight to date has been an admirable one that can make us feel proud of our Gold Coast Catholics.

"The Gold Coast Government has wonderful plans to give education to everybody," one of the Catholic educational leaders explained to me, "and for these plans, we have nothing but praise. However, certain elements employ the faulty reasoning that, if they should take the money now provided for the mission schools, Catholic and Protestant, they would be able to operate with this cash a secular school system for the Government. Of course they couldn't do that: they would, instead, destroy what they have and substitute something costlier and less good educationally. It is extraordinary how excited our Catholic people became over this threat to their schools. Not only in the cities, but out in the jungle villages, parleys were held long into the night. A thousand times over, the cry went up, 'They must not harm our schools!'"

At one of those Catholic gatherings, someone proposed that the village group send a telegram of protest to the Government. Off went the wire. The suggestion sped to neighboring villages. Soon thousands of telegrams flooded the offices of the Ministry in Accra, the Department of Education, and the homes of individual members of the Assembly. One member alone received 780 telegrams; he was desperate, for in the Gold Coast a man must sign personally for every telegram.

The Government was in a way highly pleased with what happened, because they were evidences of democracy truly in action. Here were the common people of the Gold Coast—the farmers, the laborers, the tradesmen—in every part of the country, exercising their privilege as citizens to speak their mind.

When the Assembly met, it devoted all day to this question of maintaining the present religious connection of the Gold Coast schools. The folks in the villages were very proud of the sturdy courage and the simple but effective eloquence of the Catholic and non-Catholic members of the Assembly who saw the wisdom of the Catholic contention. Those men, so new at their task of explaining their views in public, revealed fine gifts as they spoke for the recognition of religion in education. The distasteful measure was modified, and for the present at least, the day was saved.

The gratifying factor in the handling of the school question was the wholehearted vigor of the Catholic rank and file. One teacher in the little school at Akim-Swadru, Ignatius Tufuo, used his vacation to visit every center in his province—fourteen towns and cities in all —and contact all the local chiefs and the leading Catholics, Protestants and pagans, explaining to them the importance of religion in education and the rights that should be conceded to parents to insure the proper religious schooling of their children.

The backbone of Catholic education is the Gold Coast's well trained Catholic teachers. Thanks to my friend Father Erb, I had a memorable visit to a group of candidate teachers under training. When we had reached the beautiful hills of the Krobo country, we left the highway and began to climb through the village of Somanya. A few swish-brick homes of the Krobo people appeared, and then the ascent became steeper.

"This is it," remarked Father Erb, my companion; "Mount Mary, one of the top-flight teacher-training schools of the Gold Coast."

"Attractive," I commented.

"It should be," said Father Erb. "The Gold Coast Government has spent almost $350,000 here."

On a superb eminence, I saw half a dozen neatly designed buildings that provide classrooms, laboratories, library, eating hall, dormitories, auditorium, and a chapel with calm, devotional air. Great labor and pains had gone into this place, I thought to myself, as I was met by Father Daedig, the rector, and his fellow priests of the faculty. How oblivious we are at home of the mountain of effort required to create even one of these houses of formation, which have multiplied everywhere on the African continent.

One of the priests took me to the guest room that I was to call my own for the night, and threw open the window. "There across the valley is Mount Krobo," he remarked. "A symbol," he added.

"How so?" I asked.

"Mount Krobo," he explained as I gazed across the entrancing green expanse toward the rolling hills beyond, "was a short while ago a strongly guarded bastion of the chieftains of the Krobo tribe. There they carried on their human sacrifices, until finally the British flushed them out. To each young candidate teacher who comes here we can point to Mount Krobo and say, 'There is what life might have meant for you.' Then, letting him look about him here on Mount Mary, we can say, 'And here is quite another life, which with God's help may be yours if you choose to work hard enough for it.' "

That evening at eight, I met the students and addressed them in the auditorium. The sea of faces bore the same inscrutable expression that I have found on students everywhere as a stranger stands before them, his message unspoken.

"Come now," that expression seems to say. "Let's see if you can spark us!"

I directed them immediately into the heart of New York City, to a school among the skyscrapers, where a confrere of theirs of the goodly company of teachers that spans the world instructs daily in a classroom that remains forever untouched by the sun. The teacher, I explained, is a Christian Brother, who for long years has kept before him on his desk as he faces his class a printed motto that reads, "To each of these, a part of my soul." As I developed the devotion with which this teacher, fired by his motto, serves his boys, I noticed a handsome six-foot tribesman up front draw a notebook from his pocket and write a line in it. Quite as you or I might have done at the impressionable age of eighteen, this young man of the Gold Coast planned remembering the ideal of his fellow teacher in New York: "To each of these, a part of my soul."

After speaking briefly, I opened the session to questions and received very many of them. A white visitor to the quiet sanctum of Mount Mary in the Krobo hills must be prepared to face quite a grilling. He must expect to be asked questions that impugn the justice and good will of the white race, and that sometimes (as in the case of the racial discrimination in some American colleges) cannot be answered in a manner that completely clears our good name.

"I have been told," began one young man, "that there are Catholic churches in the United States that put black people in one section and white people in another. Is that true?"

I answered that years ago there were places in the southern

United States where this happened, but that there were no such churches any more.

"I've been told," said another student, "that in Nyassaland, in Central Africa, there are churches to which the African Catholics refuse to go any more, because the whites had all the good seats and the Africans had to crowd in the back."

As I understand it, I explained, there were in the past a few churches built for white plantation operators before there were any African Catholics, and the custom had grown up for the first few African converts to slip quietly into the rear seats. Now that the African Catholics are very numerous in Nyassaland, they build large churches for themselves, and the relatively few whites join them as fellow parishioners.

"Is it true," came another question, "that white men vote for Negroes in New York City?"

Yes, I replied, this happens in Harlem and elsewhere when there are good Negro candidates.

"Is it true," asked still another, "that there are Negroes in the United States who hire many white people to work for them?"

That certainly happens, I answered, since some Negroes are successful business men and engage whatever helpers they need, without regard for color; indeed, most people in the United States wouldn't notice particularly whether they worked for a white or a Negro owner.

"Why are there universities in the United States to which black-skinned people can't go?"

"Is Paul Robeson a Communist?"

"Why is the United States friendly with the Malan government in South Africa, which is so unjust to black people?"

"Is it right for British troops to kill Africans who belong to the Mau Mau in Kenya?"

"What do Americans think of Kwame Nkrumah and his African government?"

Despite the nature of the questioning, the auditorium session ended with happy smiles. After the students had retired for the night, a group of four African members of the Mount Mary staff took me to a nearby parlor, and a lively conversation, which I recall with keen pleasure, ensued. The leading spirit was Daniel Mensha, of the Ewe

The quiz kids of today's Africa are the youngsters who know all the answers when the crowd gathers in front of the village language charts.

"A Wolof takes a wife." Mark Monet and Angelique Mendy (above) beam blissfully after their wedding. Below, a little French friend of Angelique's busses the bride amid the crowd outside Sacred Heart Church, Dakar.

At the Pasteur Institute in Dakar, Africans prove thoroughly capable at painstaking laboratory tasks. There is no color bar in French Africa.

Boys and girls have to be every bit as patient in getting books at the children's library in the Gold Coast as youngsters must in the U.S.A.

Replacing Africa's old-time native medicine man with his wretched practices is the modern doctor and the pleasant and capable visiting nurse.

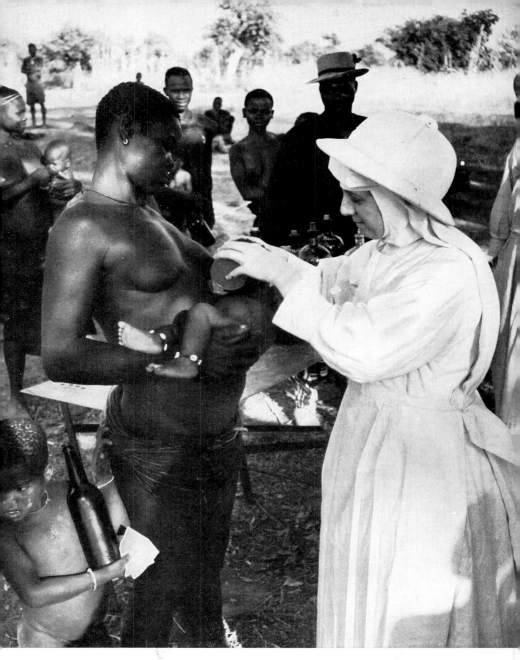

Hardy Franciscan Missionaries of Mary labor with the White Fathers among the backward tribes of the Northern Territories in the Gold Coast.

A phenomenon of modern Africa is the zeal with which the better African officials provide for the handicapped. This blind man reads braille.

University students at the Gold Coast's Achimota are proving more solid and sensible than many of their confreres at universities in Asia.

Almost every African loves music. Here a band sergeant in British Africa is teaching his earnest candidate musicians how to read the scale.

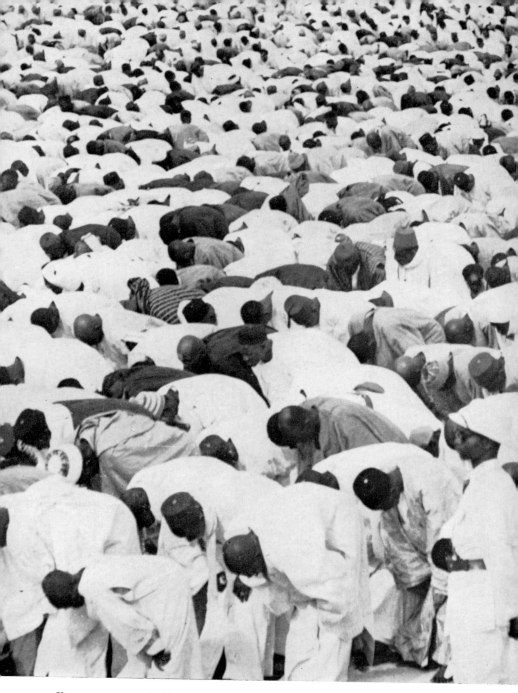

Forty per cent of all West Africans are Moslems. It is an arresting sight to witness thousands in the open on a feast day bowed low in prayer.

people. Also making contributions were George Nyinaku, of the Twi people (Kwame Nkrumah's tribe), Mark Gbikpi, of the Ewe, and Francis Abbey, of the Ga.

"I enjoyed the keenness of those students who asked the questions tonight," I remarked.

"They are really hungry for knowledge," replied Daniel. "Everybody's hungry; everywhere there's a hunger for education."

"In the cities and out in the villages, everybody wants to read," chimed in one of the others.

"But we just don't have enough books to read," added a third.

"How many village folk can read?" I asked.

"Perhaps one in ten among the grownups."

"A great many more are learning through the adult-education program."

"But most farmers don't have time."

"That's true. After they've bathed and have eaten supper, it's already dark."

"No reading lamps in the homes?" I asked.

"Not yet," explained one of the men. "Families haven't learned to get strong oil lamps. Perhaps if the Volta plan goes through, our villages will have electricity."

"Can be!" chuckled one of the group. "But many village folk just laugh at the Volta plan."

"Laugh?" I queried, puzzled.

"Yes," explained Mark Gbikpi. "I suppose to you it all sounds reasonable to build those huge dams across the Volta River, to back up the water and form a lake 240 miles long—a lake that's going to make huge waterfalls that will create all that electricity that is going to be carried by wires to every part of the Gold Coast. But many of the village people think the plan is foolish. 'All those millions and millions of pounds spent to get electricity to our village?' they say. 'That's foolish!'"

"Our native people aren't used to thinking about the good of the whole Gold Coast, Father."

"They merely think about their own village."

"And those who live near the Volta are angry, because the plan means destroying many villages."

"And people who hear that thousands of workers are going to be imported say: 'Oh, no! They can't bring foreign tribes here!' "

"And many say, 'I don't like all these new ideas, all this talk about ugly factories.' "

"How do the people like the new Government?" I asked.

"They're proud of it."

"They think we're marching right ahead."

"But I don't like a man like the Minister of Education, Botsio. He hasn't any religious principles."

"He wants to throw religion out of the schools."

"Why get rid of the Europeans if we're going to be as bad as they are?"

"We want a really great Gold Coast, a country of God-fearing men."

"I want each of my children to get a good schooling and make a good living and some day have a good family, but above all I want them to be good—and I mean good!"

"I want my children," added another, and the words rolled out grandiloquently, "to be really and truly loyal to God, loyal to their neighbors, and loyal to our beloved Gold Coast."

When I reached my room, I looked again out the window, across the valley at Mount Krobo. It stood in silence under the benevolent beams of the tranquil moon. It was a grave of the past; human sacrifice in the Gold Coast was dead. True, evil still lived there, and plenty of corruption and chicanery. Nevertheless, scattered plentifully among the citizens of this new land, were many men of simple, earnest integrity, like the quartet with whom I had just chatted. It is my guess that on these the Gold Coast will build.

The Gold Coast has an average of 2,000 faithful per priest, as against our American average of 650 Catholics per priest. And in the United States, the priests are not, as missionaries are, dedicated primarily to convert work.

Why are there not more native-born priests in the Gold Coast? There is as much intelligence and energy and piety among Gold Coast Catholics as among the Catholics of Uganda, Tanganyika, and other such areas. Why is it that 1,350,000 Catholics in British West Africa possess but 60 African priests (one to every 24,000), while 3,350,000 Catholics in British East Africa have 400 native-born priests and two African bishops, one to every 8,000 Catholics? Why, relatively speaking, has East Africa proven three times more fruitful than West Africa in building an African clergy? The question is a baffling one. Suffice it for the moment to say that missionaries in the Gold Coast are working hard at the problem since the new-born independence of that country.

Would the African people in general like to have their own clergy?

"They would be delighted!" replied an African priest. "At the Kumasi Congress, Bishop Kiwanuka brought cries of joy from thousands wherever he appeared. One youngster was heard asking a friend if he had seen the African bishop from Uganda. 'Yes, I have seen him,' replied the second youngster, 'but not enough!' "

The newest of the Gold Coast dioceses, Accra, has a Negro bishop. He is not, however, African-born, nor does he govern African clergy. He is Bishop Joseph Bowers, S.V.D., born on the beautiful little island of Dominica in the British West Indies. In his birthplace, his eighty-four-year-old father played the organ in the parish church when Bishop Bowers was consecrated for his African see. This Negro prelate was trained at the Divine Word Seminary at Bay St. Louis, Mississippi, and then sent to Rome for special studies. He was ordained in the Holy City in 1939. It was as a young priest that he first saw Africa.

The new bishop is the same age as Kwame Nkrumah, and his American background will help him greatly in the Gold Coast capital. He has a delightful sense of humor. He enjoys telling of an experience in a church in Dublin, where he knelt quietly making a visit one afternoon. A tiny Irish colleen, making a visit with her mother, passed up the aisle, discovered him, and immediately dropped on her knees before him.

After a moment the mother came by and, grasping the child by the arm, said, "Come, come, let's go."

"Sh-h, Mummy, don't bother me!" protested the little one in a stage whisper. "Don't you see that I'm praying to Blessed Martin de Porres?"

Blessed Martin's mother was likewise from the Caribbean area: she was a Negro freed woman who had been born in Panama.

Chapter 6

ZIK AND THE NEW NIGERIA

SINCE THE GRANTING of independence to India, Nigeria is the largest colony in the British Commonwealth. Its thirty million inhabitants make it population-wise the largest country in Africa. It is African Africa—there are less than 12,000 whites among the 30,000,000. It is one of the African countries in which race discrimination is at a minimum. "In Nigeria an African goes into any shop he pleases," a friend in Lagos explained to me, "to any theatre, restaurant, post office, holds any job in the country, puts his money into any bank, hires a bed in any hospital, goes to law in any courtroom, and, by decision of his own African peers, serves time in any jail—there's no color line."

Nigeria at present possesses three divisions—Southwestern Nigeria, Southeastern Nigeria, Northern Nigeria—so sharply separated from each other that they may be said to be like England, France and Germany under a common government. How substantial are the differences between the sections, is a matter of controversy. People who favor prolonged British rule seem to hold that the difficulties are almost insurmountable. Those who wish to hasten self-government insist that the divisions will quickly be ironed out if the Africans are left to themselves. One of the chief dangers is the educated minority, because its members scorn the backwardness of their fellow countrymen. Hardly more than twenty thousand people have been to high school. This minority promises to have its way; present prospects in Nigeria point to a substantial amount of self-government by 1956 or 1957.

Southwestern Nigeria is predominantly the country of the Yoruba people. It is much richer than Southeastern Nigeria and more developed politically. Some forty per cent of its children go to grade school. If it were separated from the North and the East it could make a second Gold Coast and would be about the size of the Gold Coast in population. Protestant Christianity has been strong there, and Catholicity, while it possesses excellent elements in its 185,000 faithful, is second to the Protestants in influence.

In Southeastern Nigeria, which is predominantly Ibo country, and not on good terms with the Yoruba, emancipation and advance are as keenly sought as in the West. East and West have rival political leaders; though the two southern sections stand together, against the foreigner and the North, no love is lost between them. Catholic Christians in the East are over 10 per cent of the population. The Catholics in Iboland are listened to and respected.

Northern Nigeria, counting 55 per cent of the total population, is one of the great Moslem strongholds of the continent. At one time the British forbade Christian missionaries entrance into the north; but today, both Catholics and Protestants are modestly installed. There are approximately 50,000 native Catholics, many of whom are immigrants from the south. American Dominicans from Chicago have opened a new mission field in Sokoto Province, on the fringe of the Sahara, and the project is a hardy one, worthy of their mettle. Northern Nigeria is a colorful area, with much about it that is medieval. It has the social stratification of a slave state. At the top are wealthy and powerful emirs. The Emir of Kano, for instance, receives a salary of £8,500 annually—as much as the Governor of Nigeria himself. Below the emirs is a subject mass that at the moment is illiterate, unambitious, bound only to the soil. Each man in the mass is quite happy to serve a master. "We are proud of our emirs," is the typical reply when a Hausa or Fulani is asked about the matter. The rank and file do not seem the least interested in the idea of having an individual say.

Slave though a northern Nigerian may seem to be, he feels superior to the Nigerians of the south, for he is a Moslem. The northerners know also that they are much more numerous than the southerners. A pastime of the folk in the bazaars of the north is plotting what they will do to the people of the south after the British go. *"Ba su son mu; ba mu son su!"* the northerners say quite categorically: "They don't like us; we don't like them!"

Nigeria holds a place of distinction in the annals of political philosophy because it was there that Sir George Goldie and Lord

Lugard represented the British Crown and evolved what, in their day, was revolutionary doctrine in their attitude toward the African. Lugard in *The Dual Mandate* enunciated the principle: "The governing power ought to exercise its functions for the benefit equally of the inhabitants and of the rest of mankind." [1] Lugard applied his principle of indirect rule and thus pleased the powerful emirs of the north very much, as well as the petty chiefs of Yorubaland in the south.

The port cities of Southern Nigeria, and the capital city of Lagos in particular, represent the most modern development in the country. Lagos, a city of 270,000, is to be federal territory, like Washington, D.C., in the plan for eventual self-government. Sections of Lagos are touched with elegance and charm. On the other hand, in the heart of the city are some sixty acres of notorious slums in which 30,000 people are crowded into bedraggled shacks along dirty streets with filthy open drains. The famous Idumagbo market is a riot of color and much more to the liking of the Lagos housewife than the more ordered shops. "For the last word in West Africa's huge, spectacular markets," I was told in Lagos, "you must see the great open-air emporium in Kano. The desert peoples come to it from a thousand miles away."

Ibadan, 125 miles north of Lagos, is advertised as "the greatest Negro city on earth." Its population is put as high as half a million. I viewed its astonishing vistas of tin roofs from one of the mission buildings. Today it is notable for its well-dressed citizens, its fine cars, its many taxis. It is notable, also, for its African religious life. There are many mosques; but the majority of the people are polytheists, and hence there is a predominance of *orisha* or god temples. A recent item in an Ibadan newspaper reads, "Last night the Ibadan Taxi-Drivers Association met and sacrificed ducks, goats, and dogs to Ogun, God of Iron, and prayed to him to prevent accidents and disasters."

Ogun, the god of the chase, of war and of iron, is very popular among the Yoruba, but is not their supreme being. The latter is Olorun, for whom are reserved the most respectful names, freedom from most human attributes, and remoteness from both man and the other gods. But strangely—it appears to us—the Yoruba people offer no regular worship to Olorun.

"There are no temples of Olorun," explains Parrinder, "no priests dedicated to his service, no cult-houses or convents for the training of devotees. No offerings are made to Olorun, for there are no shrines, and hence no communal prayers or sacrifices, not even the simplest libations of wine, such as are made in honour of the ancestors. Hence Olorun must be far removed from human appetites and needs." [2]

The religion of the Yoruba as well as of other peoples in Africa is not fetishism in the stricter meaning of this term; rather, it is a system of polytheism presided over by a supreme creator. But what the missionary hears most about, and the white man reads most about in the newspapers, are the lesser divinities, who get the day-to-day attention. Among the Yoruba, these are often said to be "sons" of Olorun. Thus a missionary, when he refers to Christ as the Son of God, may be told by a pagan, "So is our *orisha* (god) a son of Olorun."

The name Olorun means "owner of heaven." He is also called "creator," "the living one," "the owner of life," "the owner of breath," "the almighty one," "the all-powerful one," "the lord." Many phrases contain his name. Replying to a morning salutation, a native may say, "Thank Olorun," or, "Praise Olorun." At night the wish is expressed, "May Olorun awake us well." Dependence is shown by the expression, "If Olorun does it." For a kindness, one may say, "Olorun bless you." In distress, one cries, "Olorun, have pity!" When a great thing is accomplished, the expression goes, "It is Olorun who has done it." And finally, "Olorun grant a good end."

All of these references to a supreme being, it is important to note, were hidden from the knowledge of the pioneers who studied the religion of Africa. It was the cloud of rites and the host of wayside gods that got the attention of the early scholars. As a result, we find the *Encyclopaedia of Religion and Ethics,* in the year 1900, stating, "The most obscure and difficult question connected with the religion of the Bantu is whether they have any belief in a Supreme Being, a Creator, an overruling Providence."

For a while the protagonists of the theory that the idea of a supreme being was man-made, believed that they had evidence in Africa to support their position. Among the more primitive peoples, they said, recognition of a supreme being is not found. Gods in Africa referred to as supreme beings were, they contended, deified ancestors or personifications of the great celestial phenomena.

A major contribution to destroying the claims of the anti-supreme-being school was made by the late Father Wilhelm Schmidt, of the Divine Word Fathers. Father Schmidt was founder of his Society's Vienna institute of anthropologists and editor of *Anthropos*. For decades he was eminent in his field. Toward the end of 1925, when Pope Pius XI decided to establish the Lateran Ethnological-Missiological Museum, he chose Father Schmidt as its director. I was living in Rome at the time and had opportunity to meet Father Schmidt quite frequently. Like the truly distinguished in every field, he was simple and unpretentious. His religious community at that time forbade its members to accept academic degrees, but on a couple of occasions when accosting him I addressed him as "Doctor Schmidt." The second time I did so, this scholarly gentleman earnestly admonished me: "You must not call me Doctor! I am not a Doctor."

Father Schmidt, in his *Ursprung des Gottesidee* (Origin of the Idea of God), did much to turn the tide toward recognition of the fact that in their primitive tradition, all peoples over the globe acknowledge a supreme being. He established the theory that the religion of the oldest strata of Mankind, represented in Africa by the Pygmies (Bushmen), was genuinely monotheistic.

Other scholars with a spiritual sense find evidence in Africa of a primitive revelation, the partial vision of the Divinity given to all human beings, which vision Christianity has the mission to build on and complete. The late Father Charles, eminent missiologist at Louvain, used to say, "We finish the non-Christian religions by finishing them!" In each pagan heart is the unfinished spiritual symphony; Christianity completes the incomplete. Most appealing about Father Charles's concept, which after all is a traditional Catholic concept, is its emphasis on the *truth* that every pagan possesses, rather than on the *falsehood* that we insist on staring at so disdainfully. The truth in him may be as obscure as his very notion of the Supreme Being, but nonetheless it is precious and beautiful to contemplate.

Father Joseph J. Williams gathered data principally through Catholic missionaries, and published it in a series of monographs entitled *Africa's God.*[3] "Our findings show," he stated, "that there has been a general retrogression in matters of religion, and even where tribes have been polytheistic in recent years, there is often a clear indication of monotheistic belief in early years."

In Ibadan today, paganism is definitely on the decline. The

Yoruba religion, with its pantheon of four hundred gods, its temples and priests, was strongly entrenched when, a century ago, Islam and Christianity both entered the region. What has happened in the intervening hundred years is well described by a member of the staff at the University College of Ibadan, Doctor Geoffrey Parrinder (already quoted in this chapter), who during his residence in Ibadan has published a religious survey of the city. "Christianity and Islam are racing each other for the capture of the soul of southern Nigeria," states Doctor Parrinder.[4] In this race, he says frankly, Islam takes the lead in numbers. In the beginning, the Sunni sect was the only one represented. In 1923, the Ahmadiyya sect from India appeared, modernistic, unorthodox, advocating monogamous marriage. Islam holds great prestige in Ibadan through its following among the aristocracy.

Doctor Parrinder estimates that the combined Christian bodies number twenty per cent of the citizenry of Ibadan. Unfortunately, we Christians are characterized by our multiple divisions. Catholics and the established Protestant communities total nine religious administrations with thirty-six places of worship. "Separatist" groups total an additional seventeen organizations with thirty meeting-houses. The large total of "separatist" Christian groups, not accepting direction from Western Protestants, is notable everywhere in Africa. In South Africa, which reports between eight hundred and twelve hundred sects, the phenomenon is strongly induced by the color bar, and everywhere the desire to be free of the white man is present.

Edwin W. Smith adds another interesting explanation of the increase of native separatists. "Their success," he observes, "is due in no small measure to their adoption of less formal, more lively, forms of worship, with the use of native music and instruments . . . they approach nearer the African ethos, whereas the churches of European origin are often so distressingly European and dull."

Years ago I enjoyed the hospitality of the diocesan seminary at Ibadan, where the Society of African Missions prepares its priestly candidates. Today an African Missions priest, Father A. J. Foley, is across the city on the staff of that new Nigerian institution of special importance, the University College of Ibadan. Secondary schools, with students wearing blazers and cricket caps have long added to the academic scene in Nigeria. St. Gregory's College in Lagos is among these schools; for twenty-five years and more, Nigerian boys in natty green blazers have sauntered over its close-cropped lawns, amid simple but dignified buildings. The atmosphere makes us think of an English "public school." Now some fifty of these secondary schools are sending their graduates to Ibadan and about one fifth of the student personnel are from Catholic institutions.

"Amid the very modern buildings of this our new university," reports Father Foley, "we have a site, generously assigned us by the authorities, for a very modern Catholic chapel. The Christian cross on its tower will greet everyone who passes the entrance of the university. . . . Our Catholic boys are a fighting and self-respecting minority. Their special need is some kind of wide union with fellow Catholics around the world, from whom they may learn of other peoples' difficulties and successes."

By "the new Nigeria" is meant the Nigeria since 1935. In that year, a young African nationalist, Dr. Nnamdi Azikive, popularly known as Zik, returned home from studying in the United States. Zik is an example, like Kwame Nkrumah of the Gold Coast, of the young men who, while in the United States, pass under the appellation of "foreign student" and so often are dismissed from the thinking of Americans, with an indifferent shrug. Zik, an Ibo born in 1904, studied at Lincoln University between 1924 and 1934. Today he is one of the most important native leaders in West and Central Africa.

In 1934, Zik became editor of the *African Morning Post* at Accra, capital of the Gold Coast. Convicted of sedition, the young editor eventually won acquittal but then moved back to his native Nigeria. His family had wealth. Very shortly, with a busy press operating in Lagos, Zik had a chain of five successful newspapers operating throughout Southern Nigeria. Nowhere except in British Africa could such bitter attacks be leveled against Europeans and their government. Zik has laid down as his basic principle the idea that the European was *not* in Africa to help the African. He has consistently charged the Government with discrimination against Africans, first by the marked salary differences between European and African even when an African possessed the same degrees, and secondly by refusing advancement to Africans beyond a certain level in business and government, regardless of merit.

Zikism—the program of Zik and his followers—stands mainly for the following: (1) increased education; (2) Africanization of the civil

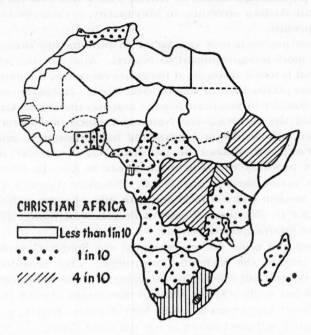

CHRISTIAN AFRICA

☐ Less than 1 in 10
∴∴∵ 1 in 10
////// 4 in 10

DISTRIBUTION OF CHRISTIANS IN AFRICA

Christians in Africa number 37,360,678 adherents, or 18% of the total population. Of these, Catholics number 16,752,127, or 44.8% of the Christian body. Protestants 12,642,785, or 34% of the Christian body, and Eastern Orthodox groups, 7,965,766, or 21.2% of the Christian body.

Among Bantu Africans, principal Catholic and Protestant strength is found in West, Central and East Africa. A substantial number of European Catholics is found in the French areas of North Africa, while European Protestants are strong in South Africa. The largest body of Eastern Orthodox Christians is found in Ethiopia.

For Christian distribution according to political divisions, see Appendix A.

services; (3) industrialization of Africa, with a free role for participation by the African according to his capacity; (4) self-government for African peoples.

Zikism has been only one factor in pushing the British toward granting more self-government to Nigeria. After all, the self-government trend is found throughout the entire continent, the entire world. Yet Zik has played a major role in West Africa. His party controls his own Ibo country in Southeast Nigeria and also the British Cameroons. It is called the N.C.N.C.—the National Council of Nigeria and the Cameroons. In Southwest Nigeria the native power is held by the Action Party, an offshoot of the N.C.N.C., the leader of which, Owolowo, probably wields as much power as Zik. In Northern Nigeria the major party is the N.P.C. (Northern People's Congress), which is Moslem and not in league with Zik. His group in the north is the N.E.P.U. (Northern Elements' Progressive Union). These various native groups quarrel bitterly.

Zikism and other factors prompted the British Government, in 1946, to propose the Richards Constitution. That provided limited political reforms but did not go far enough for the local politicos. In 1952, London made a better grant of concessions, though the Nigerians are almost unanimous in asking for still more. Nigeria will shortly have as much self-government as has the Gold Coast.

What do those who are genuinely interested in the Nigerians think of this current movement?

"We favor most of these steps toward greater self-government," said a Holy Ghost missionary of Nigeria in answer to this question. "The Church is riding out the uncertainties of the present day. The Kingdom of God is being extended in 'the new Nigeria,' which, most of us feel, will eventually become a land guided by sound spiritual ideals. At the moment we see in the picture four or five factors that oppose this sound spiritual growth."

The veteran observer of the Nigerian scene then enunciated those factors which the shrewder among the Nigerian Christians see as stumbling blocks for the future.

1—*The eye on Moscow.* There is a tendency, without formally espousing the Communist cause, for Nigerians to look toward Moscow as the champion of national self-determination.

2—*The leaning toward Islam.* Some Nigerian leaders think they will gain by making common cause with the Moslem world. The head of the Action Party, Mr. Owolowo, recently made a long journey for contacts through the Middle East and the Indian Peninsula. The London correspondent for Zik's papers wrote: "As Britain is a Christian state, and Pakistan, Egypt and the Arab States are Moslem states, surely Moslems should be entitled to claim Nigeria as a Moslem state. . . . A state with a clean majority of Moslems might add to the luster and credit of Islam as well as lessen the horrible condition of those whom Christianity has failed to save. After all, what is religion for?"

3—*The antimissionary attitude.* This attitude is not born of Zikism but is characteristic of many of the little groups of educated Nigerians who follow Zik. It is one of the galling experiences of missionaries to find those young people—who were never noted for spiritual perspicacity, and who often have had no understanding contact with Christian life or teaching—reciting the litanies of missionary sins and failures.

Much of the hostility toward missionaries on the part of educated Africans comes from the pagan secularism or antimissionary attitude of many white seculars. One day while I lunched with a European in Nigeria, he discovered red ants on the table. "We call these missionary ants," he remarked with a mischievous smile, "because they are found everywhere and are very annoying." His joke was friendly, but its origin reflects a widespread attitude. An African Protestant leader is quoted on this point in the *World Christian Handbook:* "It is one of the tragedies in the Gold Coast today (perhaps in all Africa) that very few of the Europeans who occupy the high places in the political, social, and economic life of the country are avowedly Christian or are willing to take leadership in religious life also. Our youth, looking to these men, question the value of Christianity. When one talks to the youth, one cannot but judge that a great deal of their criticism of the Church is due to the indifference of the settlers from 'Christian countries.'" [5]

4—*Antiforeign attitude.* Xenophobia is a world disease and signifies hostility to foreigners for unreasonable motives. Other hostility toward the foreigner may be reasonable and justifiable. Whatever its cause, however, strong hostility toward the foreigner in Africa cannot but do harm to the African. Education opens the eyes of the African,

and he sees clearly the improprieties in the colonial system. It is unfortunate that his anger runs so strong that he refuses to retain the
foreigner long enough to gain from him the know-how to make himself an able citizen in the world of our day.

5—Anti-African attitude. There'll never be a great Africa while
the small, educated minority of Africans in Nigeria and elsewhere de-
spises the huge, uneducated majority of their fellow countrymen. In
years gone by in Nigeria, foreign officials created resentment in the
educated Africans by displaying snobbish condescension toward them.
Today a similar resentment is being created in the ordinary folk of the
country, by snobbish conduct on the part of many of the newly educated Africans.

"But don't misunderstand," warns the man who gave me these
points, "flaws there may be, but we are marching side by side with our
Nigerians. Beneath the blatant shouting there is a hard core of earnest, God-fearing Africans who will work and pray ardently that Nigeria will be a safe and happy home for their loved ones."

Tom and Bobo, two massive Hausas, poled and paddled me across
the lazy Niger. Our boat was a long canoe, sculptured from a tree
trunk. Tom stood in the bow, a smiling but silent man. Bobo, captain of the vessel, stood in the stern. Both, attired only in abbreviated
trunks, would have made magnificent bronzes for the African Hall
of the Museum of Natural History.

First we pushed away from the bank at Asaba by means of poles
that found the river bottom and projected us out into the stream. I
sat in the center of the canoe comfortably ensconced against a wooden
back-rest set in the bottom of the boat, and let my eye rove out over
the wonderful river, third longest in Africa, that finds life in the
heights of far-off French Guinea and sweeps in a majestic arc through
interior French Africa. Now, but a short run from the Atlantic, it is
tawny from its heavy load of silt which shortly it will deposit in its
huge, many-pronged delta, larger than that of the Nile.

Once free of the bank, Tom and Bobo put aside their poles and
took up their paddles. Then Bobo really swung into action. In turn
he gurgled, hissed, grunted and sang, to set the rhythm for Tom and
himself. The billowy muscles of both men rolled syncopatingly, quite
as if they were in a dance. The river was wide and the crossing took

more than half an hour. There was time to peer at the palm-banked shore, to brood over the flowing tide of shining water, to watch the boat life, which was as interesting as on a stream in China. The ride was a delightful experience.

And then we set foot on what, with low-voiced reverence, is referred to locally as "Shanahan's country."

Bishop Shanahan is many a missionary's candidate as the greatest apostle in Africa during the first half of the twentieth century. He had the commanding moral stature of the legendary figures who went forth from the old monasteries in the great ages of the Celtic saints. He was a handsome man, with heavy but erect build; a strong body that made him, as a young priest, capable of besting the native wrestlers around the village fires of an evening; and with natural dignity and delicate courtesy that let him into every heart, proud or humble. It was Bishop Shanahan's series of fateful decisions that, under God, led to the outstanding success of the Church in Southeast Nigeria.

Today Southeast Nigeria, with but 20 per cent of Nigeria's population of 30,000,000, counts 70 per cent of Nigeria's Catholic population of 940,000. Indeed, 30 per cent of all the Catholics among the 52,000,000 inhabitants of West Africa are found in this pocket of Southeast Nigeria.

Father Joseph Shanahan joined the French missionaries in the field in 1902. He found as Christians only a few handfuls of redeemed slaves: cowardly, beaten, deceitful creatures; "pitiful foundation-stones," the priest later recorded, "for the spiritual edifice of Christianity." By 1905, Father Shanahan was named prefect apostolic with a dozen priests under him. What would he do to push forward the kingdom of God in this notoriously barren corner of Africa? His first step was to fall in love with the people. He contacted them on every occasion, learned their language perfectly, learned their ways, interested himself in all their problems.

One day for the hundredth time, an old black fellow said to him as he sought out new Christians: "We are too old to change now. Why does Father not try the children?"

The children? That's right! Why haggle with the grownups? Why not concentrate on the children? Here was the first great decision—to work through the children. But how could one organize the children? Through a school, of course. Quickly he reached his second important decision—to work at a systematic building up of schools and the training of many teachers.

The greatest among all his inspired decisions came through Ireland's national patron, Saint Patrick.

"Suddenly the vision of my native land came before me," Bishop Shanahan recorded, "and I saw how akin Patrick's problem was to mine. He had a country peopled by a wild pagan tribe. So had I. He had one great river and a few smaller ones for communication. So had I. But he did not content himself with trying to convert a few towns along the Shannon, as I was doing on the Niger. He struck boldly into the heart of the country to bring home the mystery of the Holy Trinity to all and sundry. He prepared the land for the coming of Catholic schools. I resolved to do the same."

"That was the most epoch-making decision made in his whole life," writes Father Jordan, the bishop's biographer. "With characteristic haste he summoned the other Fathers, to communicate his decision to them. He pointed out that they were touching only the fringe of paganism by keeping to the highways of commerce. They ought to aim at its heart by trekking into the depths of the bush. . . . There would be dangers, perhaps even death. But what of that? The French Fathers were filled with enthusiasm. To the bush . . . to the bush! 'Vive la brousse!' " [6]

Today the dozen priests of 1905 are now replaced in the area by 456 priests, Brothers and Sisters, foreign and African, working in five dioceses, aided by some 3,000 catechists. In 1953, Bishop Moynah of the Diocese of Calabar asked Rome for an auxiliary for his see and one of his African priests was chosen for the post. Bishop Dominic Ekandem is the first Nigerian raised to the episcopacy. There are 250,000 boys and girls in the Catholic schools, taught by almost 8,000 African teachers, many of whom are excellently trained. Thus "Shanahan's country" has become one of the wonder fields of Africa.

The great missionary is the man with a great dream. For a quarter of a century Bishop Shanahan was in the vanguard of the remarkable march into the bush country. Always before his eyes was his dream. "I felt that Christ would one day take up His residence among these people everywhere," he wrote, "and therefore I blessed every market we passed through, and every river we crossed, and every village we saw."

Chapter 7

LOWLY MAN OF THE LOST VILLAGE

WHAT OF THE lowly, common men lost in primitive villages of West Africa as yet untouched by modernity?

An interesting physician and surgeon who has worked for some years in "Shanahan's country" in Southeastern Nigeria is Doctor Louis Bertrand Gonzales. He is a product of Holy Ghost College, Port of Spain, on the island of Trinidad in the Caribbean Sea. While studying medicine in Dublin, he felt prompted to offer himself for a tour of duty in Africa. There he labored in hospitals staffed by the Holy Rosary Sisters at Emekuku and Adazi. His task gave him opportunity for devoted service among the simple folk of the vast rural areas.

"A woman with child was being taken to the hospital at Emekuku," relates Doctor Gonzales. "On the way, the party met a *dibia,* a local medicine man, who for five pounds (a huge sum here, mind you) offered to deliver the woman. After about four hours of useless beatings, and applications of leaves and so forth to the unfortunate woman, he confessed himself baffled and advised the relatives to resume their walk to Emekuku. They finally arrived at the hospital, where examination proved the child to be dead. And in spite of all we could do, the mother herself died within an hour."

Is this an exceptional experience? Or is this the normal level of general practice among Nigeria's lowly people? Happily, it represents a situation that is on the mend; but the experience is still of frequent occurrence throughout West Africa.

The area about the Emekuku hospital is particularly well off. Within the two provinces of Onitsha and Owerri—among the most heavily populated in Africa—four million people are served by a dozen hospitals. Seven of these are operated by the Government; two by the Protestants; three by the Catholics. However, only portions of this area are well cared for; other parts are completely lacking in the barest necessities. And even as regards the cared-for portions, let us have no illusions: old pagan practices are still commonly observed. By far the majority of people treated at the hospitals are pagan. They have pagan ideas and pagan superstitions, and *jujus* are connected with each of their illnesses.

"Many a patient," explains one of the Sisters, "comes in with a *juju* charm hanging on his neck. Strangely enough, the patient himself will never think of getting rid of the charm, but he will not object if the doctor or nurse quietly lifts it off. In fact, he'll merely laugh rather shamefacedly as the charm is removed."

The patient who reaches a good hospital is well cared for. But far less fortunate are the majority of natives served by the native medicine men.

"The *dibia's* knowledge of anatomy is nil," explains Doctor Gonzales; "his ideas of surgery are even less than primitive and rather more than barbarous. His skill at maternity cases is nonexistent. In maternity work we see in all its stark horror the havoc wrought by the native *dibia*, who continues cynically the practices of his forefathers of centuries ago. Two years ago at Ihiala, a woman was brought in to us in labor. After four days of the tender ministrations of fifteen *dibias*, she had six fractures, including both bones of the forearms and of the upper arms. Her body was one mass of bruises; she was cut and bleeding and swollen all over; and her eyes were closed. Her child was dead, and it was only by the mercy of God that she herself lived."

It is not brutal sadism that prompts the cruel acts of the medicine man, but rather his fanatical attachment to a paganism that attributes sickness or difficulties at childbirth to satanic forces. This belief drives the *dibia* to a wild fury that approaches madness. Often he has little concept of therapy and thus can resort only to superstitious devices.

Doctor Gonzales comments on this situation: "To see a child brought in to you in the last stages of pneumonia or dysentery, with a bit of bone around its neck and dye over its body—to see such a child expire under your eyes because its mother had taken the child to the *dibia*, who in his ignorance or malice made a few cuts on its chest or abdomen to let out the 'bad blood' and hence the bad spirits— is heartbreaking."

In the less-fortunate areas of Southern Nigeria, almost fifty per cent of the children die before they are a year old and some thirty-five per cent of the remainder never reach five years of age. But Doctor Gonzales notes that the *dibia* is not to be blamed for everything. Malnutrition and dysentery are master villains.

"In the hospital," he says, "I have from time to time youngsters who, if they were Europeans, I would say had come from the war camps of Belsen or Dachau. Their poor limbs are barely covered by skin; their ribs stand out like the bars of a gate; their bellies are swollen with dropsy; their eyes are dull and lifeless. One would need to have a heart of stone, not to be saddened at the sight of so much untold misery, suffering, and neglect."

Devotion to those struck down by disease is of great importance, but efforts in West Africa to prevent disease seem more important still. The coast of the great West African bulge has been made livable by preventive medicine. Yet thousands of natives still die through absolute neglect of the first rules of survival. Malaria, the greatest killer in the world, still runs in great part unchecked. Many parents give more attention to educating their surviving children than to ridding their villages of the causes of death. Bad diet, dirt and contamination, flies, mosquitoes, and bad water bring troubles in their wake. Superstition, fear, and ignorance still wreak greater havoc.

Two British doctors—J. A. Hamilton and M. Colbourne—toward the end of 1949, picked out a typical small village in the forest belt of the Gold Coast and made a survey of it. With a third confrere, they chose a little community called Kwansakrome, and the data they compiled made all West Africa think. [1] The following are some of the points in the survey.

Inhabitants. Kwansakrome had 250 people. Most of them were farmers; nine families had cocoa farms, and the others had food farms. Only 12 persons were employed part time in other work—as laborers, blacksmiths, carvers. There was one seamstress. Six boys went to school in a nearby town. The village had only five men between 16 and 20 years of age; the others had left, either lured by town life or to earn money to get married. The large number of children under six was telltale evidence that mortality is heaviest in this bracket; relatively few survive beyond it into higher brackets. The village women between 15 and 44 (34 in all) had borne 162 children, of whom 75 were already dead.

Water supply. The village is in a section that gets 50 inches of rain a year, almost all of it in the five months of the wet season. There are six shallow wells; during the rains they are filled, but only two are popular for drinking because the rest are salty. It is necessary to wade into the wells to get the water, and by January they are dried up. This means a walk of four miles to the nearest river, which is infected with bilharzia.

Despite the annual shortage, only five families in the village save water caught from the roofs of their houses. Not only is the water lost: as it rushes off the gutterless roofs, it works havoc by washing away soil and undermining foundations.

Homes. There are 32 family compounds, all swish-built, with corrugated iron roofs. The cocoa farmers, who are better off, can afford concrete floors and better furniture.

Latrines. At the back of the village are two latrines, fairly well kept but infested with masses of flies. These flies haunt the nearby area where the children and animals play. This arrangement is typical of the entire forest belt.

Diet. The people eat all available foods in season. These provide a certain amount of proteins, but not enough. Besides domestic and wild animals, peanuts also are a source of protein. In season, snails are an important addition to the diet.

Medical treatment. Two miles away is a Government dispensary, and 17 miles away is a hospital with a resident doctor.

Prevailing diseases. The survey showed that 95% of the people had had malaria; 77% had yaws; almost 100% were infected by one or other of the worm diseases. Some 33% of the children under five years, and 15% of all others, suffered from malnutrition.

Malaria. "The greatest killer in the world" is active over large areas of the globe, but the West African type (Anopheles Gambiae) is probably the most dangerous in the world. West African malaria does its worst in children under six; the first attacks in infancy are often fatal. The children who survive early attacks suffer constantly from fevers and general weakness, and are prone to other diseases such as pneumonia. Almost every child under six has an enlarged spleen, the sign that malaria resistance is developing. By seven, such a child is usually strong enough to throw off the disease, and the spleen reduces its size; after this fearful buffeting, malaria is not a killing disease in that particular West African. The ordinary overseas visitor, who has not fought malaria in childhood, can easily become its victim.

Yaws. This disease is not a great killer, but is responsible for much pain and ill health. It affects the skin and bones and causes many ulcers. It causes painful pitting on the feet; and in extreme cases, it attacks the bones of the face, making the bridge of the nose collapse.

Diseases from worms. The village's sufferers from round worm were 75% of the population; hookworm, 52%; schistosomiasis (bilharzia), 9%; blood worms, 21%. And 52% had had Guinea worm at one time or another.

Hookworm. Small as a pin, the hookworm egg hatches out in damp, contaminated ground and attaches itself to the feet of a passer-by. Then it burrows through the skin and moves up through the body to the small intestine. It causes a disease like anemia.

Round worm. The egg is eaten with unclean food, and hatches out in the stomach. The worm, white in color, moves all over the body but ends in the intestine, where it has the size of an earthworm. Some 30 of these parasites may flourish within a person at one time, causing no specific disease but eating up his nourishment and giving him discomfort.

Schistosomiasis (bilharzia). The incidence of 9% in this village was lower than average. The disease is caught by wading in the river or by drinking infected water. The tiny worm lives in the wall of the bladder, entering the urine and causing great discomfort.

Guinea worm. This worm is a string-like animal some two feet long; it lives under the skin, usually in the leg or foot, and for several weeks causes great pain and swelling.

Blood worm. This one is carried from person to person by a small, biting fly. The blood of 21% of the villagers was infected but no serious illness resulted.

Scabies. Some 20% of the villagers were infected. It is not a severe disease, but indicates dirty surroundings.

Venereal disease (gonorrhoea). Some 5% of the people had this. The figure for this village was much lower in proportion than the figure for towns.

Epidemic diseases. When smallpox came to the area the previous year, all the villagers were vaccinated; only one person was affected, and that before vaccination. Yellow fever is remembered as making its appearance. Dysentery tended to occur in epidemics.

Leprosy; tuberculosis. While both are found in the area, the village had no cases.

Sleeping sickness. Several tsetse flies were caught in the village, but no cases of sleeping sickness were found. However, horses and cows could not be kept because of the tsetse flies; and thus there was no milk supply; there were no meat animals raised, and no work animals used on the farms.

Malnutrition. The averages for malnutrition according to ages were as follows:

Less than 1 yr. old	*1 to 5 yrs. old*	*6 to 15 yrs. old*	*16 to 45 yrs. old*	*Over 45 yrs. old*
33%	46%	28%	18%	4%

The chief sufferers are the young children and the nursing mothers. Diseases are partly the cause. In addition, the doctors report as causes "cooking habits that waste or destroy food values, irregularity of meals, bad distribution of the food among the family where the father and the older children get the lion's share of the body-building foods."

What should be done, the doctors ask, in this and the host of similar villages in West Africa? There are three categories of people who must intervene: (1) the villagers themselves; (2) the Native Authority or Town Council; (3) the central Government. The doctors warn that would-be reformers—and this could include inexperienced missionaries—should not try to attack diseases against which greater forces than they can command must be brought into play. Speaking of their particular village, the doctors say, "At the moment, the problem of malaria here should not be tackled." They believe that the whole Government machinery must move in to battle with the malaria mosquito, working throughout the area as a unit.

However, one means they advocate most strongly; namely, education. And this must not be merely a course of "sit-down" study in a classroom. Teachers must make health education a field project for both primary-school pupils and older ones, including adults.

"The village is in need of essential education," says the report from Kwansakrome, "not primarily in order to read and write, but even more in order that its young children may live. Later, as they become literate, they in turn can help their less-fortunate friends." Thus the doctors spelled out, probably without knowing it, the program of fundamental education initiated for the backward regions of the world by UNESCO.

Hundreds of Government medical workers like Doctors Colbourne and Hamilton are on the job in Africa. Theirs is a labor of skill, but even more, it is a labor of devotion. For many of these Government officers, it is a labor of spiritual dedication.

Religious who do medical work in Africa are formed to direct their lives to the spiritual ideal of working not only for their fellow man but for God, who made the African. Let us listen in for a moment on Canon Eugene Boylan, a monk of Roscrea, as he delivers a conference to young Sisters of Ireland about to go out to Africa as doctors and nurses:

"The work of a Medical Missionary when it deals directly with the bodies or souls of others, deals with Christ. Saint Columban summed it all up in a pregnant phrase, *'Christi sumus, non nostri'*— 'We are Christ's, not our own.' Saint Thomas comments, 'Just as a tree without roots, or a house without a foundation, easily perishes, so does the spiritual edifice unless it be rooted and founded in charity.' It is by one and the same virtue of charity that we love God and love our neighbor. 'Amen I say to you, as long as you did it to one of these my least brethren, you did it to me' *(Matt. 25:40)*."

Section 2

CENTRAL AFRICA

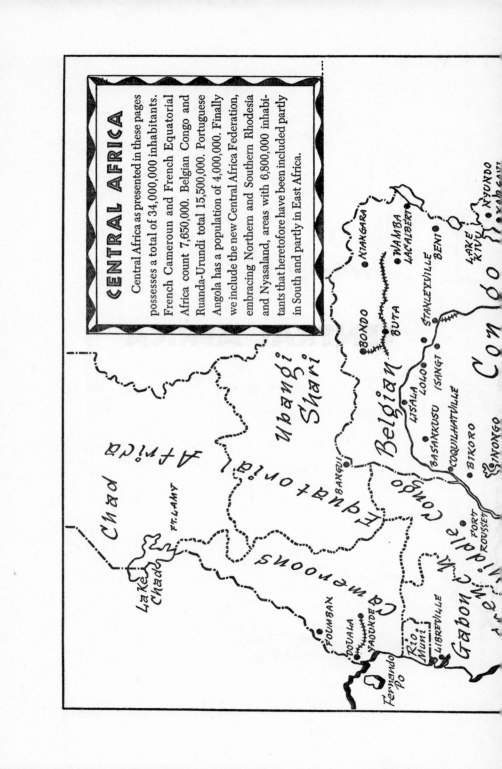

CENTRAL AFRICA

Central Africa as presented in these pages possesses a total of 34,000,000 inhabitants. French Cameroun and French Equatorial Africa count 7,650,000. Belgian Congo and Ruanda-Urundi total 15,500,000. Portuguese Angola has a population of 4,000,000. Finally we include the new Central Africa Federation, embracing Northern and Southern Rhodesia and Nyasaland, areas with 6,800,000 inhabitants that heretofore have been included partly in South and partly in East Africa.

Chad

Fr. Lamy

Lake Chad

Cameroons

Foumban

Douala

Yaounde

Fernando Po

Rio Muni

Libreville

Gaboon

Fort Roussey

Ubangi Shari

Equatorial Africa

Bangui

Congo

Belgian Congo

Niangara

Wamba

Lacalbery

Beni

Lake Kivu

Nyundo

Bondo

Buta

Stanleyville

Lisala

Lolo

Isangi

Basankusu

Coquilhatville

Bikoro

Inongo

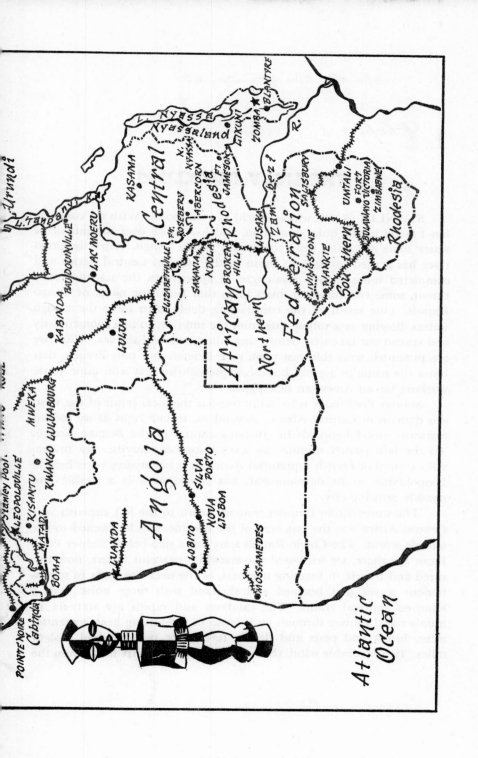

Chapter 1

THE UGLY DUCKLING

STANLEY POOL WAS as placid as a millpond. With my companion I stood in the quiet afternoon, and looked off over the mirror of water some 350 miles from the mouth of the Congo. After the great river has arched through its basin in the heart of Central Africa and completed more than a semicircle, it approaches the narrow rocky throat, some two hundred miles long, that bears the name of Congo Rapids. One result of the constricting defile is to force the Congo waters, flowing as a yellow tide from the interior, to halt momentarily and spread out lake-wise before they plunge toward the sea. Thus we are presented with this vast pool, part Belgian and part French, that bears the name of a great English explorer who first won fame while working for an American newspaper.

Stanley Pool today is in many respects the focal point of the western domain of Central Africa. Beyond us, to our right as we looked eastward, stood Leopoldville, thriving capital of the Belgian Congo. To the left, twenty minutes by ferry from Leopoldville, lay Brazzaville, capital of French Equatorial Africa; it is twenty-five years behind Leopoldville in its development, but nevertheless is a sizable and steadily growing city.

The unremitting thunder that we heard to the left explains why Central Africa was the last area of the continent to be opened to the outside world. The Congo Rapids start but a step below Stanley Pool. From the shore, we witnessed the erstwhile peaceful waters, now tortured and frantic in foaming madness, piling over the rocks in mountainous waves that boomed and shrieked with more noise than a hundred railroad trains. The cataracts and rapids are sixty-six in number and plunge through an inferno of suffocating heat, torrential rains, beasts and pests and deadly fevers, for two hundred violent miles. In a favorable wind, the roar is heard up to fifty miles from the river bank. The Portuguese, and later the other nations journeying down the western coast of Africa, easily came upon the estuary that forms the mouth of the Congo. But sailing inland, they were quickly halted—after ninety-three miles, to be precise—at the end of the viable waterway. Thus they were long discouraged from entering the interior.

One day in 1881, as Henry M. Stanley, the great explorer, worked in the neighborhood of Stanley Pool, he was astonished to encounter a young French missionary, Monsignor Prosper Augouard, laboring near the present site of Brazzaville.

"You are a very imprudent young man, Monsignor, to live without protection in these parts," admonished Stanley.

"My dear Monsieur Stanley," replied the missionary, with a bold smile, "if as they tell us, God keeps an eye of special kindliness on intoxicated folk, He must certainly watch mercifully over missionaries." [1]

"These French!" commented Stanley. "They have always the trick of turning a phrase."

How was it that Monsignor Augouard appeared at that time near Stanley Pool? Other history less well known than the story of Stanley was being enacted in Central Africa, and it involved French missionaries. We recall that, of the band of seven of Father Libermann's missionaries who went with Bishop Barron to Liberia, five were dead in a few months, one returned to France, and the seventh, Pere Bessieux, remained in the field. In September of 1844, Pere Bessieux and two lay companions landed from the *Zebra* on the Gabon Coast, in French Equatorial Africa not very far from the mouth of the Congo, and began missionary work. In 1849, the Holy See, in Pere Bessieux's words, "made me a bishop in punishment for my sins."

By the 1870's, Bishop Bessieux was a respected leader along the Gabon Coast. King Denis, the local ruler, was very friendly, although, having a hundred wives and being disinclined to give them up, he remained pagan throughout the bishop's lifetime. Curiously enough, Bishop Bessieux, who passed away in 1876, was dead but ten days when King Denis found himself likewise at death's door. No priest was handy, so the chieftain called his son and asked the young man to baptize him. What happened then was one proof that the pioneer bishop had left his mark on the primitive Gabon Coast.

"Will you promise me," asked the son, "that if you were suddenly to get well again you would declare publicly that you would keep but one wife?"

"I promise," said King Denis, and his son baptized him. "It is God's moment," declared the new Christian. "Do not attribute my death to any evil artifice, to any poisoning. I forbid you to immolate slaves for me when I am gone."

In 1878, a new leader for the handful of missionaries in French Central Africa arrived, in the person of Monsignor Prosper Augouard, the most thunderous figure in the African missionary annals of the great Congregation of the Holy Ghost. Of most missionary pioneers, the records are spare—their histories are discovered only with difficulty. In the case of Bishop Augouard, however, bibliography alone fills a volume, for he was a tireless writer, a popular speaker, and a colorful figure who made marvelous copy for everyone, friend or foe, who wielded a pen. He loved difficulties, thirsted for combat, and was never halted by the hostility of men or elements. He is unquestionably one of the great figures in the history of Central Africa.

In his youth, while a student for the priesthood in France, he was faced with a false charge of breaking the Rule. He left the seminary and joined the Papal Zouaves; but one day in Rome, he suddenly turned to a companion and cried, "Hold my gun; I must see that bishop!"

The ecclesiastic he sought was Monsignor de Segur, who arranged for his return to the seminary. One day he heard a lecture by a missionary from Zanzibar, and he asked to join the Holy Ghost Fathers. Thus in 1878 he arrived on the Gabon Coast. He was then a handsome, well-built man, noisy of disposition but deeply pious and wonderfully loyal. Almost immediately he came into contact with Savorgnan de Brazza. The latter had been born in Italy, but was a naturalized French citizen and made expeditions for France into Central Africa. Thus it came about that, while the southern bank of Stanley Pool was to be Belgian, the northern bank was to be French.

Brazza persuaded Monsignor Augouard to establish himself at Stanley Pool. Brazza accompanied the young missionary to the first cataract of the Congo, and then left him to make his own way. For some two hundred miles the newcomer directed his caravan, fought wild beasts, and overcame all the obstacles of this dangerous new country. On the site of what is now Brazzaville, he found a native village, called Mfoa.

Monsignor Augouard made friends with the chief. "When you return, you may set yourself up here with me," the African declared.

But in 1883, when the French missioner did return, he was driven from Mfoa. Undaunted, he went down the river to Linzolo, center of the Balari people. The reception he received there, however, was very cool.

"I decided," he records, "that the moment had come for strong action. I made the three chiefs enter my hut, and I attired each of them in a superb uniform jacket. Then with great pomp I had them march out among their people. The first chief—a little old man—appeared as a brigadier general; the second was a colonel of huzzars; the third, a captain of a frigate. Those three gold-trimmed jackets, topped by striking hats, despite the absence of trousers and shoes, were really imposing. The ecstatic crowd had eyes like saucers as they admired the spectacle. I was proclaimed father of the people." [2]

From that turn in the situation, came the celebrated palaver of Linzolo, in 1884, at which war was buried alive. Two guns were placed in the earth and interred, except for the tops of their barrels, which remained exposed above ground. These guns may still be seen at St. Joseph Mission in Linzolo. In 1890, Augouard was named Bishop of the Vicariate of Ubanghi, which included Brazzaville. He was then thirty-eight years old and possessed inexhaustible energy. He had a river boat brought in piece by piece, by caravan, and assembled near Stanley Pool. He called it the *Leo XIII*. A second boat, forty feet long, was the *Pius X*. Both were traveling chapels and very effective in a country that possessed only narrow footpaths through the dense rain forest.

Cannibalism was prevalent in virulent form in the French Congo of those days. Man hunting flourished, and its practices were horrible. A captive would be marched to the market place, and while he was still alive and in possession of his senses, the various parts of his body would be sold, each purchaser marking off what he wanted with white chalk. The daring of the man hunters earned them the name of human hyenas. They boarded boats on the river and at times captured whites as well as blacks. A mission Brother was killed by them, and two priests escaped only after arrows had passed through their clothing. The saddest experience of any missionary was to have to leave the market place without being able, for want of funds, to purchase the freedom of the miserable victims whose flesh was on sale that day.

Bishop Augouard was a master of the anecdote. To gain assistance for the Holy Ghost missions, he made a number of speaking tours in France and became known everywhere as the Bishop of the Cannibals, the Beefstew of the Bonjos. He delighted to relate his encounter with Pope Leo XIII—an incident that evidently lost nothing in the telling.

"Is it true," asked Leo XIII, "that your people eat human flesh?"

"Yes, Holy Father, every day."

"Up to now, among the holy martyrs of the Church," observed the Pontiff reflectively, "no one has been eaten."

"Well, Holy Father," the bishop tells us he replied, "I'll try to make a start along that line."

"Oh, no!" cried the Pope, "I wouldn't want that! Your people couldn't send us any relics of you!"

Until 1905, no great results for Christianity were recorded in French Equatorial Africa. Then an encouraging movement began. It was marked by the volunteering of candidates to the native Brother-hood and native Sisterhood. Notable was the case of Sister Peter Claver, who participated in the care of the sleeping sickness victims, caught the disease, and had to be carried to the chapel to pronounce her final vows. Those who knew her, marveled at her beautiful spir-ituality and the poetic grace with which she spoke of the things of God.

Rejected when she first asked to enter religion, she had queried, "Can we not, we Africans, love God as well as the whites?"

In September, 1952, French Equatorial Africa celebrated at Braz-zaville the centenary of the birth of Bishop Augouard. The ceremony began by an evening procession in which thousands of whites and blacks participated in dragging a huge, new altar table through the streets, to the imposing Cathedral of St. Anne. The table was of sand-stone and weighed three and one-half tons. Crude torches cast a weird light to mark the way, and tribal tom-toms reminded the older folk of the days of violence not long gone. During the next day, African athletes in relays bore a torch from Linzolo, the mother mission of the region, where war had been buried alive by Bishop Augouard and the native chiefs. At the cathedral, the Mass of the Canoe Men—an adaptation of the African choral music of the river folk—was sung by Banda choirs from Ubanghi.

St. Anne's Cathedral, a huge structure accommodating four thousand persons, has been described as African Gothic. It is adorned with ceramics depicting Old and New Testament scenes, counts twenty-one altars, and possesses liturgical furnishings executed in local art motifs. Its pointed arches resemble the bows of the long canoes that glide up and down the Congo. The way the local faithful cooperated in its construction reminds us of the manner in which Chartres and Notre Dame and others of Europe's great churches rose in the Middle Ages.

Nearby are a stadium seating twenty thousand, and a big swimming pool, which were built in 1944 by Pere Lecomte, the builder of St. Anne's. That sports center is named after Felix Eboué, Governor of the colony at the time.

Felix Adolphe Eboué stands high in the esteem of every patriotic Frenchman because he saved French Africa for Free France by siding with De Gaulle at a critical moment during World War II. He was born a Negro citizen of French Guiana, and in adult life he served with distinction as an official of the French colonial administration, in both the West Indies and Africa. When the war broke out, he was Governor of the most remote of all the French political divisions, the Chad Colony, lost in desertic French Africa. On August 26, 1940, he rallied the Chad to the support of De Gaulle and thus started a movement that brought French Equatorial Africa under the Free French.

As Governor of F.E.A., Monsieur Eboué in a famous speech, delivered in 1942 and repeated in 1944 at the historic Brazzaville Conference, established a policy for the evolution of the African along the lines of his own culture. Governor Eboué demanded and obtained an end to the "neglect and contempt in which the native political and social system has been held." He asked that the colonial peoples be enriched and developed "within the framework of their own institutions." His dream of a French federalism, of parliamentary institutions for Africa, of systematic development of African education through subsidies to Christian mission schools, became part of the body of French governmental policy. He was a true innovator and a precursor of the better tomorrow.

French Equatorial Africa has long been the ugly duckling among

France's possessions. Despite the advances, the territory is still only in
the early phases of its struggle. "Our colony is like a poor man who
sleeps on a bag of gold," remarks Bernard Cornut-Gentille, the High
Commissioner. "The greater part of its riches lie unexploited, and
the means at hand for exploiting them are insignificant."

Like many another political division on the globe, F.E.A. has an
over-all development plan. This one is a Ten-Year Plan to spend
$500,000,000 (two-thirds supplied by the state and one-third by private
capital) which breaks down into four parts:

1—Roads and routes. F.E.A. is a long, narrow area that extends
2,000 miles from the sea to the heart of the continent. It is five times
larger than France, yet has but 4,500,000 inhabitants and thus is
wretchedly poor in man power. It has rivers and air routes. The new
plan calls for trunk highways and local roads through the equatorial
forest, and through the sandy wastes and swamps of the north. Roads
will solve a primary problem. One official has put it: "We have no
roads because we have no funds; we have no funds because we have
no roads to move our products that would give us funds."

2—Power for industrialization. Water power waits to be harnessed. With workers so few, industrial plants must be thoroughly
mechanized.

3—Agricultural, animal, mining, and forest program. Present
crops are peanuts, rice, cotton, palm oil, sisal, rubber. Mechanization
is needed for farming. Scientific herding and research for care and
improvement of animal stock are essential. Gold and diamond mines
figure in the prospective development. There must be more efficient
exploitation of the great forests.

4—Social program. As elsewhere in Africa, probably respect for
man's dignity grows out of his scarcity. On the "plateau" above Brazzaville, there is a huge Pasteur Institute, where millions of vaccines
and serums are prepared yearly and where research directs the fight
against malaria, intestinal and venereal diseases, sleeping sickness, and
leprosy. Private organizations, including the missions, team up with
Government forces in operating more than three hundred medical
units. Nowhere else in Africa are health conditions among the natives so bad. Popular education in every form is promoted, though as

yet the results are but modest. The Ten-Year Plan calls for the expenditure of many millions of dollars in the field of education.

Thus we have a typical plan for making an African colony a better land to live in. The Catholic Church has similar plans on a spiritual level—but they are limited, we frankly confess, by the same poverty in means and personnel that handicaps France. Thus in a far truer sense, the High Commissioner's words can apply to the Church in the colony: it is "like a poor man who sleeps on a bag of gold"; we have a priceless legacy for F.E.A. and for all of Africa, but "the greater part of the riches lie unexploited, and the means at hand for exploiting them are insignificant."

Catholics in French Equatorial Africa total 400,000. Since the adjoining, mandated territory of Cameroun has over 500,000, the Catholics in French Central Africa are a round 900,000. The breakdown of these figures expressed in percentages tell the story. The coastal areas count one in every three, or one in every four, of their population as belonging to the Church. The remoter regions of Ubanghi-Shari have as yet yielded less than five per cent of the population to the Church, but the prospects are good. In the Moslem north, however, which counts 40 per cent of all the people in French Central Africa, Catholics total 11 per 10,000. The figure speaks with somber eloquence.

In Libreville one day, I knelt at the grave of Bishop Bessieux. In that historic mission I tasted for a moment the atmosphere of Gabon, the coastal area so redolent of the hardy pioneering that represents the finest traditions of the French in mission work. My guide was the celebrated Africanist and writer, Pére Maurice Briault, who during several decades has given us many excellent books on Africa.

"The best proof that we need no sympathy here is found in our cemeteries," remarked Pére Briault, as we examined the tombstones near Bishop Bessieux's grave. "The Blue Sisters of Castres have been on the coast since the 1860's. Here is the final resting place of Mére Edouard Prat, who died in 1927, dean by age of all the missionaries of Africa. She was eighty-seven years old, and sixty-three of those years she had spent in the tropics. Sister Cyrilla died in 1930, in the fiftieth year of her service. However, we have also had many untimely deaths among us."

Most distinctive of Gabon is its massive rain forest—which, indeed, reaches beyond Gabon, into Cameroun on one side and Middle Congo and Belgian Congo on the other.

"We priests have twelve mission stations," explained Pére Briault, "each four or five days' march from any other, and all within the unbroken forest that covers an equivalent of twenty-five provinces of France. The only open spaces are the rivers and the tiny clearings of the native villages. And as for these villages, don't get the idea that you see beautiful fields of grain around them, as in Europe. You find nothing but a few shoddy square yards of poorly kept plots, where manioc, corn, peanuts, and beans grow. Even these are not numerous. There is one journey, from Mbigou to Koulamoutou, that is 200 miles long without a single clearing." [3]

No one who has not actually entered the tropical rain forest can understand its weirdness, its horrors, and its fascination. We at home picture a forest as a park-like stretch of dense trees, with an underbrush that calls for a struggle but rewards us with charming glades and pleasant sanctuaries for a feast with our thoughts. The tropical rain forest represents original growth untouched for untold centuries. It possesses a practically continuous dense cover of massive trees, which creates a black vault stretching over more than 25,000 square miles of Central Africa. Through this the sun never penetrates, even at high noon. The undergrowth reaches far above a man's head, but the main contributors to the choking glut are giant lianas that hang in wild profusion from the trees. Lianas are supple, vine-like parasites, sometimes thick as a man's body and thirty feet long.

Contrary to popular opinion, the great rain forest holds few dangerous animals; those are found in the open grass country. The forest has feathered folk, including many parrots, but they have no song.

"Missionaries in the Gabon," explained Pére Briault, "spend 200 to 250 days a year away from the center. I can assure you that marching the paths through the tropical rain forest is a brutal experience that outrages the spirit. The long days are no time for dreaming; there are too many obstacles—fallen logs, holes, water into which one must sometimes go up to his stomach, deep descents, steep ascents, vile roots that conspire to trip you or sprain your ankle, side-slanted paths of slithering mud. There are, also, the oven-like heat and the insects. An army of huge traveler ants can mount a man's leg like a flash of flame, and if he is wounded or otherwise unprepared to defend himself, they can mean death. Dante should have known the blacks of Gabon! They have provided, as a section in their inferno, a pathless forest. Into this the lost soul is tossed, to wander eternally without ever finding its way out."

However, like almost everything else that is strange in the world, the rain forest exercises a fascination for some men who live with it. Such a person was Archbishop Le Roy, the distinguished Superior General of the Congregation of the Holy Ghost. "The forest is a jealous creature," he once wrote; "it will not reveal itself to you if you come to it with your selfish preoccupations and with fears for your convenience. It wants you to come to it for itself alone."

"In short," added Pére Briault, quoting his superior's words, "you must have regard for it, and time for it, and be free of fear of it."

As the mountains of Europe long provided refuge for hunted peoples, so the tropical rain forest saved millions of Africans from the slavers. Today Negro tribes continue to live within its borders.

The second subdivision of French Equatorial Africa, after Gabon, is the Middle Congo, the principal center of which is Brazzaville. Belgians early tackled the construction of a railroad around the Congo Rapids and thus gained access to Stanley Pool. Years later the French built a parallel rail line on French territory, from Pointe Noire to Brazzaville, 320 miles into the interior. Along this Congo-Ocean Railroad today, is gathered the heaviest population of F.E.A. interspersed with a number of the missions of the Middle Congo.

As we go still farther inland, we come to the watershed that divides the two great inner basins of the African continent—the Congo Basin on the one hand, and the Chad Basin on the other. The Ubanghi River flows into the Congo, and the Shari flows into Lake Chad. Thus we have the name of the third political division, Ubanghi-Shari. Here the great forest gives way to the grass country, throughout which trees are scattered unevenly. This is great animal country. The African is able to get meat, but he suffers from mighty beasts that often he is unable to overcome.

"As a general rule, our people are helpless as children," explained a Brazzaville missionary. "A village to the north has just gone through a period of terrible anguish. A lion entered the precincts each night for a week, forced its way through the straw enclosures about the huts, and massacred the inhabitants. Four men and two women were killed and partially eaten. One little boy was saved by his sister, who struck the beast with a stick. The animal's attention thus deflected, the youngster got away, although he had already been seized. To meet the terror, Monsieur Seguy, chief of the subdivision, brought European and African hunters to the area. At one o'clock in the morning, after the lion had already wounded another man, the patrol laid low the giant prowler, which measured nine feet from nose to tail. The nightmare was over!"

Still farther north lies the central bowl of the great Chad Basin. In the heart of this otherwise desertic region we discover Lake Chad, fed by waters from the south that roll in after the rains and, having no outlet, build up an impenetrable labyrinth of swamps and bogs that expand and contract according to season. Much of the area is useless to man but is the haunt of wild game. There, among other creatures, are found the largest elephants in the world. They prowl by hundreds, practically undisturbed, because conditions of life are too severe for all but the hardiest huntsmen.

The Chad sultanates are very ancient and their origin is often unknown. Some were erected by Arabs from North Africa who have ruled since the thirteenth century. The French fought those forces for over twenty years and completed their conquest only on the eve of World War I. The area counts as Christians a few immigrants, but very few local residents. The hardy missionary bands with centers at Fort Lamy and Garoua have need of much courage.

From this desert of the north, let us turn our eyes toward a land of prodigy, France's U.N. trust territory, Cameroun. Germans occupied this area during the brawling colonial period of the nineteenth century. In 1891, the Pallotine Fathers arrived, and from the start, all that they touched turned into a golden harvest of souls. The Ewondo people, about Yaounde, accepted the Faith enthusiastically. Success followed in the Douala area. When World War I came, in 1914, there were already thirty thousand converts in the Church. Then followed an extraordinary period during the two years from 1914 to 1916, when the Pallotines were interned.[4] African catechists took charge and their performance is one of the finest proofs of the capacity of properly trained African religious leaders. They not only held the

Catholics to a disciplined life of devotion, but also prepared thousands of new candidates for baptism.

Yaounde chiefs, uninterested in the bloody strife among the whites but impatient for Catholic priests, called for missionaries. "Send us missionaries, missionaries of *any* nationality!" they cried. In 1916, the German pro-vicar of the region passed over his powers to the Anglo-French chaplain with the simple plea, "Save these missions!"

A brave little contingent of seven French Holy Ghost Fathers took over a task that had already become too heavy for thirty Pallotines. The situation was simply hopeless. On the eve of every great holyday, the movement of Catholics toward each central mission was like a migration, with thousands on the road for miles around.

"What do you do," asked one of these veteran Holy Ghost Fathers with whom I talked, "when you see a great church packed with people calling to go to confession, and you see the great square in front of the church likewise full of people who likewise cry for the sacrament? Large numbers of these folk have journeyed two and three days. Large numbers of the mothers have babies on their backs. All that you don't finish hearing, must go back home uncared-for for another four or five months. But when I had heard 350 confessions, the day was gone and the job still remained!"

So much for the natives already within the Church. But then the catechists took the new priests out into the countryside; and in a number of places, they gathered great crowds of catechumens whom they had carefully trained.

"These are ready for baptism," each catechist stated to a marveling missionary. "You are the first priest these people have ever seen."

All this was the work of volunteer catechists. Under the direction of those volunteers, a number of chiefs had already dismissed all concubines and retained only one wife apiece. Collections of funds for the erection of churches had been organized spontaneously; substantial sums for several construction jobs awaited the harried priests. Although conditions again returned to normal, the pace here in Cameroun was so great that the expanding missionary forces never really caught up with the needs. Baptisms are still administered in almost a steady stream, and at almost any hour. I was hurried out to the font after supper to pour the waters of salvation on Marie Marguerite, fourth daughter of the Douala clerk of the court.

While I visited one evening with the Commissioner of Douala, his wife at one point in the conversation remarked to me almost petulantly: "The priests and the Sisters seem to think only of the blacks. They rush around madly taking care of them, and do very little, indeed, for us whites."

In 1925, a seminary was opened near Yaounde and was immediately filled. Today the French territory of Cameroun has the best record for native clergy in all French Africa: it counts 75 priests, and over 300 candidates in the seminary. All F.E.A. has only 35 priests. African Sisters in Cameroun number 87, as against 53 in French Equatorial Africa. These recruits to the religious ranks are no longer all from the far south. In 1953, the first priest of the Babouti people, considerably to the north, was ordained.

"In his Apocalypse," wrote lyrically Pierre Moaka, a fellow tribesman of Father John Djimbe, the newly ordained, "Saint John says that he saw before the throne of the Lamb a great multitude of all nations and of all tribes. Now we are certain that among this great host of the saved there will also be many Babouti!"

The great majority of the 514,000 Catholics of Cameroun are in Yaounde and Douala. The Diocese of Yaounde counts 49 per cent of the entire population within its confines as in the Church, while 37 per cent of that of Douala are Catholic. These two areas are among the most notable Catholic centers in the mission world today.

A Trappist monastery now marks the skyline at Minlaba, here in Cameroun. One of the Africans in the community is the priestly brother of Angelique Monet, whose marriage I attended in Dakar. The Abbey of Our Lady of Africa counts seven European and eight African members.

"Many Africans," explains Father Moulin, the abbot, "are attracted to the contemplative life rather than to the parochial ministry, and undoubtedly they will prove able for it. The average lay native is still astonished when he sees one of his educated fellow countrymen doing manual labor in our fields. We will seek to demonstrate to all the dignity and beauty of working with one's hands."

Chapter 2

THE TASTE FOR POLYGAMY

A FAMILY IN France's trust territory of Cameroun recently bought a wife for the eldest son. The "bride price" paid for the apparently much-wanted girl was approximately $5,000 in cash, plus a motor truck, plus a small herd of goats. All these items went to the young lady's parents. To her maternal uncles went smoking pipes; to her aunts went yards of cloth; to her grandma an assortment of pots and pans.

"This is an exceptional case, isn't it?" I asked a group of missionaries one evening, as we sat in a circle and chatted.

"Yes," replied one, "but unfortunately not exceptional enough. Among rank-and-file Africans, purchasing a wife today has become big business. I dare say that one year's value of what is bartered for wives in Central Africa would total millions in your American dollars. This is a huge outlay among people whose average income has less value than a hundred American dollars a year."

"My, that's interesting!" commented another. "I'm here quite a while, and I never thought of it that way before. In a cattle area, for example, the bride price will be twenty cows. A cow is worth some $25 gold. Thus twenty cows represent a value of $500. Buying a wife is the biggest operation a rank-and-file African engages in during his whole life. How true it is that, in terms of African economy, bride buying is big business!"

From Eastern Nigeria, next door to Cameroun, came recently an echo of this conversation. An African committee of legislators was appointed, early in 1954, to figure ways and means of combating the rising prices of brides.

"Prices demanded by fathers selling their daughters as brides have soared beyond the reach of the average man," stated a member of the committee. "Complaints reach us that fathers auction daughters off to the highest bidder."

A by-product of the investigation was a protest from a feminine member of the committee, Mrs. Margaret Ekpo. "The phrase 'bride price' is a shame to women," she said. "It puts us on a level with salt, pepper, goats, and other commodities. Why can't we use a word like dowry?"

But something more is needed than a change of name. Not all is well as regards family life in most of Africa south of the Sahara, despite the advances that have been made. The majority of difficulties revolve about woman's place in the family. Most of the trouble takes its start from the way that men must acquire their wives. The result in some areas is a gravely defective society.

Some years ago, a young woman of France made a brilliant record at the Catholic University of Lille and obtained a lawyer's degree with high honors. She followed her profession as a woman lawyer for a brief period, and then found that life called for much more from her than she was giving. She joined the White Sisters and, as Sister Marie-André, became a missionary in Africa. It was quite natural that the lot of Africa's womanhood became Sister Marie-André's special object of study, and her legal experience soon gained her wide recognition. Thus today she is esteemed as one of French Africa's best authorities on woman and the family.[1]

Sister Marie-André is a member of France's Superior Council of Social Affairs Overseas, and recently the French Bureau of Overseas Scientific Research arranged for her to make a fifteen-month study of the condition of woman in West Africa and South Cameroun. From this study, she lists the seven social plagues that beset woman in Africa. They are as follows:

1—The lure of town life, where all the problems of economic upheaval add to the disruption of tribal life.

2—The growth of a class of African functionaries with riches unheard-of in earlier days—riches that many of them use to "buy" wives.

3—The evils of the dowry system, aggravated by the almost-universal substitution of cash for gifts in kind and the enormous increase in the cash demanded.

4—The enforced celibacy of many young, and not so young, men who have to wait years for a wife.

5—The lack of companionship in marriage, owing to the unequal educational development of man and woman.

6—The alarming abuse of alcohol—"in course of becoming in black Africa," notes Sister Marie-André, "the gravest and most dangerous of the social maladies."

7—The destruction of tribal morality without the corresponding development of a Christian code.

Sister Marie-André has played an important role in the formulation of legislation that aims to break the grip of ugly social customs in Africa. First of these laws was the Mandel Decree of 1939, by which all marriages are invalid where there is no consent. Then there is the Jacquinot Decree of September 1951, which carries the freedom of African women further. It permits a woman over twenty-one years of age to marry without a dowry. It allows the tribunals to register marriages of girls under that age, without the consent of the parents, if the latter demand an "excessive dowry"—that is, one greater than the amount fixed in each territory by the District Administrator.

"France's decrees," says Sister Marie-André, "should free Africa from that thirst for money which has transformed marriage into a shameful traffic; they should restore to the African girl her dignity and her personality, and allow young people to found real homes, to the incalculable advantage of African civilization."

"But," remarked one missionary with a wry smile, "it is interesting to see how many young girls know these laws, though they are sometimes barely at the age of puberty, and how many resolve to use them, and yet how frequently they are baffled by one or other tiny circumstance that stands in the way."

How true this is! From lay friends and missionaries, I gathered quite a series of examples. What a tragic collection of broken hopes they represent! Let me relate as the first example the story of Margherite.

Margherite was a pupil at a small village school in the Middle Congo. Her mother, a good Christian, was married to a pagan. When the Catholic priest in his rounds stopped at her village, the woman expressed concern for her child.

"Send her to the Sisters, at the school of the central mission," proposed the priest.

The mother spoke to her pagan husband and, to win his consent, she remarked, "Margherite will be more marriageable if she goes to the mission." The husband agreed, but for reasons other than his Christian wife had in mind.

The child was delighted with the mission school. She fell in love with the Sisters, particularly Sister Barbara, and faced with dread the prospect of returning to her village.

"Whatever happens," she said to Sister Barbara at the tearful parting, "my father must get me married the right way. If not, I'll run away to the Administrator!"

Meanwhile, Margherite's mother had died, and not one but three wives were in her father's compound when she arrived there.

"Good!" the man grunted as his daughter greeted him. "I have a marriage ready for you."

"I must go to a Catholic boy, and be married by the priest," she cautioned.

"You'll do as I say!" he shouted. "There'll be no Catholic boy." A tremendous blow on the face from his open hand sent her spinning into a corner.

All through the night, Margherite planned. She would hurry in the morning to the Administrator, some twelve miles away, and explain her case: her father wished to force her to marry a pagan, and she appealed to the law for protection. From dawn on, she watched her chance and finally slipped unobtrusively from her hut. But at the edge of the village one of her father's three wives approached and took her very firmly by the arm.

"Where are you going?" the wife asked with a cold gleam in her eyes.

"Don't interfere!" cried Margherite. "I'm going to the Administrator; I've got the law on my side."

The woman unceremoniously dragged the girl back to the hut. "She was going to the French! She says she's got the law on her side." This time the man gave the girl a whipping, indeed! Then his wives tied her with lianas in the corner of her hut. Each day for many days, the father asked her if she would do as he said. Each time she refused

him, and he beat her again unmercifully. At last, one morning when
the question was put, Margherite remained silent. The next day her
father faced her again.

"Will you do as I say?" he shouted. Hungry, tired, sick, broken,
Margherite bowed her head in consent.

Two years later, Sister Barbara and a companion, traveling on
the road, passed a petty chief with his covey of several wives. "Margherite!" Sister cried as she recognized the girl.

A spasm of anguish gripped Margherite's face. She glanced
quickly at her husband and then passed the two Sisters with unseeing
eyes. Only years after did Sister Barbara learn the whole story.

"I was ashamed," concluded Margherite bleakly; "I had failed."
As one wife of a polygamist, she could only keep God in her heart.

Then there is the story of Kawa. Sister Marie-André estimates
that currently, in Central Africa, one girl in six is pledged to a man
before puberty, one in ten before the age of ten. Such was the case
with Kawa. There were many Catholic girls in her neighborhood, in
the city of Yaounde, in the south of Cameroun. At play they talked
about getting married.

"When I get married, I'll be my husband's only wife," the typical
Catholic girl would explain, with a touch of boastfulness in her voice.
"I'm not going to be merely his servant! I'm going to love him very
much, and we are going to be real companions to each other and have
a pretty home."

"Well, I'm going to have the same. You wait and see!" Kawa
would reply.

But one day when she was about twelve, her father had news for
her. He explained that, when she was only five years old, he had
pledged her in marriage to Sanokho's boy and had accepted part of
the bride price.

"Oh, no!" cried Kawa in dismay. "I'm going to be married like
the Christian girls!"

Her father did not reply; he only looked at her. Kawa saw that
there was affection in his eyes. There was a little smile on his lips, but
also, she divined, a shade of sadness on his face. She liked her father,
but she knew his great fault: he was a heavy drinker of alcohol. He
did not need to tell her—she already guessed that whatever bride price

he had received from Sanokho had long ago been spent on drink. Everything he had went for drink, and the little family was very poor.

Kawa had a good friend named Berta, and in her misery she ran to the latter's home. "O Berta, Berta!" she cried as she entered, and then with many tears she told her sad story.

While the account went on, Berta's father, who was a teacher in a Catholic school, came in and saw the pair. "Oh, my!" he expostulated. "Why such big tears?"

"Kawa can't get married the way we can," spoke up Berta. "Her father sold her when she was a little girl."

"But that's against the law now! That's not just," replied the father.

"Yes, but he's spent some of the bride price," said Kawa, through her tears.

"That doesn't matter," answered the father. "True, he's got to be honest and some day give back what he accepted. But the fact that he has a debt is no reason for his daughter to be made to suffer. The law says that all bargains by which fathers sell their daughters without the daughters' consent are forbidden."

Kawa flew like the wind back to her father. "I don't have to go to Sanokho's son!" she cried breathlessly, and repeated what Berta's father had said.

Kawa's father listened. Then he remained silent awhile, staring into space. At last he spoke, in a very low voice, as if to himself.

"Sanokho is very powerful," he said, "and he is very cruel."

Kawa watched her poor father. Whatever the law, she saw that he was in mortal fear of Sanokho's reprisals. She made no further objections.

A little time passed, and one day the girls of the neighborhood said good-by to Kawa as her father led her by the hand to Sanokho's house.

"Poor Kawa!" mourned Berta to her own father later. "She wanted so much to be married as the Christian girls are."

The new idea of monogamous marriage creates many situations that demand huge sacrifices from Catholics. It is remarkable what a large number of them make the sacrifices cheerfully.

"As soon as an African man dies," explains Sister Marie-André, "his wives are inherited by his younger brother, according to pagan custom. Young Christian men have defied this custom and refused to marry their brothers' wives despite the material advantages such a marriage offers. A Mossi chieftain, after his brother's death, inherited 150 wives. Instead of marrying them, he left them free either to become Christians and later marry Christians of their choice, or be assigned in the usual way to a pagan relative of the deceased. This heroic act is now being imitated by others, and it represents a vigorous reaction against ancestral custom. Only thus can Christianity make its way."

Sister Marie-André warns us, however, that the old Africa still rules supreme among the great majority of the dwellers on the continent. It is a mistake to become so impressed by a few brilliant examples as to believe that all the battles have been won. Foreigners who have not had the opportunity to get the pulse of Africa must understand first of all the attitude of Africans toward polygamy and its accompaniments. It is only we, the foreigners, who experience any real revulsion for the institution of polygamy as such.

"Polygamy has prevailed," explains a missionary who has lived a long time with it, "because, in the past at least, everyone wanted polygamy. It was not only the men who wanted it; the women also wanted it. Parents wanted it for their daughters. We can truly believe that only a few were interested exclusively in the bride price; far more important to the parents was the good fortune of their children."

"Explain yourself, Father," I said. "How did polygamy suit everybody so well?"

"In the first place," the missionary replied, "polygamy suited the men. 'If one wife is good, two wives are better,' they are accustomed to say. A second wife is not just a mere luxury; she is a necessity. How else get all the work done? How get the children born?

"Women, too, wanted polygamy. 'How get the field hoed when you are weary carrying the child within you?' they ask. In the pagan way of seeing things, other wives are needed. There may be quarreling, but a woman, they feel, is better off if she is not the only woman of the household.

"Finally, the tribe wants polygamy. The tribe wants progeny. The old men traditionally have wanted many young men for battle; they want an abundance of women for all the work and for child-bearing. Offspring, offspring! It has always been one of the deepest instincts among the Africans. To serve this instinct, all the wise ones argued that polygamy was best adapted to the need."

Oddly enough, the modern statistician has proved that in this respect the Africans were wrong.

"Careful investigation has revealed," states Father Marcel Pater-not, of the White Fathers, "that in a monogamous marriage a woman has more children. We refer especially to the figures given after many years of study by Colonel Jamot, director of the Trypanosomatic Clinic. Where it is a case of a monogamous marriage, there is an average of two children, while in polygamous marriages the averages are as follows: 1.4 per wife where the marriage is bigamous; 1.2 each where there are from three to six wives; 1.1 where there are ten wives; 0.6 among the polygamous households of great chiefs. These figures speak for themselves." [2]

Thus a thousand women, when each has one husband each, will total 2,000 children; a thousand women, if bound in bigamous marriages, will have 1,400 children; a thousand women, when distributed three to six women per given husband, will total 1,200 children; a thousand women, when distributed ten per given husband, will total 1,100 children; a thousand women married to great chiefs, each of which has scores of wives, will total only 600 children.

It is a popular fancy, in many polygamous areas of the Moslem world and in Bantu Africa, that women are much more numerous than men and that thus society lends itself naturally to polygamy. *Afrique Nouvelle* of Dakar recently gave a resolute answer to this, in reply to the irresponsible mouthings of a Moslem spellbinder speaking in Senegal.

"In the name of morality, be polygamists!" cried the speaker, Youssouph Athie. "From a vast documentation gathered from some of the most important newspapers in the world, I am able to demonstrate that there are eight women in the world for every man. This constitutes a grave menace to the morals of the human race. It is a situation that for solution demands polygamy."

POLYGAMY, DISRUPTER OF AFRICAN SOCIETY

A study of population by sex in French Africa [3] proves that there is a remarkable constancy in the incidence of males and females in the population. In the greater number of cases, the shortage is on the side of the female. Hence any religio-social system that encourages more than one wife to a given husband is, part from moral considerations, disruptive of African society.

COUNTRY	POPULATION BY SEX		AVERAGE PER 1,000
Senegal	Men -	587,421	1,000
	Women -	557,016	948
Mauritania	Men -	62,732	1,000
	Women -	54,254	865
Sudan	Men -	1,311,262	1,000
	Women -	1,275,900	973
Guinea	Men -	934,502	1,000
	Women -	920,288	985
Upper Volta	Men -	1,167,364	1,000
	Women -	1,155,086	990
Dahomey	Men -	340,633	1,000
	Women -	341,306	1,000
Niger	Men -	937,069	1,000
	Women -	961,823	1,026
Togo	Men -	501,414	1,000
	Women -	495,803	988
Fr. Equatorial Africa	Men -	2,049,995	1,000
	Women -	2,136,410	1,042
Cameroun	Men -	1,535,441	1,000
	Women -	1,541,723	1,004

Afrique Nouvelle had no trouble demonstrating to Monsieur Youssouph that this "vast documentation" was pure buncombe. We produce on the next page the paper's table of statistics from government records.

Such figures prove conclusively the cruel injustice exercised against the young men of a country by permitting troops of wives, up to three and four hundred in number, to rich men able to purchase them. The widespread practice of permitting two, three, or four wives to each of a relatively few privileged men also works great harm. But far more important than arguments of social or economic inconvenience, is the matter of the dignity of the individual and the sacredness of the family.

POPULATION BY SEX IN FRENCH AFRICA[3]

Country	Men	Women	Number of Women per 1,000 men
SENEGAL	587,421	557,016	948
MAURITANIA	62,732	54,254	865
SUDAN	1,311,262	1,275,900	973
GUINEE	934,502	920,288	985
UPPER VOLTA	1,167,364	1,155,086	990
DAHOMEY	340,633	341,306	1,002
NIGER	937,069	961,823	1,026
TOGO	501,414	495,803	988
FRENCH EQUATORIAL AFRICA	2,049,995	2,136,410	1,042
CAMEROONS	1,535,441	1,541,723	1,004

Toward a solution, Father Paternot directs us to enlist the African women themselves. "More perhaps than any other custom, polygamy seems impervious to the effect of outside influence and civilization," he warns. "Insofar as we do not succeed in modifying the factors that contribute to its development, insofar as the African woman does not awaken to her own personality, it is useless to count on a diminution of polygamy. Above all, it is necessary to instruct and to educate the African woman, if she is to come to the point where she will free herself from the slavery of polygamy."

Doctor H. C. Trowell, while a lecturer at Uganda Medical School, wrote on polygamy.[4] At the end of his brochure, he threw all technical considerations aside and found the basic solution far beyond the realms of science.

"Can a purely intellectual attitude to life, can reason, can enlightenment, can what Europeans call 'civilization'—by which they mean European civilization—guide Africa concerning the change in her marriage laws? No. European civilization shows cracks too large to allow it any longer to speak in a dogmatic tone to a continent whose culture, if lowly, is also lovely.

"No, only One can speak and guide . . . The Beginning and the End. For men could not climb to God. That was the tower of Babel. God could only come down to men. That was the cradle of Bethlehem."

Chapter 3

THE LAND THE BELGIANS BUILT

ANNE, THE EIGHT-YEAR-OLD daughter of the hotel cook I was visiting in Leopoldville one afternoon, came up with a big grin on her face and held out her hand to me. I took it and bowed to her quite solemnly; whereupon, she turned to her timid companions and cried triumphantly, "See, he's my friend!" I put my horn-rimmed glasses on her nose, and the little group screamed with delight.

Anne had expressed my views quite well. I felt myself very much her friend and the friend of every other African in Leopoldville and in the Belgian Congo. This was not my first visit there. Once again I was experiencing for the Congolese an attraction keener than I felt for almost any other people of West or South or East Africa. Only in Ruanda and in parts of Uganda did I find myself more completely at home.

It is in their bearing that the Congolese are most appealing. They do not compromise their dignity; they are not subservient. They hold their heads high, friendly confidence shines in their eyes, they have a jaunty air about them. Yet they seldom give the impression that they aim to be surly or overbearing. Most Congo peoples are pleasant, simple, sociable, easy to get along with. I got the impression that the heart of the representative Congolese is in the right place.

Leopoldville, the capital of the Belgian Congo, today counts some twelve thousand Europeans—the great majority of whom are Belgians —and 250,000 Africans. The city has been laid out with great care and is remarkable for its imposing appearance. A great broad avenue bordered with trees follows the curving bank of the Congo River for more than ten miles while similarly beautiful boulevards are found within the city. There are as yet few Government buildings of note but a smart modernity characterizes the business establishments.

Martin Flavin helps us to grasp the tremendous extent of the

Congo by noting that, if Leopoldville were laid on the map of Europe at Brest, the port on France's Atlantic coast, the Congo's second largest city, Elizabethville, would fall on Naples, while the third, Stanleyville, would fall on Berlin. The relative sparseness of population of the Belgian Congo is dramatically high-lighted by this super-imposition. Within the vast region of the Congo, embracing an area equivalent to all Western Europe, there dwell hardly more than ten million inhabitants.

Three figures loom large over the Belgian Congo and its people. These are the Belgian administrator, the Belgian industrialist, and the Belgian missionary. The Protestant missionaries, though including many Belgians, are in majority Americans, British and Scandinavians; while they have worked devotedly for the Congo they are not as closely bound up in the national effort. The characteristic of uniqueness to which we refer arises from the close-knit co-operation that has existed between these three figures in building the Congo.

The world's iconoclasts, so numerous in our day, will rush greedily into this opening that we seem to give them, and will say that such an entente represents nothing to be proud of; that, rather, it brings only shame on the Belgians and on the cultural and spiritual institutions that have spawned such an inglorious undertaking. After making due allowance, however, for the weaknesses and failings that creep into all the strivings of poor human beings, the achievement in the Belgian Congo must, we believe, be judged as worthy and creditable, though far from perfect. It is, too, a task that is far from completed. Indeed, it is only at its beginnings. The Belgians, I think, can be said to have made a good start in serving the Congolese. The generations ahead will judge how successful they prove in bringing their project to a creditable conclusion.

One afternoon in Brussels during September, 1876, the royal carriage stopped at the house of the Missionaries of the Immaculate Heart of Mary, a community known in Belgium as the Scheut Fathers.[1] King Leopold II got out and had a long visit with Father Vranckx, the superior, and thus made a start in getting that community, previously devoted exclusively to China, to work in the Congo as well. His repeated insistence won, also, the Belgian Jesuits for the Congo. So, too, he appealed to Cardinal Lavigerie, founder of the White Fathers, for increased interest in the Congo. French members

of the White Fathers were in the eastern Congo as early as 1879; the
King asked the Cardinal to build up a Belgian province and thus put
a heavy contingent into his field.

"I recall taking steps personally in the name of the King," notes
Count de Wiart, "to obtain the help of the Mill Hill Fathers from
London. They began work in 1905." Behind this appeal for English
Catholic missionaries was the hostility abroad against Leopold's Congo
policy.

However, despite Leopold II's enthusiasm for the Congo, the Belgians of his day never became greatly interested in this African venture
of their sovereign, except to groan at some of the bills. Years later
Leopold II's successor, King Albert I, was to win popular support for
the Congo, both as a national political enterprise and as a spiritual
crusade for Belgium's predominantly Catholic millions. Albert made
his first visit to the Congo in 1909, and a second visit in 1928.

I was reminded of the King's 1928 visit, through a curious little
incident that happened to me in the Upper Kasai Province, some
years after the King had passed through there. Two jiggers had made
their way into my feet, and Doctor Molnar of the mission staff undertook to remove them. Jiggers are tiny parasites that burrow under the
skin of the toes and become painful as they grow. I found I was in
distinguished company as a jigger victim. Doctor Molnar explained
that he had performed precisely the same operation on King Albert
during the latter's visit. He said that, after removing the parasite from
the King's foot, he placed it on the palm of His Majesty's hand, much
to the King's delight. "How wonderful!" the royal patient had exclaimed. "You must put it in alcohol for me to show to the Queen."

From the first, King Albert was a great protagonist of Christian
respect for the Congolese. At the Colonial Congress held by the European powers in 1920, he enunciated his philosophy in a concise
formula; "Every function carries with it a duty. In the colonies, he
who commands others assumes as primary duty the mission of emancipation that the mother country must fulfill towards primitive
peoples." Between 1909 and 1934, Albert made over forty public
declarations that concerned the welfare of the Congolese and the promotion of their evangelization. For a twentieth-century sovereign, this
is a distinction. On one occasion he remarked to an audience, "I

should be very happy if, at my death, not a single pagan remained in the Congo."

When King Albert died, the crucifix placed in his coffin for burial with his remains was a simple but expressive work in ivory, carved by an African craftsman of the Buta mission in the Belgian Congo.

Early in the century, the colonial administrators began to protest against irresponsible practices and to do away with them. The change to new ways was helped greatly by a huge reform movement among the Congo industrialists. Rubber and ivory collecting had become outmoded as money-making operations. Soon five huge corporations, all Belgian-controlled, were developing most of the Congo, and the Belgian Government itself had a large stake in the operation. Proper regard for the Congolese was dictated by Christian principles, but there were, also, other motives. Among these was the recognition of the fact we have already alluded to; namely, that in the Congo only ten million people were scattered over a vast wilderness, equivalent to an area from Brest to Naples to Berlin. Thus was born the Belgian philosophy of business operation in the Congo.

"Africa's most precious asset," an industrialist in Elizabethville explained to me, "lies not in its wealth in the ground or on the ground, but in its society of human beings. The white men have the know-how. Let us transfer as much as possible of this know-how methodically to these black people, the while encouraging them in every way to live contentedly and to act freely. Then we shall prosper, and they will prosper, as well."

Whether this tropical world of ten million blacks is truly prospering as it should physically, socially, spiritually, is a subject of unending discussion among Government administrators, business men, and missionaries throughout the Congo. Whatever defects those close to the problem discover, many observers who pass by have high praise for the results already attained.

"The Belgians have the most daring policy in Africa," said an American educator to me. "All you have to do is take a look at the rest of the continent to see this. Below here, in the Union of South Africa, there are big industry and big agriculture. The African does the unskilled work; he has to, because they've taken his land away from him. But he works only as an animal, with his muscles. In French Africa, the black is well treated, but he is left pretty much alone. Neither he nor the French get very much from the deal. The British give the African schooling, but don't train him much in modern skills.

"But here in the Congo, the Belgian has set himself the task of teaching the black man the white man's methods. Lookers-on scoff. 'Wait until tomorrow!' they say. 'The Belgian will then discover that he's taught himself out of a job and out of the Congo!' But as of to-day, two tremendous facts stand out: first, of all operators on the continent, the Belgian is getting the best day's work out of the African; secondly, the Belgian runs the happiest country on the continent, so far as the black Africans are concerned."

The Belgian industrialists can be happy in their turn; they are doing very nicely. Belgian Congo's gross national production is currently over $750,000,000 a year. The richest uranium deposit of the free world is there; the Congo is the world's fourth-largest source of tin, and a major copper producer. It supplies the greater part of the world's cobalt, a major constituent of the jet engine, and it produces four-fifths of the world's supply of industrial diamonds. It is a huge producer of vegetable oils.

When I read these statistics that record the annual "take" of the Belgians in the Congo, I recall a conversation I overheard between a European and a skilled Congolese garage mechanic in Leopoldville.

"Why don't you fellows get wise to yourselves?" the visitor was saying. "Don't you see the trainloads and shiploads and planeloads of riches the Belgians are carrying out of here every year? Don't you know they're bleeding you to death?"

"Listen," replied the Congolese with a quiet smile. "I know a few other things, and I don't want to forget them. I know that I was born in a grass hut in the forest, and I didn't wear shoes until I was eighteen years old. I know that my father was a tribal warrior, and my grandfather, so my mother says, used to eat human flesh. I know that today I'm a good garage mechanic; I've got a nice home; I and my wife and my children go to church every Sunday, and we are a happy Christian family. Perhaps the Belgians are taking more than their share out of here—I don't know anything about such matters. But I do know, and I don't want to forget, that the Belgians have given me an awful lot that I'm awfully glad to have."

At Luisa, in my journey through Kasai, the great province between Leopoldville and Elizabethville, the District Administrator gave me the best he had in sleeping quarters—a cot set up in his dining room. Fathers de Cock and van Oost, Missionaries of Scheut, who were my expert guides, slept with neighbors. In the morning while it was still dark, an intruding animal startled me out of my skin; it proved to be the pet pup of Joseph, the cook's boy. I jumped up well refreshed, and by half past seven, we were bounding along a good dirt road, headed for the Basala Mpasu.

"We are now in the home country of some of the most backward tribes of the Congo," explained Father de Cock, who during the 1930's, the time of this Luisa visit, was the Scheut Provincial Superior and thus greatly involved in Kasai missionary policy.

"The Basala Mpasu were subjugated only in 1929," added Monsieur Marchand, the Administrator. "They still carry the reputation of being cannibals, though we think we have done away with all that. Even yet, however, life is very cheap among them; they will kill for a trifle."

It was a land of the great unclothed. A caravan of nude women advanced in a column, each bearing a huge bundle of grass on her head. Others worked in road gangs, or leaned languidly on tools in the fields. To the women fell the work; the men walked by with spears or peered from open doors of huts, but were not discovered at manual labor. All, male and female, had a litheness about them that was almost electric. The men seemed fit subjects for museum bronzes, with long arms, long legs, rotund muscles, and something even of beauty in their figures. There were barbarism and vitality about them, a certain steeliness of eye that was cold and cruel, and yet withal, a measure of brooding earnestness and somber dignity.

I quickly dismissed the idea that the women were merely stupid, moronic cattle. I noted one woman sitting before her house as we passed, smoking her calabash pipe, every now and then spitting a long, vigorous spit off into space. She may not have clothing, I concluded, but she has a mind of her own, and probably handles herself ably when her husband crosses her.

"This forest road is as busy as a city street," I remarked.

Marchand smiled. "That is not an accident," he answered. "Roads are the viaducts of civilization," he continued a bit grandiloquently. "The first thing we do is build roads. Then we require the tribes of the forest to move their huts to the roadside."

We stopped at a village, and immediately a group of young men approached. The leader addressed me in a strong, ringing voice, but of course I could only refer him to one of the Scheut Fathers. Again he spoke his words loudly, almost sharply, and Father van Oost flung back sharp words in reply.

"What is it all about?" I inquired almost breathlessly.

"The fellow asks, 'When can we have a catechist?' I replied by asking a question of my own, 'When will you stop eating men here?' 'But we don't eat men!' cried the young man and his companions as well. 'Our fathers did, but we don't!' "

"There's an example of what's happening," remarked Father de Cock. "These youngsters want Christianity. At the moment, they see it only as the veil of respectability with which to cover up what the new generation looks back on in shame. Of course, we missionaries must be almost harsh with them under these circumstances; we must be sure that they have the will to live Christian lives once they abandon the past."

The next day we drove to Mboi, less than forty miles from the frontier of Portuguese Angola. Monsieur Serron, a thoughtful type, was Administrator there and had just returned from three months of subjugation work among the Balolo.

"The Balolo are even more handsome than the Basala Mpasu," he stated. "I believe they are now thoroughly in line, the last tribe of Kasai Province to be brought around. A year ago, two messengers went to the Balolo and were eaten. I went in with fifty soldiers, and we were fired upon. Our paths were obstructed by traps of poisoned arrows. We were prepared for this and had antitetanus serum with us, since the poison is rotted animal entrails and dung. When we first asked for the chief, we were given a 'straw man,' as is so often the case, but finally we got the right person and made him responsible."

Reputedly the most savage in all this region were the Babingi people, among whom we soon were moving. We found Ndekesha, the mission center, roaring with life. Two villages of huts, lodging a total of eleven hundred Babingi, were crowded about the mission.

"This is our current class of candidates for baptism," explained Father de Brandt, the pastor. "At Christmas the water will flow, and

DISTANCES IN THE BELGIAN CONGO

When the map of the Belgian Congo is superimposed upon the map of Europe, Leopoldville, the capital, falls above Brest on the Atlantic Coast of France; Stanleyville, 1200 miles up the Congo River, falls above Berlin, while Elizabethville, the great copper center to the south, falls above Naples.

then they will burn these villages and return home. Their successors will build fresh huts."

A sight of rare charm was Sister Maurilla, who had been in the Congo over thirty years, conducting a school of domestic science for two hundred Babingi young women. Her pupils lived in crude huts about a square enclosure. As we approached, she was directing them in the cleaning of their quarters. I noticed that a number of the girls had infants tied to their backs, and naïvely I remarked to this sweet nun, "Some of your young women are married."

"No," she answered, not the least nonplused. "They are not married; they have merely followed certain pagan customs. But their children, God willing, will not have offspring until they have received the Sacrament of Matrimony. My Babingi girls are wonderfully quick to learn and earnestly faithful to the lessons they receive here."

"Sister Maurilla is constantly defending her Babingi," said Father de Brandt with a laugh. "As a matter of fact, she is almost alone in her capacity to gain their confidence and to form them to Christian habits. She is adored by them and is one of the few persons here at the center whom they will obey. She is trying to impart her secret to the younger Sisters who are stationed with her."

"This part of Kasai Province is a showcase for you of Congo life on the lowest rungs of the ladder," observed Father de Cock. "The Government makes a clear-cut distinction between the areas where the Congolese live according to traditional customs (though almost everywhere these are being invaded), and the urban centers that practice customs unknown to the Congo region before the Belgians came. But most village people, simple though their life still is, are socially far ahead of these last few tribes of Kasai to accept modern change."

At Luluabourg, the center of Scheut work in Kasai Province, I sat ensconced in a chair near Bishop Declercq, the great pioneer of the Kasai missions.

"Here in Kasai," commented His Excellency in thoughtful mood, "we stand at the very beginning of the colossal task that the Church aims to perform among the Congolese. Of course it is the same task that the Church seeks to do among every other people on the planet. Colossal is the word for it! We are not merely signing up new members for a club or a political party. We are reaching into these people's deepest roots. We are building a complete new supernatural society. The thorough Christianization of Africa will require, as Christianization required in Europe, centuries of effort."

"Do the Government authorities appreciate what you aim to accomplish?" I asked.

"I think the better elements do," replied His Excellency. " 'Why leave behind us,' remarked one Belgian, 'a race of blacks who will curse our very memory?' "

Bishop Declercq is now dead and gone, but his reflections came back to me vividly during my recent visit to the Congo. "Operation

Colossal" which he helped me so effectively to appreciate, has become today, as applied to the Belgian Congo, something quite remarkable. Today one in every four Congolese is a Catholic, as is one in every three inhabitants of the Belgian trust territories of Ruanda and Urundi. Of the 11,800,000 inhabitants of the Congo, 3,068,284 are Catholic; and of the 4,100,000 dwellers in Ruanda-Urundi, 1,596,000 are Catholic. This makes over 4,600,000 Catholics in Belgian Africa. Since Protestants in the Congo total 787,351, the total Christians in Belgian Africa are 34.3 per cent, or a little less than five and a half million.

The close co-operation between the missionaries and the Government is the principal explanation for the fact that the Congo's institutions for education and mercy are likewise the strongest proportionately in all Africa. More than 1,000,000 Congolese children now attend 15,500 free schools; 40 per cent of the entire school-age population is at school. The best available comparative figures show 19 per cent school attendance for six neighboring British colonies, and five per cent for adjacent French Equatorial Africa. Catholic missionaries now operate 144 technical schools (which are favorite training units of the Government), with an enrollment of over 5,000 students.

Congo hospitals under Catholic auspices now total 233. There are over 200 maternity centers, which during 1952 reported more than 2,200,000 consultations. There is an impressive list of additional institutions, such as 56 leper foundations harboring over 9,000 sufferers; homes for the physically and mentally defective; asylums for orphans and the aged.

In other unusual ways, Congo missionaries have undertaken *big* projects. The Congo Catholic Cinema Center, for instance, has no counterpart anywhere else in the mission world. To date that vigorous enterprise and its affiliates have turned out over a hundred original films for mass education, all geared specifically to the needs of the Congolese. A steady supply of films feeds the two hundred projectors operated by Belgian missionaries, as a religio-social supplement to the General Government Information Service.

In Leopoldville, Brother René Reygaerts, of the Scheut Missionaries, the director of construction of the new Baudouin I Stadium, showed me his newly completed project. This huge concrete structure seats 75,000 spectators, and is but one feature of a city-wide, leisure-guidance program that the missionaries have directed in the capital since 1919. Father de la Kethulle has been the moving spirit in this enterprise. The major sports field today is fifty acres in extent and, besides the great stadium, has swimming pools with a total surface of 40,000 square feet, football fields, tennis and basketball courts. The sports association currently directs leagues operating sixty football teams in Leopoldville alone.

"Leopoldville, thanks to the generous help given by the Government to the missions, has a more comprehensive system of social welfare than obtains anywhere else in Africa," reports Jean L. L. Comhaire, now on the Social Studies staff of Seton Hall University, Newark, New Jersey. "Something more could be done for old people and invalids, but the proper care given to youth has secured the steady development of a healthy urban society. Practically all boys are at school, thanks to ample accommodation and staff provided by the missionary, and girls usually attend school, though they tend to leave at the end of their third year. On their free days children make good use of the sporting grounds and halls, where they play amid familiar and sympathetic surroundings. Specialized associations, for instance the Christian Working Youth, offers social opportunities to young persons and adults, and contribute their share in making the people realize the importance of spiritual values." [2]

In 1953, the Protestant missionaries asked the loan of the Baudouin I Stadium of the Scheut Fathers and commemorated there the seventy-fifth anniversary of their arrival in Congo territory in 1878. There are now 44 Protestant societies in the Belgian Congo with a personnel of 1,300 foreign missionaries. Their native staff totals 1,800. Protestant schools care for some 400,000 children, while their hospitals, dispensaries, and leprosy centers total over 200. "We believe that about 1,500,000 Congolese have been influenced by our efforts," explained an American worker in Leopoldville.

What evidence is there that, apart from a quantitative movement toward Christianity, there has been any improvement in the quality of Congo society?

Father Joseph Ceuppens, a leader in Leopoldville, says: "Let us make it clear that Christians in the Belgian Congo still live in a pagan society. There is nothing astonishing about the fact that concepts of family life and social traditions of clan life are still pagan. The forward march of the Congo is only in its beginnings. Nevertheless, everyone who has had close contact with the Congolese can give evidence that a good percentage among the Christians truly live by the precepts of their Faith.

"People among whom love of neighbor never meant other than clan solidarity are aware now that they owe regard to people of other tribes. 'I do not like the man next door because he is a Bakongo and an enemy of my tribe,' observed a clerk here in Leopoldville, 'but I speak to him every day. I know that as a Christian I must respect him.'

"Marriage laws are kept by many thousands at great sacrifice. Family life is becoming Christian. The observance of Sunday is helping men to live better lives in many villages. As regards worship of God and the practice of piety, the African is outstanding. In areas like Urundi, people gather on Sunday to pray, not only when a priest is on hand for Mass; in hundreds of centers, a prayer director presides, reads an exhortation, and leads in worship.

"Not only do the black Africans make good priests and Sisters; there are individuals among them who have entered Carmel and are following the great contemplatives of the ages. Belgian Africa today has three Carmelite monasteries. The two at Kabwe and Bunia were founded by Belgian Sisters who accepted African young women as candidates; now at Zaza, in Ruanda, the third monastery to be opened has an exclusively African personnel. A new Trappist monastery in Kivu hopes in time to accept African men to the contemplative life."

The first Congolese, Stephen Kaoze, to be raised to the priesthood was ordained in 1917. This achievement was witnessed by some whites with grave misgivings. But a general movement was soon under way. For the two decades from 1932 to 1952, the average of newly ordained was sixteen priests per year. Today there are over 350 Congolese priests in Belgian Africa. A few chapters hence, we shall visit an African in Ruanda, Bishop Bigirumwami, who with rare grace has assumed the role of the episcopacy. But the real miracle of Central Africa is the astounding growth of the Sisterhoods in Belgian territory. There has been an average yearly gain of 44 new native-born Sisters during the past dozen years, to bring the total to almost 675. The elevation of woman is a major problem. To convince both whites and blacks that African women have it in them to develop character and responsibility, nothing has helped more than the Church's experience with native women religious.

There is no mystery behind these outstanding achievements in the Belgian Congo. In the early days, the Government officials were hard pressed for people to interest themselves in the Africans. The missionaries entered into the task with spirit. Today we witness a common effort to provide an adequate program for the Congolese. Frankly, nothing short of a pooling of all the spiritual and temporal forces that have anything to contribute, is adequate to do a proper job for Africa's peoples. Where secular forces work alone, the efforts lack moral strength thoroughly to mold a people. Religious forces striving alone lack the financial resources and the facilitations that can be provided by secular authority.

As might be expected, Belgium has been criticized for placing so many of its institutions in the hands of missionaries. Even among the Belgian people themselves, there is an element that would prefer to keep the religious out of education, medicine, and social welfare. Outside of Belgium, there have been bitter objections by the secularists who believe that religion is long ago dead and buried and should not be allowed to pop into the main stream of life again even in Central Africa. "Keep religion in the sacristy," such critics say venomously, "where it will harmlessly rot away."

Most thinking Belgians justify the role of the missionary in the Congo on the score of the missionary's superior ability (when he is properly imbued with the ideals of his calling) to draw out the finest there is in the African, and to implant in the latter the finest there is in world culture, in order that he may eventually become a fully evolved African and a fully endowed man.

Chapter 4
_____

CITY SLICKER

FACES—FACES—EARNEST, set faces—held me fascinated as we moved from room to room. Night had come suddenly, as it does in the tropics, without a long sunset or afterglow, and lights were lit in the great quadrangle of classrooms in St. Peter's Mission in the native city of Leopoldville. Each room was crowded with full-grown men, from eighteen to fifty years of age. They were attending night school.

"All these fellows are thirsty—thirsty for education," Father Van den Heuvel remarked. "They want to know. Hence, at the end of the day's work, they come to the various missions that have adult-education courses. If they keep up their studies for six years, they finish primary school. There are some four thousand men studying this year, and a remarkable percentage of them will stick at it doggedly to the end."

"Who exactly are they?" I asked, puzzled. "What prompts them to do this?"

"Ask them," replied Father V. characteristically.

In the first grade, two big, burly blacks were at the board, each with a pointer. At word from the teacher, each man read off the pronunciation of the vowels. When they returned to their seats near where I stood, I approached one of them.

"Do you mind telling me your name?" I began.

"Stephen, Father. Stephen Mbaya."

"How old are you?"

"I'm thirty-six."

"What do you do for a living?"

"I'm a truck driver."

"Why are you coming to school?"

"I want to buy a house."

"How will school help?"

119

"If I learn to read and write, I shall be able to earn more money."

It was as simple as that. In the second grade, I approached another student. He was twenty-nine. He wanted to learn arithmetic because he needed it to take a course in mechanics.

"Why do you want to do that?"

"I want to buy a house."

"They all seem interested in buying a house," I remarked to Pere Van den Heuvel.

"Yes, a great many are," he replied. "Since the war, the Government has pushed the slogan, 'Own Your Own Home.' First of all, that is the best way to fight radicalism and the Reds; the responsible family man makes a poor disciple for communism. Secondly, from the families that settle down permanently in the towns, will come tomorrow's better-educated class. When a man returns to his village, he quickly slips back into old ways; and his children, if they come to town, have to start again from the beginning. Hence the effort to make the men resist their womenfolk—for it is the women who fret to return home. The women say that they want to eat green corn again; but they agree to stay in the city, once their husbands own houses there."

In grades four and five, I asked where the men hailed from. Practically all were from the bush or from towns fifty to five hundred miles away—Kisantu, Matadi, Luluabourg, Coquilhatville, Lemfu. The men were of many tribes. But in the mission school, they sat side by side and together drank in the magic learning. Finally we came to a smaller group, studying under the direction of my friend, Father Ceuppens, and there we were introduced to an outstanding example of a mission-educated native.

"I especially want you to meet Bernard Akiki," said Father Van den Heuvel in a low voice. "I call him my prize 'city slicker.' I do not use the term in the derogatory sense in which you use it ordinarily in English. For me, Bernard is rather a prime example of how a humble, village boy can come to Leopoldville and, by dint of hard work and sound ability, make his way in notable fashion and build up for himself a good home and family."

We entered Father Ceuppens' classroom, and I immediately found that we had left behind the primary classes of the night school. This was a special study circle for social problems; the participants in it were Africans already successful in their careers, who wished to improve themselves further. One man, for instance, conducted a program for Africans on the Leopoldville radio. Others had Government posts; some were teachers; some held good positions with Belgian business firms. Bernard Akiki was among these last.

"Bernard, come and meet this priest from America," Father Van den Heuvel called, and his model "city slicker" approached and gave me his hand. He was tall, lithe, well-proportioned; his manner was unpretentious, and his beaming smile immediately captivated me.

"How old are you, Bernard?" I asked.

"Thirty-three, Father."

"How old were you when you came to Leopoldville?"

"Seventeen."

"Bernard grew up in a little village near the great Jesuit mission at Kisantu," interposed Father Van den Heuvel. "After finishing primary school, he entered the professional school of the Christian Brothers, and he came here to Leopoldville when he had completed his training."

"Why did you come?" I asked.

"Because," Bernard laughed, "everywhere in the back country, the city of Leopoldville is talked about as the place of plenty, where food and drink are never lacking, where a man can marry a beautiful woman without too many difficulties, where everybody is free to pick the work he likes and live the new life."

"Did you find a job easily?"

"No, Father!" answered Bernard. "During the first few years, I was often very hungry, many times I was tricked, and after a couple of years I was badly discouraged. But I liked to play football, and soon I found myself known and liked by the men and the missionaries at St. Francis Church in Kintambo."

"He became quite a hero," put in Father Van den Heuvel. "He was captain of the football team that won the league trophy two years in succession."

"Did you marry the beautiful woman you were looking for?" I asked.

"Yes, I did, but not in Leopoldville! After seven years in the city, I had saved enough to pay a dowry. I went back to Kisantu, and there

the Sisters in the primary school I used to attend helped me find a
wife. After our marriage, she came back with me to Leopoldville."

"How many children have you now?"

"Five—three boys and two girls. We live in St. Francis Mission
in Kintambo."

"Bernard is head of his parish co-operative society, which is one
of the best in Leopoldville," volunteered Father Ceuppens. "It provides family help for sickness, childbirth expenses and death costs,
and pays a weekly insurance when a man is out of work."

"But my greatest pleasure is playing the clarinet in our orchestra,"
added Bernard.

"Where do you work now?" I asked.

"With a Belgian merchandizing company."

"How much salary do you get?"

"I receive 6,000 francs a month." I quickly calculated and realized
that this return of $120 a month in American currency was quite sub-
stantial.

"I am very proud of Bernard's business success," explained Father
Van den Heuvel, "because I helped him get his present work. He is
now the head of a department; he has the direction of over twenty
well-trained and capable employees, each of whom works at a desk in
a large office. It is quite different from the forest of twenty years ago,
isn't it, Bernard?"

The young man laughed heartily.

"What is your big aim just at present, Bernard?" I asked.

"I am building a house."

"What? You too! Everybody in Leopoldville is building or buying a house," I exclaimed.

"Why not look into this house-building business?" suggested Father Van den Heuvel. "Bernard would be glad to have you witness
his prowess in putting the finishing touches on his new home."

"Wonderful!" cried Bernard. "You must come tomorrow."

Father Van den Heuvel seemed particularly happy as we journeyed
home. "So many harsh things have been said against these young men
who have settled in our cities that I feel prompted to be their champion," he remarked. "True, many of them lose a taste for the better
things, but the critics forget the thousands of them who, with varying

success, are establishing good homes and thus laying the foundation for a strong Christian society of tomorrow."

Father Van den Heuvel, I was coming to realize, took genuine pride in those Africans who were making good. This priest, it was pointed out to me, is one of the distinguished figures in Leopoldville missionary circles. He is the son of a famous cabinet minister in Belgium, the first priest-member of the Government Council, and is also a member of the Commission for the Protection of the Native. He is a doctor in civil law, and thus is well prepared to watch all relations of the missions with the Government and all legislation touching social life.

"He is fearless when he gets an idea," said one of his confreres. "He carried on a one-man campaign against silicosis in mines and factories, and he won. He called on the Governor General one day and took him to the native hospitals, to show him patients sleeping under the beds as well as on them. He is currently campaigning for more street lights in the native city: 'No light,' runs his slogan, 'usually means no morality.'"

Next day Father V. and I set out for Bernard Akiki's house, and along the way, I got the story of the "Own Your Own Home" drive.

"Housing," the priest explained, "is the number-one problem in native cities everywhere in tropical Africa. In all urban areas without exception, housing is inadequate. Thus that new phenomenon in black Africa, the city dweller, lives in an overcrowded, dilapidated structure that creates medical, moral, and economic conditions far worse than anything the native knew before the white man arrived. Governments everywhere are fighting the problem, but not hard enough yet to solve it."

Since the war, housing projects in Leopoldville have added some ten thousand units in the city. First are the industrial housing projects promoted by the railroads and the port authority for their employees. After payments made during fifteen to twenty years, these quarters may become the property of the occupying family. Secondly, there are the substandard houses erected by the city for the low-salaried workers. Some six thousand such units were built in the first eight years after the war, all to become the property of the dwellers after fifteen to twenty years of small payments.

Thirdly, for the higher-salaried Africans, there is the municipal

housing-loan scheme. Best feature of this scheme is the sense of freedom enjoyed by the beneficiary. The family man applies for a plot
of land, and then arranges a building loan that comes to about $600
in American money, to which he must add a substantial contribution
of his own in cash or labor. Our African then proceeds, directed by
approved plans and constructors, to build a European-style house.
Such was the project of Bernard Akiki, whom we found at work when
we arrived. His house was completed, and he had reached the stage
of its interior decoration.

"Welcome, welcome!" Bernard shouted as we entered. He met us
with paintbrush in hand. He was clad in working jumpers, and his
European suit was hanging on a nail and protected by a newspaper.

"Oh, you've made magnificent progress!" cried Father Van den
Heuvel as he looked about.

"Yes," replied Bernard. "A few weeks more, and the Akiki family
will be in their new home. It's been a long battle, Fathers—over two
years. Do you think I have picked the right color for my dining room
wall?"

"Very good," commented my companion, evidently not intending
to become involved in details. The walls were decorated in red to
about eight feet from the floor, and above was a band of lighter color.
The house was a five-room one that would have represented a worthy
achievement in any country in the world. Bernard took us next door,
where a man and his wife were likewise completing their home. They
had varnished their hardwood floors, and everything looked immaculate. This second man was an artist, and he showed us several of his
landscapes that already hung on the walls; they were creditable works
that indicated knowledge of European technique. He told us that he
earned 5,000 francs a month.

"How will your wife and the children like this new home?" asked
Father V. when we returned to Bernard's house.

"I'm afraid the children are going to be lonely here," replied Bernard, and a shadow crossed his face. "We have been living in a very
poor neighborhood, where everybody is crowded on top of everybody
else, but we love it there. There are shoals of youngsters around us,
and there's never a dull moment from one end of the year to the other.

"After dinner every evening, for instance, men, women, old people, and children gather in our little yard around a big fire. We sing

songs, play music, tell riddles—what we call *ya moke,* the equivalent of the children's hour—and then, as the night gets on, we have those wonderful folk tales, which we call *ya molai,* the hour of the adults. There's an old Bakongo woman who's a perfect spellbinder, Fathers, a perfect spellbinder! She practically hypnotizes me, she hypnotizes me! Her stories are marvelous. And Fathers, let me tell you—those stories aren't just ordinary entertainment. Those stories are history; they hold all the rich and beautiful traditions of our people. We love them, Fathers. I love them with all my heart! Sometimes I cry when I hear those stories; sometimes I laugh and laugh with wildest joy. Because those stories are the stories that belong to my very soul, Fathers—they belong to my very soul!

"And now I'm afraid we're going to lose all those things. We're going to be sort of—respectable here, Father. I'm afraid. Maybe we're paying too much in what we're giving up."

The atmosphere had suddenly become tense. I felt that I was witnessing the denouement of a drama.

"Bernard, my boy," said Father Van den Heuvel, after a silence that was high theater, "that's why I love you! I'm so proud of you, Bernard. I'm so delighted to see that, as the years pass and as you so markedly improve your condition from a material point of view, you never lose that fine sense of integrity that God gave you and that keeps you true in your judgments of what is really worth while in life. Bernard, hold on to that love you have for your people, for your folk traditions, for the things that must remain a part of all Congolese no matter how much betterment, material or spiritual, they attain to. Pass on that love to your children. God bless you, Bernard! We'll be going now. Au revoir."

Beyond a doubt, urban life has come to stay in the Congo. In 1950, there were 850,000 black workers in the employ of industrial, commercial and agricultural firms, and by today this figure is approaching 1,000,000. The great majority of those workers today still have one foot in the city or in the location, and one foot in the country; they still cling to their villages and are on constant pilgrimage to visit their loved ones, to return even for a brief time to rural joys, free of the baffling strain of the new regime. But more and more the ties with the village will be broken. The principal influence in this direction is the Government's determination not to encourage laborers, even skilled laborers, to come to the Congo region from Europe. Officials insist that the Congolese can even today learn almost every modern routine. They face frankly the proximate tomorrow, when even managerial jobs will go to the black Africans.

More than 60 per cent of the Congolese workers have as yet no professional qualification, but 30 per cent are semiskilled, and some 10 per cent are fully qualified and furnish an output comparable to that of Europeans. At the great new industrial diamond mining center at Bakwanga, we see Africans operating the ten gigantic electric "Turnapool" tractors, worth $35,000 apiece, each with an excavating capacity of six tons. We find almost every function in the huge refinery in the care of Africans. We see the complicated high-precision machines in the great machine shop all in the hands of Africans, under the supervision of one lone European engineer.

At the great mining smelter of the *Union Miniere* near Elizabethville, less than 200 of the 6,500 workers are Europeans. Practically all of the intricate technical work in this plant, a triumph of the modern mechanical age, is handled by children of the bush, most of whose parents still run barefoot through the forest. At the maintenance shops of Jadotville, only a handful of Europeans are needed to supervise the work. Congolese operate the overhead elevators that shift the cathodic plates of copper and dip them in the 65-foot-long electrolythic baths.

So, likewise, is it at all other industrial centers of Katanga Province. So it is, for instance, at Manono, three hundred miles north of Elizabethville, where Geomines operates its huge tin mines. In the 1930's, Manono became a complete welfare state, where tender custodial care went into keeping the African worker alive, healthy, and happy. But less than a generation has passed, and obdurately the new ideas march on: the African, men are whispering, must not remain forever a child even if he prefers it; he must grow up; he must take responsibility; he must live the modern way; he must be educated; if talented, he must assume authority in the Congo's industries, plantations, and commercial enterprises.

Nor can we forget that the Congolese is free to set himself up in private enterprise. I saw plumbers, electricians, and similar craftsmen running their own businesses in Leopoldville. Several carpenters employ twenty to thirty men each. Some shops have up-to-date electrical appliances. Some Congolese merchants have trading posts scattered through entire provinces. Some Congolese planters work up to a thousand acres. However, as elsewhere in the world, it is the laborer who needs special social protection, if he is to be a man and not a chattel. Catholic labor unions have been organized in the Congo, but as yet they are not a notably strong social force. The rank-and-file missionary in urban areas is keenly aware of the social doctrines that Christianity must enunciate.

Father Van Wing, S.J., Secretary of the Committee of Mission Superiors and dean among the pioneers of Catholic policy in public life in the Congo, sums it up as follows: "It is evident that missionaries, as bearers of the Gospel message, must lose no opportunity to defend the inalienable rights of workers, which are the following: (1) a just salary; (2) a family salary; (3) humane working conditions; (4) a decent habitation for the family. The missions themselves must give good example in this respect. Dedication to the saving of souls does not excuse us from practicing social justice toward our lay helpers."

Belgian leaders frankly recognize what the missionary has done for the worker. With Doctor L. Mottoulle, director of personnel in the mighty *Union Miniere,* I went down into the Kipuli copper mines, the richest in the world; visited the company operations in the Lubumbashi Valley; and inspected the installations at Jadotville, second only to those of Elizabethville. With him I saw, also, the huge labor camps, and finally the complex of medical, social, and educational institutions, almost all in the hands of our Catholic Sisters, that are operated for the workers.

"Your company does well by its employees, Doctor Mottoulle," I remarked after several days at our rounds.

"Quite well, indeed," he agreed.

"The Government likewise follows a sound and sensible policy," I commented.

"True," he agreed again. "Thanks to Belgian law, the peoples of the Belgian Congo have been saved from destruction in the social upheaval of the last half century."

We walked for a moment, and then Mottoulle gave voice to the additional thought that my banal comments prompted in his mind.

"But in the compounds and native towns of the Congo today, we have something much more than healthy workers," he said. "We have men. We have the seed of people of character, who will be the making of a modern nation. And these men, these citizens, were not made by the industrialists or by the Government. This contribution-plus that makes the Belgian Congo distinctive in all Africa was made by the missionaries.

"The missionary, particularly in our cities, does not only preach the Gospel and teach good morals. He protects the black against a host of dangers—from without and from within. He is the black's devoted friend and tutor. He teaches the black his family responsibilities; he instructs him as to his rights; he guides him to do his duty, to build his life on discipline, to have a love for work that will bring happiness to his earthly career. In short, the city missionary is the chaplain of the laboring man. No one in the Congo knows better the Congolese and the profound aspirations of the latter's soul. No one appreciates more keenly even the economic potentialities of the black African. No one can offer sounder or more reasonable proposals to insure the future welfare of the Congolese in the life of higher civilization that lies before him."

The Belgians and their regime in the Congo have many faults, I have no doubt. But certainly in few places on earth, during this secular day in which we live, do we find more frank admission of the role of religion, and of the role of the ministers of religion, in the service of human society.

Chapter 5

CONGO MOTHER

"MBOTE, MAMA. What can I do for you today?"

"Mbote, Mademoiselle. I've come to see you. My soul is very unhappy."

"I'm very sorry, Mama! Come over here and sit down where we can talk about it."

The young Belgian social worker had met the African woman at the door, and I watched her conduct the mother to a nearby bench. Mama shifted her child from her back to her lap and began telling the social worker her story.

"It won't be a long tale," Mademoiselle van Oevelen explained to me, with a fleeting smile. We stood near the entrance of Foyer Social I of Leopoldville. "Our social workers are assigned to reach the women folk of this quarter with its fifty thousand inhabitants. We are a team of five: a directress, a social-service assistant, a nurse, a housekeeping regent, a sewing regent. Very few, you see, for fifty thousand! Mademoiselle at the door, therefore, must be generous-hearted but nimble-witted in discovering as quickly as possible how she can help each of the mothers who come to us.

"A big point in our policy, Father, is this: Each of these women whom we aid must, in some little way, agree to labor for her own improvement. Let me explain what I mean."

That was what I wanted—an initiation into the mysteries of the *Assistance Sociale*. The *Assistance Sociale* is one more of those institutions that are peculiarly Belgian in their large-scale development here in the Congo. Similar activity is found in other fields; but only in the Belgian Congo is it a main-line, driving factor in the forming of the lives of the women of the cities.

In 1953, there were 128 Belgian women working in the Congo with all the dedication of religious, in the operation of the Government-supported social centers that are the main feature of the *Assistance Sociale*. The largest number of women—some forty—were sent out under the direction of the Volunteers of Medical, Educational, and Social Service of Brussels, already a strong organization in the homeland. Almost as well represented is the *Assistance Sociale au Congo,* with headquarters likewise in Brussels but working only in the Congo territory. A third group is the *Auxiliaires Feminines Internationales,* with center in Brussels. This last organization has an American center in Chicago; Americans know it as the International Catholic Auxiliaries. Its members work in other countries besides the Belgian Congo. These three organizations operate twenty-three social centers in the Congo. In addition, there are social centers operated directly for individual missions or for industrial enterprises, by young women lay missionaries who have come out unattached, caught by the widespread enthusiasm for the missionary apostolate that grips the Belgian people.

The devoted lay worker is the secret of the huge success of the social-assistance programs. She is paid a small salary by the state and is assured proper quarters in which to live. Her mission in life is to teach the blessings of civilization, with its properly integrated Christian ideals, in the homely form of lessons in cooking, sewing, knitting, laundry, child care, to the women and children of the Congo. The Congolese are delighted to have these white women take an interest in them. They are puzzled by this new category of strangers: not Sisters, whom the Congolese have long known by their religious garb, their austere lives; not wives of colonists, whom the Congolese have come to know as part of every European venture. The African mothers crowd the sewing and housekeeping classes and welcome these kindly persons to their homes.

"How many attend your classes here?" I asked Mlle. van Oevelen as we entered the large work room.

"Over fifteen hundred women are enrolled," she replied.

"In what language do you speak to these women?"

"Some of them understand French, but the language that reaches their heart is Lingala," Mademoiselle replied. "The missionaries speak Lingala, and we follow their example."

I was already engrossed in the sight before me—over one hundred women were present to learn home-making. Each mother had left her current child in a basket cradle at the edge of the room, or with the African attendant out in the yard, whose duty was to keep the youngsters happy by means of a few playthings while their mothers attended school inside. The women were all neatly dressed in bright clothes, and they worked industriously at their tables. The sewing regent was the main center of attention, as she sat and taught a group or moved from table to table and approved or corrected each sewer's labors.

Several African young women assisted the regent. "As with almost everybody else who has a task in the Congo," explained Mademoiselle, "each of us has at least one African understudy."

Another interesting group busily at work at the center was the class of expectant mothers, each of whom was preparing her layette. A system of small payments for the cloth used is required. Nobody in the layette class is permitted to take anything home. Instead, each woman has a shelf or a drawer, and carefully piles up her articles, which remain there until the birth of the child.

"The husband enters into the picture, so far as this class is concerned," explained Mademoiselle. "We teach him how to make the cradle. Indeed, we go further with him; we take the occasion of this contact to train the husband as well as the wife, in the elementary practices that will make a Christian home. The missionaries advise us that one matter of great importance is the training of families to eat together. Only a small minority of Congolese families take their food from a common table as most white people do. In many native homes, the men eat first; and after they have left the room, then the women and children sit down. More commonly, however, the men and their guests eat in the dining room, and the women and children pick up their food in the kitchen or the courtyard. Deep social significance is attached to this and other customs. It is almost unbelievable how much effort is required to alter these practices."

"Do you get into the African homes?" I asked.

"Yes, indeed. In fact, the home can be called the front line in our great battle. Our principal conquest must be the Congo mother; she is the vital key in the task of Christian civilization. Our slogan might be worded, 'Help the family to live worthily.' Here are five aims we seek to inculcate: (1) Learn to serve meals fittingly; (2) lodge and clothe the family decently, even in the face of poverty; (3) give loving care to the children; (4) keep the elementary rules for good health; (5) use the family resources wisely."

"What beautiful rules, Mademoiselle!" I cried rather excitedly. "What appeals to me most is that you don't make a single reference to abnormalities. Problems you have in abundance here in Africa, as everywhere else. But unlike the average social worker elsewhere, you don't assume that your main task is the handling of physical, mental, and moral deformities."

"Thank you, Father!" said Mademoiselle, apparently pleased. "You are so right! We should love dearly to feel that we are not merely correcting the faults and the failures, but that we also are building—building the Congo's mothers into intelligent, educated housewives, for the countless generations of Christian living that lie ahead."

Father Ceuppens, who was by my side during all this interchange, was smiling broadly. "I share in principle the enthusiasm that you both express," he offered. "I think, Father, that great things will come from the labors of this relatively new element among us, the ladies of the *Assistance Sociale*. Doctor Spaey, a noted Belgian sociologist, believes that the greatest contributors to the evolution and emancipation of the Congo mothers will be the workers, Belgian and African, of the *Assistance Sociale* in the extra-customary cities centers, and also the religious Sisters, European or African (and especially African), in the traditional life of the villages and rural areas."

"Why do you specify so carefully that you merely 'share in principle' our enthusiasm?" I asked.

"Because," replied Father Ceuppens, laughing, "you both seem to approach with such glib confidence what is probably the most difficult single problem among all those that face us in the Congo; namely, the social elevation of woman."

"But aren't all of you old-timers being somewhat defeatist in your attitude?" I ventured.

"Why do you say that?"

"Well, among other things, I've noticed that Belgium's Ten-Year Plan proposes building four thousand new schools for boys, and only four hundred new schools for girls. You give away the victory before you begin the battle!"

"Let me explain. Government officials and missionaries are fully aware that there will be no true Christian home until the woman is free of witchcraft and superstition and is armed with at least a moderate education. It is from his mother that every boy gets his ideas during the first half dozen years of his life. But these are obstacles that can be removed only by time. These are the obstacles that today are keeping girls out of school: these, and not the Government or the missionaries. Schools already exist for girls, and in mission schools, a greater proportion of teachers is assigned to teach the girls than the boys. The fact remains, however, that in rural areas only one girl is in school for every ten boys, while in the cities there is but one girl for every six boys."

"What are these obstacles?" I asked.

"First, there is the clan, the so-called extended family to which not only the children but the individual parents are subject. Among many tribes, clan rules are very severe against any girl who leaves home before she marries, whether for school or any other reason. Doubts are cast on her virtue if the old tradition is broken. On the other hand, in some places the family asks such a high bride price for an educated girl that she goes without a suitor.

"The second great obstacle is the prospective husband. Perhaps ninety per cent of African men, of all African countries are as yet afraid to marry an educated wife. Even the educated man wants his wife to be a willing and able worker. Most educated women cannot agree to being mere beasts of burden, as African tradition makes them. Hence the need of a little time to readjust the men first, and then the women."

"You distinguish, then, Father Ceuppens," said Mademoiselle van Oevelen, "between the domestic-science training we give through the *Assistance Sociale,* and the classroom education such as women receive in the white world?"

"Yes, Mademoiselle. And of course the whole question is one of timing. We all want educated Congo mothers, but the education must move forward to be always in step with the advancing milieu."

"Today," I said, "let's keep to the *Assistance Sociale.*"

"You must visit some of our well-set-up housewives, Father," urged Mademoiselle van Oevelen, "Mademoiselle Eykens plans taking you to visit Cecile and some of her neighbors."

We walked along the busy city streets and turned in at a three-room house set in a neat garden. "Cecile, are you home?" called Mademoiselle.

"Welcome!" replied Cecile. "I've just finished my cleaning."

"This," Mademoiselle Eykens explained, "is not a typical Leopold-ville home. Cecile has been one of our star pupils; she prides herself on keeping a model home and meets every one of the requirements. She has a special aptitude for making things attractive and finds her-self at home with modern gadgets, even to the little refrigerator that her husband has bought her."

In the neat kitchen stood the spotless symbol of the ultra-ultra in home-making. "May I look inside?" I asked.

"Please do," replied Cecile.

I opened the door and had my first glimpse into a Congo house-wife's refrigerator. The shelves were neatly arranged, though the stock was meager to the eye of a spoiled American. I saw a bowl of carved portions of fowl.

"You are going to have chicken for dinner," I remarked with a smile.

"No, that is duck," corrected Cecile.

"Cecile is fortunate," commented Mademoiselle. "Duck is a rare dish here in Leopoldville. The well-to-do families may have chicken once a month, but most families feel lucky if they have a small quan-tity of meat once a week. I have seen a housewife buy two pounds of meat, including the bones, for a family of ten."

"And what is this strange dish?" I asked pointing to an unprepos-sessing item.

" A quantity of *nyong*," volunteered Father Ceuppens. "They are a large, white grub and are regarded as a delicacy."

"Are there many local foods that we should regard as unusual?" I asked.

"Some of the game in the markets would not be found in Europe or America," said the Belgian priest. "We see crocodile for sale, smoked buffalo, hippopotamus, elephant. In season there are the *mbinjo,* which are big caterpillars, and a few families eat rather repul-sive insects, rodents, and reptiles. Of course, this is much a matter of tradition. Don't forget that some European countries favor snails and frogs, which raise goose flesh on the uninitiate."

"What makes up the ordinary poor family's daily ration?" I inquired.

"Starchy foods for the most part," answered Cecile. "The ordinary family eats cassava bread and other products of cassava flour. Many eat rice almost daily. The markets sell a variety of greens, which are boiled, finely chopped, and mixed with palm oil, salt, and pepper by the cook."

"Do many people go hungry?"

"I should say," commented Mademoiselle, "that pangs of hunger are an early childhood experience for most Congolese, and for many continue all through life. The first infant born in a family is usually well fed. But when another child is born, Sonny Boy of yesterday becomes just one of the crowd. Often he has to fight for whatever he gets. Often in his desperation he eats all sorts of strange things—soil, refuse, leaves—and drinks liquids never meant for his little stomach.[1] Improvidence in families on the score of food brings disease, leads youngsters to steal, and accounts for many youngsters getting jobs to fill their stomachs."

"You and your confreres get to know the life of the city very intimately, don't you, Mademoiselle?" I remarked.

"True," replied this very capable young woman. "The social-service assistant in our team has the greatest contact with the homes in our district. We all learn to love the Congo mothers dearly. The Congolese are sweet people, much better-humored than we Europeans."

"Nevertheless, you encounter many problems, don't you?" I continued.

"It goes without saying. The latest census reveals that, in our district, there are twice as many men as there are women. This one fact alone causes mountains of woe for these poor folk."

Mademoiselle's observation recalled to me some comments made a few days previously by a thoughtful gentleman in Leopoldville.

"The Congolese woman in her home village," he explained "has, pagan though she is, a moral code. When she accepts Christianity and is disciplined in its tenets, she is armed with a new code; and in good Christian families, the Congo mother is faithful to that new code. We find many splendid types of womanhood among the Congolese in the cities. But in the case of thousands of women who transfer without careful preparation from the forest to the city, there is a sad lack of a moral code. In such circumstances, a woman absorbs with disconcerting ease a pattern of misbehavior that spells chaos for society. As a single woman, she is irresponsible; as a wife, she is easily faithless; as a mother, she is a harmful influence on growing boys and girls."

These are sobering words, surely. But two days after my visit to the Foyer Social, and my pleasant half hour at Cecile's I heard some very encouraging words. I had passed one of Leopoldville's social-service assistants, as she left a mission rectory that I was entering.

"I just encountered a social-service assistant at the gate as I came in," I remarked to the priest. "Do you think those social workers are accomplishing anything worth while here?"

"Anything worth while?" echoed the Father, by way of answer. "Decide for yourself when I tell you that that young lady has inscribed in our convert classes her seventeenth Congo mother, in the short space of time since she began her visitation work within our parish. To my mind, her work and the work of her associates constitute God's answer to the spiritual needs of the thousands of women who are adrift here without guidance. Next to our Sisters, these ladies from Belgium are the greatest blessing that has come to the Belgian Congo!"

Another group of lay apostles whom I greatly admire, celebrated recently the twenty-fifth anniversary of their work in the Congo region. They are the doctors of the A.M.M., the *Aide Medicale aux Missions,* who have sent out some sixty of their number to Africa and now operate twenty-four medical centers in every part of the Belgian Congo. While journeying about, I made the acquaintance of three of these fine men: Doctor Cochaux, Doctor Molnar, and Doctor Hemeryckx. The Government pays the salary of each, and provides an allowance for medicine; their residences and some other needs are provided by the missions.

I recall a delightful evening when a group of us talked into the wee hours with Doctor Cochaux. He is a graduate of the University of Brussels and a thoroughly enthusiastic pioneer with a generous gift of the *joie de vivre.* He told of handling two hundred dispensary cases each morning, and covering calls over a route embracing eighty villages in the afternoon. He had just completed the examination of twenty-one thousand natives for sleeping sickness.

Doctor Hemeryckx, when leaving to begin his work among the

Batetele, one of the difficult tribes, was told by his bishop, "Never forget, Doctor, that, with your medicine, you are to open God's pathway to the Batetele people."

Hemeryckx never forgot. The Batetele became to him "our people." From the jungle he wrote glowing letters of his work, to the girl he had left behind him in Belgium. During quiet nights in his African cabin, he told her of his devotion to her, but revealed hesitatingly, delicately, that he felt he should pledge his life to the lowly African people. From Belgium came a reply from his fiancée, stating that she, too, would like to devote herself to the Batetele. When arrangements were completed, she came by plane to Central Africa, and the bishop performed the marriage ceremony.

Time passed, and the Hemeryckxes were to have their first child. It would they said, seal their bond with Africa. The prediction proved true, but in a sense different from what the young couple had planned. Mrs. Hemeryckx died at childbirth. The griefstricken doctor pledged himself anew at the grave of his young wife. "Now the Batetele are indeed my people!" he murmured to one of his missionary companions. "A part of my being is here in their soil."

Today Doctor Hemeryckx enjoys an international reputation as an authority on leprosy in Africa. He is provincial inspector for leper work in Kasai and is head of the leper asylum at Tshumbe-Ste-Marie. He has been awarded Belgium's highest honors for his life of selfless service to the peoples of the Congo.

Chapter 6

AN EQUAL CHANCE TO FAIL

AT A UNITED NATIONS meeting of the Commission on Trust Territories, I heard one day the British delegate's acrid remarks, after the Soviet delegate in a long speech condemned the "colonial" powers for their incursions around the globe. The Britisher asked why the Russian presumed to consider as dependent peoples, only those who are geographically separated from the motherlands. Dependent peoples could be, said the Britisher, next-door neighbors, like some scores of contiguous peoples between Russia and the Pacific Ocean who are now contemporary younger brothers of the masters of Moscow. Most of the Britisher's hearers knew that Russia badgers unceasingly the nations with overseas possessions, but is quick to resent any nation that points an accusing finger at the U.S.S.R.

The great Pierre Ryckmans, modern fairy godparent of the Belgian Congo, was well aware of Russia's reactions, when he spoke at the U.N. on October 23, 1952. "Certain members," he said, "like the representative of the Soviet Union, who censure the acts of other states in most categoric fashion, pretend to the right to forbid every smallest allusion to methods employed against subject peoples by the Soviet administration."

A phenomenon of the times is this sensitiveness of all modern nations to references to their possession of subject peoples.

"In its traditional sense," said Paul van Zeeland, Belgian Minister of Foreign Affairs, before the United Nations on November 10, 1952, "the word 'colonialism' connotes the exploitation of populations of inferior civilization by others of superior civilization. Belgium lines up with the adversaries of this colonialism. She has fought it not only with words but with deeds . . . I hope that no one would wish to confound 'colonialism' thus defined, with another action which is quite the opposite in nature, which proceeds from high motives and con-

forms strictly with our U.N. Charter. I refer to the systematic action
pursued by an evolved people with an eye to aiding, in their efforts
toward political, economic, social, and cultural progress, the backward
native populations that fall within its administration. The U.N.
Charter itself considers this action as a 'sacred mission'; this is the term
that it employs."

Reprehensible colonialism is gone, Mr. van Zeeland asserted, while
nations exercise this "sacred mission" toward backward peoples within
their jurisdiction. "To our eyes, this sacred mission is not limited to
the few states who administer territories once called 'colonies.' It falls
to all states, whoever they be, in whose territory live native populations
with backward civilization. If I am not mistaken, more than half of
the states represented in this Assembly belong in this class."

After Mr. van Zeeland spoke, a Belgian Government publication [1]
printed in detail the complete list of nations having subject peoples.
The United States is one of these, with 394,000 American Indians.
Canada is another, with 8,400 Eskimos and 240,000 American Indians.
Sixteen nations of Latin America have 14,500,000 backward peoples
within their confines. Australia has 73,000 aborigines; New Zealand
has 115,000 Maoris. India totals some 25,000,000 tribesmen referred
to by its Government as Scheduled Classes. Indonesia has 650,000 in
miscellaneous tribespeople. Finally, for the U.S.S.R. the brochure
states, "In default of recent official data, it has not been possible to
include the backward native peoples of this country in our list."

Thus Belgium warns us not to point the finger of disdain at her.
Many nations over the earth, she notes, engage in the laudable practice
of caring for backward native peoples. This trend among governments
is all to the good. One might become impatient at this seeming attempt to put an aura of respectability about what many wish to label
as mere "land grabs" dating from the freebooting days gone by. But
the fact that the ablest men in our best nations are carefully choosing
their words to explain their philosophy toward those backward peoples
is the best guarantee that those peoples are about to get better treatment than they have had thus far in history.

Whatever the genesis of the present position of backward peoples
in the world, the fact remains that the backward peoples found in the
Belgian Congo must be regarded as fortunate, indeed. Any unbiased
observer will discover that the better elements among today's Belgians

are determined to grant to the Congolese an opportunity for the full flowering of a genuine African culture, which in the course of generations will bring out the inherent greatness, as yet all but undiscovered, that lies within the Bantu.

Superficial observers have accused the Belgians of planning merely to give the Congolese a crude, elementary schooling that will carry these Africans just far enough above the level of hewers of wood and drawers of water to make of the abler among them useful clerks and top sergeants of native labor. Some among the Belgians may in years gone by have had this plan in mind. But today the policy makers in the Belgian Congo are asking for a genuine elite and are planning for a university education that will give the most capable among the Congolese a thorough training of the whole man.

"Some people will, perhaps, be surprised," states Pierre Wigny, speaking for the Government, "to discover that a place has been reserved for the ancient classics, in the field of secondary education. Surely, the Congolese must need a more practical education. That is true for the masses. But, by establishing colleges for the natives, we wanted to prove that we were not reserving for our (white) children alone the monopoly of a high intellectual training and, as a consequence, of the professions in which it gives entree." [2]

I visited at Kisantu the simple beginnings of Lovanium, a university center that had its inspiration at Louvain, in Belgium, and that for twenty-five years has been developing under the Congo Jesuits. In 1954, Lovanium was transferred to Kimuenza, a sightly eminence fifteen miles south of Leopoldville. On the far-eastern borders of the Congo, I talked with other Jesuits, who were engaged in establishing at Usumbura what in time will be another university center. To satisfy those elements among the Belgians who ask for a complete public educational system separate from the schools operated by the Missions, a third center of university rank, which will be secular in philosophy, is contemplated for Leopoldville.

What is there in the way of a system of feeder schools, to make possible this development of universities? I put this question to Father Marcel Goetschalckx, of the Scheut Missionaries, Director of the Central Bureau of Catholic Education for the Congo.

"More has been done for postprimary education in the Congo than most people realize," Father Marcel explained. "But of course the bulk of the program lies ahead of us. The Government's reorganization of its educational program in 1948 started a truly extraordinary movement for postprimary education in Belgian Africa."

"Does anyone feel that it was a mistake in the past to limit education almost exclusively to primary schools?" I asked.

"No properly informed Belgian thinks it was a mistake," the Belgian missionary replied. "But in your part of the world," he added with a rueful smile, "there are many who criticize us." He was referring to Belgium's differences with the United Nations authorities on Belgium's policy in the Congo.

Governor-General Leo Petillon of the Belgian Congo, in his official annual discourse in 1953, stated flatly that the U.N. intervention in the name of speed was a menace. "We know these tendencies," he said. "They are inspired by ideologies that, at first glance, seem generous, but are utopian. They are built on impatience, they are calculated to incite us to do things, no matter how, in impatient haste. They are calculated to lead us to ignore the lessons of long experience, dearly acquired, for reasons of political opportunism."

Today over 1,000,000 boys and girls out of the 2,500,000 young people of school age—that is, 40 per cent of the whole—are getting a primary education. "The pattern is set," explained Father Marcel. "After the battle of the masses, now must come the battle of the elite. In the five years between 1948 and 1952, inclusive, there has been a sixfold increase in postprimary schools for boys, and a tenfold increase in similar schools for girls."

"Do you think, Father Marcel, that secondary education will eventually destroy the native languages in the Congo? All secondary education will be in French, will it not?"

"I am convinced that the vernacular languages will continue to play a great role in Congo life and culture," the missioner replied. "French will be the bridge language, for reaching the world's peoples and the world's literature, but I belong to the school that believes the Congolese will never abandon their African tongues."

"But at present they have several hundred tongues."

"Yes—but so, once upon a time, did our ancestors in Europe. Modern communications are removing the dialects and minor languages. Our schools today teach in fourteen African languages. The prospect is that these will be reduced at least to four. Lingala is the principal language in Leopoldville and Stanleyville, twelve hundred miles up the river. Kiswahili is strong in the eastern Congo, and Kikongo and Chiluba likewise have their regions. I think even our future university students must retain their native languages and thus hold their close contact with the rank and file of their people."

Only a few hours later, I was chatting with another Congo educator. His ideas on language were quite contrary to those of Father Marcel.

"I am of Flemish origin quite as is Father Marcel," this educator explained. "Hence, I hold no special brief for French. Nevertheless, I am convinced that French will be the eventual language of the Belgian Congo as, indeed, English will be of all the British areas. I believe this because of the poverty of the African languages. Africa is not India—to take a single example. In India a language has behind it an age-old culture and a literature. Here in Africa, the culture is old, true, but it is not evolved, and thus the native languages do not lend themselves to modern development. The missionaries load them with foreignisms from the French or the Flemish and so they are doomed to become unutterably ugly. I predict that, in future generations, even the children of the unlearned will absorb French at their mother's knee and accept it as their true tongue. The native languages will always have a certain cultural significance, but only that."

This gentleman's view on language is certainly not the missionary view in the Belgian Congo, and it is not the prevailing view in wide circles. As an inquiring stranger, I was fascinated to encounter in every field of thought and action in Africa so many different opinions as to where the future is to lead.

"What do the prospective candidates for the Congo's university colleges think about their opportunities?" I asked Father Marcel.

"Frankly, I assume that most of them know very little about such opportunities. The Government's aim—and we, as teachers carrying out the Government's plans, go along with the Government in this— is to avoid producing a generation of misfits, such as higher education has created in other parts of Africa. No boy here has been told, as yet, that new and great openings lie ahead for him. But why don't you talk to the boys who are scheduled to enter Lovanium, and find out what they think?"

Father Marcel's suggestion was a good one. Thus was initiated my journey to the great Kwango mission of the Jesuits, now divided into the Vicariates of Kisantu and Kikwit. A number of the stations lie along the railroad from Leopoldville to Matadi and the Atlantic Ocean, with Kisantu itself seventy miles from the capital. Fifteen miles outside Leopoldville, we came to Kimwenza, which thus is in the suburbs of the capital.

"Oddly enough," explained my companion, "the village of Kimwenza was the site of the first residence of the Kwango mission, established in 1893. The mission was abandoned in 1901 because sleeping sickness had decimated the neighborhood. It was reoccupied only in 1946, and thus is a new but flourishing station. Kimwenza has a great future."

It was not difficult for me to believe that. From the upper bleachers of Brother Rene's great sports stadium in Leopoldville, one of the Fathers had pointed out the site, plainly visible from the city. There the Lovanium University Center has 480 choice acres, with a panorama that embraces Stanley Pool, the great city itself, and the steadily growing colony of fine homes belonging to Leopoldville's wealthy families who have chosen Kimwenza as a select residential area.

"Here on this site," my companion continued, "a modest start has been made. How different the Belgians' idea is from that of the British! The latter, in the 1920's, with a generous flourish built Achimota College near the capital of the Gold Coast. That was a generation ago, when the temper of the times seemed to warrant stirring the vanity of the African by erecting a physically beautiful institution for his service. The Belgians of the 1950's are much grimmer about their project. 'Don't spoil those boys!' the authorities are warning. Indeed, it is only indirectly that the Government is helping here; Louvain University holds the initiative, working with the Jesuits. The Government's educational authorities, however, count it all as decidedly within their plan to improve the Congolese."

The highest classes established in the Belgian Congo were until 1954 located in Kisantu. In 1928, a group of professors at the Catholic University of Louvain undertook to sponsor a branch university center in the Congo, for training male nurses and medical assistants. This offspring of Louvain became known as FOMULAC, from the French name of the Belgian group of sponsors. The foundation was made at Kisantu, under the direction of the Jesuits. In 1929, a second group at Louvain sponsored an agricultural section in the Congo, likewise operating at Kisantu, with the sponsoring group employing the title of CADULAC. In 1947, a third department, the School of General Administration, was inaugurated, this also operating at Kisantu.

For a quarter of a century, FOMULAC turned out good nurses who had qualifications equal to those of nurses in Europe and America. The diploma of medical assistant was awarded after four years of medical study plus two years of internship in Congo hospitals. Some of the young men graduates were highly capable and did practically the work of registered physicians: they examined patients, prescribed treatments, handled difficult childbirth cases, operated small hospitals. But they were always rated as assistants and had to work under European doctors.

From the CADULAC foundation came, after three years of study, agricultural experts who became Government employees in organizing, developing, and protecting projects of reforestation, soil conservation, pure drinking water, and so forth. Other graduates became managers of plantations of coffee, fruit, cotton, rubber, and of similar operations. The School of Administration has a shorter history. The object of the school is not merely to train clerks and secretaries: it is also to prepare responsible administrators. The four-year, specialized course teaches law, social sciences, economics, and history. No title for its diploma has as yet been chosen.

I visited those three schools at Kisantu on the eve of their partial transfer to the University site at Kimwenza. After 1954, only the Lovanium course leading to the diploma of medical assistant continues at the old site. The Schools of Agriculture and Administration at Kisantu are now closed, and the students who were at these schools are located on the high ground south of Leopoldville, beginning a new life.

In 1954, very few native youths qualified for even the pre-university course. Only those Congolese who had a certificate for a complete secondary course in the classics or modern sciences were eligible. Even they faced one or two years of pre-university study. Thus in 1955, the first real university work will begin. Then there will be four courses: (1) medicine, leading to a full doctorate in medicine; (2) a university degree in agriculture; (3) a university degree in administration; (4) a university degree in education. It is promised that all of these courses will be essentially the same as courses in the top-flight universities of Belgium.

As I write these lines, my head is filled with mental pictures of the fine groups of young men with whom I talked during my memorable day with them in Kisantu. The rector of Lovanium was absent, but Pere Thienpont was most attentive to me, and so were other members of the faculty. In certain respects, the visit was an extraordinary experience. To thoughtful people, Lovanium represents the most portentous venture in all the Congo, so far as the Congolese are concerned. Yet there was little evidence of radiant enthusiasm, and no recitation of fine lines of deathless idealism. Among the priests, there was an appreciation of what was ahead. But there were a quiet reserve, a neatly paced maturity, that bespoke a venture that all wanted to see succeed but that all realized could go astray if, during these first few years, the young men should not be guided wisely.

"We must walk before we begin to run, before we take to acrobatics," remarked one young priest.

In other universities that I visited in Africa, I found a certain small sector of hot bloods who would be labeled at home as "smart Alecs." In all of them, indeed, I found the predominant note to be sober earnestness. At Kisantu I could find evidence only of the earnestness and sobriety. I was deeply impressed.

There was in particular the group of medical students who chatted with me before lunch: Paul, Joaquin, Ernest, Jean, Lancelot. There was the group of young men from the School of Administration: Henry, Francis, Paul, Raymond, George. Yes, they all had plans—everybody in the schools had plans—they explained. The students included youths from every part of the Congo, and fifteen of the 140 were from Ruanda-Urundi. They hoped to secure good positions; they planned to marry; and they were sure that the Congolese would be very proud of them if they succeeded. They could cite examples of other young men who had trained at Kisantu and who held posts in various parts of the Congo; not notably important posts, they admitted, but posts that proved that Congolese could do good work when they were given a chance.

But I came away with two dominant impressions.

First, I gained from these boys no suggestion that they had been led to believe that, with the Lovanium University Center at Kim-

wenza, the floodgates of opportunity were to be opened, and that
henceforth Congolese young men would matriculate into a bright,
star-studded world that would lie at their feet for easy conquest. Indeed, from the angle of opportunity, the future for them continued
to look somber and difficult. I mentioned these thoughts later, to one
of the professors.

"Perhaps," he ventured, after a moment of silence, "the Government authorities would do better to present these youngsters with some
ray of hope that there are roles in public life awaiting them, even
though limited. The fact is, the Government expects a great deal of
them but, for disciplinary reasons, refrains from expressing its hopes
publicly."

Secondly, the boys left me with the impression that their minds
are heavy with an abiding conviction of their disabilities.

"Why," asked one, "cannot we study to be full-fledged doctors,
like young men in other lands?"

"Why are we barred from all the worth-while administrative posts
in the Government?"

"Why, if we take jobs identical with those held by Europeans,
are we paid only thirty per cent of the salaries the Europeans get,
though we have the same cost-of-living problems?"

"Do blacks in the United States have the same handicaps as in
Africa?"

"Are black lawyers permitted to serve only black clients in the
United States?"

"May a black man hire a white man to work for him in the United
States?"

"Are living conditions hard for the Negroes in Harlem?"

"What do you think of the Negro Government in Liberia?"

"Why cannot Congolese go to Europe to study, as do the Africans
of French and British colonies?"

"Why are so many fine words spoken in the Belgian Congo, and
so much shabby treatment given to the Congolese?"

There was gentleness and serenity in the atmosphere, as all these
questions were asked. There were none of the venomous leers that one
encounters in African groups in West and South Africa. Evidently
there is no deep bitterness toward the Belgians. Rather, there was a
sense of frustration and a confused feeling that the Belgians, though

good people, were standing in the way of the Congolese. There was a frank admission that the Belgians were helping them, but nonetheless the conviction that things were not as the Africans wanted them to be. I came away from Kisantu feeling extremely sorry for these young men. Mistakenly, to my mind, they acted like caged animals with no great hope of breaking free.

I found it particularly difficult to give them a satisfactory presentation of their situation. It would be small consolation to them—twenty years old, on the average, and at the threshold of life—to be told: "Be patient! You'll make a modest stride forward; your children will do better; your children's children will fare still better." Who, at twenty, wants to eat such cold pie?

One boy quite naïvely remarked that the African is as capable as the white man and therefore should be given jobs like the white man's. He had a point, but in the inverse sense: the blacks as a class are as incapable as the whites as a class. Why, therefore, should either class have an automatic right to any jobs? Most whites as well as most blacks suffer from the inability to comprehend what is involved in assuming posts of major responsibility. All men—black and white—should have equal opportunity, but experience proves that all but a few are doomed to fail. A mistake is certainly made in Africa as elsewhere in the world, in favoring whole classes of men because of the color of their skin.

"Here in the Congo during the war," a businessman of Leopoldville related to me, "certain authorities proposed an officers' training school in which *all* whites would be accepted, to lead troops who would consist of *all* blacks. 'No!' I protested. 'Not more than seven out of every hundred whites are capable of being officers. Why create such a monstrosity?' My contention was that both blacks and whites must be free to strive for a commission; that we could eliminate a sense of grievance only if we would give everybody an equal chance to fail."

Capital! What an immense amount of woe we should remove from the world, if we could contrive to give everybody his chance to fail! Of course we would have to be honest enough to agree beforehand to grant equal opportunity to the few, regardless of their origin, who would prove themselves able to succeed.

Chapter 7

A MAN WITH A CULTURE

GUY MALENGREAU, A PROFESSOR at Louvain who has played a role in the development of the Lovanium University Center, makes a distinction between the immediate objectives of the project at Kimwenza and the more remote goals of an African university. Professor Malengreau states plainly that present-day plans do not envisage for now the creation at Kimwenza of a university in the proper sense of the term, oriented toward scientific research. However, all thoughtful people interested in the project look forward to the eventual development of a Central African Catholic university in the finest sense of the term.

"It shall be our task," the professor notes, "to direct the programs at Lovanium in such fashion as to avoid giving the Africans an exclusively European culture. We must prepare little by little for the blossoming forth of a distinctive civilization that will provide in some way a synthesis of the complex Bantu culture and European civilization. This will be an achievement of the elite of tomorrow."

We cannot emphasize too much the fact that all Belgian leaders now recognize that there is, in Africa, a cultural deposit that is not to be ignored but that is to be accepted in some fashion as a base on which to build. Robert Godding, the former Belgian Minister of Colonies and Director of the Belgian Colonial University in Brussels, in an address to graduates about to leave for the Congo, voices this position.[1]

"Do not," Monsieur Godding said to these young men, "when you witness native customs and traditions, conclude hastily that everything is absurd . . . What on first sight may look pretty irrational is, after all, the framework in which, in spite of everything, the natives have succeeded in living as an organized society.

"You must attempt to understand them, and when you do under-

148

stand them, you will come to love them. This is essential because no great human task has ever been performed without love."

What the government administrator learns from the scholarly leaders in his field, the missionary acquires in even more thorough-going fashion from the leaders of thought in the field of the spiritual. An outstanding missionary contributor to a comprehension of the African is a Belgian Franciscan, Father Placide Tempels, O.F.M. His volume on Bantu philosophy has been hailed not only by missionaries, but by Africanists and anthropologists generally.[2]

Father Tempels's conclusions have direct bearing on the ultimate objectives of Lovanium and all other institutions that aim to serve the African not merely by importing the culture of the white world, but by drawing forth from its hidden depths the ancient heritage of think-ing that the disdained African possesses almost without knowing it. Painstaking education of an authentic African elite will make it possi-ble for competent sons of Africa to search into their neglected heritage and, in the course of generations, to bring into being a modern African culture.

"All human comportment rests on a system of principles," notes Father Tempels. Starting at this point, he asks a question: "What is the system of principles of the Bantu?" Thus by scientific inquiry, he has sought out the fundamental philosophy of life among the Bantu. He presents his conclusions not necessarily as a definitive body of findings on the Bantu, but as findings sufficiently well established to permit him to offer to scholars a hypothesis of the system of thinking that represents the basis of Bantu culture. He begins his study with what philosophers would call the ontology of the Bantu. The Bantu has a notion of being and has a concept of "vital force" that is far-reaching in his life. Given a basic set of ontological principles, does the Bantu, Father Tempels next asks, employ critical reasoning? The questioner concludes qualifiedly in the affirmative.

The Bantu's theory of personality is next studied—his concepts on *muntu,* or the person. This and related subjects provide an outline of Bantu psychology. What norms of good and evil does the Bantu possess? Does he conceive of man as basically good or bad? Father Tempels speaks here of Bantu ethics. When a choice of right or wrong is made, what happens? What resort has man in the Bantu world, to repair harm and to accomplish good?

Father Tempels's work is admittedly sketchy. However, it brings scholars of the West a great step nearer to appreciating the true state of the African's mind. In place of outworn theories that this mind is a *tabula raza,* an empty blackboard, on which the white man has merely to write whatever he wants the African to believe and live by, or that the Bantu mind is in part like our mind and in part fundamentally different, Father Tempels offers facts that help men everywhere to accept the Bantu mind as normal, and Bantu culture as something positive and rich in its own way.

It would be too much to expect all scholars to agree with this missionary's findings, but the acceptance has been wide. "I am interested," writes Professor Herskovits, of Northwestern University (Illinois), a leader among the world's Africanists, "that so many of the ideas that Father Tempels exposes as coming from the Belgian Congo, are so close to those I have found among the Sudanese peoples of the Guinea Coast area. They are also the same ideas that we have found in such areas as Haiti and Brazil and Suriname, in the New World." [3]

Professor Herskovits would not reach all the conclusions of a Catholic missionary. The entire world of scholars is, however, united in the desire to find evidence to establish the Bantu as a first-class citizen of the planet, possessing a true culture in his own right.

Field missionaries who make no pretense of being specialists in philosophical research recognize immediately the soundness of Father Tempels's findings. There is the matter, for instance, of the influence on the Bantu of "vital force" (a theory that evidently Father Tempels and Professor Westermann, the great authority on West Africa, came upon independently but at about the same time). Sister Carmela, a White Sister working at Bunia in the Eastern Congo, on reading Father Tempels's book, recognized immediately that her experiences with the Bantu corresponded with his findings.

"Here in Bunia," Sister Carmela reported, "the black never mentions 'vital force.' But when one speaks to him of it, he says, 'Yes, we think quite like that among us.' A smile of satisfaction lights his face, and he says to his neighbors, 'She knows us!' "

"This 'discovery' that the Bantu has a philosophy," Father Tempels reflects, "may perplex us. There will be the temptation to see it as a deceptive mirage. But it cannot be denied that, confronted with this evidence, the false image of primitive man as a savage, an em-

Costuming is serious business. No Park Avenue matron is prouder of her mink coat than is this Ndekele girl of her colorful triumph in bead work.

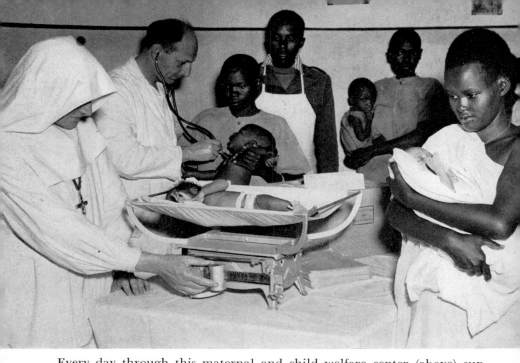

Every day through this maternal and child welfare center (above) supported by native funds at Astrida, Ruanda, over 300 mothers pass with their babes. The goggled ones (below) get ultra-violet rays in Leopoldville.

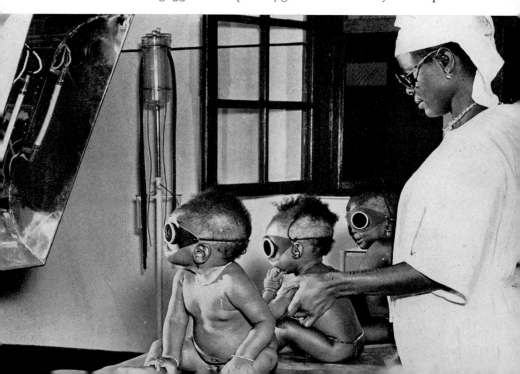

The traditional ruler in Bantu Africa counts his wealth in wives. The Fon of Bikom in the Cameroons boasted recently more than 600 spouses.

In those two remarkable countries, Ruanda and Urundi, popularly dubbed the Switzerland of Africa, prize long-horned cattle and brilliant group dances are specialties.

Every youngster in new Africa is caught by a fever, the fever to learn. These tykes (above) face teacher in a Jesuit school in Kisantu, Belgian Congo. The boy below is a promising railroad mechanic in Brazzaville.

St. Anne's Cathedral at Brazzaville is described as African Gothic. Its arches are inspired by the prows of the graceful canoes of the Congo.

A little-known side of race-torn South Africa: hundreds of women of good family lead lives of disciplined piety and zeal as Catholic Sisters.

bryonic being deprived of even the possibility of a full flowering of his mind, vanishes for good.

"Like the Biblical vision of the bones that came alive, joined together and assumed a resurrected human aspect, we discern, vaguely at first but with increasingly convincing clarity, the real primitive man that we have so grossly misrepresented. The scorned faces of the teeming masses of primitive are transformed. In place of the bestial expression that we fancied we beheld on them, of a sudden we discover the light of reason shining through.

"Henceforward these masses will have lost in our concept the mental nullity that we have falsely attributed to them. Aware that he possesses native wisdom like other men, and that his grasp of the modern world is growing, the African may now more confidently confront the West, civilized as it is but puffed up with its self-importance. The Westerner and the Bantu may now hope to face each other on a par through our distinctive wisdoms, ideals and world outlooks." [4]

"Christianity," declared His Holiness to a group of Greek journalists in 1948, "is not the monopoly of any particular form of civilization. It easily adapts itself to all, it purifies all, it crowns all with their proper character. It orients all cultures toward God, toward eternal life; and by this very fact, it perfects all in a sound and healthy humanism."

One of the most important phases in the rebirth of Africa is the hunger among the new men of Africa for cultural growth in many of the art forms: the plastic arts, decoration, music, the dance. In this they are encouraged by all educated foreigners who wish them well; that is, by Government officials, business men, missionaries.

"In a thousand ways," declared Georges Hardy, the eminent French Africanist, a generation ago, "one feels convinced that the creative forces of the black race are not at all exhausted. Rather, one is tempted to believe that they have been held in reserve and that one day soon they are going to burst forth radiantly. But we must give them time to re-establish their equilibrium, to recover from the mighty blow that European intervention has represented for them, to develop peaceably in their original milieu." [5]

Best proof of the wide diversity of opinion on this subject of the decadence and rebirth of African art, is the inability of men to agree even on the role that the white man has played on bringing about the

African's ruin. Leon Kochnitzky, who has occupied himself with cultural studies for three decades, spent 1951 in the Belgian Congo, studying this subject of its arts.

"Great as were the errors of the European colonizers in Africa," he writes, "they must be absolved from one accusation: that of having destroyed the creativeness of the Negro.

"The opinion of this writer is that artistic production decayed at the same time when the deep religious feeling that had animated the artist disappeared. A more skeptical approach to the animistic beliefs of yore, which inspired the carving of ancestor statues and ritual masks, provided the decadence of plastic arts in Africa. From that time on, artistic production was limited to decorative and utilitarian purposes. In this sphere, it still produces beautiful things. . . .

"The decadence of great African art cannot be refuted. It is comparable, *mutatis mutandis*, to the fate of religious art in Europe, where for more than two hundred years, we have not seen an artistic creation inspired by faith that can compare to a medieval cathedral, or to a masterpiece by Giotto, Van der Weyden, or Michelangelo." [6]

The Congo was just one more stop, but an exceptional one for the fifteenth century Portuguese explorers, since their master poet, Camoens, says in his Lusiads (v:13), "The greatest realm on these shores is that of the Congo." Missionaries worked zealously there and in 1491 King Nzinga Nkeuvu was baptized as John I. His kingdom embraced much of the area between the mouth of the Congo River and Stanley Pool and thus counted present-day Matadi, Kisantu, and Kwango. His capital, San Salvador, still exists in northern Angola. John I's son, Affonso, succeeded his father in 1506, as head of the Christian kingdom of Kongona Banza, and his rule until 1541 was the golden age of Christianity in this area. In 1508, Affonso's son Enrique went to Lisbon and studied for the priesthood. A few years after his ordination, in 1520, he was consecrated by Pope Leo X as the first Negro bishop of modern Africa.

Above all the period of the Portuguese was the era of the Holy Cross. In every court of justice, a crucifix was hung. Every judge wore a cross on his breast, and a scepter surmounted by a cross was driven into the soil nearby. On opening the session, the presiding judge would say: "Let not the money become black; let not Christ the Redeemer be overturned! Speak but the truth; do not shame

Christ! We, the chiefs, we will not overturn the crucifix. We swear to deliver a just judgment."

The curse of much modern missionary effort—namely, the lack of sufficient clergy for patient, systematic molding of the Faith in its new home—took its toll in the Congo as elsewhere. In a document of the year 1712, we have record of the last priest in this region for 160 years. When missionaries returned late in the nineteenth century, statues of Our Lady and the saints were being worshiped as pagan genii. No traces of active Christian belief remained. But two curious records survive of that Christian period and they have a bearing on the bygone artistic skill of the Congolese.

The first record is an intricately carved ivory tusk of monumental value. It constitutes a sixteenth century pictorial story of the joyous reception given the whites and shows individuals with crosses on their breasts. The second record is in the form of a known total of almost two hundred crucifix corpora dating from early Portuguese days, that reveal Congolese skill and feeling. Many are now among the riches of the Congo Museum of Tervueren, Belgium.

The ancient artistic productions of the Bakongo people who live in the Lower Congo Basin, are notable. Their figures of mother and child are extremely moving. The ancestor statues are celebrated, particularly those that represent men with chin in hand, like Michelangelo's *Penseroso*.

Much more important, however, than any other art in the Congo are the refined creations that have come down to us from the Bakuba. Their discovery itself reads like an adventure story. Emil Torday, a Hungarian ethnologist, was sent out by the British Museum to hunt interesting museum material. In the Congo's Kasai Province, he had the great good fortune of uncovering the very finest art specimens in Central Africa. He succeeded in persuading the Bakuba ruler to part with some of the choicest pieces (a series of statues of the Shamba rulers) for European museums.

Torday accomplished even more than this. In great pride because of his discoveries, Belgian men of culture conceived a new pride in the ancient riches scattered among the villages of the Congo Basin. "What the Congolese once did, they should be able to do again," was a typical observation; and the movement to promote cultural education in the Congo became steadily stronger. Urged by the Belgians, the King of

Bakuba became the first Congo ruler to build (at Mushenga, near Port Francqui) a brick museum, which he filled with his tribe's artistic wealth and which his people continue to control.

Henri Menjaud, a thoughtful French writer, declares, "If Negro art is destined to perish with the superstition that inspired it and that our civilization is forced to destroy, Christian Faith can bring it to life again." [7] This is the thesis which Catholic missionaries are actively engaged in making a reality in the Congo.

Strong impetus was given to the Christian-art movement by the Papal Delegate, Archbishop Dellepiane, who, indeed, merely echoed the recommendations of Rome. He actively applied the ably defined principles of the Secretary of the Congregation of Propaganda, now Cardinal Celso Costantini, a specialist in the development of Christian art within the various cultures of the world.[8] Thus in this Christian-art movement, the missions of the Belgian Congo hold a position of leadership in all Africa. The strongest single reason for this missionary interest in art is the conviction that Christianity in Africa must be engrafted into a genuinely African culture.

"Far from promoting the Europeanization of the Christians of Africa," states Father Gilles de Pelichy, scholarly Benedictine of the Lophem lez Bruges Monastery, a veteran of the Congo and editor of *Bulletin des Missions,* "the missionary, instead, must search out the elements that will lend themselves to giving birth to a native Christian culture. For the African Church of tomorrow, this is a question of life and death, a task that cannot be successfully achieved without the active co-operation of an African Christian elite."

I went one morning with Father Ceuppens to visit Brother Mark and the École St. Luc. This is the principal art school of Leopoldville, and it occupies a sightly structure that lends prestige to the enterprise located there. Brother Mark began his project in Matadi. Impressed by the results, he and his staff, which includes other Christian Brothers like himself, moved the school to the capital in 1949. The day we called, hundreds of art objects filled the high-ceilinged main hall and the subsidiary workrooms, representing studies in design, painting, wood carving, casting, and ceramics.

"The main school project this year was the furnishing of a chapel sanctuary including the designing of an altar," stated Brother Mark. We saw pieces that revealed practiced skill, while others were quite elementary. The course requires seven years of striving, and only the hardy enthusiasts persevere to the end. A few well-trained young men who have attended the school, now hold good positions in the city. None as yet rank as truly outstanding artists.

"The prize for this year's most promising creation," explained Brother Felix, "went to Benjamin Mensha, of Dahomey, for his statue of Our Lady of the Congo. See what you think of it."

"I like it very much, Brother," I said. "But I wonder what it proves as regards the success of the piece as Congolese art."

"I think we can say," observed Father Ceuppens by way of reply, "that, between sacred art with African figures and sacred art with European figures, our Congo African prefers the former. It is all too true that mere African features don't make African art. It may be generations before true creativeness born of African genius will produce genuinely great art. The mere copying of basic European or classic African designs is not enough."

"The École St. Luc is not yet turning out African art," a Belgian declared to me, quite categorically. "It is training excellent craftsmen and uncovering a certain originality, but to date the ideas of the Africans are born in the mind of Brother Mark. Don't misunderstand me; I admire the efforts that Brother Mark is making. I regard it as extremely important; the development of the black man through such projects as the École St. Luc will be remembered in generations to come, when the efforts to get the Congolese into business and administration shall have been long forgotten."

"How else can native art be developed among the Africans?" I asked.

"Pierre Romain Desfosses thinks he has discovered a way, at his studio in Elizabethville," replied the Belgian. "While painting one day, Desfosses was approached by his house servant, who asked half jokingly if he might try. The Belgian gave him paints and a brush, showed him how to use the tools, and then shrewdly left the man to himself. This was the beginning of a novel art group that, despite lack of technical training, has had its work exhibited in Brussels and at the Vatican Art Exposition in Rome. Desfosses gave his group of amateurs confidence in themselves. What they turn out lacks composition and has other faults, but often it possesses beauty that is distinctly African."

"We recognize," says Father Gilles de Pelichy, "that up to the present, our Christian conceptions cannot compare with the authentic master-pieces of ancient paganism. The native Christian artist is too often so much a slave to the European model that he is unable as yet to re-think it into terms of his own culture."

"While we are talking of art," remarked a friend in Leopoldville, "let's not forget to include the arts in which the Africans reign su-preme—dancing and music."

It was in the Congo that I came to realize how much more to the Africans than mere entertainment are dancing and music. Some mis-sionaries are strong advocates of the dance in religious drama. The Sacred Heart Fathers of Coquilhatville have made some interesting ex-periments in native Christian choreography, in connection with the great feasts of the Church year. For these feasts, the parish societies have worked out large-scale religious dances to express in this collective fashion the sacred events that they are commemorating.

"The effect has been tremendous," remarked one of the Fathers. "In that lost corner of the equatorial forest, Christianity is no longer a stranger; it has been welcomed into the tribe."

"For the African," says the scholarly Belgian, Olivier de Bou-veignes, "dancing is not an amusement; it is almost a religious act. Certainly it is an act of magic, for the dancers have in view the ob-taining of a result corresponding with the dance to which they aban-don themselves. In a war dance, it is by a kind of mime that the participants, armed for the dance, suddenly feel flowing in their veins the needed courage and lust for battle. In fictive action, they imitate daring and, catching it by contagion, they become dangerous in their art." [9]

It follows, all agree, that the end determined upon, good or evil, is served through the dance almost as a great weight is lifted by em-ploying a fulcrum. The dance provides a force that otherwise is lack-ing. Unfortunately, too often immoral ends are sought. But rather than stifle a great natural urge in the African, many thoughtful men recommend disciplining the Christian tribes to setting worthy goals for themselves in their festive dancing.

Bantu music has already found its place in the Church and, in-terestingly enough, some of its finest expressions are in the native choral music prepared for the Mass. We have already mentioned the Mass of the Canoe Men of Ubanghi, in French Equatorial Africa.

There are, also, the beautiful Ruanda Mass, and the astonishingly effective Katanga Mass composed by Joseph Kiwele of Elizabethville.

One of the celebrated choirs of all Africa is the Chanters of the Copper Cross, organized by the late Father Ansgar Lamoral, of the Benedictines of Elizabethville, and led by Joseph Kiwele. The tribes of the Katanga country used to smelt the surface outcroppings of the rich copper deposits that are now worked by modern industrialists. Of this copper they made crude crosses that they used for money. Father Lamoral adapted this old Katanga cross as part of the costume of his choir, by hammering out a rough Saint Andrew's Cross, to be worn on each singer's breast over his surplice.

"I watched Joseph Kiwele lead the Chanters of the Copper Cross at Sunday Mass," relates a friend. "The singers ranged from quite small boys to bearded men. Kiwele is short, stout, and unimpressive, but once up before his choir, he becomes a man with a dedicated mission. The experience moved me to the depths. No sacred music I had ever heard gripped me as did those strange rhythms and vivid harmonies. In the Credo, after the words, *'Crucifixus etiam pro nobis sub Pontio Pilato, passus, et sepultus est,'* the choir hummed a little lament through closed lips. It was inexpressibly poignant. It carried me off and away through space and time, to Our Lady and Saint John on Golgotha, to the sealed tomb of the Crucified outside Jerusalem. What marvelous wells of feeling these forest people have to draw from, when called upon to worship God with music!"

The Copper Cross choir is particularly celebrated for its renditions of the great, native, musical masterpieces that have come down through the generations. These are the "Songs of the Elephant," the "Songs of the Copper Country," and the "Songs of the Bayeke," with their exquisite gravity, lyric beauty, even grandeur.

It is the harmony in African music that claims the major attention of music scholars. "This harmony that impresses us as so 'civilized,' says Safford Cape, an eminent Belgian music authority, "is what astonishes us the most in native African music. We know from those who have traveled in Africa that the Bantus sing thus with great effectiveness. However, one cannot avoid the impression that some European influence must figure in it." [10]

Thus Mr. Cape politely records his lurking doubt that the African came upon his great gift of harmony all by himself. In this he follows great numbers of European scholars. But missionary specialists such as Dom Francis de Meeus O.S.B., state quite plainly that beautiful three-and four-voice harmony is common among the Africans, not in the urban areas but in the forest. "In the most savage and secluded regions," states Dom Francis, "far from every civilized center, entire populations that have had practically no contact with the European sing their traditional songs in several parts. The fact is a matter of commonplace experience among missionaries. I have myself come upon it hundreds of times. Yes, the black has an extraordinary talent for harmonic improvisation."

Dom Francis is careful not to assert categorically that this skill could not have been carried into the heart of Africa long ago by a foreigner. He ends merely by recommending that scholars study the explanation of this phenomenon. Should credit for the discovery of harmony go exclusively to the "European brain" to which the historian wishes to award the palm, or should our culture share the honors with our brother of the African forest?

I found beautiful music everywhere in the Congo. One evening at a gathering in Kabalo, far up the Congo River, a group of boatmen rendered a stirring song that thrilled me. "What is that?" I cried.

"Don't you know?" laughed the missionary. "That's the song of the Uele Boatmen. Everybody knows the lovely song of the Uele River in the northern Congo. It has become the song of all boatmen: 'Uele, Uele, madiba makasi!'—'Uele, O Uele, hard for the boatman, hard are thy rapids!' "

In the Belgian Congo, I was struck by the numerous times that I came upon people singing in solitude. One morning before our river craft left the shore in its voyage to Elizabethville, I stood by the rail and, in the brilliance of the new day, watched a lone boatman striving against the current, singing mightily to give power to his paddle. Later, as we moved over the river, we passed a Congo steamer like our own but going downstream. Alone at its far stern, facing the vessel's wake, stood a handcuffed prisoner absorbed in song.

The servant who grinds millet and the woman who pounds maize give rhythm to their work with their voice. The African sings about everything, in joy, in sadness, at labor, in idleness. He sings when he is confident; and he sings when he is afraid, walking in the night along a forest path where he may meet a leopard or the ghosts of his ancestors. He sings in the bosom of his family, for a birth, for a marriage, for sickness, for death.

"The 'burden of the white man,' " says Leon Kochnitzy, "does not consist only in bringing welfare, educational and social tranquillity, to those who, sixty years ago, were still sacrificing thousands of human victims to the spirits of their deceased rulers. In the age-old soul of the African races, the spiritual wealth so deeply ingrained must blossom anew. Then, and only then, will they retrace their steps toward creative ecstacy." [11]

This is primarily a task of the missionary. Doctor Parrinder, of Ibadan University College, states it well in words intended for his Protestant confreres. "Christian missions," he notes, "must face the issue of a truly spiritual appeal to the African mind. But this does not mean a purely intellectualist approach; the Gospel can be set forth by symbol, and touch the emotions through the use of color and ceremony. Protestants will have to work out a new technique of beautiful worship and fine churches, to replace the ugly barns and ill-translated hymns and sermons of the past. Our faith will not hold African minds until we have brought more beauty, reverence, and joy into the worship of God; something that is closer to the African's own colorful and emotional religion." [12]

Chapter 8

THE SWITZERLAND OF AFRICA

FATHER BORDENET AND I stopped by the road, in the soft green countryside, to eat our lunch. Since early morning we had been driving through Ruanda, admiring its beauty, marveling at the profusion of life along its highways, and then, a little outside Kisenyi near the fabled Lake Kivu, we had come to a halt.

We were eating but a moment when we heard a commotion down the road. Two men with the light spears that all countrymen carry in Ruanda were running toward us, chasing a small animal that at a distance looked vaguely like a tiny peacock with its tail spread. As the creature came nearer to us, we recognized it as a fat porcupine with its long, black-and-white quivers fanned out like a peacock's tail. The poor creature was waddling along desperately, with the two men pacing cautiously at its rear. About twenty feet from us, one man hurled his spear, and the roly-poly beast dropped in its tracks on the road.

"Hiya!" cried both men excitedly. They approached the animal cautiously, lest it still have any fight left in it. But it was dead.

"A fine meal!" commented gleefully the man who had thrown the spear, as he withdrew the weapon and picked up the animal by its hind legs.

"But it isn't yours!" cried the other.

"It certainly is! I killed it."

"But I discovered it down there in the field! I flushed it out and began the chase. I merely let you throw your spear at the end."

"Not at all! It would have gotten completely away if I hadn't killed it."

By this time the two arguers had climbed up the bank on the roadside opposite us. Their voices had become high and strident, and already a knot of interested passers-by had formed. For a full ten minutes the argument continued. Men, women, boys, moving to or from the nearby city, halted to listen and quite evidently enjoyed the fast and vigorous repartee.

Then as if to enlist the audience on his side, the aggrieved "finder" of the animal suddenly turned toward the crowd and wailed: "I have been cheated! I have been cheated! I found this porcupine and worked hard to capture him, and then at the last moment, this man killed it and took it away from me."

"You big baby!" shouted a young countrywoman at the back of the crowd. "If it belongs to you, why don't you take it and be done with it? What are you whining in public in that manner for?"

Everybody roared with laughter. Then the onlookers had their fling, and jollity reigned. By the time we were ready to move on, agreement had been reached to the point that the two men were co-operating in building a fire to roast the beast and thus remove the cause of their quarrel.

Father Bordenet, who is a Maryknoller stationed in East Africa, and I had been in this new land only a short while, but we were already captives to the charms of its people who, even in wayside controversy, revealed themselves as so prepossessing. After our lunch and the brief diversion, Brother Aquinas, of the all-African Josephite Brothers of Ruanda, occupied our truck seat with us as we set off on a ride over mountains, to the great mission center of Kabgaye.

"Ruanda is quite different from the Belgian Congo," I remarked to the Brother.

"It certainly is!" he replied with spirit. "I can point out a dozen ways in which it is different."

Our road was rising rapidly into the steep terraced hills above Lake Kivu, and we were momentarily distracted by the startling grandeur that opened out before us. We were traveling towards Kisenyi—a small center that is very popular with Europeans and looks like a piece of the Riviera. It is at the northern end of Lake Kivu, which in turn is a part of the western section of the Albertine Rift, that geological trench that extends south from the head of the Nile River to the Zambesi, far to the south. On the heights above the escarpment along the Rift, in what politically is western Uganda and eastern Congo and Ruanda-Urundi, are found some of the strangest physical phenomena of the globe. Here Stanley gasped in astonishment at Mount Ruwenzori, 16,800 feet high, its flanks heavy with glaciers, its head and shoulders adorned with virginal snow. A weird chain of volcanoes with hundreds of volcanic caves reaches down toward Lake Kivu. Off to the west beyond Lake Kivu lies the great Congo Forest, which embraces almost half of the entire area of the Congo.

Not far from Kisenyi stretches the huge Albert National Park, which the American explorer, Carl Akeley, was instrumental in establishing as a game sanctuary. There live the last free gorillas on earth. In mist-drenched jungle, on friendly terms particularly with the people of Ruanda, dwell the Pygmies—mystifying little people, barely three and a half feet high, possessing natural dignity, grace, and charm that makes us think of forest gnomes.

Our faces were turned generally southward, though we were twisting about many a corkscrew curve along our dizzy route. The way offered stupendous vistas that frequently included Lake Kivu. Far below lay vast pasture lands, clothed with fine herbage, where grasses mingled with choice leguminous plants like clover. Crowding every pocket-like gorge was heavy bush. Above rose the lofty hills and mountains, sometimes precipitous, sometimes gently sloped, but always rich in verdure. Our road was bordered with low bushes abloom with lavender flowers that looked like verbena. Everywhere was water: bursting waterfalls, foaming brooks, placid pools and sparkling springs. Every expanse was dotted with native farm homes. It was a fairyland vision, and it challenged the best that the earth's choicest lands can offer.

In this delightful setting, moved the countryfolk, and their herds of longhorn cattle. Small boys made us gasp by disappearing goat-like over the precipitous edges of the mountain road. Brother Aquinas and I whiled away the time chatting, as Father Bordenet concentrated on the truly difficult problem of driving. We appreciated its dangers only when we arrived at Kabgaye and heard that another truck, on the very same day, had slipped over one of the sheer cliffs and dropped through space, carrying the African driver and three passengers to death.

"You say you know a dozen ways, Brother, in which Ruanda-Urundi differs from the Belgian Congo," I said.

"Yes—at least a dozen," repeated Brother with a smile.

"Let's hear one."

"First of all, the Belgians are completely at home in the Congo. It is their colony. But the combined districts of Ruanda and Urundi form a mandated territory. Here in Ruanda-Urundi, the Belgians are only the trustees, reporting each year to the United Nations."

Yes, that was a difference, I conceded immediately. I recalled the sharp exchange in the United Nations some years ago, between Pierre Ryckmans of Belgium and Victorio Carpio of the Philippines. Mr. Carpio, a member of the visiting team of the U.N. Trusteeship Committee, insisted that Ruanda-Urundi should set up a network of official schools such as the Philippines possesses, to give "competition" to the mission schools on which the Belgians had relied up to then. The Belgians have made a small start with such official schools in Ruanda-Urundi; but they have prevented a hostile spirit toward religion, such as it found in the Filipino educational system, by placing the project in charge of the Brothers of Charity of Ghent.

"Another difference between the Congo and our land," continued our patriotic companion, "is in the matter of cattle. For all the vast Congo, there are but 350,000 head of cattle. Ours, instead, is classic cattle country. We have but one-fiftieth of the Congo's area; yet we count 1,000,000 head of cattle; that is, one for every four inhabitants. And what cattle!"

What cattle, indeed! The vast herds, grazing on a thousand hills and drinking at the full, clear streams, are one of the truly fine sights in this land. A massed herd with uplifted heads, a veritable forest of horns, is an unforgettable picture. And the Ruanda-Urundi cattle are conspicuous for size. The beasts have straight backs, long dewlaps, and a horn spread that sometimes measures six feet. The total length of a mature animal's two horns may be nine feet.

Throughout the territory, there is a cult of fine cattle that results in the building up of choice herds of so-called *Nyambo* cattle, owned in great part by the nobility. They are to ordinary cattle what race horses are to farm nags. They are tall in proportion to their length, and have delicate, slim-boned legs and small udders. Most impressive are their enormous, sweeping, lyrate horns. These cattle appear in public ceremonies. Before each great occasion, the animals' hoofs are polished, their coats are shined, bead collars are placed on their necks and bead headbands hung around their foreheads.

"At our festivals the cattle seem to be aware of their dignity and importance," continued Brother Aquinas. "One by one, they step daintily forward and placidly face our King. They are the country's greatest treasure."

"Almost all the peoples of the Congo are organized only as family or tribal groups," explained Brother. "But in Ruanda-Urundi, we have two kingdoms with fully developed societies, much like the kingdoms in Europe during the Middle Ages. A fifth of our people are aristocratic Batutsi; the remaining four-fifths are Bahutu, the principal constituent in the two nations."

"Are you a Mututsi, Brother?" I asked. (I remembered to use the prefix "Mu," which designates a single individual of a people. The people as a whole are designated by the prefix "Ba." Thus "Mututsi" means an individual Tutsi; "Batutsi" means the Tutsi people.)

Brother Aquinas smiled. "No," he replied. "I am a Muhutu. The Batutsi came from the north some centuries ago, driving their cattle before them. The Bahutu were here from long ago, engaged in agriculture ever since they drove back the Pygmies. My ancestors were glad to accept the newcomers as leaders, for the Batutsi possess a very attractive personality and a natural skill in administration."

Immediately upon entering Ruanda-Urundi, I recalled days years ago spent in Ethiopia. For in every handsome specimen of the Batutsi, is a cousin of the Ethiopians. The soundest guessing of specialists seems to establish that some five centuries ago, before Columbus discovered America, a body of shepherd people from the Ethiopian highlands set out with their distinguished cattle and moved southwestward. After a couple of centuries and a migration of twelve hundred miles, they trudged up to the Central African bastion, where today they represent the royalty and the nobility of two tiny realms.

"Have you met the King of Ruanda, Brother, the Mwami?" I asked.

"Yes, Father. All the Brothers at Kabgaye were presented to him recently," replied Brother Aquinas. "The King is very simple in his ways. As you know, he was baptized a Catholic in 1945. His Christian name is now Mwami Charles Mutara. He has dedicated Ruanda to Christ the King."

"Does he have much power, Brother?"

"The Belgians leave the local government to him and to the Mwami of Urundi. Now the Belgian Government has created a Superior Council of Ruanda, a consultative body of thirty-two natives. It happens that the first assembly of the Council is composed of thirty-one Catholics and one Protestant, an indication of the current strength of Christianity in Ruanda."

"What about the chiefs and subchiefs?"

"There are thirty chiefs and some six hundred subchiefs in Ruanda, and they continue to exercise authority."

Toward the end of the glorious afternoon, we descended from the higher mountains, enraptured by the breathless beauty of every new scene. There was in the air an exhilaration that one never experiences in the lowlands. Even in the high heavens small, billowing, white clouds raced along happily like gamboling sheep. Soon we had reached the level road of the plateau. It was night when our journey ended. The great stockade-like gates of the mission center at Kabgaye were flung open to us and Bishop Deprimoz greeted us warmly.

On my first morning at Kabgaye I began my Mass at daybreak in the dim, vaulted cathedral. When I turned toward the congregation for the first *"Dominus vobiscum,"* I was astounded to discover that the sea of faces reached back literally to the very doors and hence totaled several thousand. As the Mass progressed, the congregational prayers and singing dramatically assumed a mounting crescendo and reached a climax at the Consecration. For Holy Communion, it seemed that this entire sea of humanity surged toward the altar rail. We were four priests who distributed Communion for fifteen minutes. The men came to the rail first and were very numerous, but the women later outnumbered them.

Most beautiful were the infants in arms, who accompanied their mothers to the rail. More exactly, the majority were bound to their mothers' backs; and often, as a woman opened her mouth to receive the Host, her tiny tot stared into the priest's face, its big eyes like saucers gleaming with wonderment in the morning half light. Sometimes, instead, a little head pulled around over Mama's shoulder and gaped into her mouth as she received the Lord.

A few infants were already in jocular mood despite the hour, and chuckled grimacingly about something funny known only to themselves. Another few's mood was quite the opposite, and their mournful wails drifted aloft unheeded. In half a dozen cases the mother had quieted her Billy Boy by letting him begin his breakfast. Missionaries and Africans are very sensible people in facing nature's ways. There's no flurry in Kabgaye when a mother goes to the altar rail feeding her babe at her breast.

I noticed many women with gold bands about their heads, not only in church but later in the fields and shops and on the roads. "What does the gold band mean?" I asked a missionary.

"It's a custom we've introduced into Ruanda," he explained. "It gives special distinction to every married woman who has one or more children. It plays its part in promoting the dignity and beauty of Christian family life."

"Do you come from the town?" I asked two women after Mass.

"Town?" they repeated, with puzzled looks.

"From the town of Kabgaye," I explained.

"There is no town," they replied.

And so it proved. All the people at Mass had come in from the endless succession of farm homes that fill the countryside. Kabgaye is not a village or town, but a huge mission center. And what an extraordinary place it is! The early pioneers chose a superbly placed plateau, six thousand feet above sea level and circled by distant hills and mountains. Then they began the construction of a series of quadrangles, each embracing an area the size of a college yard. Each of these quadrangles represents a distinctive enterprise in this great nerve center of the Church in Ruanda.

"Today there are at Kabgaye sixteen chapels in which the Blessed Sacrament is reserved," stated Father Duchesne, of the publications office. "It is a world in itself."

The first quadrangle encloses the residence and offices of Bishop Deprimoz, the Church's great leader in Ruanda. "Welcome to the land of the Tornado of the Holy Spirit!" was his greeting when I arrived.

Almost immediately he pulled out the records of his flock here in Ruanda, and I quickly got the impression that he knew every one of the seventy thousand families under his care. Regarding each family in each of his forty central mission stations, he could tell me whether or not it was in good standing, whether husband and wife were separated, whether the husband had been tempted into reverting to a polygamous household.

"Here, for instance," he pointed out, "is the mission of Janja, with

1,060 families. Among these there are sixteen families in which there have been quarrels and Wifey has gone home to Mama. In ten other families, the head of the house has drifted back to ancient ways and has added at least one more wife to his menage. Thus Janja has two and one-half per cent of its families in bad standing."

"That seems very few," I commented. "Is it better than average?"

"Yes, it is unusually low," replied His Excellency. "For all Ruanda the average of families in bad standing would run as high as ten per cent."

So likewise for attendance at the sacraments—the measure of parish life—Janja ranked high. Better than 95 per cent of its 5,500 members had made their Easter duty.

"Isn't that exceptionally good?" I asked.

"Yes. The general average for Ruanda runs to about 85 per cent," explained His Excellency. "Frequentation of the sacraments is a characteristic of the vigorous spiritual life that marks Ruanda-Urundi at the present time. You saw the huge number of Communions of devotion at an ordinary, weekday Mass this morning."

My curiosity took me on a journey through the maze of quadrangles at Kabgaye. There was, for instance, the preparatory seminary for Ruanda's younger aspirants to the priesthood. A total of 224 were enrolled at the time of my visit. The seminary yard was larger than standard, and a football game was in process. The youngsters were sparkling with life.

"They have no shoes!" I exclaimed to one of the professors.

"Shoes would spoil their game," he laughed. "Their feet are tougher than their hands! Don't feel sorry for them."

Next I entered the quadrangle of the Josephite Brothers, the native community already strong in my affections since my ride with Brother Aquinas. There I met the Superior General of the Josephites and the four members of his council, who were in the course of a weekly business meeting. They made an excellent impression.

The Brothers are known locally as the *Bayozefiti*. They have twelve houses, devoted to primary-school education and to the teaching of crafts. European Brothers in Ruanda-Urundi, including the Brothers of Charity of Ghent, whom we encountered at their fine school in Astrida, total eighty.

Still another quadrangle was center for the Daughters of Mary, the *Benebikira*, who likewise have recently been approved by the Holy Father as a self-governing community of Sisters. Mama Tereza, with her beautifully expressive face of mingled intelligence and humility, is the first Mother General, succeeding the White Sister who previously directed the congregation. Mama Filomena is the assistant general; and the councilors are Mama Virginia, Mama Krysostome, and Mama Stanislaus. Their congregation, with three hundred members, compares well with our smaller diocesan congregations in the United States. European Sisters in Ruanda-Urundi now total 215.

"How is the new administration working?" I asked Sister Angela, one of the White Sisters in the quadrangle.

"Very satisfactorily," she replied. "But of course this is no surprise to us. We have watched these good women for years, and we have seen similar congregations succeed in other African regions. As you'll recall, our *Benebikira* of Uganda were approved for self-government some years ago, and they operate very successfully."

"How many African communities have the White Sisters established?" I asked Sister Angela.

"We now are training sixteen diocesan congregations of African Sisters and thus are operating sixteen novitiates for African girls. We are working side by side with 1,200 professed African nuns in hospitals, dispensaries, leper asylums and schools in various parts of Africa."

"Marvelous, Sister!" I exclaimed. What wonderful things the Africanists would learn about the secrets of the African woman's heart, if they could get inside the heads of many.

The boys' primary school occupies a quadrangle, and in another is the girls' primary school. I was struck by the sharpness and vivacity of those young girls, taught by the *Benebikira*—with the White Sisters still playing a role in the operation.

"Do you have trouble getting the girls to come to school?" I asked Sister Angela.

"Not any more," she answered. "Once upon a time when planning a marriage, family position and wealth used to be the sole criteria for choosing a bride. Now Christian parents, when seeking a wife for their son, ask about character qualities and are anxious to have a girl with some education."

The day grew old as I journeyed to the quadrangles that housed the Sisters' hospital; the dispensaries; the homes for the aged, the crippled, the mentally ill. I visited the mission's huge establishments for the closed catechumate where, for a period of six months, convert classes running into hundreds are drilled in doctrine and in the thought and action of the new life they plan to assume. Workshops for young men intrigued me; I watched students engrossed in their problems in the metal shop, the woodworking shop, and the printing plant.

"A wonderful place is Kabgaye," I concluded in summary.

"Impressive, indeed," agreed Father Duchesne. "But it is the over-all picture that really is extraordinary. Today, two out of every five people in all Ruanda-Urundi—or 1,700,000 out of 4,000,000—are either baptized Catholics or are under instruction. We follow in these two kingdoms," explained Father Duchesne, "the severe training course of the White Fathers. Despite the difficult hurdles that mark the road to baptism, we have had a net growth of over 63,000 baptized per year, for each of the last five years."

"You must be gravely short in personnel," I remarked.

"Very much so. To provide one priest for every 2,500 Catholics or catechumens, we should need a total of 680. The White Fathers have supplied almost 100 new missionaries in the last five years, and the African clergy here has grown to 128, but we still have only a little better than 400 priests in all."

"Is it possible for every Catholic to hear Mass every Sunday?" I asked.

"Oh, no! There is first of all the problem of geography. Relatively small though Ruanda-Urundi may be, the distances are too great for the Christians to come to the centers every Sunday. Many are fortunate if they can have Mass once a month. For the past dozen years, Bishop Grauls has organized the Catholics of Urundi so thoroughly that practically all of the 750,000 Christians in that kingdom gather in chapel for prayer services every Sunday. A similar effort is made in Ruanda. As you well know, rural areas everywhere in the mission world must rely on prayer services led by lay leaders. Sunday Mass is a luxury that, for many persons, can be enjoyed only in old Christian lands."

Does the African possess the inherent capability of mounting to the heights that beckon to him in the fast-changing new Africa? One day during our stay in Ruanda we discussed this question in a circle of faculty members at Nyakibanda Seminary in the suburbs of Astrida.

"One thing we can certainly say," commented a professor. "Our Catholic clergy here and in the Congo is to date the best-trained unit of society in Belgian Africa, and it measures up extremely well."

"But our clergy constitute such a tiny group," lamented Father Perraudin, the rector. "Our great weakness is the absence of educated Africans in civil life. Last year I asked my boys in class to express their views on the religious and social future of the Church in Ruanda. One boy wrote: 'Growth of the Church in Ruanda is assured because the people are well disposed. The real problem for the future is the lack of strength among our good but uneducated Catholic laity.' I thought that was a shrewd survey of the situation."

At Nyakibanda I met Bishop Aloysius Bigirumwami (Bee-gee-room-wah-mee) of Nyundo. Ruanda and Urundi have each two European bishops while Ruanda since 1952 has had a third bishop, this tall, aristocratic Batutsi, dignified in his bearing, but instinctively modest and kindly. I found myself fascinated by his softly melodious voice, his lithe, graceful hands and his engaging smile.

"His Excellency ranks among Ruanda's nobility," explained one of the missionaries. "His family record is found in the late Father Dalmas's genealogy.[1] Furthermore, his father is one of Ruanda's modern-day heroes. After World War I, he was a subchief when the British occupied his section of Ruanda. A British officer offered to make him ruling chief of all his section if he would pledge fealty to the British crown. He refused, saying that as a good Christian, and loyal citizen, he would remain true to his king. When the British finally withdrew, the Mwami of Ruanda praised His Excellency's father publicly for his integrity."

"Where in Ruanda were you born, Your Excellency?" I asked.

"I am from Zaza, which in 1904 when I came into the world was a new station of the White Fathers, only the second foundation in all Ruanda. My parents were baptized almost the same day that I was and were among the first of the Zaza converts. I recall finding their names and mine on the second page of the baptismal record. As a boy, I was constantly around the church, and it seemed to come naturally to me to want to enter the priesthood."

While at Lake Kivu, Father Bordenet and I had visited the Bishop's large cathedral, set amid rose shrubs and perched dramatically on a height that looks out for miles across the lake. I mentioned our call and His Excellency expressed regret that he was not at home.

"How many inhabitants have you within your Vicariate, Your Excellency?"

"I am told that there are approximately 400,000," he replied. "Of these, 100,000 are Catholics, for whom I have the services of forty priests."

"Are your Catholics able to support their clergy and their Church?" I asked.

"I am sorry to say that at present they are not," replied the good man. "Each farmer up to now has contributed twenty francs a year—about forty cents in American money—and I hardly dare to ask more because they have just barely enough to live. Many of the Batutsi have large herds of cattle but up to the present they haven't learned to face the problems of modern life. Thus we have not yet solved the question of local support."

"It becomes immediately evident, doesn't it," I remarked, "that a country's economy influences greatly the development not only of its political but of its religious life."

"Quite so. Our family life is strong and our people are very loyal to their faith and to the Church. They love their African priests. No one is in desperate want but we are not yet strong enough to stand alone. That will come in the years ahead."

Chapter 9

A NATION IS BORN

OUR PLANE MADE a graceful arc over the endless forest below. Everybody craned for a glimpse out of the windows.

"There are the columns of mist!" cried an English girl behind me. "No wonder, when Livingstone first saw those, he thought they were smoke from a forest fire."

"There are the falls!"

"And there are the rainbows!"

The pilot had deftly taken us within compass of the great Victoria Falls. They are the world's largest—two and a half times as high as Niagara, with a magnificent spread that we could see clearly from the air, and more than a mile wide.

The ideal spot for getting the full effect from "the Smoke that Thunders," as the Africans have long called the falls, is a nearby bank of the Zambesi River. The roar of the waters reaches the traveler ten miles away. In the afternoon, when the westering sun floods directly upon the great gorge into which the river plunges, the clouds of vapor get the full play of its rays and the rainbows are at their best. At a spot along the bank, some enterprising folk sell tea, and a special entertainment for teatime is the visit of a troupe of monkeys from the nearby wilderness. With or without your permission, they eat your three-penny cakes.

Thus I made my entry within the borders of the Central African Federation, newly created in 1953 by the union of Northern and Southern Rhodesia and Nyasaland. Geographically the new Federation is a queer-shaped creature. The Zambesi River is the border line between Northern and Southern Rhodesia, while joining Northern Rhodesia far to the east is Nyasaland. Among the missionaries, I have noted a certain reserve as to how beneficial the Federation may prove to the African. However, it is now a reality and all seem earnestly resolved to give it a fair trial.

In the Rhodesias, as elsewhere in Africa, we experience the feeling that, in terms of history, we are treading in but a narrow, cleared country that skirts a vast unpenetrated jungle of ignorance as concerns the past. In 1868, a hunter discovered Zimbabwe, in Southern Rhodesia. It remains to this day a mystery city of beautifully constructed granite walls, some thirty-five feet high and sixteen feet thick at the base. Who built it? Andrew Lang, among others, seeks to link it with Ophir of the Bible, the place that supplied the gold for Solomon's Temple.

> "Their work they did, their work is done,
> Whose gold, it may be, shone like fire
> Above the brows of Solomon
> And in the House of God's Desire."

The first Catholic missionary and first martyr in southern Africa was killed some seventy miles from Salisbury, in 1561. He was Father Gonzalo da Silveira, S.J. He had served in India and had been transferred to Mozambique. He arrived at the capital of the famous African King, Monomotopa, on New Year's Day. He received every mark of respect and was made to sit on a carpet between the King and the latter's mother. The King asked to see the statue of Our Lady that the missionary carried; and evidently the black ruler was impressed by the reverence Father Silveira showed the statue, because he knelt with the missionary when the latter asked the Blessed Mother's intercession for the sovereign's kingdom. Soon the King and his mother and three hundred of his subjects requested baptism.[1]

When Father Silveira left the royal presence, he was very happy, but tragedy awaited him. Four Mohammedan traders reached the King and convinced him that the priest was a spy of the Portuguese, and also a magician. The young sovereign believed them, signed the death warrant for the missionary, and despatched eight assassins who fell upon him, strangled him, and threw his body into a river. Father Silveira's day of martyrdom was March 15, 1561.

The celebrated Protestant pioneers, David Livingstone and Robert Moffat, appeared in this area in the nineteenth century. In 1879, the Jesuits at Grahamstown, in South Africa, were instructed to reinstitute the old Zambesi Mission. In 1880, the powerful Lobengula, King of Matabeleland, paid the Jesuits a call at their house in Bulawayo. The visit throws light on the intimacy established between the Zulu ruler and those missionaries in the last fateful years before his kingdom was destroyed under the direction of Cecil Rhodes.

Lobengula was a giant of a man, very erect, yet massive with fat, estimated to weigh three hundred pounds. His praise-singers used to shout: "Behold the great Elephant, he comes! When he walks, the earth trembles! When he opens his mouth, the heavens roar!" A French explorer, Leon Decle, said of him, "I have seen many European and native potentates but, with the exception of Czar Alexander, never have I seen a ruler with more imposing appearance."

In the Jesuit house, Lobengula seated himself in the middle of the room, with his courtiers ranged against the walls. He would not accept food in the presence of his followers, but ordered them to eat. Father Croonenberghs, the Jesuit superior, offered to take the King through the house, and as the royal visitor left the room, the courtiers chanted as always: "Behold and see, he walks! The Prince, the great King, he walks!"

Lobengula first visited the photographic studio. "You are a sorcerer!" he exclaimed, a twinkle in his eye, as he witnessed the marvels. In the second room, a pair of riding boots caught his fancy.

"Put them on," said the missionary immediately, and the King did so forthwith, unconscious of the strange figure he cut in his immense footwear, accompanied by very little else in clothing.

In the chapel Lobengula was attracted by the Stations of the Cross. He stopped a long time before the crucifix, counted the nails and thorns, and touched the wound in the Saviour's side. "And were they white men," he asked, "who behaved so barbarously? Certainly my people would not have carried on so. Bad, bad!"

Next came the pharmacy, and then the priest's room. The great Lobengula immediately sat on Father Croonenberghs' straw mattress and said, "Since my men are now outside, I'll take that food you offered me." He did full justice to what was brought and asked for a second helping.

By 1888, Cecil Rhodes's agent, Rudd, had secured from Lobengula the document known as the Rudd Concession, which gave Rhodes exclusive rights to all minerals in the Matabele realm. Armed with this,

Rhodes hurried to London and secured permission to incorporate the British South Africa Company. His activities when he returned stirred Lobengula's hostility. Rhodes then organized the Pioneer Column, which arrived at what is now Salisbury on September 12, 1890. The struggle of the whites with the last of the black rulers of Matabeleland was a brief one. Lobengula died on January 23, 1894, without being forced to bend his neck under the yoke of the conqueror. Nevertheless, he was at the time in full flight before the white man's arms.

Cecil Rhodes invited the Bavarian Sisters, Dominicans of King William's Town, to serve as hospital nurses with the Pioneer Column, and thus they reached Salisbury with the first contingent. Jesuits acted as chaplains. Rhodes throughout his life showed strong partiality to the Jesuits. He was the son of an Anglican minister, but had grown cool on religious teachings; yet he kept a basic respect for religion. He was in favor of undenominational schools but insisted that all religious bodies have the right to teach religion in those schools half an hour a day.

"Mr. Rhodes was unstinted in his praise of Catholic missionary efforts," states Father Schimlek. "The Jesuits had made a deep impression on him. He once said to a friend, 'If I could not be what I am, I would choose to be a Jesuit.' The missionaries of Rhodesia treasure the memory of Cecil John Rhodes. They value his kindness and generosity, his sympathy with them and their aims. He was their friend, stanch and true."

In 1896, the Mariannhill Missionaries reached Bulawayo. Their community remembers warmly another Rhodesian pioneer, Sir Charles John Coghlan. He had been an altar boy at St. Aidan's, Grahamstown, when the first Jesuits left for Rhodesia. After World War I, he emigrated from Kimberley to Bulawayo; and there he became the great protagonist of Responsible Government in Rhodesia, which meant the abolition of the political rights of the British South African Company. Sir Charles's opponents were the Company, the local press, Colonial Secretary Winston Churchill, and General Smuts. The fight was long and bitter, but Coghlan and the people won, and Coghlan became the first Prime Minister.

Through all his contests, Sir Charles Coghlan remained an unusually pious man. In Bulawayo he made a visit to the Blessed Sacrament every day; and because he often arrived in the evening when the church was locked, the church key was hung on a special nail in the presbytery for his benefit. He had a great sympathy for the black Africans, and since he was Minister of Native Affairs as well as Prime Minister, he served them well. He hated snobbery in all its forms and had a particular aversion to anything savoring of spiritual snobbery. Monsignor Kolbe, of Bulawayo, has given us an incident to show how this affected Sir Charles's everyday relations with the Africans.

"One Sunday morning I was kneeling in the back of the church," related the priest. "Communions were finished, but one shy little native woman went to the altar late. The celebrant did not see her and was going on with the Mass. I was about to go forward, when Sir Charles Coghlan stepped to the rail and said in a low, clear voice, 'There is another Communion.'

"Mind you, he did not say, 'There is a black woman here.' He said simply, 'There is another Communion.' Every one of us could feel that no one, including the Pope himself, had a greater right at that moment than that simple creature. I have a great admiration for Sir Charles Coghlan, but I venture to say that nothing he ever did in Parliament or in his whole career surpassed that little act of faith and charity."

On a superb site in the Matopo Hills, Cecil Rhodes established the Valhalla of Rhodesia. There Rhodes himself is buried, under the inscription, "Here lie the remains of Cecil John Rhodes." When Sir Charles Coghlan was interred there, Lady Coghlan insisted that the inscription read, "Pray for the soul of Charles John Coghlan. R.I.P."

Catholics in Southern Rhodesia today total 100,000. Of the five ecclesiastical territories, three are vicariates governed by bishops. One of the three bishops is an American citizen—His Excellency, Bishop Adolph Schmitt, Vicar Apostolic of Bulawayo—who was consecrated in Detroit in 1951 by Cardinal Mooney. Priests, Brothers, and Sisters total 750; they serve 110 parishes and outstations and are responsible for over 400 schools. Particularly praiseworthy is the network of 25 Catholic hospitals operated throughout Southern Rhodesia.

In 1885, when King Lobengula was still a mighty power in the land, he told Father Prestage, S.J., to open a mission at Empandeni. Bishop Schmitt of Mariannhill now counts that as one of his prize stations. The bishop took Monsignor Ligutti, of the Catholic Rural

Life Association, to Empandeni in 1954, and the eminently practical visitor was particularly enthusiastic about one feature of the mission.

"I saw in Empandeni," Monsignor Ligutti reported, "what I may call the finest example of Christian education for life: a two-year course in home-making for native girls preparing for marriage. Many of the girls can't read or write, but that's no impediment to home-making. There are six girls to each cottage (which are simple affairs, like their future homes). They are not taught foreign housekeeping; they are merely taught how to improve native home-making. They learn order, cleanliness, balanced diet, gardening, curing, canning, dressmaking, simple fancy work, and so forth. A very practical Tyrolese Sister has charge of the work. The girls love it, and there are 150 on the waiting list. This type of training should certainly be developed. Why should spelling be more important than living?"

The Catholic body in Southern Rhodesia is still modest in size, and hence no one expects that African candidates to the clergy or Sisterhoods can be numerous. Yet the pattern of world-wide encouragement of native mission vocations reveals itself in Southern Rhodesia. In 1953, when the Catholic African Congress met, all five clerical speakers were African priests who were outstandingly effective in addressing their people.

Bishop Chichester and the Jesuits of Salisbury, conducting the Seminary of Saints John Fisher and Thomas More, have already witnessed the ordination of fifteen Africans after their completion of the extremely demanding course of training, which extends over fourteen years. In view of the racial issue bound up with the struggle for the Central African Federation, Government leaders have shown great interest in this promotion of Africans to the Catholic priesthood. In 1951, the Prime Minister, the Right Honorable Sir Godfrey Huggins, and a former Governor of Southern Rhodesia, Sir Herbert Stanley, both addressed the guests at the ordination banquet.

Sir Godfrey Huggins called upon all sections of the community to overcome ignorance of African ways and to overcome the idea of racial superiority. "God did not make any race to domineer over others," he declared. "If only we could become a little more humble, there would be no racial friction."

Sir Herbert Stanley, a veteran of Africa, followed the same theme. "There is one injury people will never forget," he said; "a personal injury, an insult. This is the cause of so much discontent in Africa. There is never an excuse for discourtesy."

Both Northern Rhodesia and Nyasaland are much stronger in Catholic population than is Southern Rhodesia. The two first-mentioned territories count a total of 625,000, with a slight advantage in favor of Nyasaland. Interestingly enough, however, the two northern territories have only a slight advantage over Southern Rhodesia in total religious personnel: their combined figure is 810, as against 750 for Southern Rhodesia. This is because a very heavy contingent of 550 religious Sisters labors in Southern Rhodesia, an admirable figure for an area possessing so few Catholics.

The outstanding phenomenon in North Rhodesia today is the area known as the Copperbelt. Africa's great copper province, straddling the border between the Belgian Congo and Northern Rhodesia, constitutes one of the largest (if not the largest) copper-bearing areas in the world. This area runs in a southeast direction within the two countries for a distance of a couple of hundred miles with a width of forty miles. It is estimated that the Copperbelt's reserves represent 32 per cent of the world's deposits, while Chile ranks next with 30 per cent.

"Africa is no longer the paradise of lions and elephants," explains a Franciscan Conventual who works in this Copperbelt. "Our corner of Africa is now a cross between the Saar Valley and Pittsburgh. A quarter of a century ago this was empty bush country. Now it concentrates 250,000 people—a seventh of all the inhabitants in Northern Rhodesia."

"What have you been able to do there?" I asked.

"Thanks to fine co-operation from both the mine people and the Government, we think we are making big headway with the Africans. Besides all our social work, which the men seem to appreciate very much, we have the spiritual care of about fifty thousand Catholics in the area."

"But I suppose many men are spoiled at the mines," I remarked.

"Many are, I suppose," agreed the priest. "But I am constantly surprised to find that the great bulk of the men are earnest and good."

"Give me an example," I suggested.

"Take the cinema, for example. The routine is to condemn it.

Yet in places like the Belgian Congo, the Catholic missionaries do a magnificent job with the cinema in educating the Africans. I think it will do a great deal in the Copperbelt some day. The Copperbelt Negro's favorite kind of film is the American Western thriller. Why? Because it comes closest to giving him lessons that he understands in his own life. The physical conditions are similar to those he knows. There is the vast prairie, there's movement, there's struggle for life. But most important from a moral point of view, the Western classic incarnates the primacy of justice over gangsterism.

"The Negro is genuinely enthusiastic when his Western heroes come on the screen. A big cheer goes up from the entire audience when Bill Elliott, or Gene Autry, or Roy Rogers makes his first appearance for the evening. And why? Because to the native in the Copperbelt, those heroes are the people who see to it that justice is done. The Negro loves to see a good man win out. And of course the Negro is for the Negro. If a sports film from any part of the world shows a Negro in a football game or in a hundred yard dash, he gets roaring cheers. Why not?

"Only one non-Western picture has out-pulled Gene Autry or his kind. That picture was 'The King of Kings.' A good omen, don't you think? So don't sell the Copperbelt Negro short. I've found a lot of good in him while watching him at his recreations, particularly at the cinema."

The whole northeastern section of Northern Rhodesia is assigned to the White Fathers, who have by far the great majority of the country's Catholics in their care. In some of their missions, those Fathers feel strong repercussions from the man-power demands of the Copperbelt. At certain spots near Kasama, for instance, 35 per cent to 70 per cent of the local man power is at the mines.

"But we can only do our best to adjust these people to the new life," states a missionary of Fort Rosebery. "One cannot turn back the deluge! We White Fathers are quite proud of the fact that Lawrence Katilungu, the president of the Union of African Mine Workers—a union with 37,000 members in 1953—is an old boy from our St. Francis Training School, Malole. Up to the present, he has shown fine moderation and yet has maintained his leadership over the men. Here in Northern Rhodesia, the natives have a Union of African Railroad

Employees, a Union of African Transport Workers, a Union of African Shopworkers. As a missionary, I feel very sympathetic toward the efforts of these men to better themselves through their unions. I have great confidence that we shall have many very fine Africans in the Copperbelt and in other urban centers of the future."

"But don't deceive yourselves," warned Father Rene Pailloux, a splendid veteran of twenty-five years among the Babemba—one of the Northern Rhodesia's outstanding tribes. "Important though they be, the urban areas must be secondary to the rural areas. Already in Northern Rhodesia too many men are concerned with copper and lead and tobacco, and too few are concerned with food. Further, if there are to be good men in the Copperbelt, there must be fine, upright women in the bush who will be good Christian mothers."

In August of 1953, disorders broke out in southern Nyasaland. Large bands of Africans armed with spears, bows and arrows, and knives, moved about, chanting and screaming. They cut telephone wires, erected road blocks, refused to work, refused to let others work. Because there were only two thousand whites and three thousand Indians among 2,500,000 Africans, the white women and children were moved immediately to Zomba and Blantyre. The missionaries remained at their posts and quietly sought out their African people to calm them and guide them.

"What seems to be the matter, John?" a missionary asked one of his Catholics.

"The British Government is selling us Africans down the river!"

"How is that?"

"They are making us federate with the Rhodesians."

"Will that be bad?"

"Sure will! When we federate, the whites will make us their slaves!"

"Who says that?"

"The leaders say that. The Congress says that."

"Do you think they are telling the truth?"

"I don't know." John came closer and his voice dropped. "I don't know, but everybody says it's better to obey the leaders than to obey the whites. If you disobey the white man, he won't poison you! If you disobey the white man, he won't burn your hut! Everybody says it's better to obey the leaders." John hesitated a moment, and added:

"I wish we could obey you, Father. You make me feel very quiet inside."

The flurry passed after the police took the uglier among the leaders into custody. Not all Nyasalanders were as simple as John. With many who were "leaders," and with many more who had no part in politics but who had influence through their sound good sense, the missionaries as well as the civil servants talked and helped to make wisdom prevail. Nyasaland's lovely plateaus have peace again, though it is an uneasy peace. Nobody, except possibly the missionary among his flock, makes the African feel "very quiet inside."

In Nyasaland as in the rest of the continent, the missionaries continue to work with those who appreciate the role of the spiritual in life and in culture. As Nyasaland takes its dubious step into the Federation, a seventh of its Africans—325,000 out of 2,500,000—are within the Catholic Church. Over a 100,000 among the 500,000 of school age are being trained by Catholic teachers. The Anyanja people, the dominant stock in the region, are among the most intelligent on the African continent, and many Anyanja have been carefully trained as Catholics.

One notable Catholic of the Anyanja stock is E. William Chafulumira, who today is by far the most popular vernacular author in Nyasaland. One of his books, *Banja Lathu* (Our Family), which came out in 1942, became at once a best seller and has gone into nine editions, with a total run of seventy-three thousand copies. Today he is on the staff of the Northern Rhodesia and Nyasaland Publications Bureau, an organization devoted to spreading vernacular literature. Chafulumira writes in his native Nyanja, the language of the Anyanja people.

"Chafulumira's books reveal a remarkable interest in social questions," explains a White Father who admires him. "He chooses simple titles that stir the common pulse, such as, *A Good Wife, Youth, The Tale-bearer, Cooking, An Intelligent Husband.* He is an African of whom we can all be very proud."

Bishop Louis Anneau, head of the magnificent mission of the Montfort Fathers at Blantyre, spent half a century building up a superb school system that would turn out men of quality like Chafulumira. When His Excellency died, in 1950, he left behind him almost a thousand village schools as his legacy to Nyasaland.

"Don't give me any of the credit," His Excellency used to say. "It belongs to the envoy of the Pope, Archbishop Hinsley, who later was Cardinal of Westminster. Tirelessly His Excellency went up and down British Africa, repeating and repeating his famous dictum: 'The school, again the school, always the school, the school even before the church, for Africa's peoples!'"

Section 3

SOUTH AFRICA

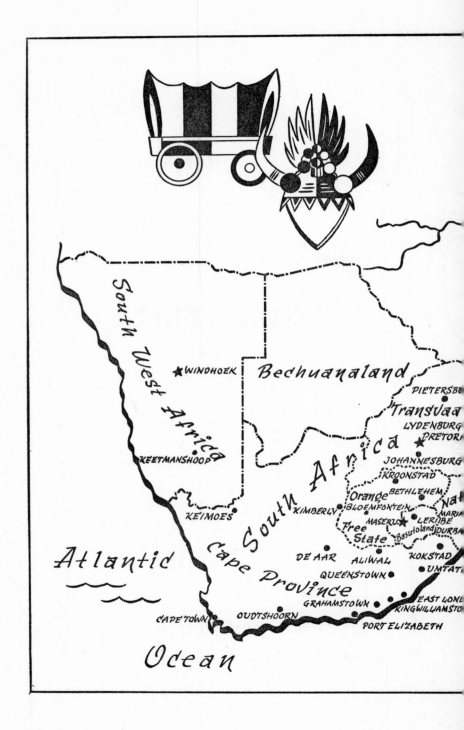

Indian

Ocean

NAMPULA
MOZAMBIQUE

Mozambique

m bezi R.

BEIRA

Madagascar

TANANARIVE

LOURENCO MARQUES
REMERSDORP

SHOWE

SOUTH AFRICA

In the geographical connotation which we accept for
the term, South Africa embraces almost 20,000,000 people.
First of all, there is the Union of South Africa with
12,500,000 inhabitants. The trust territory of Southwest
Africa plus the three British protectorates of Basutoland,
Swaziland and Bechuanaland have a total population of a
million and a half. Finally, Portuguese Mozambique counts
5,750,000 inhabitants. While this last country is sometimes
included in East Africa, strong arguments favor listing it
with the south.

Chapter 1

WHITE MEN IN SOUTH AFRICA

"HAVE YOU EVER been on a pirate ship?" I asked the eight-year-old who stood before me.

"No! Have you?" he cried excitedly.

"Oh, my, serves me right," I groaned to myself. "Why do I let these bright youngsters tie me in knots by my unwary words?" But happily, Tommie did not press his advantage. He conveniently changed the subject.

"I've seen lots of other ships," he explained. "Every summer when we go to the ocean, down near Mommie's home on the coast, we see lots of big ships, but not pirate ships. At night Daddy has his flashlight, and he signals 'Hello' with his flash, and the ship signals back 'Hello.' Then Daddy will signal 'Goodnight,' and the ship will signal 'Goodnight.' It's wonderful fun!"

"Have you many seashore resorts here in South Africa?" I asked Tommie's father.

"All along the east coast, from Cape Town to Durban, there are places large and small. We prefer the small. Durban has been called the Miami of South Africa. Tens of thousands of vacationers go there from Johannesburg during July, which is our winter season."

"But Auntie can never go," put in Tommie. "She has to stay always in Rivonia."

Tommie's father smiled. "Auntie is my sister who is a nun at the Carmelite Monastery in Rivonia, a suburb of Johannesburg."

"But we hope that Uncle Alfred can go sometime," continued Tommie, "now that he's ordained."

"Who is Uncle Alfred?" I asked the father.

"He's my brother. He is a young Oblate priest."

Later I visited the Rivonia Carmel and passed a brief hour in its reposeful calm. "Auntie," I found, was Sister Clare, a young woman

186

who, after attending the University of Johannesburg for two years and, among other things, studying Zulu to fit her for a career of usefulness, suddenly astounded her parents by announcing that she believed her calling was to a life of contemplation in Carmel.

"It was the most heart-rending experience of all my days," said Sister Clare's mother, "but we are very proud of her now."

The young nun's father made no comment. One suspected that, much as he had felt his daughter's departure, from the first moment he had understood her choice completely. He was an unusual person, a man whom the technician might label as completely integrated. He was a mining engineer, rich in life's experiences, and also a man of spiritual insight. He had a thoroughly Catholic philosophy that gave full place to both the things of life and the things of God. His daughter's career—that of the austere contemplative voluntarily immured to honor God and pray for mankind—was, one felt sure, something he clearly comprehended.

The family's elder son, Tommie's father, was a mechanical engineer working on a Johannesburg uranium project. He and his attractive wife were keen and thoughtful. I did not meet his priestly brother, but my brief encounter with other members of the fine family made a deep impression on me.

"Has South Africa many of this type?" I asked a priest friend later.

"Naturally they must be few, because Catholics as a whole are few," he explained, "but in every parish you will find people like them."

"They must exercise a strong influence on South African society," I remarked.

"That I can't promise you," my friend replied. "I take it, you refer at the moment to white Catholics. We are a triple minority—a minority of a minority of a minority—in the Union of South Africa."

"What do you mean by that?"

"Let me help you get the picture. By the 1951 census, whites in the Union of South Africa total something over 2,600,000. This, incidentally, means that we comprise five-sixths of all the whites in Africa south of the Sahara Desert. In the Union we are only 21 per cent of the total population. The black Africans are 68 and one-half per cent; the Cape Colored (which is our term covering all of mixed blood) are eight per cent; and the Indians are two and one-half per cent.

"When the million and a quarter Africans in the crown territories of Basutoland, Bechuanaland, and Swaziland, and of the mandated territory of South West Africa, are added to the Africans in the Union, we get a total of well over 9,500,000 Africans. This minority of whites in relation to non-whites is the first of the three minorities to which I refer.

"Now—no question about it—the gulf between black and white is so wide and so terrible that, relatively speaking, no other division seems of great consequence in South Africa. Nevertheless, more than in the majority of countries around the world, there is a deep cleavage here between the members of the white race. Some two-thirds of South Africa's whites are Afrikaners, and today more than ever this division must be reckoned with. Since very few Afrikaners are Catholic, all Catholics fall into the group referred to in the Union as 'the English.' This is the second of the three minorities to which Catholics belong.

"Finally, among the non-Afrikaner whites in the Union, Catholic whites represent approximately one-eighth. This is the third of the three minorities to which we belong. Thus Afrikaners total about 1,750,000; and the remaining whites total about 850,000, of whom 105,000 are Catholics."

I may note here that Catholics of all races in South Africa in 1952 totaled 835,000. This means that there are 730,000 non-white Catholics. This is between seven and eight per cent of the 9,500,000 total of non-whites in the Union and the Protectorates. The whites are immigrants from overseas or the natural growth from immigrants. The non-whites are the missionary Church. We shall begin with the immigrants and pass to the African growth.

Sarah Gertrude Millin dissects South Africa's population into its complex origins and finds that they run to a total of nineteen elements.[1] In the last analysis, however, that portion of the population that has counted the most in South Africa resulted from a combination of Dutch, French Huguenot, and German blood, which has given the country that vital body of people known today as Afrikaners. Their position looms big in the South Africa of the early 1950's. Since 1948, the evidence has become ever stronger that this element

has no intention of being a mere political party, with the non-Afrikaner whites possessing an equal opportunity to win the next election
and reverse the social philosophy that now governs the Union.

"As of this moment," said an "English" South African to me,
"the Afrikaners have won the Boer War. Never in the last half century have any of us of British origin or of non-Afrikaner sympathies
experienced such a keen sense of minority as we do today. The defeat of General Smuts and the Liberal party, in 1948, brought not
merely a political change but also gave new zest to an Afrikaner
cultural movement. That movement represents a steady growth in
language, literature, poetry, and philosophy that constantly increases
the gulf between Afrikaners and the other whites in the Union.

"Doctor Malan, the Prime Minister, has made it clear that
Afrikaners are not so stupid as to think that any country can afford
to have nothing to do with any other country in the world. He gives
at least grudging assent to the Atlantic Pact and the United Nations.
He wants a pact with other nations having possessions in Africa.
South Africa, Malan says, is ready to play her full part in the war on
communism. He intends to stay within the Commonwealth of Nations, bound in some way to Great Britain. But nevertheless, the
absorbing ideal of the Afrikaners is what is now called Afrikanerdom,
and often it is an exclusive Afrikanerdom. It is much more than
politics; it is a social philosophy that involves, among other things,
convictions regarding the non-white African that run far deeper than
those held even by the most conservative among other whites."

In the eighteenth century, the Boers grew to hate the Dutch
East India Company that held Cape Town, and in small numbers
they trekked north from the Cape to get away from the Company.
In 1795, the British, to keep South Africa from falling to Napoleon,
took over the defense of Cape Town for the House of Orange and
thus for the first time incurred the enmity of the Boers.

From 1686 to 1804, the Catholic Church was forbidden to function in South Africa, in accordance with Dutch practice throughout
all Africa, Asia, and the Americas. In 1804, however, Commissioner
General de Mist, representing the Dutch authorities, declared religious toleration. However, the new freedom was short-lived. Three
priests set out from Holland immediately for the Cape and were
given by the Dutch a room in the Castle in which to say Mass for

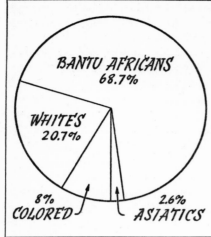

THE RACES IN RACE-TORN SOUTH AFRICA

The pie graph represents the percentual strength of each of the four racial groups in the Union of South Africa and the three British Protectorates of Basutoland, Bechuanaland and Swaziland. The statistics are as follows:

BANTU AFRICANS	8,432,032
WHITES	2,540,656
COLORED	981,896
ASIATICS	319,116
TOTAL POPULATION	12,273,700

BANTU AFRICANS 68.7%

WHITES 20.7%

8% COLORED

2.6% ASIATICS

the Catholic soldiers. After a year, however, British forces took over, and Sir David Baird ordered the Catholic priests to leave the colony. Ten years later, another try was made, and Lord Somerset gave the permission. But Bishop Slater, an English Benedictine, was refused permission to reside in Cape Town. It was not until Easter Sunday, 1838, that an enduring start was made in organizing the Church in South Africa.

Those who know South African history will remember that Bishop Griffiths, the Irish Dominican who made the start, arrived in the middle of a very historic period. He came during the years of the Great Trek, the period from 1836 to 1840, when six thousand Boers and their families set out for the great open spaces east and north of Cape Town. In 1834, word had reached the Cape that Parliament, led by Wilberforce, had abolished slavery in all the British realms. This was the last indignity, the Boers declared, that they would allow to be heaped on them by England. The participants in the mass movement away from British control were called the Voortrekkers: "Those who went before."

The Voortrekker reminds us of the man of the covered wagon who crossed the American prairies. Each Boer took his homemade wagons, his spans of oxen—eight span made up the standard team—

his horses and herds and household goods. Main routes were followed
for awhile; but soon the typical Boer broke from the crowd and
trekked away from all companion Boers, to insure himself elbow
room on the vast, empty veld. It was ordinary to establish ownership
to six thousand or twelve thousand or twenty-four thousand acres.
The Boer found a spring sheltered by a hill; built a house and
thatched it; made furniture; kraaled his cattle within fences of thorns;
planted grain, fruit, vegetables.

Each Boer became a patriarch and raised a family. His children
were not only numerous but physically large, and this physical large-
ness prevails to the present day. My spontaneous reaction, on entering
a hotel restaurant in Johannesburg, was one of admiration for the
powerful physiques of so many about me. The favorite sport of
Afrikaners today is rugby football because of the advantage they enjoy
through their prevailingly heavy build. Homestead life on the veld
was marked by hard work but developed many fine qualities as well as
sturdy physique. The Boer built up a love of liberty, a great sense of
hospitality, a calm dignity in bearing. Boer families built their lives
about the Bible, the family copy of which went out with every wagon
that left civilization. From the first, the Boers had their own clergy,
born of the soil, with strong influence over their people in every way.

When the American pioneer of the covered wagon crossed the
prairies, his most dangerous enemy was the Redskin. There is one
curious difference between the Redskin and the Kaffir who challenged
the Boer's advance. The Redskin, all concede, was at home in the
prairie. The Kaffir, as the African was properly called a century ago,
was almost as new to the South African veld as was the Boer. Both
black man and white represented great migrations. The Hottentots
and the Bushmen were already in South Africa, though few in number
and rapidly decreasing. The Bantu tribes were not there. The latter
began moving down from Central Africa almost contemporaneously
with the treks of the Boers. Fierce fighting ensued, until circumstances
made the African the Boer's servant.

Even then, the proud Bantu tribes for long admitted hardly more
than an armed truce with the white men. A typical Boer story tells of
a family that treated its African servants very well and won their affection. Eventually, rumors spread through the valley that there was to

be a Kaffir uprising, and the mother of the family faced the head servant with the charge.

"I suppose," she said, "when the revolt comes, you will kill us all."

"Oh, no, Missie!" replied the servant. "We all love the family too much for that. It has all been arranged. We will kill another family down the valley, and a group of strange servants from far away will kill you."

Whether from that fighting or from other causes, the Afrikaner has an antipathy toward the African that represents something much more than a passing prejudice. The old Voortrekker made heavy use of the Bible text, "Cursed be Canaan: a servant of servants shall he be to his brethren." The Voortrekker's son today still makes something of a religion out of his hostility to the black man. "He positively believes it his duty to humanity and civilization," says Mrs. Millin, "to uphold the difference between the children of Ham and Shem."

The Afrikaner, deep in his soul, seems convinced that he is morally justified in his attitude. Other whites may accept in some form the inherent equal dignity of all human beings. Again the Afrikaner maintains as his program of action his harsh and violent *apartheid*— aparthood. Other whites in Africa call for some form of "benevolent aristocracy" as a milder plan of unequal society.

"How do white Catholics in South Africa handle themselves on the race question?" I asked a gentleman in Johannesburg.

"Most, I should say, try hard to be Christian enough to render equal charity to all men. None, I assure you, has any chance of failing in his duty through ignorance of what the Church teaches: we have it drummed into us that no Catholic in good standing can favor racialism. In 1948, Bishop Hennemann, of Cape Town, condemned *apartheid* as unjust racialism. In June of 1952, the Catholic hierarchy published a very helpful statement on the principles of race relations. Others, such as Archbishop Hurley of Durban, called the Color Bar Act an infringement of human rights."

A number of Protestant pronouncements have been made in defense of the rights of the non-white. "Some would aver, however," frankly declares Doctor Shepherd in the *World Christian Handbook,* "that these pronouncements are more representative of the minds of church leaders than of the European rank and file. All the same, they bear the weight of official declarations. Perhaps the most outspoken and liberal of all was a long document sent out under the auspices of the Church of the Province of South Africa (Anglican), dealing with almost every phase of race relations. *The South African Outlook,* which is the official organ of the Christian Council, month by month issues its fearless comments on current events." [2]

"The Churches today have to take notice of the fact," says Doctor Shepherd, "that some of the most liberal pronouncements on racial matters are coming from circles that are openly agnostic. Many 'leftist' people are also in the forefront of efforts for African social betterment. At the same time, South Africa's most noted liberal of recent years, the late Mr. J. H. Hofmeyer, was a devout churchman and based his appeal and effort for African advancement unequivocally on the ethics of the Christian Gospel. The Churches on the whole are in the forefront of efforts for African welfare."

A factor of hostility between Boer and Briton long included differences between their religious groups. Today these differences are greatly lessened. Nevertheless, the Dutch Reformed churches, which represent 54 per cent of white Protestant Christianity in South Africa, have declined affiliation with the Christian Council of South Africa. During the early nineteenth century, British missionaries blamed the Boers rather than the Kaffirs for the Boer-Kaffir strife.

We have dwelt on this phenomenon of the Boer because, for an understanding of South Africa, it seems important to correct an impression, existing among the less well-informed in the United States, that the contest in South Africa is merely one between the conservatives and the liberals. From the Afrikaners' point of view, it is rather a struggle between those who own the country—they themselves—and the interlopers from outside. The Boer has no consciousness of a tie with any other country: he is not a South African colonist; he is a South African. Some non-Afrikaners are today as unqualifiedly attached to South Africa, but they possess much less of the panoply of a distinctive people than the Afrikaners are able to display.

When Bishop Griffith arrived in 1838 in the midst of the Great Trek, a few poverty-stricken fragments of population were the only Catholics whom he found. He said Mass in the barracks at Cape Town until he finished St. Mary's Cathedral—which stands today as the mother church of South Africa. A score of cities and towns in the Eastern Cape Town Province counted groups of Catholics. Of those,

Port Elizabeth possessed the largest. In 1852, the Oblates of Mary Immaculate arrived at Durban, under Bishop Allard, and they took up missionary work among the Africans. They began very early in Basutoland. The clergy that arrived through Cape Town thought primarily, it is true, of ministering to the Catholics; but few though they were, they made time for the non-Christian Africans as well.

Father Hoendervangers, the priest at Bloemfontein in 1852, reported: "In the forenoon, I instruct English-speaking children for two hours, and then Bantu and Hottentot children for an hour. In the afternoon, I take the English-speaking and the native children for another two hours each. I teach Bantu and Hottentots in the evening."

In the great, empty land of the old South Africa before the discovery of diamonds, the Church played a very small role. Then one day, Erasmus Stephanus Jacobs on his father's farm picked up a stone that glittered, and a trader named O'Reilly wrote to the Governor about it. That particular stone sold for £500. Within a few years, ten to twelve thousand men were digging in the Big Hole, and Kimberley was the center of the diamond market of the world.

Oblates followed the prospectors to Kimberley. Father Anatole Hidien, a French Oblate, arrived at the fields in 1871 and erected three tents at Bultfontein: one tent to serve as church, the second as school, and the third as hospital. The priest continued to live in his ox-wagon, but not for long. Before the end of the year, he died of typhus, which he caught from nursing the sick in his hospital tent. In 1879, the first Holy Family Sisters arrived at Kimberley. A bazaar was held to raise funds for their school. Catholic, Protestant, Jew, and unbeliever participated and gathered together the formidable sum of £1,450—large returns for those days. In later years Sir Ernest Oppenheimer, the great diamond czar, gave the Holy Family Sisters the De Beers Hotel and its spacious grounds, the site today of one of their fine schools.

In 1878, the Transvaal Government, suspecting that it had gold in its hills, invited Alfred Armfield, a gold-digger from Australia, to survey the Witwatersrand—the Ridge of the White Waters—from which today £80,000,000 a year in gold are extracted. Armfield reported definitely that it was "not a field for the prospector." Someone remarked on this report: "Outside disasters of death and battle, his mistake must stand as one of the most remarkable in history."

Eight years later another Australian gold-digger went out to Oosthuizen's farm on the Rand, and after looking around, wrote an affidavit that is still in existence. It reads: "I have had a long experience as an Australian gold-digger, and I think it is a payable goldfield. (Signed) George Harrison." Since today 35 per cent of all the world's gold comes out of Oosthuizen's farm and other spots within a reasonable radius, Harrison also should be in line for fame—not for any mistake he made, but for scribbling one of history's greatest understatements.

The follow-up to Harrison was made in 1886 by George Walker, in the same dramatically casual tempo. Walker had been a gold-hunter but took a job on the farm because he was hungry. He noted specks of gold in the doorstep of the barn but these specks had shown up in a number of spots—why get excited? One day, however, idly strolling about, the toe of his boot struck and dislodged an outcrop of the gold-bearing rock. He went to Oosthuizen, the owner, and uttered the historic words, "I have found the main reef."

Bishop Jolivet, of the Oblates, who was keenly alive to the significance in human values of South Africa's mining discoveries, had already despatched Father Andrew Walshe, O.M.I., to work at Pilgrim's Rest in the gold country. The next half century represented a struggle, by the Church in South Africa, to keep pace with the tremendous new day that the mining and industrial projects of the country had issued in. For those of us who have a special eye on happenings that directly touch the African, the day in December of 1922, when Pope Pius XI sent a Dutch prelate, Archbishop Gijlswijk, to South Africa as Apostolic Delegate, stands out in importance. As Father Brady the Oblate sees it,[3] that was the dawn of the third period in the life of the Catholic Church in South Africa. It spelled the end of South Africa's wretched penury in religious forces.

A characteristic of Pius XI's years as Pope was his aggressive policy for relieving personnel shortages throughout Asia and Africa. The Congregation of Propaganda Fide in Rome, through its corps of Delegates, applied itself ceaselessly to a study of the world's great checkerboard of mission territories. Constantly there was a subdividing of those mission areas; constantly in the homeland Church a search went on for new teams of workers to assume responsibility for the new units created. Thus constantly there was a stepping-up of the tempo of the apostolate: new bodies of helpers appeared, and new enterprises were launched. Thus in South Africa from 1925 to 1950, the total of priests, Brothers, and Sisters jumped from 3,000 to 7,000; the number of teachers increased from 1,000 to 5,900. The Church there was still small but possessed greatly increased vitality.

"How do the Afrikaners feel toward their Catholic neighbors?" I asked a quiet, little Irish priest in Port Elizabeth.

"Many individuals among them are very friendly," he replied. "A number send their children to our schools, which have a good reputation for hard work and strict discipline. But a rallying cry of many of the Dutch Reformed Church ministers is the *'Roomse gevaar,'* the Roman menace."

Leo Marquard, a native of the Orange Free State, in his recent book corroborates my priest informant.[4]

"On the part of the Afrikaans Churches," Mr. Marquard writes, "there has always been a marked enmity towards the Roman Catholics . . . The Roman Catholic Church appears to have plenty of money *(sic)* and has set up many excellent schools which have, rightly or wrongly, acquired a reputation as good 'finishing' schools, and of being able to 'get pupils through their examinations.' Some Afrikaners send their children to these schools, despite the warnings of the Afrikaans Churches, who fear that the children will become Romanized and denationalized. Under recent ordinance in the Transvaal, it is no longer legal in that province for parents who are Afrikaans-speaking to send their children to a Church school where the medium of instruction is English.

"Antagonism on the part of Afrikaans Churches to Roman Catholicism is openly expressed in many ways. Sermons are preached annually on Reformation Sunday, on the 'dangers of Rome.' When Mr. te Water, then South Africa's Ambassador Extraordinary, paid an official visit to the Pope in 1949, there were strong protests from synods and from Nationalist Party congresses. Finally, at a provincial congress of the Nationalist Party in 1949, it was proposed to exclude Roman Catholics from holding office in the Nationalist Party, but the proposal was withdrawn under pressure from the party executive."

The first symbol of civilization taken to South Africa was the Cross, set up by the Portuguese discoverers in the shadow of Table

Mountain as a mark of the incorporation of this new region into the realms of Christendom. Today it is a beautiful experience to journey down the Marine Drive, which reminds us of the famous Corniche Drive that hugs the seacoast of the south of France, and the Corniche Drive at Dakar that skirts the westernmost point in Africa, reaching out toward the Americas. Thirty miles below Cape Town is the boisterous meeting place of the waters of the Atlantic and Indian Oceans. There is nothing below but the South Pole.

Although almost four centuries have passed since Christians reached the southernmost tip of Africa, spokesmen for the charity of Christ still have a great task before them to make Christ's precepts live in this part of the race-plagued continent.

Chapter 2

THE BROKEN PEOPLE

"YOU MAY BE right, Arabella. Father Bernard may be a good priest. But he is a hard man. I don't like him. He is a hard man."

Thomas rose and left his hut; Arabella sat and stared at the fire. In the sermon the next Sunday and in the village meeting after Mass, the situation was unchanged. Young Father Bernard Huss faced his people unsmilingly and repeated what he had said before.

"You have been spoiled by bread Christianity," he declared. "There'll be no more of it! We missionaries are here to help the Bantus, not to spoil them. We are not here to create a generation of paupers."

Dissatisfaction was evident on the faces, and later in the words, of many members of the congregation. At home Thomas repeated his verdict: "He is a hard man, Arabella. I don't like him."

But the Zulu Christians in this Natal village of Keilands dutifully obeyed Father Bernard when he directed them in working their fields. He proved to them, unbelieving though they were, that there were great advantages in his methods of dry farming. A year passed; two years. At the end of each harvesting, there was a profit and a substantial sum was paid off on the heavy indebtedness of the farmers.

The Keilands school needed improvement. Father Bernard secured Sisters, but they were too few. Painstakingly he trained several "uncertified" teachers among the young women of the village. Barbara Ndaba, however, a candidate of special promise, he sent away to a Government normal school. On completing the course, Barbara returned as an efficient young teacher, seventeen years of age. Father Bernard went to her home to tell her father about the work she would do at the village school.

"She is not here," was all her father would say. The priest

learned the reason later. Barbara had been sold as the fifth wife of a petty chief; the price paid was fifteen cows.

Seven years passed, and all the parishioners were out of debt. The village prospered in its own modest way. All had changed but the murmuring.

"He makes the crops grow, Arabella," conceded Thomas. "But I don't like him. He is a hard man."

One day a letter came. Father Bernard had been assigned to another post. He would no longer be at Keilands, most distant of the Mariannhill stations. The people received the news with expressionless faces.

"I have been a failure!" Father Bernard whispered to himself, as he walked alone from the village.

No one appeared to bid him good-by. No one, except a school girl who ran after him with a bouquet of flowers. "Farewell, Father!" she said with tears in her eyes. "We are weeping!" And in all truth, behind the closed doors, many a tear fell for this devoted pastor who chilled his people because he was a "hard man."

Father Bernard Huss went for a week to the little outstation of Sigudu, to think and to adjust himself. He followed three lines of consideration and methodically wrote everything down: (1) Who are these Bantus, who so stubbornly resist change? (2) What could be brought into their lives to improve their culture while we preach the Gospel? (3) Where did I fail?

Soon Abbot Gerhard Wolpert talked with Father Bernard. "We must learn to think black," said the abbot, "and to feel the way the black man feels about things. The question is: How does our interference in their lives irritate the Bantus? We are bringing new ideas to Bantuland—no matter how admirable our intentions may be. We are tampering with the integrity of tribal traditions that are the mainstay of the Bantu race, traditions that have kept the Zulu in particular strong, victorious, and superior to all other tribes in Africa."

"The symbol of the Bantu," continued Abbot Gerhard, "is his ox. The ox spends much time feeding, basking in the sun, chewing cud hours on end, but then he rises and works with surprising endurance, superior to the horse and donkey. Remember the ox!"

From other well-qualified observers, Father Huss began to gather comments on the Bantus and his task with them.

"Bantu society is like a leaking tank," said Mr. Carmichael, the Native Commissioner at East London and one of the priest's friends: "nay, like a bottomless tank. The Bantus waste their land, then leave home to work in the mines, collect a few hard-earned pounds, return home, and waste their money aimlessly."

The Native Commissioner in the Mariannhill district had advice for the priest. "Father, if you priests were as eager to preach the gospel of the land as you are to preach the Gospel of Christ, then there would be a future for our Natives, and the Creator, whom you serve, would be just as pleased with your office as He is now—perhaps even better pleased."

Despite his sense of failure, in that same year of 1915, during which Father Huss left Keilands, he was chosen as rector of St. Francis College at Mariannhill. Shrewd Abbot Wolpert already saw in him the unusual qualities that eventually made Father Huss one of Africa's greatest leaders of the African.

Mariannhill represents one of Africa's important centers for creative thinking on the condition of the black man. Bishop Riccards, who invited the Jesuits to their historic center at Grahamstown, likewise had a finger in the establishment of Mariannhill. In 1879, the bishop spoke before the assembled abbots and priors of the Trappist Order, at Sept-Fons in France, and pleaded for a foundation that would demonstrate to the Africans the Christian dignity of labor.

When he finished his plea, Father Francis Pfanner, already fifty-four, rose and said quietly, "If no one else can go, I will."

Father Pfanner was prior of the Monastery of Maria Stern which he had just finished building near Banjaluka in that land of religious hatred, Jugoslavia. Years later, during the fighting in World War II, savage Red troops entered Maria Stern Monastery, tied a rope about each monk's neck, attached the rope to the sill of the window of his cell, and then tossed the man bodily out of the window to hang on the monastery wall.

In Africa, Father Pfanner and his companions made a start at Dunbrody, near Port Elizabeth, but found it poorly adapted for farming. Bishop Jolivet of the Oblates invited them north to Natal and, happily, permitted them from the first to concentrate exclusively on the Africans at a center but ten miles from Durban. One of the problems of the native apostolate in South Africa has been the mixed parish of the old white Catholics and the unwon or newly won black people. In the end, most pastors must make a choice between one or the other group.

"In my parish," a priest in the Karoo explained to me, "when I gave the Africans the greater portion of my time, as their numbers and needs dictated, whites would say to me disgustedly, 'You're just a Kaffir priest; you haven't any time for us.' The fact is, the great temptation is to serve the whites, whom you understand so much better. Then you feel you are betraying the Africans."

In the long-term planning, missionary groups like the Fathers of Mariannhill have the advantage, provided they adjust themselves to changing circumstances and improved methods. Father Pfanner's basic ideas, launched in the 1880's, continued to prove sound under Father Huss and his confreres, who were no longer Trappists but had a missionary rule adapted to South Africa. They early evolved the Mariannhill motto: "Better fields, better homes, better hearts." Today one-third of all the African Catholics within the four provinces of the Union are in the Diocese of Mariannhill.

Abbot Pfanner secured some twelve thousand acres about twenty miles from Durban, for what is now the beautiful Mariannhill center. The property stretches for seven miles through a narrow valley. On the skyline is a long table mountain adorned with a krantz of stone cliffs; this is the northern border. On small farms through the beautiful valley, some eight thousand Africans live, as Abbot Pfanner planned. The land is leased to them for the nominal sum of two pounds a year. Another thousand tenants include Cape Colored, Indians, and whites. In the center of the settlement is the monastery, with its lofty Italian campanile and its cloister walks—a dignified structure without being outstandingly beautiful. About this monastery is a village of buildings: schools of craftsmanship, St. Francis College, a high school and practice school, the pro-cathedral, likewise with a tall campanile, a convent, a hospital, an industrial school, and a mill.

Today Father Schimlek is the principal expositor of Mariannhill's philosophy and accomplishments. He is a sturdy, forthright individual, with happy memories of his younger days in the German countryside —memories that come out in his conversation.

"Long ago in Germany, when I was a boy," he recalled, "the harvesting machine came to our neighborhood, and we gathered from miles around to stare in wonderment at it. *'Ach!'* cried one old farmer and many echoed his words, 'it can't be right! No weird thing that can even tie knots can be right. I swear I'll never use it!' In talking to my Africans, I often think of that machine. If farmers in dear old Germany could fight like that against change, why should we be surprised at the African villagers?"

"What do you think made Father Huss so successful with the Africans despite his initial bad start?" I asked Father Schimlek.[1]

"I think he discovered how to convey to them his conviction that he wanted the Bantus to be a contented and prosperous people. They are not destined to be, only and forever, hewers of wood and drawers of water. They have the indisputable right to be something more than instruments for the economic advantage of other races. They have the same right and just claim for a place in the sun of South Africa as other races have."

"In his program," I ventured to say, "Father Huss seemed always to insist that it was not primarily important what the Bantu could do, but rather what the Bantu was as a man."

"Yes. He used to contend that learning alone, if their quality of living is not improved, only makes men worse. But it was his down-to-earth, practical programs that gained wide acclaim. His plan was five-fold: (1) Improve crops and stocks generally; (2) provide advice to the Bantu on farm products; (3) form agricultural associations; (4) organize agricultural shows to create initiative; (5) train a Bantu elite to guide the people."

I visited St. Francis College and admired its imposing school building, its bell tower, its airy classrooms and spacious auditorium. Nearby is a three-story boarding hall for the African boys who come from many parts of the Union. Father Huss was principal for fifteen years and reserved to himself the teaching of agriculture. Unpopular though the subject was at first, Father Huss succeeded in stirring enthusiasm in the students, and a resolve to correct the mistakes of their forefathers.

"How do the Bantus fail in their agriculture?" was his question at the end of his extensive course. Up went the hands, and Father wrote down the correct answers on the blackboard:

(1) The Bantus plant at the wrong time.
(2) Their plowing is careless and not deep enough.
(3) Bad seed is used.
(4) The Bantus are lazy; plow too small portions of land; and plant the corn too closely.

So the litany of agricultural sins went on the board. The remedies were written down next.

Each student had an individual plot and also was required to work with his companions in common fields. The double aim of Father Huss was to awaken at one and the same time the competitive sense and the spirit of co-operation. The boys' yearly efforts concluded with an Agricultural Show, and an annual show continues to this day to be a part of the Mariannhill technique. The whole countryside participates in the festivities as each school year closes. Very popular is the song Father Huss encouraged his young farmers to sing—their own praise-song of learning in the style of their traditional Zulu *izibongo:*

> *Take up the weapons,*
> *The weapons of learning.*
> *Attack the enemies,*
> *Dispel the darkness,*
> *Abolish diseases,*
> *Prevent starvation.*
> *The gloom of hunger and sickness*
> *Is caused by ignorance only.*
>
> *Oh, people! nations advance by learning.*
> *Send your children to school*
> *To draw from the well of wisdom,*
> *To guard against the foes of the people.*
> *Let them learn to work with their hands,*
> *Let them use the gifts of their mind.*
> *The salvation of our Bantu people*
> *Depends on the store of their knowledge.*
> *It will be the end of all sorrow,*
> *It will be ended by learning.*

Doctor Loram, Chief Inspector of Native Schools for Natal, had been observing Father Huss and his work for a long time and one day called on him. "Father, I have watched your method of teaching agriculture," the Inspector said. "I think it is just what our Bantu boys need. You must compile a book on your theory, with suggestions on its practical application. We will then prescribe it for all the Native schools of Natal. I have already arranged with Longmans Green of London for the publishing."

Thus came into being Father Huss' *Textbook on Agriculture,* which has been studied by hundreds of thousands of Africans in the Union. Father Bernard had learned well how to preach the gospel of the soil as proposed to him by his friend Mr. Carmichael. He preached it in the simple words and humble patience that he had acquired from his years of failure at Keilands.

When the Dutch landed at Cape Town in 1652, the Bantu tribes in their migrations from Central Africa had probably reached what is now the northern border of the Cape Province. A hundred years later, or about two hundred years ago, first contacts were made between the white man from Cape Town and the Bantu. During the following hundred years, from approximately 1750 to 1850, the major fighting took place, and at the end of that period the white man had become master. To understand South Africa, it is important to recall that we witness in that country today the dispirited drifting of a broken people, a people who, like the Indians of our Golden West, once pridefully turned their faces into the singing winds of the open plain and strode as free men in their own land.

Mrs. Millin says of them: "Today the children of the race of Chaka, the King of the Zulus who 'ate up' whole tracts of Africa, who 'wiped his spear' in the blood of more than a million people; Dingaan, his brother, who murdered the trusting Voortrekkers . . . of Moshesh, the wise and wily Basuto who knew when to make war and when to make peace—today they are all, all the black people who were friends or enemies to each other and challenged the march of civilization—they are all the charges, the servants, the dependents, the victims, the problems, the danger, of the white men." [2]

Henceforth the white man decided what the African could have. Thus the Native reserves came into being. In the twentieth century, when the Union of South Africa was established, nation-wide legislation was enacted on the question of the reserves. Three pieces of this legislation are worth recalling:

1—The Land Act of 1913. This was a temporary establishment of the Native reserves. It gave 7.3 per cent of the land to the Africans, who at that time numbered 78 per cent of the population.

2—Beaumont Commission 1916. This group of gentlemen, working toward a permanent disposition of the land, recommended too generous an allotment to suit the whites, and twenty years of wrangling followed their decisions.

During this period matters became desperate. The African heightened his own sufferings in two ways: (a) he maintained his traditionally primitive methods that represented definitely bad farming; (b) he continued addiction to his "cattle cult" and heavily overstocked his grazing areas with badly bred animals. The results were catastrophic. They included great losses in acreage through erosion; steady decline in per-acre productivity; steady increase in malnutrition.

3—Native Trust and Lend Act 1936. This commission made realistic proposals to increase the reserves to 12.4 per cent of the land in the Union. Again the proposals were blocked. By 1945, the Union had allotted 9.6 per cent to the Africans, and a small amount more has since been added. There is hot opposition in any neighborhood whenever an attempt is made to buy usable acreage for the blacks.

Today these crowded, hopeless, forlorn lands, the Native reserves, hold one third of South Africa's nine and a half million blacks. A second third work on the white man's farms. The final third are workers in the cities and in the mines.

"I can see," I said to Father Schimlek, "that, with so much wretched living among the black Africans of the reserves, Father Huss had to fight hard to get those people to earn their own bread and to stop looking to the missions for handouts."

"Decidedly!" agreed Father Schimlek. "The early missions made the mistake of giving too much to the Africans. It came to be so that, instead of asking what religion a man belonged to, one black man would ask another, 'Where did you dress?' The answer would be given, 'I dressed with the Church,' meaning the Anglicans; or 'I dressed with the Americans,' meaning the Protestants; or 'I dressed with the Romans.'

"Father Huss tried to cure this way of looking at things by encouraging the development of socio-economic institutions that required the African to take care of himself. All of these proved useful; but for the most part, they succeeded only because we missionaries kept the direction."

"How do you mean?"

"For instance, Father Huss founded the Mariannhill Bank with initial deposits of four pounds sterling. Today the deposits are £70,-000. Several level-headed Africans are today members of the board of directors and give a good account of themselves. Nevertheless, I am convinced that it is the hard-headed good sense of Father Edwin, the missionary treasurer, that guarantees sound administration, and not the advice of the African directors. There is too little here of the climate that breeds responsibility."

"Have you organized co-operatives?"

"Father Huss received from the Carnegie Foundation a grant that permitted him to visit the United States. When he returned to Africa, he set up a center at Mariazell, near Umtata, from which he organized co-operatives. By 1941, he had fourteen societies, and they continued successful so long as he exercised careful direction over the African leaders. The ideas that Father Huss brought back from St. Francis Xavier's College, at Antigonish in Nova Scotia, set the pattern; although he got, also, help from co-operative movements in Europe, as well as from our own *Eerste Volksbank* of Pretoria, which had proven conclusively the suitability of the co-operative movement to South Africa."

"Looking back on the co-operative movement of the last twenty years, what do you conclude?"

"So far as our experience goes, I would say that our savings and loan co-operatives were successful under European direction; our selling co-operatives were successful on a small scale; our buying co-operatives did not prove successful."

With variations, this is the story on co-operatives as I heard it in many places in Africa. In a few instances, as among the Chagga people in Tanganyika, the idea is outstandingly successful. In the missions of the Congo, for instance, twenty-two co-operatives are reported as operating with an enrollment of five thousand members. Everywhere there is the call for more experience, throughout a continent on which experience in all such matters has hitherto been lacking.

"The most important thing about Africa's neglected rural life is its neglected African," remarked Father Schimlek. "A meager third of Africans can read and write, and the great majority within this third have had only a couple of years of vernacular education."

Of approximately 1,900,000 Africans of school age in the Union, almost exactly a third (640,638) were at school in 1946. Half of that number were in the two substandard grades; that is, were below grade one as reckoned in the South African school system. All of the remainder were in the six grades of primary school. Some 17,000 Africans were in classes above the sixth grade.

Have the Catholic schools taken care of their share of African children? In 1952, there were 149,368 African children in our schools, exclusive of 22,351 Cape Colored and 3,542 Indian children. The African children represent 7.8 per cent of the estimated total of the school-age African population of the Union. Since African Catholics total something over seven per cent of all Africans in the Union, it would appear that the Church in South Africa is educating the full 100 per cent of its quota. This means that the Church's performance is three times greater proportionately than the general performance in the Union.

The heavy contingent of over 4,100 European Sisters and 600 teaching Brothers in South Africa explains in great part how the Catholic Church is able not only to conduct over a hundred higher schools for European pupils—some of these schools among the finest in the land—and also operate 68 higher schools for non-Europeans. The total of Church-conducted schools is an unusually good one, probably not equaled by any other voluntary organization. Now a Catholic university for Africans has been opened in Basutoland, as we shall see in a later chapter.

A visit to any one of the hundreds of higher schools that dot Africa is a happy experience. I recall a bright Sunday afternoon when Bishop Hugh Boyle, of Port Elizabeth, took me to Marymount in Uitenhage, an attractive boarding school for African young women. We spoke to the students in informal assembly on the front lawn.

"How many are going to be nurses after graduating?" I asked. The great majority raised their hands.

"It is the most promising career for an African girl here in the Cape Province," one of the Sisters explained.

"How many will be teachers?" I asked. I was surprised to see relatively few hands.

"How many will be housewives?" I then queried. There was a wave of laughter, and two or three had the courage to commit themselves.

"You can be sure," said the bishop, "that the overwhelming majority will quickly move in that direction."

University education for black Africans was initiated in 1916, when the South African Native College was opened at Fort Hare. Students at Fort Hare take the examinations of the University of South Africa. African students are admitted, also, to classes at the University of Cape Town and Witwatersrand. Father Huss trained the African who became the Bantu race's first doctor of literature in South Africa. He was Benedict Vilakazi, who studied at Mariannhill. Under the guidance of Father Huss, he secured his B.A. degree with honors. He attracted sufficient attention to be appointed assistant professor of Zulu at Witwatersrand University—the first such appointment in South African history. Then followed his other degrees of M.A. and D.Lit. A brilliant career was cut short by Vilakazi's death at the age of forty-two. He is buried near Father Huss in the Mariannhill cemetery.

While at Mariazell, Father Huss coached Henrietta Jezile, a young woman of Umtata, and through his guidance she became the first Catholic Bantu doctor of medicine in South Africa. She secured her B.Sc. at Fort Hare, and her doctorate at Witwatersrand.

"Henrietta was one of Father Bernard's most loyal students," Father Schimlek told me. "She was at his deathbed in 1948 and, when nobody else could understand his words, Henrietta was able to interpret his last wishes. She atoned in great measure for the disappointments that some other students had caused Father Bernard."

In South Africa as in other parts of the continent, among the most carefully trained Africans are the native members of the Catholic clergy, who currently total about fifty. The tremendous racial struggle in the Union probably explains why we find so few evidences of buoyant enthusiasm for the developing of a black-African clergy. Candidates who might be encouraged in a land where the racial battle is less intense, do not make safe subjects in South Africa.

Typical of the unusual young men who are pioneering in the priestly ranks in South Africa is Father Boniface Legwate, the first black priest from the Diocese of Pretoria. As a boy, Boniface grew up in the picturesque Transvaal village of De Wildt. His father was the minister of a separatist Protestant parish in the village, and Boniface was brought up in his father's beliefs. From early childhood, however, the boy experienced a strong fascination for the cluster of buildings, on the mountainside above De Wildt, comprising the Catholic mission. Finally the pull became irresistible: Boniface told the missionary on the mountain that he wanted to become a Catholic and that some day he would be a priest.

"I was astonished," related that pastor later. "I had never dreamed of getting a native African vocation in De Wildt."

Boniface kept his word. He went to the African seminary in Basutoland and was ordained as an Oblate of Mary Immaculate. In 1950, he had a triumphal homecoming to De Wildt.

"He is an example of the hardy specimens that must build the black African people and their religion," comments Father Le Dreau, the shepherd of souls in De Wildt.

Today Pretoria harbors the National Seminary of St. John Vianney, but that receives only white candidates. African candidates in the Union attend St. Peter's Major Seminary at Donnybrook, near Mariannhill. St. Peter's is proud of its alumni and never tires of recounting their experiences.

In the spring of 1954, one of these graduates, Bonaventura Dlamini, was consecrated Bishop of Umzimkhulu, a division of the Diocese of Mariannhill. Bishop Dlamini was the first African ruler of a diocese within the Union.

While I was in South Africa, one of the young graduates of St. Peter's received a telephone call one morning with this urgent message: "Accident. Send a priest and the holy oils."

The young native priest was alone; the white pastor and white curates were out. Without hesitation he set off with the oils. At the street intersection indicated, he found the accident victims—two white men dying from a traffic crash.

"Can I be of assistance?" asked the priest. A white passer-by who

was helping the victims turned—and hesitated as he saw the African
with the Roman collar.

"Are you a Catholic priest?"

"I am sir."

There was no further hesitation. "These men are dying, Father,"
the man said quietly and respectfully. "You must work quickly."

The young priest anointed the first victim, already in a coma. But
the second, though suffering keenly, had the strength to resist when
the black man knelt beside him. All the instincts of a life's experiences reacted in the African; he stood up immediately and stepped
back several paces.

The white helper saw the situation in a flash. He dropped to his
knees, took the dying man's arm, and shouted in his ear: "A Catholic
priest! He's a Catholic priest! He wants to anoint you."

The victim looked at the black man, at the little metal box with
the cotton wool, and a smile lit his eyes. "Try again, Father," urged
the white helper.

There was no objection that time. As the priest carefully made
the sign of the cross over the dying man's head at the end, there was
an audible sigh from the gathered crowd. The African levite started
to rise to his feet, but the victim grasped his hand and kissed it fer-
vently.

"It was at that moment," said the young graduate of St. Peter's
later on, "that I knew as never before that in my priesthood I had
entered a world that is above all color."

Chapter 3

DOCTOR AT DUNCAN VILLAGE

THE WOUNDED BLACK man was brought into the clinic. Sister Gracia, Sister Aidan's African assistant who served as medical orderly and kept everything spotlessly clean, watch with professional concern as drops of the man's blood fell on the floor.

"Close the door and lock it," called out Sister Aidan.

She spoke just in time, for at that moment several husky Africans arrived, knocked sharply, and demanded loudly to be admitted. Another thirty seconds, and a hundred angry men were shouting outside.

"There's been a tribal faction fight, and those men want this fellow's skin," said one of those who had carried in the wounded man. The black faces of that little group were gray with fear.

Sister Aidan, the doctor of the clinic, worked deftly and with calm. But the noise outside became a mounting crescendo. Friends of the wounded man had now arrived, and the fight with the hostile group was on anew. Suddenly Sister Aidan left the table and telephoned the police.

"Please send the ambulance immediately to St. Peter Claver Clinic at Duncan Village," she said.

"Anything serious?"

"Yes. A critical situation around the clinic," she replied, glancing out the window.

The milling crowd drew aside as the ambulance arrived, and no one attempted to enter the clinic as the door opened wide for the stretcher-bearers.

"It's knife wounds, bearer," explained Sister Aidan. "He won't die unless this crowd gets its hands on his throat."

"I understand," answered the chief bearer. The crowd vanished as soon as the ambulance whirled away.

"That makes it a day, Sister Gracia," said Sister Aidan. "What is our total?"

"Including the man you just saved from being cut to bits, it is 132," replied Sister Gracia.

St. Peter Claver Clinic was in the heart of Duncan Village, the name for the East Bank location (segregated area for Africans) on the outskirts of East London. East London is a beautiful city at the mouth of the Buffalo River, three hundred miles south of Durban. It is South Africa's fourth-largest port—after Durban, Cape Town, and Port Elizabeth. It is a popular seaside resort with lovely blue vistas of the Indian Ocean that delight the eye and fresh expanses of green grass that calm the heart. Few tourists, however, get to Duncan Village.

Set appropriately amid the squalor of the East Bank, Duncan Village is the residence of forty thousand urbanized Africans, required by law to dwell within its precincts while working in East London. For over three years, Sister Aidan had directed St. Peter Claver Clinic. It was part of St. Peter Claver's Mission, which twenty-four years earlier had been founded within the location and eventually possessed an attractive ensemble of church, school, convent, and rectory. Father O'Malley was the pastor and had as mission helpers two European and five African Dominican Sisters of Kingwilliamstown. Sister Aidan and Sister Gracia took care of the clinic, and the other Sisters operated the school with its four hundred city-born children. Father O'Malley had some twelve hundred Catholic parishioners in the location.

Sister Aidan was head of her group. But she was far more than that: she was a legend.

Elsie Quinlan, who became Sister Aidan, was born in County Cork, Ireland, in 1914. In 1937, she took her degree in social sciences at University College, Cork. Then she caused a flurry among her friends by announcing that she intended to join the Dominican Sisters of Kingwilliamstown, South Africa. As Sister Aidan, she received her religious training in historic "King" and made her profession as a member of a sturdy community that had its origin seventy-five years ago through a pioneer group of seven who went to "King" from Germany.

Typically, her superiors gave Sister Aidan a heavy task—to make of herself a doctor of medicine. In 1946, she received her degree at the University of Witwatersrand, Johannesburg. Her first assignment was to the mission hospital on the celebrated Glen Gray Native Reserve.

Then she practiced in Far East Rand Hospital in the Transvaal. In 1949, she opened the St. Peter Claver Clinic.

"A woman!" the Africans scoffed. But soon she became known as the wonder woman. The crowd of Africans grew larger and larger, and journeyed to her little consulting room from a wider and wider radius of miles. Before Mass was over in the morning, the knots of patients were forming in the yard. Sister's day's work began at eight. She had her lunch in the clinic and remained with the sick until the late afternoon. But even then the calls continued into the evening.

Not only her skill, but her smile, the twinkle in her eye, the depths of her sympathy, were reported from mouth to mouth. Her mother-wit and tact were as of high order as her medical technique. Her ability to probe into the depths of native thought and emotion was as great as her surgical skill. All types of patients received satisfaction from her. She was a passably easy touch for the wandering hobos. Mothers and their babies claimed her special attention; she did much to cope with the high rate of infant mortality in the location.

There was seldom a day without a special case. One day an African lad, out of work and hungry, stole a bottle of milk, and the milkman who gave chase delivered him a crushing blow on the head. The wounded boy was carried into the clinic, and Sister Aidan labored over him long hours, but he died as evening fell. Another day a weary old man shuffled in. "Sister," he whispered hoarsely, "I am very, very tired." With that he slumped in death at her feet. To all comers, she gave the service of her hand, her head, her prayerful heart.

Yet of course, by the measure of worldly fame, Sister Aidan created no stir. There are a score of Catholic clinics like St. Peter Claver's, serving the Africans in the Union. There are forty-four Catholic hospitals in South Africa, most of them devoted to the Africans. Throughout the African continent, hundreds of religious like Sister Aidan live for Africa's ailing millions. Sister Aidan, however, was due to play a dramatic role, not alone in revealing the rare nobility of all who follow her great vocation, but in throwing into vivid focus the brutish agony of the herded millions who dwell in South Africa's cities.

In 1952, a deepening crisis fixed its grip on South Africa through Government action aimed at establishing then and forever the political, social, and economic inferiority of the non-whites. In answer to that legislation, the details of which we need not go into, the small

voice of the non-whites was raised through such organizations as the
African National Congress. These organizations announced a cam-
paign for the defiance of unjust laws. The campaign was to start on
June 26, 1952, and the leaders called for ten thousand volunteers who,
on that date, would make passive resistance to the objectionable laws.
"We do not hate the Dutch or the English, but we hate the oppressive
laws under which we are compelled to live," declared Doctor J. S.
Moroka, President-General of the African National Congress.

The campaign was actually launched. By September, over three
thousand Africans and Indians were arrested for defying "unjust"
laws. Doctor Moroka was arrested under the Suppression of Communism Act of 1950, which makes it an offense to "advocate . . . the
bringing about of a social, economic, or political change in the Union
through violence or unlawful disturbance." Passive resistance, however moderately it might be employed, was against the law in any case.
But in point of fact, moderation was too difficult an achievement for
the over-wrought campaigners. In October there were riots in Kimberley and in Port Elizabeth. Uneasiness spread everywhere except—as
can well be understood—among people such as the Sisters of St. Peter
Claver's Mission, who were very close to the Africans.

The Sisters were uneasy, but for quite a different reason.
"Wouldn't it be too bad," they said, "if the Government or our superiors were to get worried and decide to move us from the location and
close the clinic!"

In consequence of the Port Elizabeth outbreak, the Government
on Friday, November 7, issued a ban prohibiting all open-air meetings in the Eastern Cape, which included East London. As a protest
the Resistance Movement, as it was called, proclaimed a general strike
to begin the following Monday, November 10.

At St. Peter Claver's Clinic, Friday, November 7, was a banner
day; Sister Aidan treated 170 patients. But in Duncan Village, excitement ran high. These were no ordinary days, the villagers felt; these
were great days. These were days when wonderful things were going
to happen!

Erastus Dubula said they were going to happen. "No longer are
we just nobodies, my friends," declared Erastus, sitting in the street
on a crate, his pudgy hands on his knees like a chief. "No longer does
the white man push us around! Now we have leaders. The voice of

these great leaders rings out like Gabriel's trumpet. 'Be warned, white man!' cry out our leaders. 'Be warned! You say no meetings; we say no work!' Wonderful! It's wonderful to have leaders. And if the leaders say no work, there'll be no work. No work, understand?" And his voice roared out like a bull's as he glowered about the circle.

"That's all right, no work, Erastus," said Mrs. Seme, a calm woman, "but what do we do when there's no food?"

"Foolish woman!" snorted Erastus. "Always something foolish like that. No food!"

"Be still, Mrs. Seme! You don't understand," called a man in the crowd. "This is our great day! You'll see—there'll be food."

"Afrika!" cried a teen-ager and leaped into the circle, thumbing the sky with the victory sign of the Resistance Movement. "Afrika!" cried the crowd with rollicking shouts, their thumbs into the air.

Everywhere in the location, conditions were similar. There were speakers; there were tense faces of listeners; there was loud laughter, the laughter of hate, of disdain. There was mischievous whispering of clever plots in the making—plots that were soon to be carried out, and that would set everybody free. Occasionally one heard the nostalgic cry, *"Mayibuye iAfrika!"*—"Let Africa come back!" Again, groups of Christians sang such songs as *"Nkosi sikelel' iAfrika"*—"God Save Africa!"

Then came electrifying news. There would be no strike on Monday; the leaders had voted that in East London there would be work on Monday. But instead, the chairman of the African National Congress Youth League, who had gone to the District Commandant of Police, announced that a meeting could be held, after all. The meeting would be held at half-past two Sunday afternoon, in Bantu Square in Duncan Village. True, the permission was for a *prayer* meeting. The District Commandant told the League chairman that the chairman himself could not speak, and that the meeting could not in any way be political. If it should prove political, the meeting would be dispersed immediately.

By whatever name, it would be a meeting. In a matter of minutes, members of the Youth League had assembled and were at work on crude placards for the meeting. Bugles were brought out, and in groups the organizers paraded among the forty thousand dwellers in the location. By Saturday night the noise had become a bedlam, and it was three o'clock Sunday morning before exhausted mothers finally had sufficient quiet to tease their plaintive children to sleep.

"It doesn't seem to me that these rascals are the kind of folk to get excited about going to prayer meeting," volunteered one weary mother.

On Sunday afternoon it was found that the news had reached well beyond the precincts of Duncan Village. Strangers were in the crowd, and there was a glint in many an eye that indicated an ugly spirit. The clock reached half-past two, but things were not ready. The police—both white and black—were on hand in force, and endless queries were in progress. Some villagers hazarded the guess that the commandant had come to doubt the wisdom of his grant of permission. After a two-hour delay, an attempt was made to start the meeting. But when the speakers began, neither their words nor the atmosphere was prayerful.

In less than fifteen minutes, the officer in charge declared the assembly at an end. "Break up! Break up! Get moving!" was the police cry.

"No! No!" came the angry roar. "Africa for the Africans!"

Someone in the crowd threw a rock at a policeman; a shot was fired. Soon there was head-on combat, in which blood was shed. The crowd was broken into groups of frenzied creatures, angry and disillusioned in defeat, as they were pushed by the police from Bantu Square into several nearby, narrow streets of the location.

About four o'clock that Sunday afternoon of November ninth, Sister Aidan left St. Peter Claver's in her little British car, to do an errand in East London. All was peaceful around the mission, because the meeting was in Bantu Square, some distance away. A Sabbath quiet hung over East London. As Sister Aidan returned to the location about five o'clock, she passed two members of her Dominican community and gave them a little wave.

She was about to enter the location when a policeman hailed her. "There's trouble in there!" he warned.

"Oh, they all know me," she replied with a smile, and drove on.

She was entering by a back way, probably to reach the mission in time for Benediction, and came along narrow Bantu Street that abutted on the square. Suddenly she found herself moving into an infuriated mob, its anger beyond all reasoning. A mad-eyed black man, pouring out a torrent of abusive words at her, stood directly in front of her car and forced it to a standstill. The seething crowd had already seen blood; it had already helped spill blood. At that critical moment when the Sister's car was stopped, someone touched off the spark that ignited the general, insane lust for violence.

"There's a white woman! Let's kill her!" shrieked a voice.

Strangers were numerous in the crowd, undoubtedly. Yet many local persons recognized her. "That's the good doctor," something whispered vaguely inside them. "But no matter," the tiny voice continued; "she is a hated white!"

A huge, wild-eyed fellow threw a large stone that crashed through the windshield and struck the Sister in the face. A hail of other stones followed—fourteen of them were later found in the car. Undoubtedly Sister Aidan was knocked unconscious at the start. A witness told the court that, at the first blow, she covered her face with her hands as one sometimes does to pray, and in this attitude of prayer she met her death. Her rosary beads were entwined around the fingers of one hand.

After the volley of stones, the mob charged the car, dragged the Sister from it, beat her with clubs, stabbed her, horribly mutilated her body, and dismembered it. Dark visions of abandoned tribal orgies suggested themselves, and in a trice portions of the Sister's flesh were cut off and devoured.

"We're eating the flesh of a nun!" was reportedly the exultant cry of one of the profanators. We are made to think of the torture and death of the Jesuit martyr of North America, John de Brebeuf, whose flesh was also eaten. Hideous though the practice be, it represents admiration for the victim because it expresses a desire to absorb the spirit of the fallen one.

Their fury vented, the attackers tossed some portions of the mangled body back into the car, applied a torch to the automobile, turned it over on its hood, and made off. A police officer passed a few minutes later, but the gasoline-fed flames were so great that he could not even approach to identify the vehicle. Inhabitants of nearby houses on the narrow, tarred street fled in horror of the scene and through fear of the flames.

The mob was not through with its anti-white work. It rushed to St. Peter Claver's Mission. Two Catholic boys, who were distant witnesses of the atrocity on Bantu Street without knowing who was killed, had run swiftly to St. Peter Claver's with the warning of violence, and a police van had taken off to safety the six Sisters who were at home. Father O'Malley had removed the Blessed Sacrament from the church and had closed his quarters.

Thus the flourishing, twenty-four-year-old Catholic center in the heart of Duncan Village was waiting meekly and unprotestingly when the angry men with torches arrived. At half past eight that Sunday night, the sky of East London became lurid with flames as the church, the rectory, the school, the convent, the clinic, were completely burned down.

Only a great outdoor crucifix that faced the school yard remained, standing amid the desolate wreckage.

Chapter 4

MR. CHEAP

JOHANNESBURG IS THE biggest thing in Africa. It is a mining town with a million people in it. Its core is the congested business center, fringed with crowded apartment and residence areas such as we know in our American cities. Then to the north fan out the attractive suburbs: communities like Houghton where, in the radiance of a California morning, we ride through winding, tree-lined avenues, past expensive homes, country clubs, tennis courts, golf courses, swimming pools. But to the south, lies an infamous arc of appalling slums that rank with some of the worst in the world. Everywhere are the mines, the mine dumps—the hallmark of Johannesburg—the pit-head gear, the paraphernalia of the battle for gold.

A friend loaned me his car and an African acquaintance of his was my chauffeur. Thus I met George Maruku, a young man whose family came from Basutoland more than a generation ago, and whose relatives today are very much at home in the Golden City. George was an interesting individual, a graduate of the Native University at Fort Hare and a writer for Bantu papers. He accepted his place in life, with no illusions about any bright opportunities that might lie before him.

"The gold mines of the Rand are the biggest single employers of African labor in Africa," George observed as we rode. "The eternally pounding stamp-batteries of Johannesburg, which crush the stone that holds the gold, are called the heartbeat of the nation. Every day some 350,000 able-bodied adults, called 'boys' by the white men, are lowered into the shafts. Thus far, they have taken out over six billion dollars in gold."

"How much are they paid, George?" I asked.

"They average the equivalent of fifty cents a day in your money, plus their keep," replied George.

"As a man learns his job, does he get a raise in pay?" I asked.

"Very little!" said George. "That's the key to the whole labor problem. You have heard that gold is the most precious thing in South Africa. But the real wealth of the country is cheap labor. Deprive the Union of cheap labor, and it would become bankrupt overnight. The great commandment of the mine owners is, 'Thou shalt employ only cheap migrant labor.' Each of us Africans has a big tag tied to him, or better, a brand on his hide. It reads CHEAP. Every African is named 'Mr. Cheap.' By any other name, no employer wants him."

"But are you sure that, even if a man gets experience in the mines, he can't earn more as time goes by?"

"I'm quite sure of that, Father. While I was at Fort Hare in 1943, there was a statement by the Chamber of Mines, which represents the owners, asserting categorically that this had to be their policy. The statement was much discussed by us Africans. The statement said that the ability of the mines to maintain their Native labor force by means of tribal Natives from the reserves at rates of pay that are adequate for this migratory class of Native but inadequate in practice for the detribalized urban Native, is a fundamental factor in the economy of the gold-mining industry."

"The mine boy, then, is a special class of African," I observed.

"Yes, that's right. Among us Africans, the mine boy is the simple rube from the country. He lives in the mine compounds, one of which you are going to see at Sophiatown. Most of us Africans around Johannesburg live in locations. There is a third category of urban African, the domestic servant. He is regarded by many as the best off, since he lives in quarters supplied by the master and is not confined to the compound or the location."

"Why do the mine companies speak of migrants?"

"Because almost literally that's what the mine worker is. The system brings only the young workers from the kraal. They sign on for 350 days in the mines, during which period each man is well fed and well doctored but, as you will see, has no more home than a concrete bunk in a large dormitory building. He leaves his wife and children back in the reserve, so that the wife can continue to work their little plot of ground. After his term of service, the mine boy goes back to the kraal."

"Does he have anything to take with him, out of such a small salary?" I asked.

"Perhaps the first time back he doesn't have much. When he's green, he makes a particular fool of himself in the city, spending the first money he's ever had. He returns to the reserve with a pathetic collection of flashy and worthless junk, in a tinseled box that he has paid a terrific price for in the bazaar. He takes back, too, a contempt for the old tribal ways and an impatience toward the local chiefs in the reserves. After several trips to the city, he takes home less junk and, if he hasn't learned to gamble, more of the $175 that he has earned in his 350 days."

"Why do the mine workers migrate for fifty cents a day?" I asked.

"Frankly, because the African's economy is so rigged that he has to, to keep from starving. Some white men will tell you that the country boy, the young man from the reserve, comes to the city for adventure, for escape from the cramping restrictions at home. Some will say that a young fellow has to go to Goldieburg for prestige; until he does, the girls of the reserve point the finger of scorn at him and tell him he's not fully blooded yet.

"But apart from these contributing factors, most fellows are at the mines because they have to be. A married man with a plot of land in Transkei Native Reserve, which is one of the best, can with the help of his wife get about $50 a year from his land. If he has five children, the Native Reserve authorities say he needs a minimum of $160 a year. He can hope to get that much money only by leaving home."

We were outside Johannesburg by then, and turned off the main highway for a short run along a tree-lined road that soon brought us to the Durban Deep Mine. Before us stood a group of neat, one-story, brick buildings, the administration offices of a busy enterprise that employs some ten thousand men on three shifts a day, six days a week. I had penetrated into the bowels of copper mines in Elizabethville and hence I declined the 9,000-foot ride down the shafts to where the boys from the reserves were blasting out the gold ore.

Instead, I joined a group of visitors because I wanted to see that rather forbidding African institution, a mine labor compound. We journeyed about a quarter of a mile past the volcano-like mine dump, ochre in color, every ton of which the black laborers had extracted from the earth. Then we passed through a gateway in a long one-story building, and entered a yard about three acres in extent. Rows of small brick houses, boxlike structures crowding each other, lined three of the four sides. The open area in the center formed a court that was bright green with lawn and spangled with well-kept flower beds.

"The company is proud of this compound," said the white official who accompanied us. "Every man is well housed, clothed, and fed."

He led us along a path beside the garden, to one of the houses. There was where our Joe from the reserves—where twenty-four such Joe's, as a matter of fact—hung their hats for their 350 working days. The house consisted of a single room, sixteen feet square, in the center of which stood a little iron stove. This furnished heat in the winter and served the lodgers for cooking their meat. The bulk of the room was taken up with bunks, tiered to the ceiling.

Several men were sitting or lying on their bunks. They seemed shy and uneasy at our intrusion. The place was clean and in perfect order, suggesting immediately to me that there was some reigning mind that ruled rigidly in the name of neatness. Each blanket, for instance, was folded with military precision, each fold exactly the same size, the tidied coverlet resting on the bunk in each case at exactly the same spot. Life wasn't like that for those men back in the reserves.

In the compound there was a large cafeteria, and although it wasn't mealtime, a small trickle of early eaters served to demonstrate how things operated. Each eater took for himself an empty pan; waiters with spotless aprons were ready as each man advanced. With expressionless faces, the waiters ladled huge servings from the enormous caldrons until the pans were filled. One caldron held mealies, the African corn-meal mush which equals our potatoes; a second caldron held beans; the third contained a finely diced vegetable stew. Meat is served only every three days, and then is given out raw, each man to cook his own as he likes it. In a special section, Kaffir beer is served—a sour, tepid beverage of two per cent alcohol that requires a locally cultivated taste.

"Each man gets 4,400 calories a day," said our guide. "He goes back to the reserve fatter than he came."

That particular compound has several small play areas and a first-aid room. A company hospital and large play fields for football and tribal dances are located nearby outside the compound, for the joint use of the entire body of Durban Deep's ten thousand exiles from the veld.

Later I had a chance to ask one of Johannesburg's excellent team of Oblate missionaries a question: "Does a priest or minister ever get into these compounds?"

"Yes," he replied, "and we find instances of boys who are quite exemplary in keeping up the religious practices that they brought with them from home. For the most part, however, the compound is a wretched chamber of horrors that breeds unnaturalness of many kinds."

"I suppose little can be done from a religious angle for the Africans in the cities," I remarked.

"Quite the contrary!" burst forth my priest friend, as sharply as if I had struck him. "While the compound is not a place for much profitable work, the locations as a whole are responding in tremendous fashion to the religio-social program inaugurated by Bishop Whelan here in Johannesburg. Today thinking men declare that the key to success in religious service in South Africa is the urban location. Rural work alone is a waste of effort. In the movement from the country to the city, rural missions must be able to refer their boys to location priests. These should be numerous and alert, as we try to keep them here in Johannesburg.

"The surprising development of recent years is the flow back to the reserves of a considerable number of boys who have gotten religion in fine healthy fashion while in the city. There are many difficulties for religion in the city, it is true, but men who are trained in the city develop a certain initiative that proves a fine influence back in the villages. Among the urbanized Africans, a very promising element of middle-class citizen with a strong sense of responsibility is growing up. He is proving a good homemaker and an active Church member."

Later in the car with George Maruku, I repeated to him this last remark about the middle-class urbanized African and his promising characteristics.

"Father, neither my two brothers, both of whom are married, nor I find it gravely difficult to maintain a happy family life here. This is because each of us has been able to carve out a career that, though not brilliant gives an income that permits us to pay for what we need. I do well with my newspaper work; one of my brothers keeps a shop;

and the other is a medical practitioner. The medical practitioner has an income of twenty pounds a month.[1] But we are as yet rare exceptions. Urban Africans vary greatly in their financial condition, but most are very poor. Some miserable families have but a few shillings a month. The few who are successful run to fifteen and twenty pounds a month as does my brother. Of course there are some who live on wrongful gains and do far better.

"But there are two maddening conditions that govern the lives of all Africans in Joburg (as we call the city for short). First, there is the calculated and systematic prosecution of a Government policy of deficit living imposed on the Africans. This not only keeps us poor but also keeps us in humiliating subservience. The whole scheme of wages presupposes our dependence. Ordinarily the urban African can't have sufficient income to pay reasonable prices for elementary necessaries. For instance, the ordinary African can't pay enough rent for his home to give a reasonable profit to a property owner. As a result, there are few property owners in the ordinary sense of the term who rent to Africans. The Government must erect the homes in the locations and take a loss on the investment, if Africans are not to be without roofs over their heads.

"The second maddening factor in our economic situation is the complete inadequacy of housing in Joburg. In 1946, after the war, it was stated that there was a shortage of 42,000 houses in the city. In 1949, the shortage was 46,000 houses. The condition is very near to that today. The Union holds Africans to unskilled occupations and refuses to let us learn the skilled trades; it pegs our wages so low that families can't live by them without help. Quite honestly, then, the Government declares that people with such wages can't pay proper rents, and it undertakes to build houses for us. But of course it can't find the money to build 46,000 houses! Thus there have been times in the recent past when as many as forty thousand people have slept under the sky of a winter night, on the open veld."

"In other words," I commented, "Mr. Cheap is low-priced for the Chamber of Mines, but not for those who have to support him practically as a ward of the nation." [2]

"But just how do people live under such conditions?" I continued.

"Let's drive to a few of the great locations around Joburg and you'll see," George proposed. "No city in the world has anything like

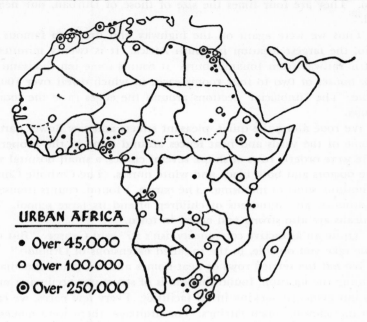

URBAN AFRICA

• Over 45,000
○ Over 100,000
◉ Over 250,000

THE MOUNTING CITIES OF AFRICA

Never before the nineteenth century did cities contain such a large proportion of the world's peoples. In Africa, the so-called retarded continent, cities are still few. Cairo and Johannesburg are the only two large cities. The accompanying map graph, prepared by Doctor Jean Comhaire, indicates a total of 82 urban centers on the continent.

	Over 250,000	Over 100,000	Over 45,000
N. AND N. E. AFRICA	5	11	18
W. AFRICA	3	4	13
C. AFRICA	1	5	7
S. AFRICA	3	3	4
E. AFRICA	–	2	2
INS. E. AFRICA	–	1	–
	12	26	44

them. They are four times the size of those of Durban, our nearest rival."

Thus we were again on the highway and drove to famous Orlando, the largest location in South Africa. It is twenty minutes by electric railway from Johannesburg. It counts some ten thousand red brick houses of two to four rooms each, in which dwell over 100,000 people. The "unofficial" sections around the edges raise the total to 150,000.

We rode along the quiet, pleasant streets and saw flower gardens in some of the yards and neat fences around some of the properties. There were orderly rows of shops, several clinics, a small hospital with white doctors and both black and white nurses. The Catholic Church was nothing short of imposing. The parish, I found, counts thousands of Catholics, and hundreds of children attend its large school. The Anglicans are also strong and active in town.

"Quite an attractive community, isn't it?" said George. "But now let me take you outside, to the so-called extensions of Orlando."

We left the serried rows of neat homes and, on land immediately adjoining the location, found thousands of structures occupying many acres but evidently lacking in all facilities. Every few paces, we came upon malodorous, open latrines. For drainage, there were makeshift gutters running with filth. The small houses consisted of rows of so-called "breeze-block shelters" motley and unkempt.

"This is Orlando's shanty town," explained George. "Every location has some similar form of construction that clings about its edges like a mass of barnacles on a ship. Ever since 1944, these shanty towns have been growing up outside the locations, as desperate answers to the homelessness and rooflessness caused by Joburg's rapid growth."

On the road north to Pretoria, about ten miles from the center of Johannesburg, is a great gray township with closely packed houses that supply living space to another 100,000 Africans. This is Alexandra.

"Alexandra is interesting," said George, "because it is not a location. It had its start early in the century but became a huge squatters' camp after World War II. My brother Joseph lives here and keeps his shop here."

"Let's visit his home," I proposed.

It was evident that Alexandra was new and was suffering from the same acute overcrowding as its neighbor communities. Many of the houses were unkempt; many looked as if they were used as multi-family dwellings though hardly large enough for one family.

George's brother was away, at work, but his wife Edna greeted us. Her home seemed above the average in its attractiveness.

"Do you rent this house from the Government, Edna?" I asked.

"Oh, no, Father! Alexandra is not a location. The Government approved it as a freehold Native township. We have over twenty-five streets in town, and along these streets are about four thousand stands of land, all owned by Africans. Alexandra's a very special place! The word 'location' is an ugly name for an ugly way of living. We are very happy that we don't live in a location. We're not strangled inside a location fence."

"How, then, may I ask, did you get the money to build?"

"My husband keeps a shop, Father, and he was able to borrow some money. We have an extension out behind our house, and another family lives there; the rent helps us to repay the loan. We have to work hard, but we dream of the day when we'll completely own our own home."

"Were you born in the city, Edna?" I asked.

"Yes, in Pimville."

"Do you like the city?"

"Oh, yes, I'm proud to be a city girl! Father Coleman says we should be proud to be city people. Father Coleman is our pastor, Father. He makes us feel so proud to be good and upstanding and progressive. Father Coleman is wonderful!"

I missed seeing "wonderful" Father Coleman or his curates, but I perceived reasons for him to be proud of St. Hubert's Church which stands at the entrance to Alexandra. Nearby is a huge school for two thousand children. Sisters of the Holy Cross, both European and African, and lay teachers provide a total staff of thirty-seven.

By far the most impressive shanty town in the environs of Johannesburg is Moroka. In 1947, when squatting was widespread around Johannesburg, the city council decided to introduce "controlled squatting." It set aside some 1,500 acres, twelve miles southwest of Johannesburg, and established an emergency camp to accommodate eventually 100,000 people. This was Moroka. Batteries of pit privies were erected; water was provided in batteries of stand pipes; refuse-removal service was organized, as well as an emergency medical service. Plans were made for butchers' stalls, general dealers' stalls, clinics, administrative buildings. All this was a far cry from the accommodations that the better thought among the Europeans now requires for locations: roads, lighting, house-piped water; even libraries, swimming baths, and other recreational facilities.

The Moroka squatters, before being legally recognized, began erecting what the South African calls Hessian shacks. These are miserable huts made of gunny sacks. Meanwhile, however, the authorities organized a brick-making plant, supplied roofing material, and encouraged the people to build their own homes. The results are quite remarkable in many parts of what has today become a community of 75,000 residents.

"Do you see those beautiful houses?" asked George. "Those were built by the squatters."

"Which prompts me to ask, George, why this whole housing crisis is not solved by putting the Africans to work on their own homes."

"The building unions have fought ferociously against it," replied George, "even though white carpenters and other tradesmen are hopelessly too few. The unions oppose giving the Africans any opportunity to get their foot inside the door of the skilled-labor world. However, in various ways the officials forced to meet the housing crisis have worked out methods to circumvent the unions."

"I'd like to meet the Catholic priest," I remarked.

"I know him," said George. "He is Father Paulsen, whom the people like very much. Moroka was still a center of riots and death when Father Paulsen arrived."

We found Father Paulsen's rectory to be an unimpressive, two-room house in the outskirts of Moroka, with no road leading to it. Immediately in front of the rectory was a jumble of rickety shacks set in continuous rows and housing 1,200 squatters. The pastor was not at home, but we saw his large school with its 600 children. The school employs ten teachers, of whom five are paid by the Government and five by the Catholic community.

Later a priest acquaintance spoke of the missionary work being done in this shanty town, Moroka. "Father Paulsen," said my informant, "is carrying on one of the most inspiring pieces of religious work in the Rand. He has become a major focal point of religious life in Moroka. Every morning some two hundred people attend Mass and approximately a hundred receive Holy Communion. This would be a good record even in the heart of New York City.

"Worth watching are his neighborhood centers. He has thirty-two centers in Moroka, where people meet every evening for night prayers. Sixty volunteer African catechists direct these centers. The men of the parish are organized into the Society of the Sacred Heart. They give their attention to the integrity of married life. They employ their good offices in settling tiffs between husband and wife, using their wiles to persuade families to stay together. The women are organized in St. Anne's Association. They visit the sick and the needy—giving not much in alms, since money is scarce, but giving what a lot of people need more than money; namely, motherly affection and neighborly kindness."

As we rode home from Moroka, I asked George a question.

"What should you say, George, is the thing that the African wants most?"

George thought a moment. "Some people say we'd like most to have cattle and lie in the sun. Others say we want education, money, opportunity. I don't really think that to possess things—either the things of the old Africa or of the new—will really satisfy us, any more than merely possessing things satisfies the white men. I think that we really yearn most to *be* something, rather than to *have* something.

"I think we desire tremendously to be free from the world's disdain. Then as we analyse this desire, we see that merely being externally free of that disdain won't be enough either. I think that, in the end, we want most of all not merely to be free of other men's disdain. We want to see, by looking deep inside ourselves, that we *deserve*, by the right way we do things, to be free of man's disdain. And then, as well, of God's disdain.

"We don't see all this right away. But I think this is what the African wants most of all."

I found myself silenced.

But why be astonished that Mr. Cheap, quite as well as any other man on the planet, should exercise his right to spiritual insight? There is in the African a stronger appeal for the non-material than many of us whites realize. A story that David Adam told me in Johannesburg illustrates this truth.

A white man had shot and wounded a buffalo. The beast charged, pinning the man to the ground and inflicting a nasty wound in his thigh. His Matabele servant rushed in with a hunting knife, stabbed the buffalo in the throat, and carried the wounded man back to camp.

Later, when wounds had healed, the white man sent for his servant and said, handing him a pound note, "This is very little, but I am not a rich man. You were very brave and saved my life."

"Please, will you take it back?" was the black man's reply. "That was not an affair between master and servant but an affair between men of honor."

Chapter 5

THE DISINHERITED

BROTHER NARZISSUS AND A class of boys from St. Francis School were planting a row of Natal mahogany trees. One day the dark green, leathery leaves would supply beautiful shade for the playground at Mariannhill. Father Bernard Huss, reading his breviary nearby, glanced up and saw a man approaching.

The bell of the monastery campanile began to intone the midday Angelus. The convent bell in its dome-shaped belfry chimed in, high-pitched and ladylike, and the bell of the St. Joseph Pro-Cathedral followed with its deep reverberations. *"Ingelosi yenkosi . . ."* began Brother Narzissus in Zulu. The boys stopped their work, took off their caps, joined their hands, and recited the responses of the prayer in unison.

At a distance the approaching stranger likewise stopped, removed his hat, and bent his head in reverence. When the bells were silent again and the boys had returned to their tree planting, Father Huss advanced toward the stranger and extended his hand with a greeting. He saw that the man was slight of build, dark of complexion, with quick, gleaming eyes—an Indian.

"Gandhi is my name," said the stranger. "I should like to see Mariannhill, Father."

"Welcome, Mr. Gandhi. I am Father Huss, the principal. I have heard about you and about the efforts you have made to help your people. Congratulations, Mr. Gandhi."

"Thank you, Father. As a matter of fact, I am just as interested in the lot of the Bantus in this country. Recently I prepared an article for my magazine, *Indian Opinion,* in which I said that nothing was being done by the white man for the Bantu Race in South Africa. A friend who read the manuscript suggested that, if I would visit Mariannhill, perhaps I would modify my statements."

231

The two men spent the day together, inspecting the college; the workshops; the school garden with its orange trees, its neat beds of vegetables, and its beautiful flowers. At times they talked animatedly, and at times walked in thoughtful silence. In the church Mr. Gandhi stopped before the crucifix and remarked in a low voice: "It is patient suffering, Father, that will save us—the Indians as well as the Bantus. Your crucifix preaches a great sermon to the world."

At the day's end, Gandhi seemed deeply impressed as he took leave of the Fathers he had met. To Father Huss he said: "Before I go, I should like to mention something. I once said that I liked Christ and His teaching, but did not like Christians. Today I wish to correct this statement. If I had met more people like you, I think I should have liked the Christians, too."

Mahatma Gandhi at that time was at the end of a twenty-one-year stay in South Africa and was about to return to India. Many who know of Gandhi's lifelong fight for Indian freedom overlook this substantial period in his career when he fought—for the most part in vain—for the rights of Indians in South Africa. He won a number of small battles, but lost the great war of principle that he waged. In later years he fought South Africa's Asiatic-exclusion Act. He approached General Smuts with an argument that could be summarized as follows: Let the South Africans admit in a year only six Indians— not more than six—but let there not stand against all Asiatics, nominally at least, the grievous Act of branding them as the equivalents of criminals.

General Smuts, in fighting vainly for this concession, quoted, on the Assembly floor, Gandhi's words: "Do not dishonor us! We recognize that there must be distinctions, but do not cast a stigma upon us in the laws of your country." The appeal was refused. The case resembled greatly the Japanese Exclusion Act voted by the United States Congress in 1924.

Today Indians in South Africa number 300,000. Of these, 78 per cent are in Natal, where they are more numerous than the whites. While in Durban, I enjoyed the hospitality of Archbishop Hurley and the delightful company of three American Oblates, Fathers Ceuppens, Hill, and Shelden Kelly. With Father Hill I visited the Indian quarter in the heart of the city. That quarter now surrounds Emmanuel Cathedral, and a great Indian market is directly opposite the cathedral.

In the market is a Moslem mosque, and in the vicinity are numerous Hindu temples. Little, sad-eyed Indian mothers walk the streets with their little, sad-eyed children.

"It is the Indian children whom the whites fear most," explained a Durban friend. "There are so many of them! There are 44 births per thousand Indians, and but 26 births per thousand Europeans. It is calculated that in fifty years there will be 800,000 Indians and 300,000 whites in Natal."

We visited St. Anthony's Church for the Indians, which the Oblates have conducted since 1902. Another St. Anthony's in Pietermaritzburg, is likewise devoted to the Indians.

"Are Indian Christians numerous?" I asked.

"Out of every twenty Indians," one of the group explained, "fifteen are Hindu, four are Moslem, and one is a Christian. Protestants number some ten thousand, and Catholics five thousand. Seventy per cent of all the Catholics are in Durban."

"Do any of your Indian Catholics enter the religious life?"

"Some half-dozen Indian young women have become Sisters. One Indian religious, Mother Cecilia, who died a few years ago, is credited with building St. Anthony's Day School for Indian boys and girls. This is a three-story edifice on Centenary Road."

When in South Africa we speak of Indians, we include the Pakistanis, who are strong among the Moslems. There are a number of Indians of wealth and of good education. One of Durban's big department stores is owned by them, and they are prominent in transportation. They hold title to a third of the privately owned land in Greater Durban. But this success of a relative few obscures the fact that the great majority of Indians are wretchedly poor.

The poor are confined to the Indian locations, which are wretched slums, possessing little or no drainage, no sewerage, no footpaths, no lighting, great swarms of mosquitoes. Among South Africans 5.2 per cent of the whites live below the so-called Poverty Datum Line, 28.8 per cent of the Bantus, 58.2 per cent of the Colored, and 70.6 per cent of the Indians. Thus seven out of every ten Indians live below the minimum subsistence level. No wonder that there is five times more tuberculosis among them than among the whites! Severe working restrictions are the cause of this poverty: today 70 per cent of all

Indians are domestic servants; some 8 per cent are farmers; and 7 per cent are merchants.

Whatever the hardships of the past, they promise to become accentuated as South Africa's Group Areas Act is progressively enforced. First steps were taken in 1951. The new laws displace many persons, especially non-whites, from land on which they are living or from which they make a livelihood. India and Pakistan are still fighting the discriminatory legislation before the United Nations. South Africa refused to recognize the UN's authority to deal with the case.

"What is the great complaint against the Indian?" I asked my Durban friends.

"I'll tell you what a man remarked to me the other day," replied one. " 'The Indian does not play the game,' he said; 'he works and makes all the members of his whole family work disgracefully long hours.' We recognize the objection as a legitimate one, since conceivably the Indians might destroy the entire way of life of South Africa. However, the remedies taken against the evil must be just."

"The Indians seem to have a tremendous capacity for application," remarked Father Shelden Kelly. "For instance, there is a Moslem boy who lives just below my window at the rectory. He is learning the Koran, and he practices reciting it hour after hour. His high-pitched intonations drift up to me endlessly, from morning till night. It would be a rare white lad who would study in that fashion!"

Perhaps one of the hardest blows of all to the Indian was to discover that he was an object of the savage hatred of the African. That hatred was frighteningly demonstrated by a happening of January, 1949.

A Zulu boy had a quarrel with an Indian boy in an Indian shop. The Zulu boy struck the Indian boy, and the Indian shopkeeper intervened by striking the Zulu boy. From that blow the Zulu boy fell against a glass window, which broke, shattered in pieces on the Zulu's head, and without injuring him seriously, covered him with blood. The little incident caused a reaction among the Africans like that of dry straw bursting into flame from a spark. Confreres of the wounded Zulu saw his blood flowing by the hand of the Indian—and there followed three days of earth-shaking massacre, rape, arson, and looting, that brought maiming and death to Indians by bullet, knife, bludgeon, fire.

Father Hill was stationed at the cathedral at the time. He told me of some of the barbaric slaughter that he witnessed from his window. It was only when the Government flew in companies of police, from Pretoria and Johannesburg, that the killing could be halted.

Once again the less evolved among the Africans were puzzled by the actions of the white men. In a score of ways, the blacks had learned of the whites' hostility toward the Indians. Then they saw that, when the Africans undertook to drive the Indians out, the white men stopped the blacks and punished them. An Englishman told me of an Afrikaner with four sons, who herded the Indian farmers of his neighborhood into his large garage and set up an armed guard to protect them, he and his sons serving by shifts, day and night, until the riots ended.

Natal represents the heaviest concentration of Indians in Africa, but the entire eastern area of the continent is a field for their activities. They are a trading element in the cities of East Africa, quite as the Syrian is in West Africa. In Kenya, they are three to one over the whites; in Uganda, they are ten to every one white; in Tanganyika, four to one. In Kenya they are an intermediate element between the white man and the black. An African engine driver, for example, gets one-third the salary of the white engine driver, while an Indian engine driver gets two-thirds the salary of the white. Indians conduct many of the small hotels in places like Mombasa and Dar es Salaam and give them the cachet of hostelries in Karachi or Bombay. In Nairobi, white residents are constantly losing more and more property on swank Delamere Avenue to the Indians.

But it is in the remote rural areas that the Indian proves a most interesting phenomenon. In many a tiny village of the bush, we find a hut occupied by an Indian set amid the huts of the Africans. This trader makes the endless circuit of the periodic market days, which are an established institution of every small center of the countryside. He and others like him, almost lost in the wilderness, are minor-league players of the big-league operators who live in the city; those outpost workers look forward to moving one day into larger posts, nearer civilization, though many end by making their small territories large enough, through their own resourcefulness, to prompt them to remain there permanently. In either case, the outpost trader exercises a real influence on the surrounding Africans.

At an isolated spot in rural Uganda, one day, we stopped for gas, and the young fellow who served us was chatty. "Do you do well here?" I asked.

"Always better!" he replied. "When I came, these black folk had nothing. The men and the women stared at my bright cottons and fancy goods, and between themselves I heard them say, 'I like that.' To me, then, they'd say, 'I want that.' I'd tell them what it cost, and they'd go away. Sometimes it would be weeks before they'd come back. They had gone out and worked—a thing they had no reason to do before—and they had earned the price of the goods. Now they're growing double the amount of coffee that they used to grow, a few years ago, because they want things."

The Government authorities and the African leaders bewail the Indian penetration. Bishop Kiwanuka, African Bishop of Masaka, in Uganda, drove me to see the fine homes of Indians and he remarked, "Those are the men who take our people's money."

The Indians are not dismayed by the obstacles they meet. One afternoon at Kakitumba, on the border between Ruanda and Uganda, I watched an elderly and very suave Pakistani gentleman and a very uneasy Pakistani young man, as they tried their best to wheedle from the Belgian border officer a thirty-day pass rather than a fifteen-day pass for the young man. The latter had just arrived from Karachi and was to "visit" the older man at Nyanza, a center in Ruanda where we had paid a call.

"With thirty days' margin rather than fifteen," explained my companion, "the young man has a better chance of losing himself inside the country, and thus ending as a lifetime resident of Ruanda. The Belgians do not want any more Indian traders!"

The older gentleman approached me. "Do you know the Fathers in Nyanza?" he asked.

"We visited them a few days ago," I replied.

"Wonderful people," he observed, "wonderful people! I like to deal with them. I came out from Lahore twenty-five years ago, and I've known the Fathers from the beginning."

I glanced at the anxious, perspiring young man, who was pleading earnestly for two more weeks to visit his friends. In my mind's eye I could see him, twenty-five years hence, calmly telling someone like myself, as the polished gentleman before me had just told me, that he had been a quarter of a century in Nyanza.

The Irish Holy Ghost Fathers told me of their work among the Indians in Mombasa. Bishop Blomjous, of the White Fathers in Tanganyika, stated that he hoped to secure an Indian priest from India for his diocese. "These Indians are my people," the missionary bishop explained. "I want to do all I can for them."

One day while I was a guest of Bishop Boyle, of Port Elizabeth, we took a beautiful ride into the veld. We stopped to see a little school His Excellency had just completed near Kirkwood, and on the grounds we came upon a quartet of Xhosa children. Although shy, they were most engagingly charming. The bishop passed a bantering word or two with them, and then I asked them if they would sing me a song. The effect was electric. Their faces lit, their eyes danced, and excitedly they went into a huddle as to what they might offer. Ivy took the lead, and Maria, Esther, and Celia formed the chorus. With the most evident delight, they swung into a rhythm, their voices somewhat fragile but exquisitely sweet.

Meanwhile, a little knot of three other children stood nearby. Rather than seem to neglect them, I suggested to the bishop that we speak to them, also. It became immediately apparent that they were quite different from the Xhosas. As we approached, they became frightened, their wan little faces set stiffly, and they could only stare vacantly at us. Their tongues were tied, and getting a song from them was impossible.

"What forlorn little midgets!" I remarked to His Excellency.

"With your inexperienced eye," he answered, "you would not know, but these last children are Colored. Quite obviously, they are not Cape Colored, for they are so completely spiritless. There is a substantial difference, you know, between the Cape Colored and the children of a first generation of a casual union between white and black."

We drove through Kirkwood with its jackaranda trees, which are breathtakingly beautiful when their blue flowers are in bloom. We stopped at Mary Immaculate School, a secondary boarding school for both kinds of colored girls. It was with new interest that I observed the pupils. I asked one of the Sisters—a Dominican—to point out the differences among them.

"Of course we treat all pupils alike," she explained, "but the Cape Colored regard themselves as quite a distinct people with a definite physical type, a characteristic accent, a characteristic laugh. Their home language in Cape Town is usually Afrikaans, though socially they prefer English."

I had an opportunity to meet some of the finer elements among the Cape Colored when the bishop took me to visit the new Institute of St. Rose of Lima. The community is an exclusively Colored one, of local origin, and the religious have their motherhouse at Uitenhage.

"These Sisters will specialize in teaching in our Catholic schools for the Colored," said Bishop Boyle. "They will play an important role if the Government insists on its legislation that each group must be taught by teachers from among its own people."

Before leaving South Africa, I had acquired quite a clear concept of the Colored—a distinct group among the disinherited minorities of this extraordinarily race-conscious land. Although in the United States we use the word "colored" to designate a Negro, in South Africa it signifies always a person of mixed blood. The Colored in the Union are something over a third as numerous as the whites. Ninety per cent of these Colored live in the Cape Province; and the great majority of them are in the western division of the province, principally around Cape Town. That area they consider their ancestral home; their presence in it dates from the century of the Pilgrims and Plymouth Rock. Thus a distinction is made between Colored in general and the Cape Colored, who are also referred to as Cape people.

And what strange combinations of blood they represent! The early Hollanders married the primitive Hottentots and Bushmen, peoples whose forefathers were probably the earliest inhabitants of the African continent. Today eleven per cent of the Colored are known to have Hottentot blood, while those with Bushman blood are less than one per cent. Other strains were added by the slaves whom the Cape Towners brought in: they included captives from Bantu East Africa, Negro West Africa, India, Malaya, Indonesia, China.

"It is important to remember," a sociologist explained to me, "that some of our Colored don't have a drop of Bantu blood in them.

Some of the ancestors of our Cape Colored included beautiful women from the East, endowed with delicate features and the lustre of jewels in their eyes. Many Colored of the present day possess quite an allure when done up in their finery."

Unfortunately, few Colored people can possess much in the way of finery, since as a group they suffer from economic strangulation. They are restricted by law to low-pay employment as dockers, laborers, leather workers, domestics. Thus two out of every five live below the so-called Poverty Datum Line.

"There are 200,000 Colored in Cape Town," a Cape Towner explained to me, "and each year several thousand of their boys and girls start life by hunting for a job. Not more than thirty or forty out of all these can expect to become skilled workers, because never can a larger number be taken on as apprentices. This is heartbreaking for the Colored since for generations before the new legislation and the white labor unions, the Colored workers prided themselves on being the skilled artisans of the community."

The Government supplies schools. Government-aided private schools, including our Catholic schools, are available to the Colored, but there is no compulsory education. Poverty decides the school question in most families. All too often, little Tommy has to quit his classroom to earn a pittance as an errand boy, and little Ida bids teacher good-bye to become a minor servant girl. Socially, the Colored occupy an intermediate place between the black Africans and the white. They are welcome neither in the home of the white nor in the kraal of the black.

Now Prime Minister Malan sets out to destroy the last vestige of the Colored man's self-respect by destroying the few effective political rights that he has inherited from a more generous past. For long he has been able to vote in the Cape Province and Natal. But the pendulum is swinging in the opposite direction. The Colored man is to be disfranchised in the south; he continues to be without political rights in the northern provinces.

General Hertzog, whose views we regarded as quite severe twenty years ago, said of the Colored man: "The time has come when the northern provinces also should recognize his right to be represented in Parliament through his vote. To deny him this would be in the highest degree unjust and unwise."

The great majority of the Union's Colored are Christian. Catholics among the Colored represent eight per cent of the group, or 75,000 among 920,000. Though almost half of these live in Cape Province, several dioceses outside the Cape have sizable contingents. Those dioceses provide special institutions for the Colored; but naturally, the best-organized Catholic institutions among the Colored are in the Cape Province.

One center that I remember in particular is in a section of Port Elizabeth known as Schander Township. There St. James' Colored Mission has an attractive church and well-organized primary and high schools. The schools are conducted by the Assumption Sisters. Of special attraction for me, however, was St. Anthony's Dispensary, in charge of Sister Celestine of the Little Company of Mary. This community, which in Port Elizabeth counts a considerable number of Australian members, operates St. Joseph's Hospital, a 75-bed institution that is the finest in the area. From St. Joseph's as her base, Sister Celestine visits the Colored of Schander Township, and a great part of her time is given to tending the sick poor in their homes.

"What is there about these people that impresses you most?" I asked Sister.

"That's an easy question to answer, Father," Sister Celestine replied immediately. "I never cease to be surprised by the examples of spiritual beauty that I find among these folk who eke out such a precarious existence in their wretched hovels. It is always a new experience. One day it will be a slip of a girl who is cheerfully struggling to get the money to take care of her sick mother. Another day it will be a mother, already burdened with several children, who sacrifices to the bone to take care of the sick child of a neighbor. Again it will be a mother deserted by her husband, who patiently labors long hours to keep her invalided son at home in their bleak, two-room flat.

"We read in books about the angry and embittered Colored people who are rebellious against all society. They are being wronged, it is all too clear. But I wish some of the people who write about them could stand behind me, as I knock on their rickety doors and go into their poor homes. Amid the squalor, I discover the lovely peace of Christ. It brings tears to one's eyes."

Chapter 6

JOURNEY TO BASUTOLAND

ORANGE FREE STATE is called the Prairie Province. It stretched out before me, mile upon endless mile to the far horizon, with all the indefinable beauty of the veld in the brilliant sunshine. My train for Basutoland had left Bloemfontein shortly after eight o'clock that morning. I had found the city, the judicial capital of the Union, a place of quality and dignity, endowed with good climate, good architecture, and attractive South African gardens, rich with thick hedges and abundant shrubbery. Even the Bloemfontein location was something special, boasting of houses built thriftily by the Africans with municipal aid. Father Guntur Hegenbart, of the Oblates, the location pastor, drove me through its maze of streets and showed me his new chapel. "A servant girl in America is building it with her savings," he explained.

My train chugged placidly eastward and ever gently upward, for Basutoland is, among other things, the Union's principal watershed. The portion of the plains over which the train journeys was once within the Basuto realm, but the Boers took possession of it. Today three-quarters of Basutoland, a country the size of Belgium, is mountainous. Four-fifths of the population of 600,000 live in the remaining lowland quarter, into which we were then moving.

At one point as we rolled along I was treated to one of the most interesting sights in South Africa, a classic, eight-span ox-wagon sauntering along a country road that paralleled our route. A heavy-built black man, who I am told is called the voorloper, walked ahead of the lead animals. The eight pair of red oxen made their way with serene majesty, slowly, methodically, rhythmically, their horns flashing in the sun. The driver walked beside his wagon, which must have been twenty feet long.

The Basutos are not as tall and handsome as the Zulus, the best

241

known of South Africa's peoples, but they are brave and intelligent. They pride themselves on never having been conquered, though certainly they suffer terribly from the nineteenth century strife that weakened all of South Africa's tribes. The four most important South African peoples are the Zulu and Xhosa, who form one family, and the Basuto and Bechuana, who form a second.

Moshesh, the great Basuto leader, one of the shrewdest figures in the South Africa scene, kept the backs of his warriors to the mountains and was never unprepared for an attack. Eugene Casalis, a French Protestant missionary, was with Moshesh and his men when Moselkatze, the mighty Zulu, sent his forces against the Basutos. The latter, in their famous natural fortress—Thaba Bosigo, a great, cliff-fringed hill with a plateau top large enough to quarter an army—watched the Zulus approach. The Basutos gazed down calmly as the enemies in the valley prepared their ornaments, sharpened their weapons and executed their war dances. Then the terrific battle began.

"Accustomed to victory," relates Casalis, "the Zulus advanced in serried ranks, not troubling to notice the masses of basalt rock that came leaping down on them with tremendous noise from the top of the mountain. An irresistible avalanche of stones, accompanied by a shower of spears, sent back the Zulus with more rapidity than they had advanced. We could see the chiefs snatching the plumes off their warriors' heads and trampling them down in a rage. Another attack against the formidable rampart succeeded no better than the first.

"Next day the Zulus returned home to their sovereign. As they departed, the Basuto drove some cattle to them with the taunting message: 'Moshesh salutes you. Supposing that hunger brought you into this country, he sends these cattle so that you may eat them on your way home.'" [1]

Moshesh displayed magnificent courage and was in the forefront of every battle that his men fought. Casalis, when he first saw the Basuto leader, felt at once that he had to do with a superior man, trained to think and command others, one who "bestowed on me a look at once majestic and benevolent." During all his reign, Moshesh desired to rule and live in peace, but always was faced with war. In his late seventies, when the Boers were menacing his people, he pleaded with Britain to take the Basutos under British protection.

After his plea was granted in 1868, he wrote to Queen Victoria, "I am glad that my people have been allowed to rest and live in the large folds of the blanket of England."

This is the origin of what General Smuts used to refer to as "those anomalies" on the map of South Africa: the three British Protectorates of Basutoland, Bechuanaland, and Swaziland. The native peoples of all three territories had asked Great Britain to take care of them. When the Union of South Africa was established, in 1910, Smuts took it for granted that Britain would hand over the three to the Union as a present. But Britain didn't—and even today hesitates to do so. To-day the peoples of these areas are more anxious than ever to have Great Britain as their protector. Their peoples are much freer than if South Africa's laws were brought to bear on them. The Government in London has issued a White Paper indicating that Britain does not favor transferring the territories to a regime with a racial-discrimination policy such as that of the present South African Government.

The negotiations continue, with most missionaries feeling that the protectorates serve better the welfare of the Africans. Most feel, how-ever, that it is at best but a matter of time: Britain's tenuous hold will not continue indefinitely against South African insistence.

A fourth territory, that of Southwest Africa, remains technically a trusteeship under the United Nations. Ever since World War I, how-ever, the Union has administered that territory and regards it as in-corporated within Union borders. The Anglican, Father Michael Scott, championed before the UN the tribes in Southwest Africa whose rights he considered infringed, and thus he reminded the protectorate peoples what they may expect from the Union when annexation comes.

The last mile of the train ride from Bloemfontein is actually within Basutoland's borders and is the only mile of railroad track in the entire country. But who thinks of railroad track, once his eye obtains the vision of Basutoland's ten thousand peaks? The country, someone had told me, is called the Switzerland of South Africa. I had vaguely expected the standard mountains and standard valleys that prompt people to apply such a name to a hundred places over the globe. But here during the next few days, I found a scene quite unlike anything I had beheld anywhere else on earth.

"People call it the devil's dumping ground," said an Englishman on the train.

But they are wrong, I decided. It was not the devil but the Divine

Artist, who had convulsed this gnarled knob on the surface of the globe so successfully as to make it one of His most striking achievements. Basutoland is not beautiful in the ordinary sense. It is awesome in a majestic, mysterious, haunting way. It has valleys, but they seem never to follow the ordered pattern of ordinary valleys. It has peaks—forests of them—but never, it seems, formed into neatly regimented companies. It has krantzes of stone cliffs, but they seem in hopeless disarray. It has colors and shadows which etch the blue basalt giants into weird shapes, their eeriness compounded when the wind blows and the clouds scurry across the sky, creating ever-changing silhouettes.

What is it, above all, that projects into every landscape of Basutoland an air of brooding loneliness? It is, I decided, the predominant barrenness. True, the valleys have vegetation, and the fields when fat with crops are smiling. But much of the vast uplands are denuded. The carelessness of man, then, has created ugly seams of erosion in areas that should be gently sloping grasslands.

My mountain meditation was suddenly interrupted by our arrival in the little station of Maseru. Father Jacques met me and drove me immediately to his busy mission of Loretto. It is in the outskirts of a town that, principal community of the land though it is, looks like a pioneer settlement in the foothills of the Rockies. I quickly plunged into the saga of this extraordinary mission of the Canadian Oblates. Bishop Allard and the saintly Pere Gerard of the French Oblates were the first to enter there in 1861. They traveled hundreds of miles on horseback from Maritzburg. In the neighborhood of Leribe, they found several families of Irish farmers who had not seen a priest for years. They called on Molapo, Moshesh's son, who was the chief at Leribe, and were graciously encouraged to make a foundation. This was the start.

"In the early 1930's," Father Jacques related, "the French province had some 50,000 Christians here, but was badly short of personnel. The French invited the Canadians to take over. Our Canadian superiors promised to send ten missionaries a year, for ten years, and as ample funds as possible for support. The people of Quebec more than did their part in helping with offerings. Today we have 125 priests here, including the Basutos. The Catholic body numbers 225,000, or 37 per cent of the entire Basuto nation, and the year's total of baptisms now averages 10,000. For the work in Basutoland, we have

550 foreign and Basuto Brothers and Sisters and almost 800 lay cate-chists. People who know, tell us that this is one of the most flourishing Catholic missions on the globe.

"Recently the Holy Father named a Basuto, Emmanuel Maba-thoana, to be Bishop of Leribe. This is a new ecclesiastical division, with Basuto priests as well as a contingent of foreigners to help the bishop. The new diocese counts 40,000 Basuto Catholics. Bishop Mabathoana is a third-generation descendant of Moshesh, the famed founder of the Basuto nation."

Thus once again we hear the story repeated: vigorous and en-thusiastic Christians in the missionaries' homeland, contributing spir-itual and financial strength, execute an outstanding performance when they take up a missionary job. Those of us who know the love of the Quebec people for their Faith, well understand the wonderful backing they have given the young, energetic Canadian Oblates.

"I hope I shall be able to meet some of the Basuto priests," I re-marked as Father Jacques and I sat chatting.

"That will be easy," he replied. "The first Catholic priest of the Basuto nation, Father Raphael Mohari, is stationed in Maseru. We will take him with us on our journey to Mazenod and Roma."

At Maseru we picked up Father Mohari, a kindly, dignified gen-tleman who had been ordained in 1931. The Basuto countryside came alive as he sat beside me during our ride.

"What handsome horses!" I cried when two mounted men gal-loped past us just out of town.

"Oh, yes," said Father Mohari, "the Basutos love their horses like their sweethearts. They take pride in owning well-fed and well-groomed animals. Before Basutos ride, they don clean and colorful clothes and wrap themselves in gaily colored blankets."

"There seem to be many cattle and many herds of sheep and goats, in this region," I remarked.

"Yes. All our people are farmers or herdsmen, or both. Some spots are shockingly overgrazed, but people who know tell us that the land as a whole does not have more animals than it can support. Basutoland is really a fine stock country, with natural mountain pas-tures that are unsurpassed in South Africa."

"Do the herds cause the erosion?" I asked.

"In some sections they do. The Basutos understand that bad

grazing practices cause great harm. They try to keep certain lands for the drier seasons, and give their herd boys instructions on where to go. Of course many of the boys misunderstand or don't do what they're told. I know, because I was a herd boy once."

"It must be monotonous work," I said, and I let my eye drift out over the scene before us.

At that moment, there were about a dozen herd boys within sight, each clad in little more than a loincloth. Some boys stood idly, leaning on their staffs. A few were moving their flocks of sheep, gently prodding them as the animals grazed slowly and peacefully in the rolling, green, hill country. I turned toward Father Mohari and found him smiling, gazing at me with a twinkle in his eye.

"No, it is not really monotonous," he said. "Not for Basuto boys. I suppose it would be for American boys."

"Then you didn't find it monotonous," I ventured.

"No. For I and my companions were really kept quite busy. I helped tend my father's flock of five hundred sheep. For a time, with other boys I helped care for my uncle's flock of over a thousand sheep."

"What did you think of, out there on the hills?" I asked.

"Well," Father Mohari replied, with, I suspected, a moment's hesitation about telling me, "while I was out in the open all day, the idea came to me that I wanted to go to school."

"What did you do about it?"

"For a long time I did nothing. I was afraid. My father was a pagan, and I knew that he was opposed to school. He said it spoiled a boy to get book learning. My mother was a Catholic, and I had been allowed to follow her religion. At last I went to her and asked her to intercede for me with my father. My mother was a wonderful person; she had no fear. She knew how my father felt and what he would say, but she went to him anyway. As she and I expected, he became much incensed. He even struck my mother with a rod.

" 'You vain creature!' he shouted. 'You want to crow about having a boy in school.' He forbade her ever to speak to him of the matter again.

"I continued to tend the sheep, thinking always of my desire. One day when I was fifteen, I stole off to school and had myself enrolled. But the teacher was very cool with me. 'We have a lot of young fellows like you,' he said, 'who get a notion to come here, and then they don't have the backbone to stick at it.'

"That night my father sent for me. 'I was looking for you today and couldn't find you,' he said. 'Where were you?'

"I was greatly frightened, but somehow I answered, 'I went to school, and the master put my name in the Government book.' To my surprise my father did not beat me. Instead he railed disdainfully about my putting my name in the Government book. 'Now the Government's got you!' he kept repeating. 'Your name's in their book.'

"I could not decide what my father's attitude was. I didn't sleep that night. Next morning at daybreak I went out of the hut, ready for school, but I just stood out in front, uncertain what to do. After a short while, my mother came out. 'You are like all the rest of the lazy loafers!' she cried. 'Yesterday you enrolled in the school, and to-day you have not enough energy to go.'

"I took one astounded look at that dear woman, and started for school on the run. 'Wait,' she called, 'let me give you some food.'

" 'No,' I replied. 'Father may see me and keep me from going!' So I started my happy years at school, and eventually I became a teacher."

"That's a perfectly wonderful story, Father Raphael!" I exclaimed. "What, then, made you think of the priesthood?"

"The idea did not come at once. At the school where I taught, we used to see a great deal of an old French missionary. He was always kind to me. He was most flattering in his praise of me because I tried hard to help my pupils. He lived a life of great self-abnegation. He got me thinking. If this man, I would say to myself, can come here from afar, and live his life so completely for us, why shouldn't I do more to help my people? Finally I asked him if I could become a Brother among the Marists in whose school I taught.

"The Marists had no place to train Basuto members. A little while later, the old missionary said to me, 'The bishop wants to see you.'

"I was astonished when the bishop said he thought I might try for the priesthood, in the new seminary he was opening at Roma. That was in 1924. There were three of us that first year in the seminary, and one of the three is the new Bishop of Leribe, Bishop Maba-thoana."

"Did you know the bishop before you met him in the seminary?"

"Yes. He was a herd boy like myself, and at eleven he entered the school where I taught. I had him in class."

"Did you know his family?"

"Yes. His father had become a Christian at fifteen years of age, and his mother was born of Catholic parents. The father and mother were present at his episcopal consecration, in 1953."

"Is he quite a capable person?" I asked.

"Very much so! I was always a dull old ox, but he was as bright as a sovereign. He is an eloquent preacher and an accomplished musician. He has written the music of a Mass entitled 'Mass of the Uganda Martyrs,' which he has put on records. His great specialty is Bantu languages, which he taught at Pius XII University. Besides our own Susuto he knows four native tongues, as well as English, French, and Latin. He has worked on a comparative grammar of our African languages. He studied a year in Rome, and had a sojourn in London. All Basutoland went wild with joy when he was made a bishop."

Later during my visit, I met Bishop Mabathoana and found him quite up to my expectations. He is slight of build, with incised features and warm, intelligent eyes. With his quiet demeanor, he will take on stature as the years pass.

We made a brief stop at Mazenod, the great literature and Catholic Action center of the mission. As the sun went down we reached Roma—a remarkable place that represents no developed town but a very unusual concentration of Christian institutions of a high order. It took me the better part of the next day to visit them. Here is the tally: (1) Roma College, a teacher-training college headed by very capable Brother Jules, with a staff of a dozen Canadian and American Brothers of the Sacred Heart; (2) St. Mary's Institute, a boarding and day school for African girls, a training school for African women teachers, and a novitiate for African Sisters, all conducted by the Holy Family Sisters; (3) Pius XII Catholic University College, the only institution of its kind in South Africa, devoted exclusively to the higher education of Africans; (4) St. Augustine's Major and Minor Seminary for African clergy; (5) St. Mary's Juniorate, for training African Brothers of the Sacred Heart; (6) St. Joseph's Hospital, staffed by Holy Family Sisters.

Deep in the mountains, 150 miles due south of Roma, Father

Andrew Blais, an Oblate from Massachusetts, has built up Eagle's Peak College and Teacher-Training School for Africans, at Qachas Nek. Mazenod has a Teacher-Training School and Industrial School for Africans; Mekaling has an Industrial School for Africans. At Thaba Tieka, in the heart of the mountains, is a second hospital. Finally, at seven different centers in Basutoland, are houses of training for the hardy African Sisters who are meeting with such resounding success in the country.

Heading this assemblage of institutions and the entire Diocese of Maseru, is a young and alert missionary leader, Bishop Joseph Des Rosiers, O.M.I., who gave me a royal welcome.

"I am here but a few hours, Your Excellency," I remarked, "but I see North American drive and enterprise at every hand."

"We try to keep our thoughts on the work that is not yet done," replied the bishop. "We have a strong center here, and some fifty stations throughout the mountains, but we are constantly bewailing our inability to cover the ground. We have 360 schools, but that total is only three-fourths of the number needed. I am particularly proud of the young priests who live at the distant mountain posts, talking Susuto. You must arrange to see how the people live in the villages."

The opportunity soon came to me to accompany Father Guilbeault, now rector of Pius XII University, and Father Coté, into the nearby hills to Nazareth. There on a rolling crest set in superb scenery, we walked among the villagers.

"Is the ordinary family able to make ends meet here?" I asked.

"Not from their land or their herds," replied Father Coté. "For that reason Basutoland is, practically speaking, like one of South Africa's Native reserves. We are told that from fifty to sixty per cent of the men, year in year out, follow the road of enchantment to work the mines in the City of Gold or to work on the farms of the Free State. We are said to average 100,000 men away from home most of the time. The men of a village often take it in turns, one team doing the needful at home while the others are away. People here have acquired tastes that call for more than merely keeping alive, and hence they have to go abroad to get the extra money."

"Do you think some of these people would let me visit their homes?" I asked.

"They will feel complimented to have us call," Father Coté answered. "Let's stop in here."

We approached two huts just off our path. "This is one home," Father Coté explained. "One hut is the residence proper, and the second is the kitchen hut. Note that the whole property is fenced with sisal plants."

Between the two huts was a smooth, clayed surface, hard as cement. Near the kitchen hut was a shallow, bowl-like declivity in which a slow fire burned. On the clay lay a skin with drying tobacco on it. The two huts were circular, built of wattle and daub painted an ochre color. The neatly shorn, thatched roof made each hut as smart-looking as a Dutch boy who has just had a haircut.

"Imelda!" Father called.

"Welcome, Father," answered the housewife, who was all smiles as she stepped out of the kitchen hut.

"Father is a stranger and would like to see your home, Imelda."

"Oh, what an honor!" replied the little lady, ready with the apt expression.

We found Imelda's residence as clean as any house at home. The circular wall was painted a light yellow, up to six feet from the floor. Then there was a band of red, stenciled with a repeating design. Above this were pictures, one of them of Père Gerard, the saintly apostle of Basutoland whose cause of canonization is being promoted. Two small windows provided the hut with light. Furniture was scarce, but there was a hanger loaded with clothes, shawls, and blankets in South African designs. Rolled up sleeping mats stood in the corner.

"How long will it be before Joseph returns?" asked Father Coté.

"Another three months," replied Imelda.

"What a wretched situation, to have a young wife and her husband separated in this fashion for almost a year at a time!" the priest remarked to me.

Nearby was the cattle kraal, empty because the animals were grazing. A discreet pile of fuel dung cakes stood at the fence, gathered from the fields or cut from the floor of the kraal. For want of firewood, this precious manure was kept from the land. Government experiments have shown that manured lands will produce 1,100 pounds of mealies per acre, in place of the 300 pounds per acre that the unnourished soil is rendering while the manure is used for fuel.

"The farm agents assure us," noted Father Coté, "that Basutoland could feed a much greater population if the people would use modern methods."

Down the path was Constantia's household. On her wall, also, was a print of Père Gerard. Evidently her husband had done well from the sale of his wool, since the hut was much better furnished. He was not away in the city, though he was momentarily absent from the house. In his place we met tiny Emmanuel, whose only article of clothing was a stomach band of bright-colored beads.

"Thank you for your call," beamed Constantia. "Every time our priests visit us, we remember it for many years."

"How do you explain that such lovely people as you have here in Basutoland have become notorious throughout the world for their frightful ritual murders?" I asked a group of missionaries that evening.

"It is not the lovely people, as you call them, who engage in the ritual murders. However, even otherwise decent folk can become involved in them. The superstitious power that magic exercises over all the black folk who have not completely broken its grip on them is terrific."

"Who exercises the magic?" I asked.

"The witch doctors are to blame. But even they are not entirely as evil as they seem. What they do, they have learned to do from the past, and they believe in it implicitly. The wretched deeds that they prescribe are, as the term 'ritual murder' indicates, formulas that they are convinced are necessary.

"Behind the witch doctors are the chiefs. The chiefs want to keep their power. They see themselves losing power, and they ask the witch doctors why. The witch doctors tell them that it is because they are flouting the ways of their fathers. Acting for the chiefs are their henchmen. These men are not necessarily evil; sometimes there are even Christians among them. But they feel completely at the mercy of the chiefs, and they have to do what the chiefs direct. I know, from talking with some of them, what an agony it has been for them to carry out the ugly orders of the chiefs. They say they must obey, in order to save themselves and their families."

"Apparently the murders still go on," I remarked.

"Yes. Recently, for instance, back in the mountains a week's journey from here by horseback, a chief was setting up a new village for his son. He wished to do it in the best way possible. He consulted the witch doctor. The witch doctor, as is the routine, prescribed that a calabash horn of living blood from a designated human victim must be planted in the new village, to insure good luck to the son. Then a team of the chief's henchmen was ordered to bring in the victim, who was a strong, healthy, and rather successful farmer with a fine family at home.

"The man, mad with fear, tried to plead with the chief: 'Take my oxen, take my wife to be your wife, take my children as your slaves, but let me live!' 'I don't need your oxen, I need you,' answered the chief. 'Men, do your work.'

"A crowd of women gathered around and set up a hideous shouting, so that the victim's shrieks could not be heard. Blood was drawn from him while he was still living, to fill the horn. The shrieks stopped only when the man's throat was cut. Later the British authorities got the story of the crime and found the perpetrators, but could not get any testimony that they could use in court. The chief is still free."

I was out riding with Bishop Des Rosiers and he gave a lift to a teacher whom we met along the way. The matter of ritual murders came up in the conversation with our fellow wayfarer, an earnest family man.

"Teacher," said the bishop, "these ritual murders do Basutoland harm throughout the whole world. What can be done to end the custom?"

"It is difficult to say. The chiefs are the ones who are to be condemned."

"Teacher, don't you think that a strong Christian country could do away with ritual murders?"

"Yes, a strong Christian country would do away with ritual murders. If we had a strong Christian country, we would no longer suffer this shame."

Bishop Des Rosiers and his confreres in the South African hierarchy are quite convinced that their people will never possess properly able leadership until they can be given a thoroughly Christian higher education. Behind this conviction lies the development, at Roma, of Pius XII Catholic University College. The undertaking is a tremendous one, for no Government grant can be expected, and no diocese in South Africa is financially in a position to render substantial assistance.

Years ago when the idea of university education was first discussed, the Catholic bishops considered the erection of a residence hostel at the South African Native College at Fort Hare, which the Union supports for non-Europeans. Three hostels already at Fort Hare had been erected by the Methodists, the Presbyterians, and the Anglicans; but difficulties arose when the proposal was made to add a Catholic hostel. Then the Oblates responded in magnificent fashion to the plea of the hierarchy, to assume the huge burden of building and staffing Pius XII Catholic University College within the precincts of Roma. The Oblates must pin their hopes on finding the funds in North America.

"I wish you could tell me the secret for raising a million dollars to build our university," remarked Father Guilbeault, who carries the financial responsibility.

The physical structure is as yet on the modest side, though the plans are ambitious. The Oblates have won great respect in Canada through their good work at the Catholic University of Ottawa, which is their achievement. Valued staff members from Ottawa have gone out to Basutoland.

"It is a daring and difficult undertaking," explained Father Quirion, the staff's professor of commerce and a man with clear ideas. "We are all enthusiastic about it because we see that Africa needs leaders with Christian principles. Either we develop such leaders, or we lose Africa."

As yet there are relatively few young Africans who can qualify for the college classes at Roma. In 1953, the enrollment was thirty-five. Since the opening in 1945 fifteen young men and a young woman have obtained the B.A. degree.

"The most important thing in the university is the student body," remarked Father Quirion. "I see three different types among the students, resulting from their differences of origin. The Basutoland boys show the least acquaintance with modern life but the best qualities of heart. The Union Africans, who come principally from the locations, have been hardened by their experiences; they have paid a price for living in a world of high tensions. The young men who come from Rhodesia, Uganda, or other places in Africa, reveal the most mature characteristics: evidently they have grown up in a social climate that has encouraged them to develop greater self-respect."

I was well impressed with the lay members of the university staff. Most distinguished is Doctor Harold Jowitt. Doctor Jowitt spent thirty-three years in the British Colonial Service. As Director of Education in Uganda in 1934, he made recommendations that led to the founding of Makerere University. While serving in Uganda he decided to enter the Catholic Church and was finally received by Bishop Fleischer of Mariannhill.

I spent a very profitable morning listening to Doctor Jowitt. "I admire greatly the Catholic Church's sound teaching on race," he stated. "I think that a good number of African leaders who are developing today have intelligence and courage. I hope we can do a great deal to provide strong spiritual foundations to many of these men who desire ardently to accomplish good for their people."

A preparatory student at Pius XII University is Constantine Bereng Seeiso, the future Paramount Chief of Basutoland. "He is a promising young man," one of the staff told me. "While at Roma College, he was leader of the college's first Scout Troop, a member of the college band, and one of the best players on the college tennis team. For years he has been a daily communicant."

Some decades ago, Constantine's father, the late Paramount Chief Seeiso Griffith, created quite a sensation by his spiritual conversion from a profligate life and his entry into the Catholic Church. When he first asked Father Foulonneau what the conditions were for becoming a Catholic, his reputation was so bad that the missionary did not take him seriously.

"Chief," the old priest said, "it means giving up the bottle and renouncing all your thirty-eight wives except one."

"But I have two that I really love," protested the chief.

"One only!" repeated the missionary tartly.

Chief Griffith succeeded eventually in leading an exceptionally exemplary life. His wife Victoria, who accompanied him always to Mass and Communion, was likewise virtuous. At sixty years of age, the chief began learning to read in order to use a prayerbook. He and Victoria instituted for themselves the practice of rising each morning at one o'clock to recite the Rosary and to make the Way of the Cross. Thus a strong religious strain has persisted in the descendants of Moshesh.

Section 4

EAST AFRICA

Somalia

Indian

MOGADISCIO
★

Ocean

EAST AFRICA

East Africa as treated in these pages possesses a population of 18,000,000. It embraces Uganda. Tanganyika, Kenya and the coastal island of Zanzibar. The southern provinces of the Anglo-Egyptian Sudan, Somalia (British, French, Italian Somaliland) and Ethiopia comprise Northeast Africa which with Insular East Africa (Madagascar and other islands) is heavily Bantu. Space limitations prevent our consideration of these areas. North Africa, which belongs to the Arab world, is beyond our purview.

Chapter 1

CONVERSATION IN MASAKA

THERE WAS A twinkle in the eye of Bishop Kiwanuka, as he led me into the neat, modern office of Chief Alexander Kironde. The two men had been schoolboy companions, and their meeting was always a signal for friendly repartee.

"Here he comes," said Chief Alexander, who as a dutiful Catholic made the gesture of kissing the bishop's ring; "the best man in Masaka for getting things done."

"Not a bit of it!" replied the bishop. "Here is where I come every time I want to see how to be a wonder-worker."

Bishop Joseph Kiwanuka, now in his late fifties, was the first East African-born ruler of a diocese when he was named head of Masaka, in 1939. After fifteen years of service and his passage into middle age, he had taken on a degree of flesh that filled out well his purple-piped soutane. But he still wore habitually his huge smile and walked with an agile, easy stride that was almost a swagger. He governs well in his diocese of over 150,000 Catholics, with its eighty priests, sixty of whom are native Baganda people like the bishop himself.

I found Chief Alexander a handsome specimen of a man, tall, large-bodied, and big-boned, with a strong face. It was immediately evident that he was vigorous and clever. He wore the *kanza*, a flowing white robe of Arab origin, and a smart English-style jacket of gray tweed, the accepted dress of a local dignitary. He governs the county of Masaka, in the native state of Buganda, which is ruled by the *Kabaka*, Buganda's traditional king.

We were in the heart of East Africa. On a rainy Monday morning, my gracious hosts in Johannesburg, Fathers Lewis and Dalton of the American Paulists, had driven me to the airport where, by Comet, I leaped the two thousand miles from Johannesburg to Entebbe, in Uganda. Thus I was halfway along the 4,000-mile transit from Johannesburg to Cairo. (Distances are enormous on the African continent.)

Entebbe is a little paradise of English country homes, neatly shorn green lawns, and gorgeous flower beds, nestled on the banks of Lake Victoria. It is the seat of the British Protectorate of Uganda; twenty miles away is Kampala, seat of the native state of Buganda and principal business center of the country. Father Paul Bordenet, of the Maryknoll mission in Tanganyika, who was to be my *fidus Achates* through much of East Africa, met me with a mission truck. We hurried through bustling Kampala and covered a zigzag route toward Uganda's western border. We were now in the countryside around Masaka, some eighty miles from Kampala.

"Bishop Kiwanuka tells me, Chief Alexander, that you and he were boyhood neighbors," I remarked.

"Yes," replied the big man. "We were both born in the parish of Mitala Maria, only a few miles outside Kampala. It is an important old station of the White Fathers; we are proud to belong to it."

"I know the place quite well," I observed. "I made my first visit there twenty years ago; and when I stopped there this time, its great church was still teeming with children, who swarmed inside and out of it like ants."

"Our parents helped build that huge structure years ago," put in Bishop Kiwanuka. "The people gathered 35,000 shillings for it, in days when the shilling was quite precious. Today there are 30,000 people in the parish, of whom over 18,000 are Catholics. The Mohammedans number 5,000, and the pagans only 2,500. The Protestants, who are much stronger in many parts, number 4,000 there."

Mitala Maria is a typical parish in a part of Uganda where Christianity is very strong. Today the country as a whole counts 5,000,000 inhabitants, of whom a half are Christian. Twenty-five per cent are Catholic.

"You are very smart and business-like in your set-up here, Chief Alexander," I said.

"Thank you, thank you," he responded and smiled. "It is quite the vogue, you know, to gripe about the British, but we Baganda like forms and filing cabinets and red tape as much as the British do. Thanks to their presence, we have many unusual features in Uganda, for a country that has almost no European settlers. For instance, there is a golf course at almost every administrative station in the country, and there are 7,500 miles of all-weather roads.

"On the other hand, Buganda and the neighboring states are very much Africa. There are big herds of elephants in northern Buganda and in the West Nile country. At spots like Murchison Falls, one can see thousands of elephants, hippos, and crocodiles. As one drives along the main highways, everything points to an inhabited country, but we can show you jungles as well. We have beautiful mahogany trees as much as 180 feet high, containing twenty to twenty-five cubic tons of timber."

"Is Buganda a province of the country we in America know as Uganda?" I asked.

Chief Alexander looked quickly at Bishop Kiwanuka, and the two smiled. "Buganda is to the Baganda people," he replied, "what Ireland is to the Irish. It is our homeland. To the British, we are a province; to ourselves, we are a nation. In the British Protectorate there are four provinces, one of which is Buganda, which embraces one-third of the total population of the protectorate. True, the British give special consideration to Buganda because our ruler, the *Kabaka*, has high precedence as a hereditary ruler in direct treaty relationship with Great Britain."

"As I understand it," I said, "from the beginning the British recognized the Baganda as quite an extraordinary people."

"When Speke and Grant, the first English explorers, reached the court of our ruler, Mutesa, almost a hundred years ago," said Bishop Kiwanuka, who now spoke up, "they were astonished to find themselves among an unusually well organized and intelligent people who had a great deal of dignity and courtesy. The two explorers reported these facts to London. They mentioned in particular that the people clothed themselves very modestly with a copper-colored bark cloth. Today cotton has supplanted the lovely bark cloth our mothers used to make from a local tree of the fig family, but the cloth can still be bought in shops in the larger centers."

"And what about the people's modesty and dignity and courtesy?" I asked.

"Our country people have retained it to the full," replied the chief. "I confess that many in the cities have lost the traditional charm of our people."

Certainly the Muganda housewife, with shopping basket in hand and a bottle balanced easily, almost carelessly, on her head, is an unfailingly fascinating sight everywhere along the way. Such a sense of balance explains the splendid carriage of these people. The country dress is simple, but in the city the women are strikingly ornate.

"The women of Buganda are for the most part magnificent," says Elspeth Huxley, whose critical judgment deserves a quote.[1] "In Kampala they ride the streets in gorgeous purples and magentas, golds and puces and verdurous greens, like oriental galleons crowded with sail of silk and satin. . . . Their backs are straight as palm trees, their heads are high and they walk with the pride of an empress: often puffing, as they go, at a clay pipe with a long slender stem. The men in their white robes, or their clean drill suits and gleaming topees, are a foil for the women's garish, Moresque coloring. Men are to be found in rags here, as in most places—though the rags, being clean, seldom look squalid—but by and large you could not see such a gaily dressed and well-fed collection of people today in any European city."

"May I ask where you stand in the Buganda government, Chief?" I inquired of our host.

"I am neither high nor low," he replied. "At the top is our *Kabaka* who, according to the so-called Uganda Agreement of 1900—the document on which the British base present relations with us—has three principal ministers. These are the Prime Minister, the Chief Justice, and the Treasurer. Oddly enough, in our Constitution it is specified that the Prime Minister is to be a member of the 'Native Anglican Church,' and the Chief Justice is to be 'Roman Catholic.' The Treasurer, then, is usually a non-Christian, though this is not specified in the Constitution."

Throughout Uganda one encounters similar division of civic offices. At Mbarara, for instance, I met Father Coté, superintendent of schools for Bishop Lacoursier in the great diocese of the White Fathers, which covers the western province. After the coronation of Queen Elizabeth, Father Coté accompanied, to an audience with the Holy Father in Rome, the *Mukama* of Toro in the western province, King Rukidi III, and his Chief Minister. Since the King is a Protestant, it has become a tradition in Toro that the Chief Minister must be a Catholic—as is the case with the present incumbent, Thomas Mbema.

"Who else makes up the Kampala Government, Chief?" I asked.

"There is a rash of officials on Mengo Hill! Then there is the Buganda Parliament of eighty-nine members, two-thirds of whom are appointed by the *Kabaka,* and one-third elected."

This movement toward the development of an elected governing body is involved in the contest now in course between the British authorities and the *Kabaka* and his followers. The present *Kabaka,* Mutesa II, is a young man of gentlemanly comportment who while at Cambridge University, acquired a strong liking for English ways and for English exercise of free will. In November of 1953, his recognition as ruler of Buganda was withdrawn by the British, for "obstructionism." He and his followers gravely suspect (and probably are right in their suspicions) that the British are attempting to weaken the old regime in favor of a popular electorate that would embrace not only all Uganda but all British East Africa.

Mutesa II now resides in London. The restriction is not a great penance for him personally, but it is a source of distress for his subjects, who smart under this categoric evidence that they are still far from being a free people.

"And what of your position, Chief?" I asked.

"I am the county or so-called *saza* chief for the county of Masaka," replied Chief Alexander. "There are twenty such county chiefs in Buganda. I have the supervision of the district or gombolola chiefs, while below them in turn come the parish or muluka subchiefs."

"Do you encounter British officials in the fulfillment of your duties?"

"The only British official now within Buganda is the British Resident at Kampala," replied the chief. "The entire Buganda Government is native. However, we encounter Britishers who render valuable technical services to our Baganda people."

"You are internally, then, a self-governing people," I said, summing up our conversation. "From the financial angle, are you a self-maintaining people?"

"In your American sense of providing great public institutions for our people, we are not," answered the chief. "Our people meet our general operational expenses. Every Muganda pays a head tax of fourteen shillings a year, which is a substitute for labor services that he used to render in bygone days. All this tax money goes into the Buganda treasury. Every man also pays fifteen shillings a year poll tax to the British, a quarter of which comes back to Buganda. Thus each Muganda pays a yearly tax of twenty-nine shillings, the equivalent of four American dollars. This is about the highest personal tax paid by men of any country in Africa. But burdensome though this is for our peasant people, they manage to pay it. They are a nation of successful farmers."

Bishop Kiwanuka and I took cordial leave of Chief Alexander Kironde. "He is very loyal in his defense of the Baganda people, as are we all," remarked His Excellency when we rode away. "But I don't agree with him when he says that we are a nation of successful farmers. We are not yet successful. Look at that field of neglected banana plants, for instance! The owner of that field is lazy. I repeat and repeat to my people the sad fact that they are lazy, that they lack the spirit of industry. We are not yet successful; we are only beginning to be successful. We shall fail if we do not study more, if we do not work more, if we do not take more care to maintain a life of the spirit in the simple family life of our countryside."

Uganda is a land that smiles, I decided once again, as we drove through the farming country about Masaka. Everywhere it was green as emerald. Though on the equator, it has a subtropical climate because of its elevation, and it enjoys a happy combination of warmth, cool breezes, and temperate nights. Everywhere there is unusual evidence of elementary comfort. We rode through well-forested, thickly populated country, with banana, coffee, cotton, cassava, and sweet-potato patches lining the road and running back into every valley.

"Tickle Uganda with a hoe, and she will smile with a harvest," I said to His Excellency, repeating an expression I had read in a book.

"True and yet not true," countered the bishop. "There are tremendous farming problems that grow more grave each year. It is for this reason I am so anxious to train my priests to handle the social problem. They must stir my people to live better in the conduct of their temporal affairs as well as their spiritual. This is why I sent two of my priests to your American University of St. Louis to study sociology under the Jesuits. In a certain sense, Father, we have already left behind the days of missionary pioneering in this diocese. Now the need is intensification of Christian living on the part of our good people."

He interrupted himself with a sudden idea: "Ah! I know what we should do. We are near the home of Martin Mulanga. Let us visit him. He is a simple, hardworking man who earns only a modest salary, but he knows well what we are facing among our farmers. Driver, stop here at Martin's, please."

The driver turned the bishop's car from the highway, and slowly we moved along the narrow dirt road to Martin's home. Several youngsters were playing in the yard.

"The bishop! The bishop!" they cried, and dashed toward the automobile. "Welcome! Welcome!" they shouted, their eyes and every muscle in their bodies dancing in unfeigned delight.

"Is your father home?" asked the bishop.

"He has just arrived this minute," one boy replied.

"Tell him I have a visitor for him."

But Martin needed no messenger. He stepped out almost immediately from one of the cluster of several huts that made up the domicile. Indeed, from every hut poured a surprisingly large number of folk, young and old. When all were accounted for, I found that Martin evidently was responsible for a wife, seven children, some cousins, and a number of other relatives. It was beautiful to witness how thrilled everybody was to have the kindly prelate of their own race pay them a call.

"Welcome, Bishop! Welcome, Fathers!" cried Josefina, Martin's wife, who was dressed in the gay cotton robe of the Baganda.

She directed us into the small, unadorned front room of one of the huts, which evidently was Martin's parlor. With the poise and grace of a queen, she brought chairs. The bishop took one chair and lifted a young tot to his knee; Martin had another chair; Father Bordenet, a third; I, a fourth; and Josefina, the fifth. The room was crowded. Youngsters filled the center of the floor, and the other women folk craned through every doorway.

"I must explain to you," the bishop said to me, "that fifteen minutes ago these children came from school wearing good clothes that made them look quite prim and neat. Then the first thing they did was to hang the clothes carefully on hooks for tomorrow. After that, they donned these tattered play rags. All these families make the school clothes last by hanging them carefully on the hooks after school hours."

"If we didn't," said Martin with a rueful smile, "there'd be no shillings to buy food!"

We had a happy visit with this charming family, the bishop carrying the conversation since naturally it was all in Luganda. His Excellency interpreted for me the choicer bits of the gay chatter. Then the women withdrew, the youngsters ran away, and Martin and I entered into our subject, the bishop assisting as translator.

"May I ask, Martin," I queried, "what is your precise position?"

"I am an assistant agricultural agent in the Masaka county," Martin replied.

"Martin and his brothers are not among the lazy folk I spoke of a few moments ago," interposed Bishop Kiwanuka. "He has one brother who is an assistant inspector of police, another who is an auditor, and a third who is a middle-school teacher."

"Do many people operate their own farms, Martin?"

"Father, Buganda is a land of family-sized homesteads, or *shambas* as we call them, most of them less than ten acres. As you go along any road, you see these small holdings, with their neatly hoed patches of coffee, cotton, and sweet potatoes. Each holding has its clump of plantain trees, which produce our cooking banana. All this land belongs to us Africans. Sale of it to non-Africans is not permitted."

"But surely not everybody owns his own land," I said.

"True. The workers of the land are not always the owners, but they are not serfs, either. For the most part, their shambas are on rented land. The big chiefs who own much of the land are our Baganda aristocracy. Many of them own the fine homes you pass, with retinues of servants. The motor cars that pass you on the highway are theirs. The dignified women in Kampala and our provincial towns are the wives of our rich.

"We are envious of those people, but we are proud of them as well, because they are our own. 'See,' we say to the white men from afar, 'our great men have handsomely dressed wives just as you have!' "

"Bravo, Martin!" I responded with a laugh. "You talk just as an assistant agricultural agent would talk in Kansas or Iowa, in my country."

Later I learned that the Baganda aristocracy of which Martin spoke represents definitely a great factor in Uganda. An illustration of this is the case of Leonard Bassude, a young member of the national legislative council. Leonard was educated in Uganda Catholic schools and went to a Catholic college in Ceylon, as is the custom for a number of the sons of rich Africans. With money from his family, he has developed a coffee plantation of some hundred acres along the highway between Masaka and Kampala. Besides being prominent in politics, young Mr. Bassude is a member of the coffee growers' association, which markets about one-fourth of Uganda's coffee production. He drives a good car, has a home that any American would like to own, produces his own electricity, and manages an income of about $25,000 a year from the profits of his enterprises.

Mr. Bassude is proof positive that Africans can make their own way. The Africa of naked savages and wild tribal rites is steadily disappearing. Men like Bassude talk about Maritain and Bergson, trends in modern music, tomorrow's political problems. Perhaps for many, the new culture is as yet but a veneer. The old ways go slowly. As one modern black man said, "It takes time to get things out of the blood."

"What is your principal crop here in the neighborhood of Masaka?" I asked Martin.

"Coffee," he replied. "In Buganda as a whole, cotton had been the great means of livelihood for half a century. The railroad to Mombasa was finished over fifty years ago, and immediately the British made plans for things to sell. They discovered how good our soil was for cotton; since then, we have exported as much as 400,000 bales in a year. But Kenya taught us the value of the coffee plant. Here in Buganda we grow what is called 'hard' coffee or *robusta* coffee. Now we are rivals of Kenya in the coffee business. At other places in Uganda, they grow the mild or *arabica* coffee."

"Does coffee growing require much work?"

"Quite the contrary!" replied Martin. "*Robusta* is a perfect crop for the lazy farmer. The trees need no pruning or special care other than mulching. The coffee berry requires no preparation other than being left out in the sun. The crop has no enemies other than a single borer worm. The mild, enervating climate of this warm, moist, easy country makes the fertility almost ooze up out of the ground. The trees raise to a great height, with many straggling stems that mean lots of berries."

"What is the principal sustenance crop, Martin?"

"It is the cooking banana. Bananas and coffee—coffee and bananas—that is the pattern around here. The Muganda lives from the cradle to the grave on *matoki,* boiled banana mush. And there is a banana beer that he loves to drink."

"What is the Muganda peasant's choicest dainty in the line of food, Martin?"

"Have you noticed along the paths the towering cones of red clay, covered with twigs? Those cones, as you know, house the white ants. After the rain, the winged ants rise in clouds from the ground. The Muganda is ready for them with his sacking, which he throws over them. He collects them by the quart, and then he takes them home and fries them in fat. We have an old proverb that says, 'A true friend is a man who will even share his fried ants with you.' "

"But this all sounds quite wonderful, Martin," I said. "Where are your problems?"

Martin's face clouded. "There are very serious problems here, Father, and the sad fact is that some are completely of our own making."

"Explain yourself."

"Well, note these various points. First, we have a soil so fertile that plants almost grow up under our feet and trip us. Secondly, we have a 50-inch rainfall that never fails. Thirdly, we have a sweet, good sun that warms the earth and never scorches it. In spite of all these advantages, the soil of Buganda will fail us if we do not cease our careless ways."

"How do you know this?"

"The official word of the agricultural officer, which word we agents are carrying to every farmer in Buganda, warns that Buganda's crops threaten to decline faster than all our lessons in better farming are helping. I mentioned that one year we produced more than 400,000 bales of cotton. It is true that the world market is not always good, but our acreage has risen steadily. Yet many farmers secure less and less per farm acre."

"Why?"

"It is not entirely because our farmers are careless. It is because the owners of the land don't have the courage to treat the land right. It is because they think they need money so badly, that they won't take a present loss to rest the land in order to make a future gain. They let out plots of land so small that the individual farmer pushes his lot hard and is squeezing it to death. The Government's great experimental station at Kawanda has worked out wonderful information about handling tropical soils, and that information is valued all over the world. But nobody can really force the Muganda to use this information, and so in many instances his soil spoils right before his eyes."

"Isn't anybody at all doing the right thing?"

"Oh, yes; don't misunderstand. Many are practicing mixed farming, strip-cropping, and so forth. But too many are not."

"Is this abuse of the soil the only cause for worry?"

"No. Another grave problem is not the farmer's fault, but needs a great deal of help from the farmer to fight it properly. This is the constant threat of the tsetse fly and the killing of our cattle."

"Is Uganda in the tsetse-fly zone?"

"About a third of the country is regarded so. The Government must do much of the fighting. But at the moment we are pushing the British to get out! This means that our Buganda Government officers, up to now easy-going and unscientific, must become skillful and disciplined and must spend big sums of money to find good methods and then to apply them."

"You don't sound very hopeful."

"We need Buganda leaders. We need to give our farmers confidence in the leaders. This is one reason why people like Bishop Kiwanuka and his priests are very important. The people trust them. They will listen to them. The priests do not need to be farm experts, but they need to know enough to encourage their people to believe and obey the Buganda farm experts, who must be this province's leaders soon."

Chapter 2

IN THE SPAN OF A LIFE

I HEARD THE SOUND a drum as Bishop Kiwanuka and I approached Kitovu, the parish at which His Excellency maintains his residence. "We shall be just in time for evening Benediction," remarked His Excellency.

When we arrived, there by the side of the church I saw the mounted drum. It was quite novel to find a youngster happily engaged signaling the prayer call on that distinctively African substitute for a tower bell. As we entered the church, school children by hundreds, and a goodly number of men and women from the neighborhood, were making their way into the well-built edifice—a typical construction of the White Fathers, from whom Bishop Kiwanuka inherited his Diocese of Masaka. When we knelt in the sanctuary, we heard the patter of many bare feet in the aisles, making music like a running stream. The congregational singing was melodious; the praying was hearty.

That evening at supper, Father Bordenet and I were the only white faces at a spacious table about which sat eight Baganda clergymen. Their topics of conversation matched well those which a similar gathering of clergymen might discuss in a large rectory of London or Munich or Milan or New York. There were reported bits on happenings about the parish; there were items of good news and bad, from Kampala and other spots in Africa and overseas.

"Queen Elizabeth is coming for the dedication of the hydroelectric dam at Owen Falls," one priest remarked.

"That means we'll soon be flooded with electricity," someone else commented. "It means factories, and factory workers."

"Which means that they'll spoil the simple pastoral life of our people," said another.

"But our people need a few of the right kinds of factories for

269

employment," replied the first speaker. "The way the population is growing, many men will soon find no land for farming."

The conversation continued for a brief period after the meal. Then at a signal, we went to the chapel for night prayers. In the still of the evening, we returned to the residence.

"How proud Archbishop Streicher must have been to see your diocese carrying on during his last days," I remarked to Bishop Kiwanuka before we parted for the night. "How proud he must have been of you, Your Excellency!"

"You could not have said anything more gracious," replied this Muganda prelate very warmly and simply. "Archbishop Streicher still lives in every corner of this diocese; he is still loved by every man, woman, and child here. Besides all he did for Uganda, it was he, you know, who opened the first mission here in Masaka."

"It is in places like Masaka," said one of the priests, "that we really know how Buganda has grown in the last seventy-five years. Most people who come to Uganda give all their time to Kampala, the capital. But in the rural areas, is the real heart of the country. In all his life here, Archbishop Streicher kept his eyes on us; his heart was with us."

Thus the pulse of Masaka beats in unison with the pulse of every other community and countryside over the world. Everywhere there is the same hunger to be thought of, to be recognized, to be respected, to be remembered.

Cardinal Hinsley, who was Apostolic Delegate to British Africa when I visited the continent a score of years ago, characterized Archbishop Streicher as one of the truly eminent figures among the Church's leaders on the Dark Continent. Like most great men, he was very simple and gracious. Spare and small of build, he gave a first impression of being physically frail. Instead, he had both physical and moral toughness. He had spiritual depth and vision. He was severe with himself and called upon his missionaries to place great emphasis on self-discipline. Yet he exercised great kindliness toward every individual, whether weak or strong. His career was marked by unusual far-sightedness in resolving the many spiritual problems of Uganda.

When Archbishop Streicher died, in 1952, he was eighty-nine years old. Thus he had been born about the time when Speke was reporting to London on those remarkable people of Uganda. Young Father Henry Streicher sailed from Marseilles on July 12, 1890; and on November 25—four and a half months later—he got his first glimpse of Lake Victoria.

"When from the summit of Mount Scopus the pilgrim gets his first view of Jerusalem," the new arrival wrote lyrically at the time, "he dismounts, kneels, kisses the ground, and intones the *Lauda Jerusalem*. A similar sentiment possessed us. Neither our knees nor our lips touched the ground, but at sight of the Great Blue Lake, a cry of joy burst from us, a cry that Heaven itself must have heard, for it was a cry of gratitude and of Godly love."

Henry M. Stanley gets credit for the extraordinary fashion in which missionary work was begun in Uganda. A letter of his in the London *Daily Telegraph* spoke of the "enlightened reception by King Mutesa of the Gospel truths" that Stanley had imparted to the Buganda ruler. Stanley was badly mistaken as to the effectiveness of his words on the King.[1] But there was no mistake about the effect of his report in Europe. An enthusiastic band of six Anglican missionaries journeyed over Arab caravan routes through hundreds of miles of Tanganyika—a region unoccupied by missionaries at that time except along the coast—and reached the court of King Mutesa in 1877.

Cardinal Lavigerie also was impressed by the extraordinary reports from Uganda. His first band of White Fathers journeyed the same long route and were received by Mutesa in 1878.

Both Protestant and Catholic missionaries made only modest headway during the early years. First fruits of the White Fathers' work were four royal pages at the court of Mutesa, who were baptized in 1880. Mutesa died in 1884 and was succeeded by eighteen-year-old Mwanga, who showed hostility to the Christian strangers from the beginning. In October of 1885, King Mwanga murdered Bishop James Hannington, of the Anglicans. A month later, he ordered the beheading of Joseph Mukasa, chief chamberlain of the court and a Catholic, who had remonstrated with the King for killing Bishop Hannington.

The young Mwanga was addicted to unnatural vice, a practice not common in Uganda but taught the royal youth by Arab debauchees. Most of the court pages, sons of the best families in Buganda, had become Catholics, and they refused all of Mwanga's improper advances. King Mwanga became infuriated. A climax was reached when he sent for a young page named Mwafu, who told the King he was studying to be a Christian, and would obey the Christian tenets.

"Who is teaching you?"

"Denis Sebuggwawo."

"Call Denis!" cried Mwanga. When Denis entered the room, the angry King thrust a spear through his throat.

The Christian pages then knew that trouble was approaching for them. Charles Lwanga, who had succeeded Joseph Mukasa as chief chamberlain and was the Christian leader among the pages, that night secretly baptized four youngsters who were catechumens. Early the next morning, all the pages of the court were drawn up before the King. He ordered the Christians to step forward. Led by Lwanga and Kizito, the oldest and the youngest, fifteen pages did so. They were joined by two others under arrest, and two Christian soldiers. Mwanga asked the group if they intended to remain Christian.

"Till death!" came the response of all.

"Then put them to death!"

The members of the little band were bound, and then led thirty-seven miles to Namugongo—where a memorial chapel stands today. "The heroic little band passed within a few feet of me," wrote Father Lourdel, the superior of the mission. "Little Kizito was laughing and chattering . . . I was so overcome that I had to support myself against the palisade."

On June 3, 1886, each confessor of the Faith was stripped, bound, wrapped in a mat of reed, and thrown as a living faggot into the huge execution pyre. Only one was not alive when fed to the flames; he was Mbaga, son of the chief executioner. His father had begged Mbaga frantically to renounce Christianity and be spared, but the boy had refused. "Break his neck!" ordered the father, as the guards bound his son. Thus the youngster was cheated of the burning.

Uganda was still under the spell of the valorous witness of the King's pages, when Father Streicher arrived four years later. Indeed, the holocaust is rated, by many white men and black, as the greatest religious event in modern Africa. Preachers in their pulpits, teachers in their classes, mothers to the children at their knees in huts throughout the continent, relate the story of those heroic African youths who did not falter. Even the cynics who call religion a delusion, recognize the moral power of this deed of constancy.[2]

Few countries in the world have had a Christian religious history so weird as that of Uganda during its early decades. The story includes bitter wars, which saw Catholics drawn in on one side and Protestants on the other. Years later Governor Bernard Bourdillon conferred on Archbishop Streicher the order of Commander of the British Empire in recognition of the prelate's part in trying to assuage the sufferings in the strife.

Father Streicher was consecrated a bishop in 1897. He bought his episcopal ring from an Indian trinket huckster in Mwanza. Father Izidore Bazin of the White Fathers, who for years has written brilliantly of events in Uganda, singles out six key points of policy that made Archbishop Streicher's leadership outstanding.[3]

1—Catechists. In the beginning, it was the Catholic chiefs who were the great promoters of the Faith. "I myself," says Father Bazin, "saw whole villages led to the missionary, from tottering old men and women to infants nestled at their mothers' breasts. 'They all want to pray; give them enrollment medals!' the chief would cry. We were exhausted from baptizing."

But of course this manner of procedure could go on only in early pioneer days. By 1902, Bishop Streicher had directed that training, discipline, and spiritual life must be built up before baptism. A four-year religious course was instituted, and a carefully conducted school for religious teachers was established. Thus in 1897 there were 243 catechists; in 1902, there were 997; in 1933, there were 2,097. Archbishop Streicher's first notable achievement was the building up of this army of disciplined lay workers.

2—The Bannabikira. Bishop Streicher soon discovered among many Baganda women, who though without book learning, had already become profoundly Christian, an innate power of forgetfulness of self, tact, delicacy, unusual understanding, and a strong sense of duty. To a group of White Sisters led by a gifted religious from Holland, Mother Mechtilde, the bishop said, "Make religious teachers of these women and—who knows?—perhaps religious."

The Bannabikira, the community of African Sisters that grew out of this directive, is probably the first in Africa in date of foundation (1908) and, since today it counts almost four hundred members, the first in size among such groups. Many who know the vigorous spirit of simple austerity that Mother Mechtilde bequeathed to the community, and the high incidence of college degrees among its members, place it among the first in quality in all Africa. It is now completely self-governing.

3—Reparation for Sin. In beautiful Entebbe, by Lake Victoria, Bishop Streicher established in 1913 a convent of enclosed contemplatives, the Sisters of Mary Reparatrix. The bishop lived in a land and in a day that vibrated with spiritual triumph, but he sought to deepen his people in holiness by emphasizing the ravages of sin. "Now," he declared when these Sisters arrived, "night and day, prayers and mortifications mount to Heaven in reparation for the sins of Buganda."

Baganda young women understood the need so well that today a carefully trained body of some fifty choice daughters of Africa are members of an Institute of African Sisters of Reparation, independent successors on African soil to the original French foundation. Throughout the continent no other institution with the same objective approaches it in size and development. But thoughtful men everywhere have long recognized the aptitude of the Africans for deep spirituality.

4—The Press. Bishop Streicher played a distinctive role in building the press in Uganda. In 1911, he founded *Munno,* the first periodical in the country, a vernacular newspaper that today has a circulation of 9,000. Modest though this figure is, it approaches that of the top independent paper of the country, *Matalisi,* which each week prints 12,500 copies. Today Uganda has fourteen newspapers, twelve of them in the vernacular, nine printed in or near Kampala.

5—The Bannakaroli. Catholic schools were increasing, and lay teachers were needed by thousands. But Bishop Streicher wanted an elite of religious men dedicated to this work. He found in Father Richard the proper man to build up a community of African teaching Brothers, the Bannakaroli, who today number eighty.

6—Baganda Clergy. The White Fathers knew very early that they had in the Baganda a people who could provide their own clergy. One of the Archbishop's tasks, as a young priest under Bishop Hirth, was to open a preparatory seminary in 1893. In 1913, the first two Baganda priests were ordained.

"They represented the sole survivors," the Archbishop told me when I visited him, "of the 280 candidates whom we sought to form in the course of twenty years." African priests in Uganda today number 160.

Emotions of joy indescribable marked the great event of ordination, which took place at Villa Maria. Villa Maria is the ecclesiastical village, with flowering hedges to mark its avenues, that resembles Roma, the Oblate center in Basutoland. It lies within Bishop Kiwanuka's Diocese of Masaka and is the principal center of the White Fathers in Uganda.

Bishop Streicher reached in the ceremony the point where the ordaining prelate chants, *"Ut hos electos benedicere digneris"*—"Deign Thou, O Lord, to bless these elect ones." The tension was too great for the dear man; his voice broke and tears of happiness poured down his cheeks.

The two newly ordained, Fathers Basilio Lumu and Victoro Mukasa, went from church to church at the principal mission centers in a festive pageant participated in by the populace with delirious enthusiasm. "I was present when they visited Mitala Maria," recalls Father Bazin. "One sang the High Mass and the other preached. The young preacher began with the greatness of God, described the prodigies of His creation, the major events of history. 'And now, my brethren,' he concluded, 'admire the greatest of all God's prodigies, that He has raised up a Muganda to His divine priesthood.'

"Those words, so humbly spoken, stirred the Baganda to the depths. 'It was tremendous!' they said afterwards. 'We had to press our hands to our mouths, to keep from shouting and clapping in wild applause.' "

In 1932 the Archbishop, already seventy years old, received permission from the Holy See to resign and resume the work of a missionary of the line at the outlying post of Ibanda in western Uganda. He had still another satisfaction awaiting him. He had spoken to me of it as a possibility, when I visited him.

"If we can supply from our ranks such officers as the Chief Justice of the country, there is no reason why one of the more gifted among the Baganda clergy cannot govern as a bishop," he had said.

In 1939 the Holy See took this last step. A telegram from Rome arrived one day at the major seminary of Katigondo addressed to one of the professors, Father Joseph Kiwanuka. After a distinguished record as a seminarian at Katigondo, Father Kiwanuka had spent four years in Rome in the study of canon law and had returned to Uganda with a doctorate. On reading the telegram, he reacted like a man visited by tragedy: he reached for a chair, sat down, and wept.

"What is it, Father?" a passing confrere asked in alarm.

Silently the young priest handed the telegram to the inquirer. East Africa was to have its first African bishop of the black race. Archbishop Streicher was co-consecrator in Rome with Pope Pius XII. Afterwards he returned and resided in Masaka. There, while he worked among the lowly as a simple priest, he witnessed in Bishop Kiwanuka's successful disposition of diocesan affairs the realization of his fondest dream.

In the march of events during the past three quarters of a century, the Mill Hill missionaries, whose motherhouse is in the suburbs of London, have shared in the sufferings and the triumphs of the White Fathers and today are responsible for a third of the Catholic body in Uganda. The Missionaries of Verona have worked for three quarters of a century along the Nile in the Sudan. In 1910, they moved over the border into Uganda. With headquarters and a beautiful cathedral at Gulu, they have a flock, comprised principally of tribes close to the southern Sudan, that represents a fifth of Uganda's total of 1,300,000 Catholics.

The marvel is that this extraordinary achievement in Christian penetration has taken place practically all within the lifetime, long life though it was, of a single apostolic leader. Still more dramatic, however, is the fact that pioneers of Uganda, who reached the shores of Lake Victoria but a few years after Archbishop Streicher, talk openly today not so much of the times of their arrival, but of the future day, not far distant, when the foreign worker in Uganda will terminate his role of responsible administrator of the Church and will, not necessarily leave the country, but turn over to the Africans the direction of this portion of the kingdom of God on African soil.

Douglas Hyde flew out from London to the international congress of Catholic lay leaders, held in Uganda in December of 1953. One morning Mr. Hyde stood gazing at the beautiful, rose-brick seminary at Kisubi near Kampala, the seat of the congress. Archbishop Cabana, of Kampala, joined him and likewise gazed admiringly at the structure.

"It was built entirely by the Africans," His Excellency said proudly. "The builder himself was a black man who learned his trade in our own technical school. It is an all-African affair."

Then the Archbishop added significantly, with equal pride though perhaps just a little wistfully: "And long before its life is finished—the life of buildings here in the tropics is short—it will have passed over to the Africans, and we missionaries shall have gone back home. The non-Christian Africans now know this, too. They are coming to realize that we are genuinely here for their sakes, building for them, and only concerned to help them materially and spiritually."

Chapter 3
———————

FIVE LITTLE WOMEN

FIVE LITTLE WOMEN whom I met at Nyenga, in eastern Uganda, I remember with sentiments of deeper sympathy than I experienced toward anyone else in Africa. Their names were Bertha, Modesta, Teresa, Perpetua, Francesca. They were lepers. They were, furthermore, either professed Sisters or candidates in preparation for the religious life, who had been transferred to a leprosarium after the dread disease had been discovered in them.

Father Paul Bordenet and I had driven to Owen Falls, just below the headwaters of the Nile. There we saw that huge dam, almost half a mile wide, which, as the Department of Information hand-out says, will generate enough power through the hydroelectric plant to equal "the entire electricity requirements of Britain before the Second World War."

Father Paul and I ate a late lunch in a grove of eucalyptus trees, near the fifth hole of the Jinja Golf Course. It was an enchanting spot on the bank of Ripon Falls. During our long jaunt through East Africa, we carried food in the truck and thus spared ourselves the search for kind friends or dubious eating places. That day we used *pate de foie gras* as a sandwich spread, and drank carbonated water that had survived a thousand miles of jolting.

"This golf course has a ground rule found nowhere else outside East Africa," remarked Father Paul.

"What's that?" I asked.

"If your ball falls into a hippo's footprint, you can move the ball without penalty."

Quite a reasonable rule for a neighborhood that is densely inhabited by those rather amiable four-ton beasts. Particularly at night the hippopotamuses come up out of the lake and wander over the golf course.

Africa counts many fine Christian leaders. Ewald Munseri, of Bukoba, is the able publisher of the first independent newspaper in Tanganyika.

Father John Schiff of New York City (above) holds his Luo boys under the spell of his harmonica. Below, Bishop Laurean Rugambwa talks to Monsignor Grondin the day he ordained Maryknoll's first African priest at Musoma.

Tanganyika's traditionally most valuable crop is sisal, a vegetable fiber important on the world market for making rope and other products.

In northern Uganda and Kenya are Nilotic peoples, the main body of whom now falls under control of Moslem Egypt as Britain withdraws from the Sudan. This is a typical Shilluk village.

Masai, most dreaded tribe of old East Africa, dance the "lion grunt,"
awe-inspiring routine executed in perfect time to the shuffling of feet.

Yesterday's warrior today sits at a table; his children eat meal mash
from tin plates. What prospect replaces the ancient thrill of battle?

Herds of four-ton hippos, mighty elephants, millions of running game require acreage. Africa will soon begrudge it to them. Mr. Hippo, beware!

The ancient culture of Arabia and the Persian Gulf once prevailed along East Africa's coast. This rich doorway still stands in lovely Zanzibar.

From this idyllic scene we drove to Nyenga and the five forlorn little women, but with no foreknowledge that we were to meet them. Years ago I visited Nkokonjeru, the Mill Hill station where Mother Kevin maintained her wonderfully interesting headquarters for her community of European Franciscan Sisters. I had been following the accomplishments of that dynamic little woman ever since. The work of the community in its care of the lepers has been outstanding. Father Bordenet and I intended to visit their leper settlement at Buluba, which houses 600 in-patients, or the St. Francis Leper Camp at Nyenga, which is smaller. Finally we picked Nyenga because I had been asked to visit Mother Kevin's first American candidate, Sister Peter Mary; that religious had served the lepers for twelve years at Buluba, but for the past two years had been pioneering at Nyenga.

Many things about leprosy puzzle the doctors, who still feel that they are only at an early stage in their researches. One unsolved mystery is why Uganda should have the highest percentual incidence of leprosy in all Africa. Leprosy in the world today counts by conservative estimate approximately 4,500,000 victims, and thirty per cent, or about 1,350,000 are in Africa.[1] Leprosy is found in almost every country of the continent, but in highest frequency in warm, humid areas of dense population where overcrowding gives prolonged contact with infected human carriers. East Africa has over 250,000 cases, of which 80,000 are in Uganda—62 cases to every 1,000 inhabitants.

We left the main highway and drove through rolling country, past the Mill Hill preparatory seminary, where I had been a guest of Father Wheatley some years ago. We found Nyenga mission bright with flower gardens and bursting with life, for the school children were at play. One of Mother Kevin's African community, the Little Sisters of St. Francis, greeted us with a toothsome smile and directed us to the leper settlement.

"You are not very isolated here, Mother," I said to the superior.

"There would be no great sense in trying to be!" she replied. "We have 340 in-patients, who are the most severe cases; but in the hills about us, are some two thousand others, who come in for treatment as regularly as we can persuade them to, and who mingle with their relatives and friends with only half-hearted efforts at segregation."

"Is that good?"

"It's dreadfully bad! But if we have seventy or eighty thousand

lepers in Uganda, thousands in Kenya, and probably 100,000 in Tanganyika, how conceivably could the Government segregate them so completely that the disease could die out through lack of new victims?
Happily, since 1945 we have the new wonder drugs. We don't know,
frankly, how effective they are to prove, but by present prospects, we
shall have gained a victory over leprosy in twenty-five or thirty years."

"Under the present living conditions, I should think that literally
millions would become infected," I remarked.

"No. Because, contrary to popular opinion, leprosy is not highly
infectious. It is believed that not more than one-third of the victims
can pass the disease to others. Nevertheless, segregation is important.
It is sad to note that children under ten are particularly susceptible."

Doctor R. G. Cochrane, now Medical Secretary of the British Empire Leprosy Relief Association (BELRA), a fine Christian gentleman
who has devoted his life to leprosy work in India, insists, I find, on a
campaign of protection for children. Leprosy in England disappeared,
he says, because strict segregation kept the disease from the children.[2]

"We are hoping to have a word with your American, Sister Peter
Mary," I said.

"That you will," Mother assured us, "but the lady doctor, Doctor
Wanda Blemska, is here—she comes for three days, every two weeks—
and Sister Peter Mary is deeply involved organizing her patients for
their tests. We'll go down to the clinic and see her there."

We went out through the convent garden, garnished with small
flower beds along the gravel paths. "Our lepers tend the flowers," explained one of the Sisters. "Some are quite mystified because we are
fussy about perfectly useless plants that can't be eaten, but they are
glad to do whatever we ask them. We keep as many as possible of our
in-patients at work, since it is important for their morale. They tend
the fields or do other chores, some hours each day."

"This seems to be the current vogue everywhere in Africa now,"
I remarked. "The old-fashioned asylum-prisons are disappearing."

After we had walked about a quarter mile, an interesting sight
opened to our view. Before us stretched some acres in the wide valley
that contained the camp. Arranged in rows on either side, were over
fifty circular huts of standard, local construction. The space between
was a broad parade, in the center of which stood the clinic—a crude

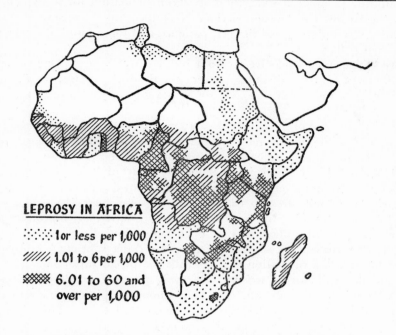

LEPROSY IN AFRICA
∴∴ 1 or less per 1,000
///// 1.01 to 6 per 1,000
※※※ 6.01 to 60 and
over per 1,000

INCIDENCE OF LEPROSY IN AFRICA

Approximately 1,500,000 of the estimated 4,500,000 cases of leprosy in the world are found in Africa. Almost 400 leprosaria, governmental or missionary, are operated on the continent, though they care for only a small percentage of the sufferers. The highest rates of infection in Africa occur in warm and humid places of dense population. Africans, while very susceptible to the disease, seem prone to develop a milder form. Nigeria is credited with the highest number of lepers on the continent— 400,000. French West Africa and the Belgian Congo have each some 200,000. The worst-off country percentually is Uganda, with more than 60 victims per thousand inhabitants.

building in modern style, the only recommendation for it, evidently, being its low cost of construction. Near the clinic were several small dormitory buildings for the bed patients, and those buildings likewise lacked frills.

"The in-patients live six to a hut," said Mother. "One of each six serves as group corporal. Except for the bed patients, we attempt to keep living conditions as near as possible to the normal ways of home."

At one end of the clinic, we saw a sprawling crowd of a hundred or so patients, and discovered on closer examination that they constituted a zigzagging queue that was moving toward a door. We went among them, and I was struck immediately by a fact that is not at all surprising. Almost everywhere in Africa, a crowd means good nature, expressing itself often to the point of boisterousness. In that crowd of patients, however, high-voiced chattiness, hilarity, mischievous repartee were absent. There was no open expression of woe, even in the way of sorrowful faces. But there were a quiet sobriety, an absence of buoyancy, a suggestion that beneath the placid surface was a common denominator of tension. By every popular standard, this was quite as we might expect. We were among people of a race that is inured to adversity, but theirs was a special adversity. Those people were constantly aware that they were in the grip of extreme misfortune—they were lepers.

Then we went through the door and found a very capable and highly diligent American religious carrying on singlemindedly a most complicated technical task under very primitive conditions. Sister Peter Mary is the laboratory technician of St. Francis Leper Camp; she is the only trained resident operator in this project that seeks to serve almost 2,500 lepers.

I admired the Sister from the moment we met her. She was happy to see us and to have a brief contact with home, but it was abundantly evident that she was a completely integrated devotee of the task at hand. She was a consecrated woman in every sense of the term.

"Don't let us interfere," I said as we entered. "We only want to watch you at work."

"These people are not in a hurry," the technician replied with a smile, as she adjusted the garment of the woman she was examining. "Doctor Blemska is in the front of the building and has a good supply of prepared patients to keep her busy. I'm delighted that you are able to come here and see my laboratory! I want to show you everything." Father Bordenet and I will not soon forget what we saw.

"Conditions have changed so enormously," Sister Peter Mary began. "What a revolution we have witnessed in this world of leprosy since I arrived in Africa fourteen years ago! It was wretchedly trying each day when, from morning till evening, we were occupied with administering those painful injections of chaulmoogra oil. My heart used to bleed for the poor creatures. The specific gravity of chaulmoogra is such that the dosage caused aches and pains that persisted for days."

"Did chaulmoogra oil really cure?" I asked.

"Some fifty per cent of our early infective cases could be rendered free from infection in about two years. But in the advanced cases, all chaulmoogra could do was slow down the progress of the disease. As time passed, we experienced increasing disappointment at the number of persons supposedly cured who came back as relapses."

"How long ago did workers among the lepers—workers like yourself—begin to get excited about the new wonder drugs?"

"I should say that it was toward the end of the Second World War. We had long heard reports of various more effective therapeutic remedies known as sulphones, but our tendency was to be skeptical of them. At Carville, Louisiana, where the Sisters of Charity are in charge of the nursing, the U.S. Public Health Service tried out promin and after a couple of years published reports of outstanding success against even severe forms of the disease. Doctor Muir at the Government leprosy hospital in Trinidad, in the British West Indies, was successful with diasone. Workers in British Guiana and in India found sulphetrone effective. Then came DDS,—the abbreviation for a long medical term."

"Did you procure those new remedies as soon as you heard of them?"

"No, not in proper quantities to do an effective job. The reason was that in the beginning they were hopelessly expensive. Today, the battle for low-price production has been won in great part; but in the case of a settlement like ours, that must operate on a shoestring, even a greatly reduced price may still be too high in relation to the money on hand. However, we are using a number of these remedies, with

DDS most in vogue at present. The sulphones have changed the whole face of things so far as our work is concerned."

"Should you say that the specialists in leprosy feel that they've broken through the ignorance barrier and have the major problems licked?"

"Not at all! The fact is, the researchers feel that they are as yet only at the threshold of a true understanding of the disease. In the recent years, they have been concentrating on drugs to kill the bacillus, rather than studying the disease itself."

"What happens next?"

"Research and more research! They tell us that there are over a thousand Sisters like myself plodding away with lepers, giving them the best remedies that we can find.[3] There are an immense number of Protestant workers and hundreds of others, serving in leper asylums around the world. But even now with all our progress, there are still so many unanswered questions that at times we are tempted to feel like squirrels on a wheel, furiously spinning out our days and, so far as really solving anything is concerned, getting nowhere."

"Some among you have made really great contributions. You certainly can be proud of a co-worker like Sister Marie Suzanne of Makogai."

Sister Marie Suzanne, I recalled, had begun work in the Fiji Islands, in the heart of the Pacific, much as Sister Peter Mary was beginning at Nyenga. At Makogai Sister Marie Suzanne and a companion member of the Missionary Sisters of the Society of Mary opened a small leprosarium for twenty patients. Twenty-five years later, when she was called home to France, her leper hospital had expanded to care for 900 persons and was among the largest and best equipped in the world. While in the Fiji Islands, Sister Marie Suzanne had built a small laboratory and made an intensive study of the disease. In France she continued her researches at St. Louis Hospital and Pasteur Institute. Then the Society for the Propagation of the Faith set up a laboratory for her at Lyons, attached to a small hospital for lepers.

One of the patients at Lyons was Father Chaurire, who had contracted leprosy in the mission field. He asked the Sister to use him as a guinea pig in her experiments. Accepting the priest's offer, Sister Marie Suzanne did two things. From the diseased body of the veteran missionary, she took infected skin and discovered a new germ, now named by science *Mycobacterium Marianum,* which has been developed into a vaccine. Secondly, she so successfully treated Father Chaurire with the new sulphone remedies that the priest completely recovered his health and was able to return to his mission field.

Sister Marie Suzanne's vaccine was tested at the Nden Leprosarium in French Cameroun, by Doctor Blanc and Nurse Prost. They reported as follows: "Marianum vaccine has produced Mitsuda positive reactions in 100 per cent of the cases of healthy children. Among lepers, the change from Mitsuda negative to positive was verified in 83 per cent of the cases."

Sister Marie Suzanne continues her researches. Perhaps some day we shall read of the immunization by vaccination of all the children in the hills about Nyenga, where children's lives are now in jeopardy through the presence of almost 2,500 lepers in their neighborhood.

"I'm afraid," commented Sister Peter Mary, "that the daily work here is too completely all-absorbing, for me personally ever to find time for research. I hope, however, that the people at home know how all-important it is to engage the finest minds in science to fight leprosy wherever it may be found."

"How do you handle a typical leper who comes to you, Sister?"

"First there are tests that are prepared for the next visit of the doctor. In each case, there is some simple medication that can begin immediately. Then there is the opening of the case history for each. We photograph each patient on arrival and then keep a photographic record of the case up to the day when, please God, we can dismiss him or her as cured."

"You say 'we.' Who does the photography?"

Sister Peter Mary laughed. "It was the editorial 'we.' All these photographic entries are part of my day's work."

During the conversation, Father Bordenet and I had been eyeing the cases heavy with blood specimens, and also the bulky card files. Then we saw the voluminous records with the long series of photographs. A few of the photographic series—some of the most dramatic in their evidence of the effects of the sulphones—were posted on the laboratory wall and revealed the metamorphosis that certain particularly wretched-looking creatures experienced within periods of six months to a year.

"Let me show you my photographic darkroom and apparatus," volunteered Sister Peter Mary.

"Isn't it hot working here?" I asked as we entered the suffocating cubbyhole.

"Very much so! I spent some days building those vents in the roof, but then had to close them again because the light spoiled my negatives."

"Do these photographic records of cleared-up skin signify that the patient is ready to go home?"

"No; though unfortunately, for most of our patients, the cleared-up skin is the sole criterion. As soon as that stage is reached, the men in particular make a break for freedom. A year or two later, many return to us, worse-off than ever. For each cleared-up case that can be persuaded to remain here, the doctor gives tests every three weeks; afterwards, if there has been a satisfactory period of negative reports, the patient is given a fond farewell. Many of us believe that there should be a law requiring patients to remain segregated for a period of, say, two years after they are declared negative; and that law should be in effect until we know more about the disease."

"Are there still some cases that do not react to medication?"

"Yes. Let us take a moment and go over to a few huts where we'll see some of the really advanced cases."

We crossed the parade, Sister Peter Mary saluting the passers-by along the way. The Baganda greeting is a very beautiful one, though unusually complex, and there was a lovely pathos in its soft and slightly sad lilt as the lepers made the exchange with the sister. Each time both parties made a momentary halt and slight bow.

"Even though we meet a dozen times a day, we must repeat most faithfully that little litany," Sister explained. "I must confess," she added with a rueful smile, "that as an impatient American I find it trying at times, in the midst of heavy work, to go through the formality. It is a fine test for one of my temperament to adapt my ways to the leisurely pace of these people."

We entered the huts of some of the graver cases and found men and women with flesh lesions that no longer would heal, and with putrefaction that produced a repellent stench.

"This advanced state of the disease is due to neglect or to the attempt to hide its existence. In days gone by, there was no hope of cure; hence, on discovering that they were victims, people sought madly to fight off a revelation of their dread condition. With the disease so common, there is a general knowledge throughout the countryside of tricks of concealment, which can be practiced for a while. There is a local plant that provides a black juice that can be painted over the initial sores quite effectively. Finally when it is too late, the poor creatures are dragged into us by their relatives."

"The reports of the new medicines must be changing this attitude," I commented.

"Yes, but too late for many folk. Here is Bertha, a lovely old lady who is a burned-out case. As you can see, the disease did great havoc before it was halted. Until infirmity made it impossible for her to move any more, the old dear hobbled to Mass every morning."

Bertha was an aged woman, sitting placidly outside her hut, in the sun. She would hobble no more, for she was handless, footless, and blind.

"Are all these patients from among the peasant farmers?" I asked.

"Father, leprosy knows no boundaries. Some of these patients belong to families that are in comfortable circumstances. The most unique hut on the property is one that harbors five young women who were already professed as Sisters, or part way through their religious training in a novitiate, when they were discovered to have the disease."

"Five religious who are lepers!" I cried. "May we visit them?"

"By all means! Naturally, they do not wear their religious habits. And among the residents of the camp, not all of the five are known for what they are, since some of the young women prefer to live unnoticed."

Raphael Brown in his survey of leprosy reports that 109 Catholic missionaries (64 priests, 6 Brothers, 39 Sisters) contracted leprosy in modern times, and that 42 of them were still living in 1951.[4] The heavy incidence of leprosy in East Africa is high-lighted by this concentration of five religious victims at Nyenga.

The house reserved for the religious was better constructed than the standard huts, but still very simple. As we approached, two of the residents were sitting at the door, chatting.

"I have two American priests who wish to pay you a visit," said Sister Peter Mary in the vernacular. "How many are at home?"

"Modesta is inside, but Perpetua and Francesca are not present," came the reply.

"Please call them for a moment. Fathers, this is Sister Bertha, who was a professed religious for a number of years in Tanganyika before her illness was discovered."

Sister Bertha was spare and hardy. She gave us the impression that she could take care of herself.

"What was her assignment before she came here?" I asked.

"She was a schoolteacher. Now she acts somewhat as the mother of the group, since she is the oldest. Nobody is completely reconciled to being a leper, but from the start she has been very sensible in accepting her lot."

By this time, a gentle little miss had come out of the house and now stood with us.

"This is Modesta," said our guide. "She is from Uganda. She speaks English, Father, so you must give her some good advice. She was a second-year novice in her community, and she made a grand little candidate. She is extremely homesick for her convent; and because she yearns so to go back, she takes her plight badly."

"Modesta," I said, "you must remember that, before we can give anything worth while to God, we must love it so dearly that being deprived of it will break our heart. Isn't that true? You've loved dearly the beautiful life that God gave you, particularly the happy years in the novitiate. Thus you possess the perfect gift to offer Him with the Biblical prayer, 'The Lord giveth and the Lord taketh away; blessed be the name of the Lord.' You really do say that prayer, don't you, Modesta?"

"Father," Modesta replied falteringly, her eyes hauntingly sad, "with my lips and with my heart I sing that prayer a hundred times a day, but with my eyes I cry it all away again."

I felt that if I attempted to say any more I'd be shedding tears myself. Fortunately, Teresa returned at this juncture with Perpetua.

"Perpetua was a postulant in Uganda," came the next report. "She is wonderfully helpful in teaching the children." Perpetua smiled.

"Have you many brothers and sisters at home, Perpetua?" I asked.

The smile turned to stone. I tried similar questions but evoked not a monosyllable of reply.

"Perpetua never talks about home, Father," said Sister apologetically. "You have not yet met Teresa. Teresa is a postulant from Kenya."

Teresa was a pleasant person who wanted to talk. "I dream every day of going back to the Sisters, Father," she said. "It will not be long now."

"The saddest days of all lie ahead for girls like Teresa," explained the Sister as we walked away from the group. "There is such a popular horror of leprosy that it is practically impossible for one known among the people as a victim of leprosy to be effective thereafter as a religious."

Francesca then appeared, large of build and easily the most vital of the five. "Francesca," the Sister said, "is a member of the Luo tribe in Tanganyika and was a postulant at the novitiate of the Maryknoll Sisters in Musoma. She is a fine, sensitive person who feels her affliction dreadfully."

"Francesca,"—Sister said in the vernacular of the girl—"these two Fathers are from Musoma."

"Oh, I must go back with you!" Francesca cried excitedly. "I must go back with you!" Then she put her face in her hands, and with a great sob cried, "But I am not yet ready."

"Three weeks ago," Sister Peter Mary told us, "the doctor pronounced Francesca negative, and she was walking on air. Yesterday, however, the doctor found her positive again. She went to Mother and wept as if her heart would break. Two Maryknoll Sisters visited her recently from Musoma and made her immensely happy, but the reaction after they left was sad to see."

"Sister," I said, "lepers are very much people, aren't they?"

"Very much, Fathers! One of the most horrible things in all history is the spectacle of the suffering leper driven out by men and cursed as unclean. There are other diseases equally as terrible but none carry the social stigma of leprosy."

"Sister," I commented, "more people should meet lepers. More people should witness the pathetic sight of these five religious, suffering from the disease itself, surely, but suffering especially from what to them is the dreadful catastrophe of being outcasts as unclean."

Raphael Brown quotes good advice from the chaplain of a leprosarium in the Philippine Islands: "The worst thing about leprosy is not the disease, but the shame of having it. All too often, victims of leprosy are branded as outcasts, living dead, smitten by God . . . Leprosy is not a crime or a disgrace, but just another ailment of the human body, and should be treated as such. Let us not stigmatize these unfortunate patients."

Sister Catherine Sullivan, a veteran of Carville, gave some good advice in a conference to seminarians in Louisiana: "In your sermons, do not use the word leper as a synonym for sin . . . adding to the burden of misrepresentation and tragic misunderstanding already much too heavy for those who are its victims."

The Fifth International Congress on Leprosy, held at Havana in 1948, recommended that preachers and writers avoid altogether the use of the terms leprosy and leper. It recommended the employment of the term Hansen's Disease. The suggestion has merit, since it is true that the very appellation evokes horror. However, the impracticalness of the suggestion is evident in the fact that the Congress itself, when it met in Madrid in 1953, still found it necessary to employ the word Leprosy in its title.

Father Paul and I bade good-by to our five new-made friends in the leper camp at Nyenga. When we drove away, they followed us to the gate. I looked back and saw Modesta and Francesca waving after us disconsolately.

Chapter 4

BAGAMOYO AND BEYOND

TWO MEN, one black, one white, squatted facing each other on the open savanna in the shadow of Africa's highest mountain, Kilimanjaro. The black man was Fumba, chief of the Chagga people; the white man was Father Alexander Le Roy of the Holy Ghost Fathers, pioneer in East Africa. Beside the chief stood his uncle, a venerable elder, while beside the priest was his guide. About the little group sat a wide circle of Chagga braves.

The dignified figure beside the chief spoke out: "The white man of the tribe of the French, Mapeh-Roua (the local name of Father Le Roy)—the man who reads, writes, looks at mountains, heals the sick, tells everybody to pray to God—Mapeh-Roua has come to visit Fumba. He has said that he will build his house at Kilema, that he will live there, that he will accomplish good. This is why he wishes to be the brother of the Chief."

"Yes, the brother of the Chief!" exploded the braves in unison.

"But if Mapeh-Roua is a liar, a thief, a traitor"—and the old man glowered ferociously at the young missionary—"may he die!"

"May he die!" echoed the chorus.

"And you, Fumba, listen," continued the old man. "If the Father, his brother, his family, are able one day to say, 'Fumba has deceived us!' death to your father, your mother, your wives, your children, your goats, your sheep, your cattle!"

"May his banana trees perish!" cried the chorus. "May the water of the mountain dry up! May his fire go out forever! May his beer be poisoned, and may he die!"

Then said Fumba to the missionary, "Mapeh-Roua, will you drink my blood?"

"Surely," replied Father Le Roy.

"If you vomit it, you are my enemy. If you retain it, you are my friend."

"So be it!" agreed the missionary.

The old uncle then took a dagger and made an incision in the forearm of the chief, and a similar one in the forearm of Father Le Roy. Chief Fumba tore a piece of flesh from the roasted white goat by his side, rubbed the flesh in the incision in his arm, and pushed it into the mouth of the missionary. The white man struggled bravely with the huge morsel and finally was able to consume it. The chief fed his visitor three such servings. Then Father Le Roy in his turn rubbed pieces of the goat in his own incision and put them into Chief Fumba's mouth.

With a beaming smile, the chief cried out, "The ceremony is over: we are brothers!"

This blood-bond between African and missionary was sealed on August 14, 1890. Father Le Roy—who later was a bishop in French Equatorial Africa, then Superior General, and finally the venerable Archbishop Le Roy, a great, beloved figure in both France and Africa —had journeyed to Kilimanjaro from Bagamoyo. It was from Baga-moyo, the mainland base opposite the island of Zanzibar (colorful Arab emporium and notorious slave market), that early settlers, sol-diers, and missionaries advanced into Tanganyika. When the new port of Dar es Salaam was developed, Bagamoyo ceased to be the chief base for contact from the outside world with the heart of Tanganyika.

Today Tanganyika is a trust territory of the United Nations, governed by Great Britain. It is rated as the most backward country in East Africa. Tanganyika has but fifteen thousand Europeans (with nearly five times as many Indians), and Great Britain evidently has no intention of building up white strength there. "The Africans can have Tanganyika for the asking," I was told, "as soon as they can prove that a withdrawal by Great Britain will not make the land a sitting duck for some conquering power."

At present Tanganyika counts some nine million black Africans. It is neither preponderantly the homeland of any great African people nor the political home of any union of African peoples. Certain peoples of Tanganyika are outstanding. The Chagga of Kilimanjaro are among the most advanced in Africa. The Basukuma of Mwanza and the Bahaya of Bukoba are vigorous and progressive. Some tribes in the southern highlands of Tanganyika are ranked as outstanding.

While in Bukoba, I asked a group of Bahaya leaders how far their interest in their neighbors ran. "We feel friendly toward the Baganda," one replied, "and are related to the Bahima of Toro in Uganda. We are on good terms with the Banyakusa, who are our eastern neighbors on Lake Victoria. Beyond that we are not interested in anyone else."

That attitude is typical. Tanganyika is a mosaic of unrelated tribes who if they are going to unite in a nation must develop common bonds of friendship and interest. "At the moment," an informant remarked, "there is hardly an African alive who would fight and die for the honor and glory of Tanganyika. The country is a creation of the foreigner."

"What is the African attitude toward union with Kenya and Uganda?" I asked.

"In all three countries, those men advanced enough to have an opinion are bitterly opposed to the idea. The principal fear is that the whites of Kenya would control everything. The Indians of Tanganyika froth at the mouth at mention of the project, because they now enjoy much freedom. Africans with spirit, like the Baganda, are opposed because they face the prospect of being submerged. My guess is that time will prove the idea a good one; in the atomic world of the future, fragmentation of political entities will no longer be desirable."

Ever since 1860, when the Holy Ghost Fathers on Christmas Day celebrated their first Mass in Zanzibar, a train of Catholic missionaries has been moving in, first through Bagamoyo and then through Dar es Salaam, to work among the Tanganyika tribes. Today over 1,500 priests, Brothers, and Sisters from overseas are at work in Tanganyika, co-operating with 700 African priests and religious. African Catholics today number 903,000, over ten per cent of the total population.

The Chagga of Kilimanjaro have the distinction of being the first tribe in Africa assigned for evangelization to American Catholic missionaries. They were the object of my first visit in the country. During my journey with Father Brouwer, it was still early in the morning when before us, as we rode, rose the blue gossamer mountains, the twin peaks of Kilimanjaro. On their summits lay the eerie adornment of eternal snow, like delicious icing on a cake. Despite the vicinity of the equator, three great peaks in East Africa are crowned with unfailing snows: Kilimanjaro, in Tanganyika; Mount Kenya, in Kenya; and Mount Ruwenzori on the borders between Uganda and the Congo.

The gray bush through which we had ridden since dawn gave way to green, for we were then in a land where water is plentiful. Beehives hung everywhere. Bees are prized for their honey, but chiefly because they fertilize the coffee trees. We made the beautiful ascent to the plateau amid the lush growth that speaks for the deep, rich, volcanic soil, the generous rainfall, the singing streams fed by the snows and glaciers. Chattering waterfalls in the labyrinthine depths off the road seemed to call out almost garishly, "This is a fat country; here we want for nothing." The air breathes life and prosperity on this sprawling mountain and its surrounding massif which constitute a total area of 1,300 square miles.

In Africa's native world of modest finances, the Chagga enjoy prosperity. From what I can learn, they deserve it, since it is their unusual ability to work together (and this despite bitter local rivalries) that accounts for their success. While riding with some of the Fathers between Kilema and Kibosho, I spied a small network of canals.

"I suppose the British taught them that," I remarked.

"Not at all," one of the priests replied. "The Chagga for centuries have been experts in the making of irrigation canals. They go deep up into the mountain forests and tap the rivers. By ingenious and skillful arrangement of furrows, they bring the water to their district, two or three thousand feet down the mountain. Secondary furrows lead to the individual farms. A sort of water board in each district fixes the day and hour when each family can use the furrow."

"Aren't there many fights?"

"Surprisingly there are not. Furthermore, the very experience the Chagga have had with their canals has taught them the value of co-operation in other matters. A boy here on the mountain learns that a person can't run a canal by himself, just as a boy in the United States learns that he can't win a ball game without co-operating with other boys. A canal takes team work. The families who share a furrow must unite to keep it clean, and must co-operate for careful timing in opening and closing the sluices. Many people will tell you that the Chagga success in the coffee co-operatives comes from family co-operation on the canals."

Certainly the Chagga have experienced success with their coffee. There are 12,000,000 coffee trees on the mountain and its neighborhood. In the early days, ignorance and lack of discipline led to carelessness in growing methods. This created hostility among European coffee growers, who quite rightly feared dangers to all concerned, because of disease and low quality in the coffee crop.

"The men of Lyamungu and Mr. Bennett get much of the credit," I was told in Tanganyika. "Lyamungu was founded in 1933 by the agricultural officers, for the purpose of testing and selecting the finest quality trees and in other ways improving production. The Kilimanjaro Native Co-operative Union, one of Africa's most successful co-ops, was the answer of the natives to the challenge of the Europeans. The organizer of the Union was a Mr. Bennett, whose special genius was that he could bind together twenty-eight separate societies of native growers with 30,000 members. The gross annual turnover of this organization now represents a value of almost a million pounds."

"We are quite proud of the men who at present are operating the K.N.C.U.," says Father Joseph Noppinger. "The President and Manager are both good-living Catholics and other important officers are outstanding Protestants. Plans are made to use coffee profits to build in Moshi a $150,000 commercial school for 250 pupils. The K.N.C.U. has a special school for training coffee cultivators. In this and in other ways it aims to insure enduring success for this Chagga enterprise."

The temptation of the European resident in Africa, when he hears a transient acquaintance express enthusiasm about any evidence of African ability in a business enterprise, is to mention the dozens of examples of African failure in co-operatives and other undertakings. My mind, I found, went back rather to the barbaric scene on the open savanna—the scene of August 14, 1890, when the Chagga chief Fumba made his first blood bond with a white foreigner. Whatever the failures in new Africa as a whole, it is certainly extraordinary to find Fumba's sons and grandsons, in less than seventy years, able to spend tens of thousands of pounds on handsome buildings in Moshi, the Chagga coffee center, for education and recreation and other useful purposes. Let's give these people credit for what they've done, even if the road they have still to journey be a long and difficult one.

The missionaries play their part in encouraging those relatively advanced Africans to improve their family living conditions, but great numbers continue in the old ways. With Father Brouwer, I had gone down the hillside at Kilema and visited a *shamba*—a native home of typical cone-shaped dwelling and accompanying cone-shaped wicker-work granaries. The dwelling possessed no windows and was almost hermetically sealed when the door was closed. The left half of the interior was occupied by five cows and calves.

"Those animals have been there all their lives," my companion explained, "night and day, summer and winter. They are almost blind and have long, claw-like hoofs. They are stall-fed, raised in somewhat the same way as the Long Island ducks that leave their wire cage only to go to the housewife's pot."

The murderous tsetse fly of the plain is the cause of the system. Lines of women and girls move down and up the mountain, endlessly bringing the grass fodder. In the hut we were visiting, the grass supply was stored next to the beasts. Alongside stood a skin bed for the family. In the center of the hut were three stones for the fireplace.

"Here they cook," explained my guide, "and here they talk and chat. Around the hut fire, most young Africans are educated. Smoke and many odors make the atmosphere unbearable for us, but not so for the Chagga. To them, the atmosphere is that of home."

"Is family life changing with the schooling of the women?" I asked.

"Up to the present, there hasn't been much schooling of women. These women with the grass on their heads represent the problem. The older generation says that, if the girls get schooling, they won't carry the grass for the cattle, and they won't work the fields."

"But don't the educated men want educated wives?" I asked.

"At first, most didn't. Today many do, and in time that desire is going to play a big part in changing the position of women. The missionary knows that, in the new Africa, a moderately well-educated mother with strong religious principles is the key to a strong African home."

It is some years since I visited that Chagga hut. But even today, my Holy Ghost friends tell me, only a small percentage of Chagga men have built new-style homes. There is no hurry.

Those who know the Chagga people as difficult and quarrelsome, find a visit to one institution in this mountain world a thought-provoking experience. This is the motherhouse and novitiate of the African Sisters of Our Lady of the Snows, at Hauruma. Physically the property is a veritable paradise, with its tidy acres of farming and grazing land. Under the direction of the Precious Blood Sisters of Princeton, New Jersey, eligible Chagga girls receive a thorough training as religious. They show themselves well adapted for the life, for they are intelligent, humble, and generous. Religion, the visitor decides, brings out in these young women great charm and suppleness.

Unfortunately, I was unable to visit Tanganyika's southern highlands. There a crisp, healthy climate and beautiful, upland cattle ranges promised once to become a white settlers' development to duplicate the Kenya highlands. The several hundred miles of costly transport to the railroad killed the idea, and a changing world now makes a large white invasion highly improbable.

In the highlands the celebrated Bavarian Benedictines of St. Ottilien conduct their superbly organized missions among the Wangori, the Makonde, and other tribes. Peramiho is the principal center. There on African soil have risen an Old-World Benedictine monastery and superb cathedral, out from which the missionaries journey systematically, just as did the monks of the West from their monasteries of Fulda and St. Gall and many other centers of northern Europe in the early Christian centuries. Ndanda is a companion center to Peramiho. Almost 200,000 carefully trained Christians, a fifth of the Catholics of Tanganyika, are now in the care of the Benedictines.

The Makonde people have a strong tradition of native art. Thirty years ago the monks called in some of the best of the tribal artists, gave them a workroom, and encouraged them to continue in their traditional carving, which features the female body but also depicts elephants, lions, leopards, birds, and snakes.

After a short time, the monk director gave the artists a new subject. "Carve the figure of the Crucified Saviour," he said.

"The results were astonishing," he relates. "Although the artists had seen European crucifixes, their own work was far removed from the European style. The face of Christ was typically Bantu and almost masklike. The individual parts of the Corpus were out of proportion and stylized according to Makonde tradition."

Later a request was made for a Madonna and Child. "The artist produced an ebony statue of the Blessed Virgin in native clothing, holding the Child Jesus in the manner that native mothers carry their children. The expression on the face of the Bantu Madonna was gentle beyond all description."

The director of the art group reports interesting reactions from the African Christians. "Our native Sisters," he says, "could not be persuaded to accept for their chapel a very beautiful crucifix in native artistic tradition. But they were delighted with one that was anatomically correct though with the Saviour represented by a typical Bantu face. Christian artists wish to free themselves from the old tradition. As Christianty takes deeper root here, the true artists of the tribe will revert, we think, to their traditional native artistic style even for Christian subjects."

Tabora is the key to western Tanganyika, where the country's largest population is found. I stood in the boiling sun at Kouihara, outside the city, and looked at the remains of the old fort or *tembe* (a rectangular habitation with an interior court) in which David Livingstone resided before beginning his last journey. A little monument commemorates his presence. There, too, the first caravan of White Fathers camped, in 1879.

Behind the African hospital in Tabora, I saw the glaring white cross with its bronze tablet to the memory of the first White Fathers to give their lives in that territory—a total of five between 1879 and 1882. Today all western Tanganyika is the responsibility of that missionary society. In their 93 stations, they minister to some 300,000 Christians—a third of all the Tanganyika Catholics—in territory extending from the beautiful southwest highlands and Lake Tanganyika to the Uganda border. This admirable body of missionaries, currently possessing a personnel of 2,100 men in Africa, is the largest Catholic sending society at work on the continent.

At Ujiji, on Lake Tanganyika, I had my first sight of a victim of sleeping sickness. The Sisters had placed him on a cot outside their small hospital, and his fixed, glassy stare met me as I approached. He was a young man of about twenty, who was at an advanced stage of the malady, tremulous from head to foot, and no longer possessing the use of his senses.

"We can do nothing for him," one of the Sisters remarked laconically.

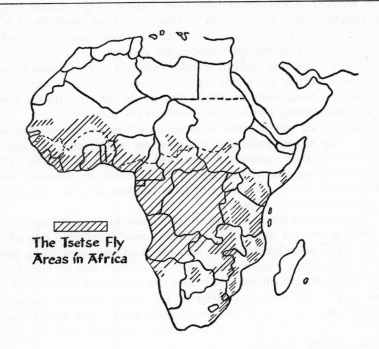

The Tsetse Fly
Areas in Africa

AREAS OF AFRICA INFESTED BY TSETSE FLY

A great hindrance to stock raising in large areas of Africa is the presence of the tsetse fly which, while ineffective in the case of wild game, works havoc on domestic animals. A species of the tsetse fly is the bearer of sleeping sickness.

It is remarkable what influence the tsetse fly has had on the political, social and economic history of the continent. In the religious domain, a factor in the failure of Moslemism to advance strongly toward the south has been the fear of the tsetse by the dominantly pastoral Moslem tribes of the north, who otherwise would be inclined to migrate southward.

A number of Europeans have been victims of the disease but in most instances have been caught in time. We were speaking of it in Mwanza because at Tinde, not far from Lake Victoria, Tanganyika's sleeping-sickness-research laboratories are located.

"The world's best medical scientists are still as vague about sleeping sickness as they are about leprosy," remarked one in our group. "Progress has been made at Tinde, but as yet we are without a vaccine for immunizing human beings against the disease."

"Despite all our modern achievements," remarked another missionary, "the Government has at times no other recourse than to declare certain badly infected areas closed to human habitation. That means that man, the master, solves his problem by running away. Hundreds, sometimes thousands of local residents are put aboard lorries and transplanted elsewhere."

"What chance has a man when the disease hits him?" I asked.

"There are two forms of sleeping sickness," explained one of the group. "The slow form doesn't become fatal for years. The rapid form is fatal if not caught within a month. Both can be cured only if the injections are introduced before the protozoon has entered the spinal fluid. The last long sleep of the victim reminds us of the modern spinal injection of the anesthetist's needle; but in the case of sleeping sickness, all the senses are blacked out and from the effects there is, to date, no recall."

The villain in the piece is the tsetse fly. Human beings are victims of only relatively small detachments of these insects. The major object of attack is the world of domestic animals. The fact that wild game is immune encourages us to expect the discovery some day of a protecting vaccine for livestock. Two-thirds to seven-eighths of Tanganyika are declared to be uninhabitable because of the tsetse fly. To date, the scientific efforts to halt the advance of the fly have on the whole failed.

"Two-thirds of Tanganyika constitute a lonely wilderness," Bishop Blomjous, of Mwanza, explained to me. "Causes are the lack of water and the abundance of the tsetse. Soil and climate are not good enough for a purely crop-raising economy. The African could get along on all of this land, however, if he could raise cattle. In the final analysis, therefore, the great destroyer is the tsetse fly."

Near Shinyanga, in the Mwanza area, is an experimental station for tsetse fly control. Most interesting in this part of Tanganyika is the Sukumaland Federation, which represents, in substance, a test of the ability of the African tribes to organize and participate in this tsetse fly campaign. The Sukuma count approximately a million Africans living at the southeast corner of Lake Victoria, just south of the famous game reserves, the Serengeti Plains. Life has been harder and harder for those tribesmen because such a great portion of their land has been conquered by the tsetse. Faced with the alternative that they organize or die, fifty tribes or so have united in the Sukamuland Federation. Government experts on water conservation, forestry, agriculture, and veterinary techniques are co-operating, with extinction of the tsetse fly a major objective.

I found Bishop Blomjous to be one of the African's warmest and wisest friends on the continent. After conversations with him that went into many hours, and after a careful perusal of what he has written, I am presuming to distill his philosophy of Africa into six principles. I hope they do him justice.

1—The African's rights and obligations. All elements should unite in encouraging in the African the exercise of a sense of responsibility founded on his basic rights—political, social, economic, spiritual—as the indigenous inhabitant of all those parts of Africa that he can properly claim as his own.

From these rights, flow obligations on the part of the African to himself, his family, his community, his country, his race, and to world society.

2—Active participation in betterment. All elements should encourage the African to active participation in the betterment—political, social, economic, spiritual—of himself and his race. Anything less than such encouragement makes of the process a strife-producing contest. Such strife as already exists can only harm both African and non-African.

Only by such encouragement will Africans of intelligence, prudence, and integrity be present in such numbers in African movements as to balance the hotheads.

"When self-government, whether it be near or far, arrives in Tanganyika," remarked His Excellency, "I want the best among my own African Christians to be well up front in advocating everything that is good for the country."

3—Training to true wisdom. All elements should strive to give African leaders, in addition to practical technology, the broad cultural education that is the surest path to true wisdom. Such education must signify service to their people and to the world. Our Christians must be trained specifically for public life, or their Christian principles will easily be forgotten when they encounter situations that have been completely unforeseen.

Similarly, our African clergy and their episcopal superiors must be trained specifically to social action, or they will ignore or shy away from this all-important field of their ministry.

4—The tribal culture. All elements should recognize the importance of the tribal culture of Africa, to which the native language is the key. Africans must be proud of the good things in their heritage, and build on this heritage. At the same time, a world language is important for all who in any capacity would span the bridge to other cultures, the substantial (though not exclusive) source for present-day Africa's needed knowledge.

5—World Christianity an essential to African culture. All elements should recognize the devastating effects of secularism (the rejection of the spiritual) on African culture. The basic teachings of Christianity, like truth itself, remain the same for all mankind; but in its leaders, and in many of its externals, Christianity in Africa must be African and must correspond to the call of the African spirit.

The extreme of advocating spiritual values in terms of native African rites, as proposed by anti-Christian European scientists and by nativist movements like the Mau Mau, is similar to the Nazi advocacy of ancient Teutonic rites.

6—An African philosophy for the foreigner. All non-African elements (settlers, political administrators, business men, missionaries, visitors) should recognize that they are working at cross purposes with a movement of importance to world society, when by their words or actions they ignore or flout the current movement among Africans toward assuming their rights and obligations.

"So far as my missionary priests are concerned," notes Bishop Blomjous, "I tell them that in Africa the days of the patriarchs are ended. Their role is that of John the Baptist; they must decrease in order that the Church of Africa will increase. Naturally, in many places it will take generations for the local Christian society to become completely self-maintaining, self-propagating and self-governing under the Holy See."

My visit to Bukoba as guest of Bishop Lanctot was an invigorating experience. However, it was when we left that charming city on the banks of Lake Victoria, and mounted by steep roads among the rolling ridges above, that our enthusiasm reached its peak. Gone were the arid, treeless plain, and the dusty cattle tracks of the endless bush country of central Tanganyika. The new scene was one of rich, tropical landscape and tall trees, the product of a rainfall twice that of Mwanza. From Kanazi, we saw the region of Lake Victoria as a superb panorama. The road was alive with Africans, the women in bright and fairly expensive clothes. The area grows an abundance of bananas as sustenance crop, and coffee as the money crop; the Bahaya are rivals of the Chagga in enterprise, and their *robusta* coffee likewise rivals the Chagga output.

We were on our way to visit the first African prelate of a see in Tanganyika, Bishop Laurean Rugambwa. The last few miles were over a secondary road that ran westward from the lake, up a majestic escarpment that made us feel we were approaching a medieval castle. Amid the cool, grassy uplands, we found the bishop's pro-cathedral and his completely African rectory and mission compound.

Shortly after World War I, a non-Christian from Bukongo, Kihanja District, a mile and a half from the Rutabo church, began studying the doctrine. His name was Pushubirera. The man was a *musita,* a member of the clan whose privilege it is to give the chiefs to Kihanja District. His wife was a *muhinda,* a cousin of the present chief, Henrico Berogi. The man was baptized in 1920 and received the name of Domitian. His wife and children followed his example soon after, the wife receiving the name Asteria, and the eldest son the name Laurean.

After completing the necessary years of study, Laurean entered the major seminary at Katigondo, in Uganda. He had unassuming piety and was serious, sociable, and endowed with good spirits. Ordination came in 1943. Then Laurean did mission work among his fellow Bahaya around Bukoba until, in 1948, he was sent to Rome for three years of disciplining in canon law. He was a curate at the busy station of Kashozi when, on Christmas Eve in 1951, word was received of his appointment to govern a new diocese, which would be formed by cutting off an area containing some of the 120,000 Bahaya Catholics of Bukoba.

From village to village, all along the Kagera River, the Catholics exclaimed, "We have a new bishop, and he is one of ourselves, the son of Domitian Pushubirera!"

Domitian and Asteria were up at dawn on the great day of the consecration. They dressed with care, and left early for the Rutabo church. "What strange things God does, Asteria," Domitian said in a low voice as they trudged among the trees. "We walk this mile and a half from our little house to Rutabo, and when we return our son will be a bishop!"

"It is not even a century ago," said the African preacher at the consecration, "that God made known to us the true religion, and now already He is choosing one from among us to be our head. God has loved our country." The police had to be summoned to lead the new prelate through the excited thousands outside the church.

When the bishop greeted us at Rutabo, I noted his tall and slender figure, his beautifully supple hands. Born of the blood of chiefs, he had an easy but lofty bearing. If his ordinarily sober mien permits a smile, it is warm and engaging with a strong evidence of teeth.

When we spoke of his people, Bishop Rugambwa waxed enthusiastic. "They must understand all that their religion means," he said warmly. "Even if they are poor and have little, if they understand their religion and appreciate it and fight for it, then we have the Christians we want."

After a distinctly African evening meal we chatted a while in the light of the lamp. We spoke of the African clergy in Tanganyika, who now number 165, and of the African Sisters, who total over 500.

"Do they have considerable influence on their people?" I asked.

"In Tanganyika, the best persuaders are African persuaders," replied one of the priests with a smile.

Then a member of the circle took the lamp, and the group of African clergy at the bishop's house that night—accompanied by Father Bordenet and me, the lone foreigners—strode across the courtyard in the moonlight, to the cathedral, reciting the *Miserere*. Kneeling in the sanctuary, we had night prayers by lamplight, our voices echoing through the empty church. There was a crude solemnity to the little ceremony, an atmosphere such as probably marked the pioneer days of centuries ago, when those monks of the West to whom we have alluded built the Faith in northern Europe. These are pioneer days, too: a new dawning when Africa's society of peoples looks forward to a fullness of life of its own.

Chapter 5

LAND OF THE TWELVE TRIBES

AN HOUR AFTER leaving our Lake Victoria steamer at Musoma, I was listening to Father Robert Moore preach his Sunday sermon in Kiswahili. Within another hour, I was listening to Father Thomas Gibbons, in Nyegina, preach his sermon in Kikwaya. This is a tip-off on Maryknoll's Prefecture of Musoma, on Victoria's eastern shore: it is a land of many languages. Indeed, the Maryknollers, after lunch that first day, listed for me twelve different language groups within the territory. Added to this dozen of tongues is a thirteenth, used as the lingua franca throughout Tanganyika; namely, Kiswahili. English, the ambition of every African youngster who gets a chance at schooling, makes a fourteenth.

Adjoining the Prefecture of Musoma at its south, is the Prefecture of Maswa, also a Maryknoll mission field. Thus Maryknollers are responsible for the east coast of Lake Victoria, from the Kenya border to the border of Bishop Blomjous' Diocese of Mwanza; and inland, south to the now celebrated town of Shinyanga, "the Kimberley of East Africa." At Shinyanga in 1940, a Canadian named Williamson discovered what was to become the largest privately owned diamond mine in the world.

But most interesting to us for the moment is the matter of the languages in the region. North of the Musoma border, in southwestern Kenya, is a large portion of the Luo tribe, numbering almost a million. Some fifty thousand of them spill over into Musoma; but among the Mill Hill Fathers on the Kenya side, those Luo people provide the solid phalanx of a single language. In the Prefecture of Maswa, to the south, the greater portion of the people are Sukuma, speaking a single language. Thus sandwiched between rather large tribes, is this linguistic curiosity, the Prefecture of Musoma: a relatively small patch of land along the lake, with 250,000 inhabitants who speak a dozen tongues. This strange potpourri of tongues is a rather common situation in Africa along the borderline between the Bantu and Northern languages. And because of this tangled skein of language, neither social progress nor Christian progress is as far advanced as it might be. Hence, lest we conceive the notion that all East Africa has already reached a greatly advanced stage, let's take a brief journey through this relatively backward area, which the Maryknollers, latecomers on the African scene, are now undertaking to tackle.

Modest in make-up though it appears, with little more than a few traders' shops, Musoma is the metropolis of that eastern-shore world. It has its "foreigners" in the way of elements from other tribes, in town for short or long stops. Hence the necessity of a Kiswahili parish despite the fact that Musoma is within the home territory of the Bakwaya people.

Father Moore's chapel is new, and his command of Kiswahili is a new achievement. He had already learned the language of the Luo people. "Either we like languages in a polyglot field like Musoma," remarked one of the young priests, "or we find life dreary indeed! The largest single language group in the territory numbers less than fifty thousand. In most cases, a change of station means a change of language."

There is something charmingly casual about a house of worship in backwoods Africa. While Father Moore preached, a tiny tot in his birthday suit toddled about among the women, chattering happily. Another youngster played with his mother's rosary for a while, then pulled the ear of the child beside him. Strangely enough, the second youngster, instead of letting forth a howl of pain, only jabbered back good-naturedly. Meanwhile, the women on their side of the church, and the men folk across the way, listened to the sermon.

Nyegina, the oldest mission station in the territory, is eight miles out of town. We rode through heavy bush and plantations and suddenly came upon the neat establishment, set on an eminence that provides a wide horizon out over Lake Victoria. It is a scene of idyllic peace.

"Progress has been slow among the Bakwaya," explained Father William Collins. "They are a matrilineal society in which the man does not pay a large bride price at marriage. Curiously, this leads to loose marital ties, and this low respect for the marriage bond has carried over to a degree among our Christians. At the moment, perhaps as many as thirty per cent of our Christian Bakwaya are in the spiritual 'dog house' through bad marriages."

"How do those Christians take it when you tell them they are in the black book?" I asked.

"Oh, we continue to be the best of friends," replied Father Collins. "They make no defence except to remark philosophically that it's the way things go. They are stubborn as a tribe; their neighbors call them the hard-headed ones. But they are very likable. We hope that, by means of schools and intensified Christian living, we shall be able to get the younger folk to take pride in building up the right kind of Christian homes."

"That's the pity of it all," put in another of the priests. "Until the countryside has a good number of outstanding examples of what fine Christian home life is, it will be very hard to convince these people to give up their old ways. I chat often with a farmer down the lane from me. I remarked a short while ago to him that he was a good fellow, why didn't he become a Christian?

" 'Oh, you wouldn't have me,' he replied. 'I've got three wives.'

" 'Well,' I said, 'why not choose the one you consider your first wife, and put the others away?'

" 'Come inside a minute, Padri,' he answered with a twinkle in his eye. 'I'll tell you why.'

"When we were inside, he called to the three wives, two of whom came from the fields. All three were in late middle age, as was my farmer friend. They shuffled up to me slowly, pleasant smiles on their faces, and saluted me warmly.

" 'Now, Padri,' began the farmer, 'these are my three wives. We have lived here together for many years. We do all the work in the fields together. We get along wonderfully together—don't we?' he finished, turning to the three.

" 'Surely do!' they replied, laughing.

" 'Now, Padri, I ask you,' continued the old fellow. 'What would you do if you were in my place? Supposing you had three fine women like these, and you wanted to become a Christian, which two of the three would you send away, Padri? Which two of these three would you send away?'

"I saw immediately that the situation required for the moment, at least, a gracious withdrawal. I made a noncommittal reply and congratulated all of them for being loyal, one to another, during all the years.

"In a 'new' country such as ours, a man like my farmer friend will appreciate the higher beauty of Christian society, only when he can get to see that we are not interested merely in taking away from him something that he considers good and proper. Rather, he must see that we are ready to give to him and his people something much finer than what they have heretofore known."

After a day in Nyegina, Monsignor Gerard Grondin and I began the circuit of this checkerboard of peoples in the Musoma area. First, there was the ferry ride from Musoma across the bay to Kinesi. We two were the only whites who sat in the soporific calm of the sunny deck as the crowded vessel chugged away from one bank, across the placid water to the other side.

"Where are we now?" I asked the Monsignor.

"Now we are in a new country," he explained. "This is the territory of the Basimbiti, one of the best peoples in the area. They are friendly, and anxious to better themselves. In times past, they've had some harmful practices but the older Christian leaders now discourage them. They've practiced child marriage, but British civil law forbids it, and it is passing out. The people are fairly well off, through fishing and cattle raising."

We had lunch in Father Edward Bratton's prefabricated, aluminum house, at Komuge, which was to be replaced by the more permanent structure he was building when we visited him. Then we walked in the hot sun through arid, open country, to visit Chief Johannes, ruler of all the Basimbiti, who now number some thirty thousand. The chief was building a better house, but the one he was living in was a crude, wattle-and-daub structure with a clay floor. We met his wife, Christina, and his daughter Katherina.

"Katherina failed in the examination at the Mwanza school," said Father Bratton. "But she's a likable child; she'll make a good wife for some lucky fellow, one of these days."

"Thank you for coming, Fathers," Katherina called after us, with a sudden burst of courage as we moved away.

Next we visited Cosmos, the catechist. He proudly led us into his untidy hut, where chickens ran about the floor. In a corner burned a fire, over which Cosmos had just cooked a pot of millet for himself and his daughter. A decoration on his wall was a page from an American newspaper, which carried about thirty photographs representing the principal communities among the 120,000 Sisters in the United States. My eye caught the name of Sister Mary Mercy of the Sisters of Mercy, whose family lives in my home town of New Bedford, Massachusetts.

Scattered over the open country were clusters of huts, some of which housed the catechist's prospective new Christians. We dropped in on one family and were greeted cordially. Three huts were neatly centered in an area hedged with sisal plants. On either side was a line of five storage bins on stilts, stuffed with food and family treasure. Gathered in a cluster near one of the huts, sat the family.

"This Father has come here all the way from America," the catechist said, introducing me to the group.

"He must be very tired," commented one of the women, looking at me with concern.

"She thinks you walked," explained one of my companions. "When she makes a journey, that's what she must do."

For miles, then, Monsignor drove our truck through the nagging anonymity of thorn scrub, the heritage of the vast dry areas of Africa. Occasionally there was the exhilarating flick of a bright bird, and occasionally the splash of a bright flower, usually the purple hibiscus.

"Now for the next on our list of tribes," announced Monsignor Grondin, "the Luos. They are the liveliest people in the prefecture. We are arriving at Kowak."

Immediately I was all attention, for we were touching the realm of one of the most interesting peoples in East Africa. True, we were only on the outer fringe, since the Luos in this corner of Tanganyika number less than fifty thousand, in a body of two million that extends through Kenya, Uganda, the Sudan, and beyond Lake Albert into the Congo. Bishop Blomjous calls the Luo tribe the hope of Christianity in East Africa.

"They love to talk, laugh and joke," said Father Joseph Glynn, pastor of Kowak. "They are frank, candid, and very hospitable when we call on them. They have a dash about them. 'Wan wa Luo,' they say—'We have the Luo way.' They are tremendously cocksure. Before a football game, they'll declare, 'We'll win: we're Luos!' Whether or not it is meant as a compliment to us, people call them the Americans of this part of Africa. They stand together in extraordinary fashion. 'Kinship sticks to one's bones' is a favorite Luo saying."

The Kowak church is one of the most primitive I saw in East Africa. The White Fathers who built it had to employ the local materials—mud and straw. The walls are of mud, and the confessionals are mud bays protruding into the outside garden. The kneelers, for which there are no pews, are likewise of mud. There is no glass in the windows, and birds fly in and out in very friendly fashion. But the edifice was well filled for the early, weekday Mass, and the congregational chanting was well done.

Quite as I expected, life boomed at Kowak. Father Glynn took me to the catechumenate, where I heard a class of adults singing their lessons on sanctifying grace. The dispensary of the Maryknoll Sisters was a busy spot, with ceaseless come-and-go about the convent. With Father Glynn I visited a number of Luo homes. They were not as neat and shiny as, for instance, the homes in Basutoland, nor did they have much in distinctive furniture.

"The Luo passed directly from no clothes to European clothes," said the missionary, "and thus he has no distinctive mode of dress, and no distinctive ornaments. He has an abundance of traditions and customs, but few distinctive implements. He uses a four-ox plow, which the smaller farmer rents from the larger. The husband does the plowing, and the wife does the cultivating."

"The Luo woman has a mind of her own," put in Monsignor. "When a Luo girl marries a non-Luo, the man always ends by learning his wife's language."

Besides Kowak, there is a second mission station in Luo territory, that of Masonga. The site of Masonga is a choice one, overlooking Lake Victoria. The place is 3,700 feet above sea level, and the mountains of Kenya are visible, eight miles away.

At the mission, we found noise and life aplenty. Monsignor and I were met by a reception parade several hundred strong, followed by an entertainment, which included several narrative dances by the boys. Vincentius Atudo, a clever teacher, led them in an animal hunt that was delightfully vivid. Then Gallus Omolo, another very capable teacher, directed a large chorus in excellent singing and plain chant.

"Singing is the specialty of the Luo," explained Father John

Schiff, the Masonga pastor. "Celebrated in the tribe is the man who renders his ballads to the accompaniment of the *nyadungu,* a harp-like instrument."

Father Schiff took me about among the gathered populace, and we met Agnes Achieng, first wife of the chief and a fervent Catholic. Her spouse, whom we also met, Chief Nyatega, is a good man who goes to daily Mass. However, he has an unsolved problem of nine wives.

"He is not greatly attached to them personally," the pastor told us, "but he cannot face the financial burden of getting rid of them."

Father Schiff and I walked through the village of grass houses that sheltered the catechumens and the families of employees of the mission. Everywhere the reception was joyful to the point of hilarity. Noticeable was the propensity of men and women to joke and badger.

"How long will Father stay?" asked one woman.

"Only for the afternoon," replied Father Schiff.

"Too bad!" she shot back. "If he were here over night, I'd give him a hen for his dinner."

"You have no hen," objected the pastor.

"I have. It's that one right there," said she, pointing to a clucking creature a few yards away.

"Not at all!" cried out another woman. "That's my hen!"

"Well now, why the fuss?" laughed the first character. "The Father is not staying, anyway."

"The Luo would have made good companions to the Spanish conquistadors," said one of the Fathers at Masonga. "They are out for gold, glory and Gospel. They want material possessions and a good name as well. Once Christian, then, they become militantly so, proudly displaying their religion."

From the Maryknoll Sisters, whose convent at Kowak is their first foundation in Africa, we had heard more about Luo traits. "We have been advised to make our community of African Sisters, which is now in formation, intertribal," said Sister Rose Miriam, the novice mistress, "but we find the Luos gaining principal attention, for one reason or another. They have a tendency to be domineering, and we have to keep them in their places. At the same time, they are wonderfully dynamic; they have the stuff of greatness. A perfect Luo would, I believe, be a great saint."

"How do you get your candidates?" I asked.

"Ordinarily their vocations are cultivated at the various missions. But young girls have come to the convent door with nothing but what they were wearing, saying that they wanted to become Sisters.

"Some face a big battle, as did Hannah, a Luo. Hannah, we discovered after she was with us, had run away from home. Her mother stormed in on us one day, but Hannah hid for hours in one of the Sisters' rooms. Her father stormed in also. Although a Christian, he could not content himself with losing a dowry of twenty-five cows, which would have a value of $500. That sum was the greatest wealth that a small farmer like him would receive in his whole life. The noisy visits continued, and each time Hannah hid until her parents had wearied and gone. Never a comment from Hannah, except a quiet smile and the words, 'I want to be a Sister.'"

Reluctantly, Monsignor and I went on our way. "Wonderful people!" I remarked, still under the glow of the Luo. "Where now?"

"Now to the land of the Bakuria," answered my guide. Our road mounted steadily as we entered North Mara, a portion of the prefecture that has generous rainfall. Toward evening we reached the mission of Rosana. It is perched dramatically on the edge of an escarpment 5,500 feet above the sea, where there is always a fresh breeze. The view over the great valley is breath-taking.

"Welcome!" called out Father Joseph Reinhart, as we arrived. "Have you seen the cattle rustlers?"

"Cattle rustlers?"

"Right. The whole district is in a dither! A gang of Bakuria are reported to have stolen eight hundred cattle from the dreaded Masai, the world's greatest cattle thieves. The Masai, it seems, drove their cattle to the Bakuria water holes some thirty miles from here, because of the drought—and lo! their cattle disappeared!"

The Bakuria take the prize for primitiveness among the twelve tribes of Musoma. We saw them everywhere, wearing colorful bead necklaces and bracelets, heavy brass bands on arms and legs, and a minimum of clothing. They hunt with bow and arrow. While the Luo people are strong on singing, the Bakuria are celebrated for their beautiful, costumed dance routines. The Bakuria prayer chants have great charm but are not as melodious as those of the Luo.

"Our Bakuria, though kind and hospitable, can be tough," com-

mented Father James as we talked through the long evening. "Their
great opponents are the Masai, to whom they refer simply as 'the enemy.' But our Bakuria will be model ladies and gentlemen some day."

Next morning, though we were but a few miles from the equator,
I wore a woolen pull-on under my cassock during Mass, so low was the
thermometer. The entire eastern border of the Musoma Prefecture
lies within the great game country of the Serengeti Plains, one of the
most celebrated regions in Africa.

"We expect Father Wille to arrive in about an hour," said Father
James at breakfast. "He is on his way to the Mara Valley, to hunt fresh
meat for the workers at Komuge. Why not go along with him?"

So it was arranged that I should go into the wonderland of the
Serengeti. Great areas of Africa teem with game, but few compare with
this Kenya-Tanganyika region, the heart of which lies in the neighborhood of Arusha, west of Maryknoll's prefecture. Ngorongoro, the most
celebrated base for hunting parties, is 150 miles from Rosana. With
the morning still young, we drove down the long escarpment road
past a small gold mine, one of several in the Musoma region. Soon the
road ended, and we were in the trackless savanna, classic home of the
running game and the animals that prey on it. Over the open country
are trees of the flat-topped acacia family, scattered unevenly and looking, as someone has said, like a poorly planned orchard. Every now
and then there is a thicket—convenient spot for animals' lairs.

Without long waiting, we were soon driving with one, two even
six, herds of various animals on our left or right or before us. When
we surprised them, we saw them at their prettiest. Then the antelopes
would dance their graceful ballet as, tingling in every nerve, they flew
away from us. The exquisite impala flashed in the sun, as he rose
easily over a ten-foot thorn bush, fright intensifying his beauty. Clown-
ish zebras were there by the hundreds. So, also, were specimens of
the gentle topi, the wildebeest, reed buck, hartebeest, and that tiny
globule of spurting mercury, Thompson's gazelle.

"Aren't there any of the really dangerous species here?" I asked.

"Apparently they're all on holiday today, though they're all seen
regularly in these parts," replied Father Wille.

"Which do you consider the animals to watch most carefully?"

"I've always heard the buffalo listed as the hardest one to deal
with," replied Father Wille. "A professional, J. A. Hunter, has just

written a book in which he puts down the leopard as the most dangerous, and then the lion, buffalo, rhino, and elephant, in that order.
But your foe today will be easy to manage. You have only to avoid
getting buck fever."

I glanced at the hunting license as I rode, and found it like the
catalogue of a zoo. The Tanganyika general permit lists fifty-five species of animals, and regulates the killing of all except poor Mr. Ba-
boon, who is regarded as a public pest and gets no protection.

Soon a moment quite unforeseen in my plans arrived, and I was
called upon by Father Wille to earn the price of my outing! He insisted that I undertake to bring down the first animal.

"Off to the right, there is a herd composed entirely of topi," he
said. "They do not frighten very easily. Walk quietly toward them,
through the trees, pick a target, and do your duty."

I did as my experienced companion directed. When I moved, the
herd noticed but merely stood gazing at me. The topi is among the
sturdier animals of the antelope family; while not so lissome as some
of the more delicate varieties, it, also, is a beautiful creature. As those
twenty or thirty beasts stared at me, it seemed a wretched thing to
think of striking one of them down. Hopelessly bad shot that I am,
I made an inglorious job of despatching my quarry, but finally a lone
topi—two hundred and fifty pounds of meat—lay still on the savanna.
The others of the herd were far-off, over the hill, melancholy mourn-
ers of their fallen comrade. Later in the day, Father Wille killed a
second topi, and possessed of what he came for, we started home. As
we rode, I preferred to think of the several thousand quick that had
met our breathless gaze during the day, rather than of the two dead on
the floor of the truck.

"What is our next tribe?" I asked Monsignor Grondin that evening.

"We now head for Iramba," he replied, "and visit the Bangorimi."
Iramba is well situated in green hill country, with rich valleys that are
excellent for crops but cursed, so far as cattle are concerned, by the
presence of the tsetse fly.

"We have had several human victims of the tsetse here," Father
Louis Bayless, the pastor, said later. "One of our catechumens died of
sleeping sickness recently."

The Bangorimi are related to the Bakuria, but are further advanced and wear less ornamentation. They live in clusters of crude circular huts near their fields. Each hut has a cooking fire inside, and bough beds suspended above the floor. Family supplies are strewn about the hut in disarray. On the hard bough bed in one hut, little Angela was sleeping, and with unforgivable carelessness I disturbed her. She awoke with a frightened wail, and I retreated, as a wretched intruder should who pries curiously into the sacred precincts of other people's private worlds.

Five of the twelve tribes of Musoma remained as yet unreached. They were the Bakizu, Bashashi, Bakoma, Banata, and Basenye. Some are quite small in membership. Father William J. Murphy, of the Maryknollers, was in the process of founding a mission station among the Bajita. They are a promising tribe, whose members have shown great interest in Christianity and whose converts already number seven hundred baptized.

"On the other hand," observed Monsignor Grondin, "the Bazanaki, who live in rough, hill-billy country, have shown practically no interest. We are tackling them also. Curiously, one of the best-educated Africans in Tanganyika, Julius Nyerere, belongs to the Bazanaki. He is a Catholic young man, who has an M.A. in history and economics from Edinburgh University and who now teaches at Pugu College, near Dar es Salaam. He has already gained recognition as an African leader in Tanganyika."

"We are apt to picture these humble tribesmen as mere unwashed savages," continued the Monsignor. "A man from the Bakoma people dropped into Nyegina the other day for a meal. He had an artificial leg, and one of the priests asked him if he moved around much on it. 'I come into Musoma every month to collect my twenty shillings of war pension,' he replied. 'I am a veteran of the Far East; I lost my leg there in the fighting.' He had probably seen more of the world than many a college president."

On my last morning in Nyegina, the fife-and-drum corps of the grade school marched several times under my window, with a couple of hundred youngsters parading snappily behind it. Remarkable is the resourcefulness the Africans display in making music. For equipment, this band had half a dozen fifes (the only instruments that had been purchased) half a dozen crude drums made of animal skins, a series of homemade wooden clackers and a triangle made of an oarlock. The lithe little youngster who led the parade carried a baton that was a stick of wood ornamented with the owner's carving at the top.

"They want a holiday in honor of the visitor," announced Father Collins. What better proof that everywhere today it is the same one world?

Chapter 6

SOPHIE AND THE TRAGEDY OF KENYA

SOPHIE, A YOUNG schoolteacher and Catholic Kikuyu wife, was put to torture by a Mau Mau gang to force her to take the dread Mau Mau oath, one of the seven prongs of which required her to renounce her religion. After many beatings, a leather knot was placed around her neck, as if to strangle her. As they tightened the knot, the torturers demanded, "Do you consent?"

Sophie replied with a stifled voice: "For all the gold in the world, no! If you say that it is to regain our land, I also am *Mokikuyu,* a Kikuyu like yourselves. But if you include my religion, you are wasting your time. Kill me!"

A sister of Sophie sat in the room, Sophie's six-month-old infant crying in her arms. "Consent, Sophie!" the sister pleaded. "For the sake of your child here, consent."

"I cannot! Not even for my child."

The Mau Mau torturers became even more enraged. "Do you promise that you will not work any more for the missionaries?" they asked, referring to her position in the Catholic school.

"I will still work."

"Do you promise you will never set foot again in their church?"

"I will always go there."

"Do you promise you will bring us the head of your sister, the nun?"

"No, never! I promise nothing," she replied with a smothered voice, and then lost consciousness.

"Sophie is a symbol of the glory of the Kikuyu, of their bitter woe, and of the tragedy that drags down all Kenya in its destructiveness," records Father Octavus Sestero, of the Consolata Missionaries of Nyeri.

By the middle of 1954 over a thousand Kikuyu had met violent death, at the hands of their brother tribesmen of the Mau Mau, while several score of non-Africans had been murdered. Much valuable property and many herds of the Europeans had been destroyed, but far more ruin had been visited upon their own countrymen by the Mau Mau. True, in direct financial loss the Europeans were the greater sufferers.

However somber the future may be for the Kikuyu, the dark clouds of doubt hang heavier still about the white settlers of Kenya. The latter has been convinced as recently as 1952 that they had, in this East African colony, a paradise on earth, on which the dawn of fair promise smiled brightly. But many are now disillusioned. "So far as I myself am concerned I can fight this thing out," commented a typical planter, "but I am not sure that I should make my wife and children fight it out."

At the turn of the century, Kenya for the British was not important in itself but was, rather, the roadway to elsewhere. The elsewhere was Uganda. A military railroad was built from Mombasa, Kenya's port and the finest on the East Coast, to Kisumu on Lake Victoria. In the course of its construction, British settlers discovered Kenya. The railroad administration picked Nairobi, at approximately the halfway mark, as site for the railroad shops; but they had hardly set up their machines before settlers intruded on the scene, and the march of a small but vigorous white empire was launched.

The great attraction was the Kenya highlands: in that period, boundless, empty lands, airy and magnificent, sublime in their mass and color, gifted with a livable climate, equipped with a roalroad that, though not built for Kenya, was just the thing for turning lonely uplands into an English countryside. Good family stock from the British Isles, sometimes well supplied with capital, venturesome folk looking for the right kind of new land, sailed out through Suez to Mombasa.

The wonder is that they persevered amid the numerous setbacks. In 1903, Lord Delamere, the most influential among the pioneers, took 100,000 acres of land so unpromising that people thought him foolish to agree to pay £200 for the yearly rental. He began with sheep, and they died by hundreds. His cattle withered away to skin and bone. There was no water until miles of pipe were installed to bring it from a borehole at a far corner. But in the midst of catastrophe, the difference between Africa and Britain revealed itself. Lord Delamere brought a team of experts from Scotland, to find out scientifically the reason for his woes. The precise answer was discovered by a chemist from New Zealand, who found that a shortage of cobalt in the feed was causing all the trouble. Today the pedigreed miracle herds of this region are fed unfailingly a weekly cobalt ration.

This procedure of Delamere was outstanding, but was not exceptional. The Europeans in Kenya who succeeded (and not all were able to succeed) did so at cost of a long series of grain failures. As thoughtless charges today are hurled against them for having ridden roughshod over the Africans, it is important to make clear the truth that, as a body, they achieved their results through unusual enterprise. Their shortcomings toward the Africans have been the same shortcomings that whites everywhere have committed when encountering men of color.

Africans in Kenya, particularly in the highlands, were few in those early years—no one questioned why. The sturdy Wakamba people were observed east of Nairobi; the Kikuyu were found in the glorious country about Fort Hall and beyond; the Luo prevailed in the vicinity of Lake Victoria. Among the whites, principal interest in the blacks concerned their value as field workers, cowherds, house boys.

Into the Kenya region even before the white settlers, missioners had entered. By 1913, the date of the Kikuyu Conference (named not after the tribe but after the Church of Scotland center outside Nairobi) there were eight Protestant groups in Kenya. Protestantism today counts some 300,000 members in the country. In addition there are independent African bodies whose members preach Christ but have no ecclesiastical connection with traditional Christian groups.

Catholic missionaries in the country represent three separate points of origin. The Holy Ghost missionaries from Zanzibar established themselves at Mombasa and Bura in 1892; today they are responsible for Nairobi and southeastern Kenya. The Mill Hill missionaries from Uganda began work in Kisumu when the railroad made that city important; care for all western Kenya at present falls to them. These missionaries have been particularly successful among the Luo and now count 265,000 of the 410,000 Catholics in Kenya. The third Catholic group, the Consolata Missionaries—a small, new society from Turin, Italy—holds particular interest for us because from the first it has labored almost exclusively among the Kikuyu.

On June 28, 1902, Father Perlo, a Consolata priest, reported saying in the Aberdare Range "the first Holy Mass ever celebrated in this wilderness." He continued: "I consecrated to the Virgin the poor souls of this country, beseeching her to plead with her Divine Son, so that in the not too-distant future we may reap an abundant harvest for eternity. We ascended the slopes, and at 8 a.m. were ten thousand feet above sea level. Stretching out at our feet was the rolling country of the Kikuyu. For the first time, we gazed upon that breath-taking view, snow-capped Mount Kenya, straddling the equator."

From that beginning, a solid nucleus of Catholics was built among the Kikuyu. A portion of the effort of the Holy Ghost Missionaries was likewise given to the Kikuyu. Thus in 1952, in a population of 5,000,000 Africans in Kenya, Christians totaled approximately three quarters of a million, of whom 410,000 were Catholic. The largest tribe in Kenya was the Kikuyu, with over a million members. Of these, some 200,000 were Christian. Catholics among this 200,000 totaled 75,-000.

Father Perlo (whose arrival in Kikuyuland we have mentioned above), by the evening of his first day, had pitched his tent in Tuso, the village of Chief Karoli, the great leader of the Kikuyu. It was Karoli who captained his people against the incursions of the Masai. He it was who led the Kikuyu braves in glorious victories over the trouble-makers, Wang'ombe and Ndione, and gave peace to the tribe. From the first, Karoli was friendly and helpful to Father Perlo and his companions.

A dispensary was opened at the mission and news of it spread like a prairie fire. Hundreds of patients arrived, some from great distances. With a simple Kikuyu grammar written by Father Hemery, of the Holy Ghost missionaries, the Consolata pioneers acquired the difficult native tongue. Practical men of North Italy, they quickly harnessed a mountain stream to run a sawmill and thus had timber for their buildings. Their work grew. A simple, outdoor school was opened, and Chief Karoli was among the first pupils.

"Let me teach you to write your name," proposed Father Perlo. The idea pleased the chief immensely, and he followed every lesson attentively. He was intrigued by the mysterious marks on the paper; he wanted to solve the puzzle.

It was this urge to know, this peerless simplicity in the finer types among the Kikuyu, that early gave proof to the missionaries and to the more perceptive among the settlers that the Kikuyu tribe possessed unusual qualities. Wisdom and moderation were characteristic of the Kikuyu of that day. A tribal discipline safeguarded the rights and property of each member of the community. Thieves or trespassers had little opportunity to prosper. Violence and murder were infrequent, and offenders seldom escaped justice.

In 1915 Chief Karoli, then aged seventy, asked for baptism for himself and his wife Wanjiro. For the festivities he invited his friends Chiefs Njili and Moriranga and many others to be on hand. It proved a memorable occasion when many of the great ones of the tribe, even though not embracing Christianity, showed their respect for the things of the spirit.

From the first, the Consolata Missionaries aimed to train native leaders as teachers and religious. For many years, candidates were prepared for the priesthood, and in 1927 the first two—Fathers James Camisassa and Thomas Kemango—were ordained. They were the first Africans of Kenya to be raised to the altar.

"See! They were wearing the same vestments as the Europeans," noted their people in satisfaction.

Some years ago I made an interesting visit to St. Paul's Seminary for the Kikuyu where promising candidates for the priesthood pursued their studies in full view of the Kikuyu's beloved Mount Kenya. As for the religious life for women, strong Kikuyu family practices made vocations a foregone conclusion. The first three candidates presented themselves in 1918. Training began under the Consolata Sisters at Mogoiri, and in 1929 the first group of Kenya's native candidates were professed. In 1946, the Holy See approved the establishment of the Kikuyu Sisters, known as the Sisters of Mary Immaculate, as an independent community. They were some eighty members, and the group elected Sister Julia Wamboy as its first Mother Superior.

I watched those daughters of the Kikuyu in admiration, as they taught youngsters in school, directed playground drills, and chatted with the Kikuyu parents who came to take their children home. Particularly noticeable was their buoyant good humor. Their religious habit, a peculiar tan, was chosen because it is a predominant color in the local native dress.

At Teto, one of the earliest stations in the Kikuyu country, I watched six hundred Christians come in from their villages to Sunday

Mass. "A generation ago, when we made this foundation," said Father Benedetto, "these people went about in the nude. From the beginning, however, we knew that they were not primitive savages. They are among the keenest and most intelligent peoples in Africa." Their faces reflected their pastor's words. There was a sparkle in their eyes and a freshness in their mien that reflected the rich vigor of the mountain country in which they lived.

"Let me see your prayerbook," I said to a woman who passed.

"Gladly, Father," she answered in English, and visibly pleased, handed me the book.

My attention had been caught by the cover—skin cut from an antelope pelt, bound neatly about the little volume. On the flyleaf, that black woman, a teacher, had printed the words, "As the hart panteth after the fountains of water, so my soul panteth after thee, O God."

"It fits our wonderful Kikuyu country, Father," said my thoughtful acquaintance.

By the side of the church, corralled like prancing ponies, behind a pole fence toddled almost a score of young children, guarded by a Kikuyu maid. The infants went inside with their mothers. Hundreds of the congregation approached the rail for Communion, and many a mother had her infant on her back. A teen-age boy sang a solo in the organ loft until his turn came to go to the rail; then he and the organist hurried down the middle aisle.

"The Kikuyu are a very attractive people!" I exclaimed enthusiastically to Father Benedetto as we walked toward the rectory.

"Yes," he replied without enthusiasm. "But they have us very much worried at the moment. So many of them feel disaffected toward the Government for the loss of their lands."

The loss of their lands! In Kikuyuland in the 1930's I had heard for the first time the story that has been on so many lips since 1952, the story of the tragedy of the Kikuyu.

Earlier in this book, when we were in the Gold Coast, we rehearsed the story of the Golden Stool. We were astounded to learn that, because no white man in authority in the Gold Coast had known enough cultural anthropology to understand and interpret the significance of the Golden Stool, Great Britain had fought a war with the Ashanti tribes to obtain possession of the stool. For decades thereafter, the British Government had infuriated the intelligent black people by its unwittingly sacrilegious offensiveness. After Captain Rattray and his anthropological team had, in 1920, interpreted to British authorities the significance of the Golden Stool, peace was restored in the Gold Coast.

It is a coincidence that in Kenya, in East Africa, during almost the same period of years, events were developing that needed the attention of cultural anthropologists. In point of fact, able anthropologists from Europe, including Professor Lindblom of Sweden and the celebrated Malinowski, studied the history and customs of the Kikuyu people early in the twentieth century. Their findings might have guided events to avoid the present savagery in Kikuyuland. The significance of their conclusions was ignored. A multitude of factors have now joined to create an almost hopeless tangle. Taken in good time, the key factor, the flouting of time-honored ways among the Kikuyu, could have been recognized and acted upon.

All through Africa—in the Gold Coast, in the Congo, in Basutoland, in Tanganyika—I recall long sessions with scholars and missionaries, in which deep regret was expressed by wise and experienced leaders that greater attention has not been given to a systematic employment of cultural anthropology for a proper understanding of Africa's peoples. Government administrators can be forgiven for overlooking such a matter. Business men and settlers are not expected to care enough about people to doubt the superficial evidence of their eyes and to probe more deeply and delicately into the inner man of Africa in order to know him properly. But how explain this negligence on the part of all but a very few missionaries?

Now scholars like Professor Leakey of the Coryndon Museum of Nairobi (a cultural anthropoligist and leading expert on Kikuyu law and custom), have given such studies to the public.[1] Though probably too late for efficacious action, what they uncover provides a sobering object lesson in the harm that can be done through our ignorance of a people like the Kikuyu.

In 1900 and thereabouts, when the European settlers first entered Kenya, they found the vast Kenya highlands unoccupied. Professor Leakey explains that this phenomenon came about through the fact that during the previous ten years the Kikuyu had suffered four colossal disasters that had reduced their numbers by fifty per cent. Those disasters were the following: (1) a rinderpest epidemic that killed most of the Kikuyu cattle; (2) a decimating smallpox epidemic; (3) a famine after a long drought; (4) a plague of locusts. Great numbers of Kikuyu who did not die, particularly of the highland region of Kiambu, fled to seek escape among their clansmen at Fort Hall and Hiari. As a consequence, parts of the Kikuyu country were almost empty of people. Thus it happened that the British Government in all good faith transferred considerable tracts of land formerly occupied by the Kikuyu tribe to the white newcomers from Europe. Those white newcomers in turn negotiated in all good faith for this land. Had they not seen with their own eyes that it was vacant?

By about 1920, the Kikuyu tribe had recovered from its disasters. Its leaders, who then had a smattering of education, began to demand return of the lands that were dotted with profitable European homesteads. By Kikuyu law, no man could sell his land, even if he wanted to, without giving first refusal to one of his own family or tribe; certainly no one could sell the property of an absentee. This and a score of other arguments convinced the Africans that they had been cheated and brought resentment among the Kikuyu to fever pitch. Some of the expropriated landlords united in a society called the Kikuyu Central Association.

Lack of political experience soon led the K.C.A. into difficulties with the police. The society's president, Harry Thuku, was arrested in 1922; and during the riots that followed in Nairobi, some Kikuyu were killed. Feelings moved up several notches from hostility into hatred, deep hatred, against the whites.

"Unfortunately," explains Father Sestero of the Consolata Missionaries, "this hatred of the stranger was turned in great measure against the missionaries and their works. They were in fact the element that was easiest to fight, because they did not have guns and askaris as the Government did. A K.C.A. slogan was '*Gotire Mothongo na Mobea*' ('There is no distinction between the white man and the missionary')." [2]

The names of Jomo Kenyatta, Jesse Kariuki, and Joseph Kangetha soon came into prominence, and the hostility of those Africans to Christianity was strong from the beginning. "There is little doubt," says Professor Leakey, "that they regarded themselves as men with a mission; that they were fired with a burning desire to help their people and to set right the wrongs, both genuine and imaginary, that had been done to them."

Kenyatta, called by his followers the Burning Spear, was as a boy a skinny, little cowherd with a big smile, who enrolled young in a Protestant mission school. During the 1930's, he was a leader in promoting independent Protestant churches, which enabled religious Kikuyu to continue church life and yet break with the foreigner. One of their tenets was, "No intervention by white missionaries." Independent grade schools, many of which received Government grants-in-aid, were advocated by Kenyatta. Ironically enough, such schools were promoted by the Kenya Department of Education, whose officials were anxious for any turn in affairs that would strengthen the non-mission schools. Independent schools became a large-scale movement in 1934.

"A group of strayed Protestant Christians asked the Education Department, in the 1930's, for the registration of independent schools free from interference by Christian agenies," states a Kenya missionary. "The application was promptly granted by the department, in the hope that the natives themselves would secularize the schools on their own initiative. In no time the country was dotted with independent schools, which deteriorated into hotbeds of communism, unsound patriotism, and gangsterism. At the time the Government suppressed them they numbered two hundred and had twenty thousand students."

Peter Koinange, during the Nineteen Thirties, founded the Kenya Teachers College at Githunguri, which proved an important feeder for K.C.A. leaders, particularly after Jomo Kenyatta became its principal. This likewise has been suppressed by the Government. After World War II, Kenyatta returned from a visit to Europe, during which he studied communist techniques. He was more respected by his followers and more bitter than ever toward his chosen enemies. The K.C.A. had been suppressed during the war, but a substitute, the Kenya African Union, was founded; and for five years in secrecy, it organized a much more dreadful instrument, the Mau Mau movement.

By far the most important grievance of all Kikuyu, whether moderate or radical, whether God-fearing Christians or men professedly of no religion, was the loss of the Kikuyu lands. Exaggeratedly false and fantastic stories of new "land thefts" were constantly appearing in the vernacular press. The original claims, however, were impressive

THE DISRUPTED LANDS OF KENYA

The Kenya Highlands represent but one-fifth of the total area of Kenya. Much of the remainder of the colony is barren and unpromising. Except for the vast plateau of Ethiopia, the Kenya Highlands are the most considerable tract of open, habitable land exceeding 5,000 feet in tropical Africa. The popular understanding among the white settlers who took title to portions of these highlands (see graph) was that they were held only nominally by Africans who were not interested in them. It is the contention of the Africans that from time immemorial they have been very much attached to these lands and that they never had any intention of alienating them to the foreigner.

Thus these disputed lands figure so prominently in the Mau Mau uprising in Kenya.

enough to win the sympathy of all fair-minded persons, African and non-African.

In addition, other important factors stirred Kikuyu wrath and prepared the way for the Mau Mau. Those factors were seven: (1) suppression of independent schools; (2) increase in population, which heightened the land crisis; (3) widespread pauperism embittered by demands of the young, not only for bare sustenance but for the better living that they had come to consider their right; (4) deteriorated living conditions for the squatters on foreign-held land; (5) disappearance of ancient customs that previously had been a protection against a breakdown of the Kikuyu social system; (6) discontent among Kikuyus returned from foreign military service; (7) increased consciousness of the white man's color-bar philosophy.

The Mau Mau movement, which was the old K.C.A. and the new K.A.U. in battle garments, had three elements in its make-up. They may be described as follows:

1—The military inner circle. The bitterest enemies of the Mau Mau confess to admiration at the dastardly effectiveness of its operating techniques.

2—A religio-political bond embracing all Kikuyu. This interests us much and calls for an explanation of (a) its tremendously powerful pressures on all Kikuyu and (b) its dread oath.

3—An anti-white program creating peril to life and the pocketbook. Evidently this was conceived as a long-term program, on the theory that time is on the side of the African. Relatively few whites have been killed, but all are forced to maintain a state of tension and alert that farmer families could not possibly continue over a period of years. Kenya, a wealthy colony for its size, could easily afford the emergency expenditures of the first couple of years, but would be bankrupt if the outlay had to continue for a decade or more.

Their plans evolved, Kenyatta and his assistants began moving among their own people, to organize secretly a thoroughly homogeneous unit unswervingly dedicated to destroying everything foreign to the Kikuyu.

"It is a commentary on how seriously out of touch the white authorities were with Kikuyu life," a highly placed personality in Nairobi explained to me, "that this organizing movement went on for years before its significance came to light. A lack of knowledge of the difficult Kikuyu vernacular is an important factor in this. Everybody did business through black interpreters. There were the court interpreter, the educational secretary interpreter, the police interpreter, the business man's interpreter. At times the Mau Mau conspired with some of those interpreters to have anti-Mau Mau leaders condemned by the authorities as enemies of the whites!"

"Half of our trouble," expostulated the Honorable E. A. Vasey, the man handling Kenya's finances, "is that we whites and the African don't understand each other."

Kenyatta began his now-famous secret harangues in Kikuyu territory by clever use of ridicule. "The white man dresses you as he dresses his women!" he cried disdainfully, referring to the ankle-length skirt, in general use by house servants and waiters. "You do all the work. But only your women used to work. Are you women? The white man calls himself 'mister'; or 'sir'; or 'lord.' What does he call you? *'Boi-ee!'* he shouts, and you run. You used to be Kikuyu and warriors, and owners of fine cattle and far lands. And today? You've got no cattle, you've got no lands, and you're not warriors or even Kikuyu. What shall I call you? Women and boys? Go serve your masters, you women! *Boi-ee!* Grovel in the land that is rightfully yours!" [3]

Against Christianity, Kenyatta railed with similar disdain. "Jesus Christ is an Englishman!" he told his listeners in the stillness of the Naivasha forest. "Shut your eyes in prayer, you Christians. When you open them, you'll find he has stolen more of your land!"

Then came the religio-political bond of a dread oath, taken under frightening and humiliating circumstances that, by playing on traditional superstitions, made the victims, even if they acted under duress, feel that there was no turning back from the unhappy new course. The oath was administered at first only to a few; then a wider swath of the population was introduced to it. Finally all Kikuyu, willing or not, were to be subjected to it. This stage was reached in 1952, and it was then that the movement became clearly known for what it represented.

The Mau Mau oath is composed of a mystical seven points, which summarized are as follows:

1—I renounce belief in Christian teachings, in the practice of prayer and the reception of the sacraments. I regard missionaries as a menace to be liquidated or removed.

2—I will boycott all whites.

3—I renounce all alcoholic beverages made by whites.

4—I reject all Government policies regarding education.

5—I pay my initiation fee to the society and promise all future payments as made on demand.

6—I will never report a Mau Mau to the police for any offense or crime.

7—I will reveal this oath to no one.

The frightening conclusion is, "May God strike me and my family dead, if I fail to obey this oath!"

"You can imagine how stunned and shocked we were," related a Consolata Missionary, "as reports came in of great numbers of our people forced to take this oath."

Numbers of the more valiant Catholics, like Sophie, with whose story we began this chapter, resolutely withstood the Mau Mau demands. The cost was great suffering and sometimes death. Typical of the intimidation that conquered most resistance is the experience of Magdalene Wayiki, who now is a refugee at a Consolata mission.

A messenger called at Magdalene's house one evening and invited her to accompany him to a nearby house, where a party was to be held. Unsuspectingly, Magdalene followed the man. At the house, she was ushered inside and there found other village women already gathered. Men armed with pangas (huge, two-foot-long banana knives) guarded the door. Magdalene was informed that she was to take the Mau Mau oath. She objected, and was told by the men with the pangas that she would be killed if she refused, and those present would drink her blood.

One by one, the women were led from the hut. When Magdalene's turn came, she was ordered to remove everything that was foreign— her sandals, her medal, her rings. She was led to another hut, which was in semidarkness. Men were gathered around the wall, and she saw her husband sitting in fear in one corner. A loop of grass was thrown about Magdalene's neck, and some Kikuyu earth placed in her hand. The oath giver made a circle seven times around her head, with a mixture of goat's blood and earth. He then handed her a banana flower and told her the oath she was to take.

Magdalene refused to take any oath renouncing her Christian religion. The leader slapped her several times and made obscene threats of what would happen to her if she should continue to refuse. Magdalene looked to her husband for help, but he was too terrified to speak. When she continued to object, the man obtained a rope, tossed one end over a rafter, looped the other about her neck, and hoisted her off the floor until she lost consciousness. When she was revived, she continued in her refusal, and again she was hoisted off the floor.

How long that torture went on, Magdalene has no idea. She remembers that, during one period of consciousness, she mumbled the Mau Mau oath. She was then sent home. As soon as she was able, Magdalene fled to the mission. Fortunately, she understood that the oath she was forced to take did not bind her. Nevertheless she was too frightened to inform on the individuals who had abused her.

Most of the Catholics in the Nyeri, Fort Hall, and Kiamu Districts were forced to take the oath. A few of the lukewarm freely took it and left the Church. Archbishop McCarthy, of Nairobi, and Bishop Cavallera, of Nyeri, announced that all such were excommunicated. Naturally, sympathetic understanding was shown toward the weak characters, and special "Days of Return" were held when missionaries, aided by faithful Kikuyu elders, tried to persuade as many apostates as possible to renounce the oath. Like Magdalene, some Catholics took the oath under duress and knew that they were not bound by it. Still others like Sophie refused to take the oath even under torture. Of these latter, some have been killed, some beaten and wounded, some burned out of their homes.

"Among those murdered were some of our best Catholics," reported one of the Consolata priests. "Among them are three men—Mariano Wacira, Domeniko Nyota, and Joseph Gacera. One day they may be honored as the first martyrs of Nyeri. All three belong in Gekondi, a center of violence. Through it all, the three served the mission with great devotion. The Mau Mau ambushed these three fine men at a ford in the Gekira River. They hacked them to death with pangas and threw their bodies into the water.

"Mariano Wacira, a catechist for forty years, had just been awarded the Pro Ecclesia et Pontifice medal by Pope Pius XII. He was killed before the honor could be formally bestowed on him. At a meeting of the elders of the Nyeri missions, to study ways and means of defending their Faith against the Mau Mau, Mariano had said publicly: 'This is the time for us to show our faith. We must all be ready to shed our blood.' At a Legion of Mary meeting at Gekondi, he had declared: 'I feel that I shall be killed for my Faith. However, the Mau Mau can kill only my body; my soul will live forever with Christ!' "

This anti-Christian factor in the plan has proven the Achilles heel in the Mau Mau program. Otherwise, feelings were running so high among Kikuyu of all persuasions on the score of tribal injustices that a formidable solidarity might have been obtained against the white men. It is not surprising, therefore, that retribution should be taken by the Mau Mau against Christian missions. After a while, Kikuyu Home Guards were systematically organized by the populace to protect the missions.

Imenti, the central station of the Consolata Diocese of Meru, was attacked by a band of fifty Mau Mau. Sister Eugenia, a European sixty-one years old and thirty-two years among the Kikuyu, was killed by clubs and pangas. She was hideously slashed, and one of her hands was amputated. In the same attack, Father Edmund Cavicchi was wounded. Father Patrick J. McGill, of the Irish Holy Ghost Fathers, a worker for twenty-five years among the Kikuyu, stirred the ire of the Mau Mau by his fearless condemnations of them. They made three attempts on his life, during one of which his curate, Father J. J. O'Donoughue, barely escaped death.

Kikuyu priests, Sisters, and lay teachers were objects of special hatred. On October 15, 1953, a band of terrorists attacked the all-African mission of Baricio. One of the two African priests succeeded in escaping to the forest; the other was captured and beaten senseless. Of the five African Sisters, two were killed, two were badly beaten and one escaped. By the middle of 1954, fourteen Kikuyu Catholic teachers had been killed, and twenty-five Catholic schools had been burned down.

"The full weight of the tragedy," declares one of the Consolata Missionaries, "falls upon the very tribe from which the Mau Mau springs. The Kikuyu peasant in the quiet countryside or in his lonely hut at night may open the door to welcome a friend and find there the hideous Mau Mau killers. It is the tormented rank and file among this wonderful people that holds my sympathy."

Has the Mau Mau movement a Communist connection? It would

appear that it has. Michael de la Bedoyere, a thoughtful philosopher of London's Fleet Street, reminds us that it does not require much Communist intrigue to make the Mau Mau work for the Red cause.

"If Professor Toynbee is correct," says De la Bedoyere, "in calling the impact of the West on the East a form of Western aggression, this kind of aggression was far more obviously marked in the impact of Europe on Africa. It is only in still recent history that a great, dark, uncivilized continent was parceled up by the Powers for the purpose of economic exploitation. . . .

"And now Africa is full of agents whose job is to dot the i's and cross the t's for any African who is slow in picking up the idea that he has not exactly had a fair deal. Never was the way made easier for the astute propagandists of Moscow, who need never mention the word communism at all. By causing disaffection among the natives, many of whom are now sufficiently educated to feel a genuine enough grievance, they set the white minority and the Powers responsible for them a problem that is likely to become graver as month succeeds month. . . .

"In Kenya, the open Mau Mau criminality involves a self-defensive police action which cannot be disapproved by the world if wholesale massacre is not to be tolerated. None the less, the long-term problem is equally puzzling for a white minority in the midst of a people which, albeit still primitive, has legitimate economic grievances which will be increasingly encouraged by Communists and their agents among the better-educated African leaders.

"The only possible answer to these explosive situations in Africa must lie in working toward making a reality of the spiritual strength which Christianity alone can give to the West in its battle with Communism. . . ." [4]

Chapter 7

EAST AFRICA GOES TO SCHOOL

WHILE MRS. BEACHEY busied herself with the noon meal, I sat in the library of the Beachey family's very attractive home and read passages from Winston Churchill's book, *My African Visit.* The Beacheys are from Canada, and Doctor R. W. Beachey is a lecturer in the history department of Makerere University College, Kampala. With his assignment, he has fallen heir to one of the European-style residences on the campus, where he lives with his wife and two children. "We should hardly be better fixed, were we at one of Canada's fine universities or colleges," commented the lady of the house.

Churchill wrote *My African Visit* in 1908. In it he expatiated enthusiastically on England's rule "over the whole of the northeast quarter of the African continent under the influence or the authority of the British crown." Sir Winston has lived but a normally long life, yet long enough to see his vision consummated and an entirely new concept take its place; namely, the progression of East Africa from British colonial status to responsible self-government.

A pastoral letter of the Catholic Bishops of Tanganyika, published in 1953, reveals the trend of the times in this respect. The letter, signed by all seventeen members of the Tanganyika hierarchy, is a doctrinal instruction and by no means of political nature. Yet there is a section entitled "The People of Tanganyika and their Political Aspirations." A couple of paragraphs from this document help us to appreciate how far the people of Africa have come since 1908, when Churchill and the leaders of his time could think of Africa as primarily a field of political achievement for the European powers of their day.

"Africans have begun to see themselves and others more clearly in the light of Christian revelation," declares the pastoral, "and they grow daily more aware of their dignity as men. And among those especially who have enjoyed the benefits of education, there is an increasingly strong demand to play an active part in the development and direction of their country. Nobody looks back with greater joy on the advance of Tanganyika than the Church, which has spared no pains to try to bring to Africa what is best in Christian civilization. . . .

"Tanganyika is a country of many semi-independent tribes, each with its own dialect, laws, customs, elders, and chiefs. The present Government is responsible for the development of political institutions and for guiding the destinies of the people as a whole, in order to insure for them now and in the future the progress and security that is necessary for independent nations in a highly complex and competitive world. *For the goal desired by all is a self-governing Territory*, and the preparatory work in view of this is proceeding at a gradual but ever-quickening pace." [1]

No place in East Africa is better suited for an appreciation of the promise and the pitfalls before the peoples of East Africa than Makerere. This is an autonomous University College which, although situated in Uganda, serves the whole of East Africa. The students there are now able to take the external degrees of London University; the first candidates sat for their degrees at the end of 1953.

Kampala's seven, flat-topped hills lend an intriguing complexity to the city. On the summit of each hill, we find ourselves in a miniature world separated from the general community. There is Rubaga, with its huge Catholic cathedral and surrounding properties, calm and reserved like a great, wall-less cloister. There is the hill of the Anglican cathedral and nearby institutions, including the large C.M.S. hospital. On a third hill, rise the diaphanous minarets of the Aga Khan's Moslem mosque. Mengo, a fourth hill, bears the cachet of Buganda's royalty. So likewise, Makerere, occupant of one of the seven hills, seems to live to itself, once we mount the rugged road. Centered on the hilltop plateau is the main block, with its impressive ivory walls and green tile surrounded by smartly trimmed, picture-book lawns, fine trees, flowering shrubs. Dark-skinned students in shorts and shirts move in and out noiselessly, some with the set step of men errand-bent, some strolling in casual, low-voiced conversation with companions. A brilliant sun gives an almost magic glamour to the scene.

"Beautiful, isn't it?" remarked one of the professors to whom Mr.

Beachey introduced me. "There is a perilous unreality about it all, if we take the physical Makerere for what it might seem to mean in England. Of course, no sensible person makes such a mistake. Makerere is tremendously important, not for what it has actually done as yet, but for what it can mean in East Africa's tomorrow."

Two simple and attractive chapels flank the main block, identical in construction. One is Catholic; the other represents the rest of the Christian world. In Uganda, non-Catholic Christianity is overwhelmingly Anglican; but in Kenya and Tanganyika, a large number of sects are represented. There is likewise a Moslem mosque on the campus. Evidently a frank acceptance of the Deity is a rule at Makerere. On the beautiful school shield, which I found emblazoned in the main foyer, appears the text, *"Deus illuminatio mea"*—"God is my light"—the motto of Oxford University.

There were some four hundred students at Makerere in 1953, the majority in lower classes. Of the total, one-quarter were Catholic.

"Our Catholics showed up very well, indeed, in the examinations," reports Father Carney, their chaplain, a Mill Hill missionary who is also an instructor on the faculty. "Of the five science students accepted into the Medical School, four are Catholics; and among them is Miss Josephine Namboze, from Namagunga School, who is the first girl ever to be accepted. Miss Namboze was also among the prize winners with two other Catholics, Miss Namuli and Miss Valentine Eyakuza, both from St. Mary's of Tabora, Tanganyika.

"During 1952, we experienced a student strike at Makerere. Naturally, some Catholics were among the leaders chosen by the student body, but it is to their credit that not one took part in the student meetings without first consulting his chaplain. Indeed, during those days almost every Catholic sought the advice of the priest. The result was that the more courageous among them publicly asked the other students to obey the authorities.

"The spiritual life of the students is vigorous and attendance at daily Mass very good. A setback was experienced at the beginning of the troubles in Kenya: two or three Kikuyu Catholics neglected their duties for a time, and tried to influence others against the practice of religion but without success. On the other hand, a Kikuyu boy from Mangu asked for Baptism and was confirmed by Bishop Rugambwa, who visited us and addressed the students in the chapel. One of our lower-class boys desires to try his vocation to the priesthood.

"I am confident that the vast majority of Catholic students now passing through Makerere will return to their homes prepared to be active in their religion, provided that they receive that little encouragement and sympathy so necessary to young men commencing a career."

It was a pleasure to register Father Carney's sentiments, since everywhere, among both Catholics and Protestants, one of the first questions asked regarding a Government-operated institution of higher education is the effect that such an institution is having on the spiritual life of the Africans.

"Both at Makerere and elsewhere," said Father Peter Rivard, one of the fine leaders among the White Fathers, "a great deal of devastating harm is done to the blacks by contact with whites who are completely secularized. As does every well-balanced European, the African conceives religion as integrated with life. It seems to be an obsession of many secularized whites to seek to destroy this concept in the Africans. One youth at Makerere returned to Bukoba very much upset, because one of his professors had kept repeating to him that there was no God, that God was only an idea cooked up by the missionaries."

"How are you impressed by the students?" I asked Doctor Beachey, who gave me generously of his time and introduced me to a number among the school authorities.

"As a group, they have something very fine about them that makes me like them very much," the doctor replied. "They come to Makerere with a sense of bewilderment much greater than British or American students experience when they enter a university. First of all, the difference between Makerere and home is enormous for the youths. Very many of them have lived in mud-and-wattle huts. Many go back from here each year to bare feet and tribal ways. Their life is quite distinctly a dichotomy. Part of our job is to help them to avoid becoming maladjusted to their society.

"In their studies, even after good secondary-school courses, they are under enormous handicaps by the complete isolation of their environment from the requirements of a University of London degree. In history, for instance, we start with the Elizabethan period. But very

seldom has a student here ever heard of 1066. Every historical allusion
that one makes, every aside that the professor drops, requires explanation. Particularly during the first year, the students are in a daze; they
deserve a great deal of patient, sympathetic treatment."

"As they move into the higher classes, do they keep their heads?"

"Quite as in Canada, they can be spoiled by stupid vanities. A
certain element even among the faculty gives them the line, 'You are
the patricians; you must maintain your superiority.' This makes some
of them silly. I saw one boy, for instance, hire a servant to carry his
small handbag from one building to another when his room was
changed."

"What prospects await these young men after they complete their
studies?"

"The opportunities are tremendous. The great question is the
graduates' capacity to fill them. On analysis, we find that it is more a
moral question than an intellectual one, a matter of character that
will guide a young man to adapt a certain amount of awkwardly adjusted equipment to the requirements of real life. Few of our graduates go in for teaching, though many African teachers are needed for
the higher schools. A few give promise in the arts, though East Africa
has little tradition in this field. In the professions, medicine is most
popular. I try to encourage boys to enter business because most East
African business is in the hands of foreigners, principally the Indians.
The Africans are poor in business but primarily I think, because
they've had no experience at it. With two or three generations of intensive effort behind them in this field, I'm convinced that there will
be less cause to wail about their helplessness."

"I see very few young women among the students," I remarked to
Doctor Beachey.

"There are less than a score of them here," he replied. "As in the
rest of Africa, far fewer girls than boys are educated. In East Africa
the Baganda are best in this respect; they have almost as many girls
as boys starting school—though most girls do drop out early. In
Tanganyika and Kenya, the average is one girl to four or five boys, in
the grade schools."

I was particularly interested in Josephine Namboze, who was mentioned by Father Carney as due to be East Africa's first woman doctor.
Her family lives not far from the Mill Hill mission center and the

residence of Bishop Billington, on the other side of Kampala. Her father, as we might guess, is an educated man, professor in a Catholic normal school, who has inspired his brood of twelve children to make something of themselves. Naturally the financial burden he bears is herculean.

Josephine is a soft-voiced, gentle girl endowed with unusual intelligence, who speaks precise and beautiful English. She decided to become a doctor when she was only thirteen years old.

"At school we were assigned an essay to write, on what we wanted to be," she explained as she sat in her little home making a dress to wear at Makerere. "I looked out the window and saw the nurses at work in the nearby Catholic hospital, under the supervision of a doctor. I decided then and there that I wanted to become a doctor—not a nurse, because they seemed to have all the difficult work. I know better now, but I still want to be a doctor. I feel that is the way I can best help my people."

Josephine's ideas tumbled out as she talked. The place to teach equality is in the school. Boys should learn to treat women as their equals. They should be taught that the woman is the heart of the family.

"After all, an educated boy needs an educated wife if he is to respect her," she declared, giving the wheel of her sewing machine a spin. "We are raising up many educated boys, but where will they find wives? An educated boy doesn't want to marry a woman who believes in old tribal taboos, who won't eat eggs because they will deprive her of fertility."

"Do you think your people will accept you as a doctor?"

"I doubt if the men will accept me," she replied frankly, "but the women will. It is to help our women that I am becoming a doctor. They need much help."

East Africa already has a number of young African doctors who give great promise. At the Fort Hall hospital, in the territory of the Consolata missionaries, there is a tall, sturdy Makerere graduate, Doctor Likimani, who is said to be as skilled at surgery as many of the European doctors in Kenya. In the back country beyond Tabora, in Tanganyika, people speak of a very devoted Makerere graduate, Doctor Mwaisela, who is a credit to his profession. The pattern is forming.

Makerere depends for its candidates, naturally enough, on the feeder schools throughout East Africa. Each time I visited one, I found myself trying to envision the boys and girls moving up and out, into the fast-changing world around them. One such school is under the direction of an old friend, Father Doyle of Mill Hill. He is rector of the Senior Secondary Boarding School at Namilyango, not too many miles outside Kampala. It sits on a sightly eminence among lush green hills, and possesses a group of buildings that could be the envy of many a small college anywhere in the world.

"You'll recall," Father Doyle remarked, "that we came into being at the turn of the century, to train the sons of chiefs. The office of chief is not as important in this part of Africa as it once was, but we are still getting the sons of chiefs as well as other boys who represent the best elements in many of the tribes. At the present moment, we have 178 students from twenty-one tribes, and we are very proud of the type of boy we graduate."

"I suppose the accent is on classical studies," I said.

"Not exclusively. We have two sections: the academic, which prepares for Cambridge examinations; and the commercial, which prepares for the London Chamber of Commerce examinations. Our boys likewise take the Makerere entrance exams."

A game of soccer was in progress. "What about the accent on sports?" I asked.

"We give sports their due, always with an eye to what they can contribute to build up vigor and to teach teamwork to our young hopefuls. Britain's battles, so it is said, were won on the playing fields of Namilyango."

Indeed, Namilyango has sporting victories that are won elsewhere than on sports fields. In the later afternoon, the campus cleared of all human life as everybody gathered in the gymnasium. In the center of the gym floor stood a regulation boxing ring, and as we entered, a class in boxing was already in progress.

"We owe all this to that English gentleman in the ring with the boys," explained Father Doyle. "He is a businessman in Kampala, Mr. Holcom by name, who for the past seven years has come out here every week, without fail, to coach the boys."

"Do they take to the sport well?"

"Like ducks to water! This year Mr. Holcom organized a Uganda

Boxing Team, made up preponderantly of Namilyango boys, and arranged a meet with the Kenya Boxing Team. The Uganda Team won, six contests to four."

"Who are those boys now in the ring?"

"The taller one is the son of the Prime Minister of Bunyoro, and his opponent is a Muganda."

Mr. Holcom declared this first contest a draw. A second bout was staged, between a Kikuyu and a Muganda. The Kikuyu took the decision. It was a delightful experience to witness the explosive glee, the wild enthusiasm, the hearty good fun, of the tightly packed crowd of student fans. The majority of them participate, at one time or another, in the bouts, by an established system of rotation. "It helps to make fine young men of them," said Father Doyle, "good losers and gracious winners."

Namilyango's prize among its buildings is its chapel, an architectural gem designed by Father Doyle himself. Said he: "Its construction was arranged by a Government educational officer who, in an address to the boys, drove home very compellingly the argument that religion is the basic foundation for all education. I talked with him some days later, and he agreed that this meant a chapel for every college."

Everywhere in East Africa, educators talk about the shortage in trade schools and agricultural schools. In times past, there has been a great tug of war in educational circles between leaders who would emphasize the academic and those who wanted to stress practical training for earning a living.

Few of the missions, either Catholic or Protestant, have maintained in outstanding fashion this emphasis on manual training, in particular on crafts and agricultural techniques. The high cost of equipment has been one reason. Monsignor Ligutti, an advocate of systematic agricultural training and of rural social living for all non-urban areas throughout the world, greatly lamented the weaknesses of the missions of Africa in this respect, during his recent visit to the continent.

A fundamental mistake by the builders of Africa was made, we are told, the day that they fixed a clerk's wage as higher than that of an artisan. A fundamental mistake by the builders of all civilization throughout the globe was made the day that the white-collared man was given economic and social superiority over the farmer. Certainly Africa is suffering greatly today through the lack of status for the artisan and the farmer. Educators would dearly love to put into the hearts of African artisans and farmers the proper pride of position that they should possess for their happiness and well-being.

Makerere University College has helped give recognition to farming by creating a faculty of agriculture. It has purchased the Kabanyolo Estate, a 340-acre holding, ten miles from Makerere and five miles from the Namulonge Government Cotton Research Station. The college authorities have no illusions about the task that faces it to build up a readiness among qualified East Africans to follow a career in scientific farming. But they are encouraged by the fact that the Belgian Congo and other countries in Africa have had success along this line. The missionaries of Verona are rated as having, at Gulu, both technical and agricultural schools that rank among the best in Uganda.

"Agriculture is, and will continue to be," says Sir Andrew Cohen, Governor of Uganda, "the major industry of Uganda. It must be treated as such in Government policy, and in all the efforts of those concerned with the economic development of the country."

"We have problems with our technical school program," admits Father Gaffney, Uganda Educational Secretary General; "nevertheless, our mission centers have always been the pioneers in this branch of education."

Father J. O'Meara of the Holy Ghost Fathers, Educational Secretary General in Kenya, notes the trend toward academic studies. "During the first three decades," he says, "the results achieved in Kenya by insistence on practical education based on Christian principles were astounding. Kabaa, in Ukamba, was founded in 1925 to help meet the great need for teachers, and it also had a strong technical bias. Carpentry, brick making, masonry were all included in the curriculum. But the swing was already toward more academic forms of training."

Bishop Holmes-Siedle, of Karema, reports enthusiastically on the "courageous break-away from the academic syllabus" in Tanganyika. "Africa is and must remain primarily an agricultural country," he says, "and the African should remain in his tribe, for his own good and for the good of the country. But the old educational system was going exactly contrariwise to these elemental principles. The new program seeks to remedy this. The boys will be taught to be useful citizens in their own milieu. They will learn to raise their standard of living and make money without leaving their homes. At the same time their training, with its agricultural or handicrafts bias, will not prevent a certain number of them from going on to secondary education."

Europeans and Americans have no realization of the large enterprise, relatively speaking, that grade-school education represents for Protestant and Catholic missions in Africa, particularly in British and Belgian Africa.

"When you go back to New York," a missionary leader in Tanganyika remarked to me, "remind the people of the United States that the Catholic Church in Africa has almost as many pupils in its schools as the Catholic Church in the United States! Thank Heaven, we don't have to build any million-dollar buildings, and we get generous Government support for much of our work. Nevertheless, for our puny backs the burden is mighty heavy. Here in East Africa alone, for instance, we have 950,000 pupils in our schools, and we employ 12,000 African teachers, besides having the services of 2,000 teaching Brothers and Sisters."

Certainly, a great deal of fine intelligence is devoted to the school system. In Kampala a modern two-story brick building is the administration center for Catholic education in Uganda, under Father Gaffney, of the White Fathers, and Father Fraupel, of Mill Hill. In the chancery building in Nairobi, I visited the Catholic educational center for Kenya, under Father O'Meara of the Holy Ghost missionaries. Father Richard Walsh of the White Fathers directs the national headquarters for Tanganyika, at Dar es Salaam. Together these men constitute a top-flight educational team in East Africa, though they'll admit that the work that counts most is done at the grass-roots level.

"The present panorama of school life in East Africa seems quite imposing for a pioneer country," remarked Father Gaffney, as we chatted in the airy quarters of the Kampala secretariat. "But big changes are ahead. British Africa's educational top brass was called to meet at Oxford University, in September of 1952, and a number of us missionary representatives were included. On every side, we heard that changes are necessary to keep pace with the times. Naturally, we missionaries want no changes that will squeeze the things of the spirit out of the African school system."

"Just at present, the missions are the principal school operators, are they not?" I observed.

"Yes. Back in 1925, eighty-five per cent of the schools in East Africa were missionary. In that year, the *Report of the East Africa Commission* was published by the British Government in London and became the bible of the educational officials out here. It has largely directed the school policy in the tremendous developments of the last quarter of a century. Now the ideas in the Oxford conference [2] will probably play a great role in the new era ahead."

"How did they feel at Oxford, about mission schools?" I asked.

"To put it briefly," answered Father Gaffney with a smile, "they said, 'Thank you—and now good-by!' If you'll look at the Report, you'll see that they duly note that, as regards education, African and European alike willingly acknowledge how much the territories owe to the efforts made by the voluntary agencies (which means the missions) in the years before the Government developed an organized school policy. 'It is equally clear,' the Report goes on to say, 'that in future the voluntary agencies have a changing role to play in African society, particularly as it affects education.' [3] The reason they give for this is accepted by many as sound enough; namely, that in Christian circles, whether Protestant or Catholic, the black Africans are taking over more and more. Competent though Africans may be in their own way, the Government contends that they haven't either the economic strength or the educational experience to assume to the full the direction of systems embracing hundreds of grade schools. The Government wants to take over, and of course this will mean shortly that local African authorities will be in charge."

"This means, then, that our Catholic schools will become secular schools?"

"Not if we can prevent it!" replied Father Gaffney with spirit. "In some instances, the Catholics will be strong enough to keep full-fledged private schools. In other instances, the authorities talk of the so-called Scottish system and the Quebec system, which in one way or another provide what is called the uni-denominational school. This means that the Government will own and operate the schools and control the curriculum, but a religious body will have a voice in the choice of the teachers and in the religious instruction of the boys and girls."

"What did they say at Oxford, on that idea?"

"Curiously enough, they incorporated its good points in the Report, though without advocating acceptance of the idea. 'It can be claimed,' the Report says, 'that the school in which the best kind of Christian education can be given is not the multi-denominational but the uni-denominational school, for two main reasons: first, because in such a school all subjects in the curriculum can be taught as aspects of religious education, and so the false dichotomy of religious and secular education can be avoided; secondly, because the close relationship of a school to an adult religious society enables an easy and natural transition by the boy or girl into the adult religious community.' "

Chapter 8

AFRICAN THANK-YOU

SEVERAL DAYS LATER, Father Paul Bordenet and I were riding through the drab, thorn-scrub country of Tanganyika. As we jogged over the rough dirt road, we came upon two ten-year-old boys, evidently going to school because each carried a packet of books.

"Let's give them a lift," I proposed.

Father Paul took pains to let them see that we were Padres, and then slowly stopped. "Jump in!" I signaled.

They hesitated a moment. Then their eyes gleamed, and they scrambled aboard. We immediately found that they knew neither my English nor Father Paul's Kikwaya. But they spoke with their eyes.

Evidently it was a thrilling experience for them, to stand in the body of the truck, holding on to the back of our seat. Each boy wore a tiny white shirt and neat shorts, passably clean, but no shoes. One carried three little paper-covered books; the other had two little books and a small pad of paper. One had a cheap strap about his; the other had a piece of string. Both boys gazed animatedly out at the thorn scrub, now on one side, now on the other, and then at the road ahead that our truck swallowed up so quickly. They looked at us, at what we wore, at our hair (so different from theirs), at our faces. And as my eyes caught theirs, they would break into a big, white-toothed smile and a gleeful laugh. "Hi! Hi!" they cried at last. We were reaching their stopping place. A hundred yards back from the road, stood their little school. Out of our truck they leaped in a jiffy. Then they bowed graciously and showed us their teeth again. As we drove away, they stood and waved after us.

There was Africa of tomorrow, I thought. How tickled those boys had been! If only we could succeed in winning the affection of such as they, and make them understand that we truly wish to help them.

If only they could be convinced that we have a genuine love for them, it would be very easy to guide them wisely.

The thought was not mine. I had picked it up from one of the men I admire most in East Africa, Father Michael Witte of the Holy Ghost Fathers. Twenty years ago I had driven with him seventy miles from Nairobi through the unfertile Wakamba wilderness while he talked incessantly about his boys of Kabaa.

At last we saw before us a verdant eminence topped by a building, isolated like a Cistercian monastery.

"It must be an oasis!" I exclaimed.

"It is," said the intense Father Witte, a glint in his eye. "It is, because fifty of the smaller boys water the thirsty ground for two hours every day. It is an oasis because it has been made so. Kabaa means 'bald-headed': the hill was once almost arid. It is an example to these boys, if they will catch the lesson, that whatever they touch in any line will flourish if they will give it hard work."

This was the key to Kabaa. Kabaa was a campaign against the lassitude that is born of immemorial lack of discipline.

The boys gave us a lusty greeting as we arrived, and I instantly observed their admiration and even affection for Father Witte. The three hundred of them lived in well-built but modest houses, not very different from their own homes. The central building was a staff house, constructed of one hundred thousand bricks, which had been made on an opposite height and carried down dale and up hill for two miles. In this primitive country, every such project seems as colossal as building the Pyramids.

We arrived in time for supper. In the evening Father Witte gathered his large, chattering company about an open fire, in a clearing near the staff house. A thin moon rode high overhead. Father Witte and I sat on chairs, and around us were concentric circles of black faces lighted by the glow from the fire. Suddenly Father Witte stood and lifted his arm imperiously; there was dead silence. Then the arm moved—and I gasped as a surge of music filled the air.

It was exquisite! *Ave Maris Stella* was the hymn, in an arrangement that I had never heard, in which the soprano voices climbed long delicate slopes, against a background of the deepest bass. Father Witte, I discovered shortly, had been a choir master in Holland; and on that African hilltop, he had prepared singers with great technical skill. But it was the ineffable richness of the Negro voice that made memorable the night. The boys thus entertained me for more than an hour.

Another special memory is that of a visit, the next day, to the boys' quarters at the time of their noon meal. We found no fancy dining hall. There were twenty-five out-door fireplaces, each consisting of three stoves so arranged as to hold a simple grill or a vessel for boiling. Each boy was required to bring in enough firewood daily, to cook his own meal, and during one week in every six, he and another boy must do the cooking for a squad of twelve. I saw one boy carrying to his fireplace a skinned animal that looked like a rabbit, while other boys were roasting similar pieces of meat.

"Many catch small game and share it with boys in their particular groups," explained Father Witte.

We saw the gardens, the tailor shop, the carpentry shop, the student court. A good part of the afternoon, we spent in the classrooms and study halls of the grade school, the high school, and the teachers college. "Though study has its problems," commented my guide, "as a matter of fact, it is the easiest of the nuts that we must crack.

"In Africa, the system is wrong!" Father Witte continued, in a burst of impatience. "There is too much instruction, but too little education. What young Africans need is a big tablespoonful of education and a small teaspoonful of instruction."

"What precisely, do you think a boy needs most for good results from his schooling?" I asked.

"I think," replied Father Witte, reflecting a moment, "that an African boy must feel—and he is capable of feeling sharply—that he is really loved by his teachers."

Many years passed before I contacted Father Witte again. He had had a number of assignments, because he had unusual skill in organizing. But Kabaa, I could see, still held the focus of his heart. He remembered the Kabaa boys best of all.

"Those boys can show gratitude, too," he remarked. "A few years ago, I celebrated my silver jubilee in a mission north of Nairobi. About fifty of my old boys, who held good positions in or around the capital, heard of it. They put their heads together and invited me as a guest of honor to a dinner in a Nairobi hotel. The chief judge of the Colony and the local magistrate (both white men, but good Catholics who know no color bar) joined us at table. The sincere speeches of the boys, made in simple, fluent English, were the fine sauce for the meal."

"I'm glad to hear that," I commented. "Men say so often that the African is never grateful."

"He is always grateful!" insisted Father Witte. "Sometimes it is in European fashion, as with the boys who invited me to dinner. Most often it is in African fashion."

"How is that?"

"Once at Kabaa I called a boy into my room because he had not shown any outward sign of satisfaction with a gift that I knew he appreciated. 'Can't you at least say a word of thanks, my boy?' I asked.

" 'Oh, Father, you white men always show your gratitude. We blacks keep it in our hearts, but it is there!'

"Somehow, between the European way of the wonderful group who invited me to the jubilee observance at the hotel, and the African way of that shy little shaver at Kabaa, I remember the African way with even deeper feeling."

Someone asked Father Witte what was the main reason for his great hold on the hearts of the Africans.

"It is just an accident," he replied.

Yes, an accident born of all-embracing love. When every design and calculation has failed, it will be this accident that will win the day for those who would help guide the new men of the world of Africa.

APPENDICES

APPENDIX A

Statistics of the Religions of Africa
Compiled By Doctor Jean L. L. Comhaire

COUNTRY	CATHOLICS	PROTESTANTS	EASTERN ORTHODOX	MOSLEM	ANIMISTS AND OTHERS	JEWS	TOTAL
NORTH and NORTHEAST AFRICA							
RIO DE ORO and IFNI	1,000	—	—	40,000	—	—	41,000
TANGIERS	[1]	200	—	36,500	50,000	7,000	100,000
SPANISH MOROCCO	263,000	100	—	943,500	159,500	14,200	1,374,000
FRENCH MOROCCO	365,000 Un. 1,000 [2]	5,000	1,500	7,858,500	20,200	243,800	8,495,000
ALGERIA	864,000	1,600	—	7,696,000	207,400	140,000	8,909,000
TUNISIA	280,000	400	—	3,140,000	—	105,000	3,525,000
LIBYA	45,000	—	—	1,060,000	15,000	4,000	1,124,000
EGYPT	55,000 Un. 81,000	163,000	950,000	19,411,000	174,000	40,000	20,874,000
SUDAN, ANGLO-EGYPTIAN	111,600	12,400	—	6,175,000	1,983,000	—	8,282,000
ETHIOPIA	23,400 Un. 18,190	43,400	7,000,000	3,750,000	4,153,010	12,000	15,000,000
ERYTREA	48,500 Un. 33,300	3,300	2,500	560,000	470,400	—	1,122,000
BRITISH SOMALILAND	100	—	—	523,000	900	—	524,000
FRENCH SOMALILAND	2,585	50	500	75,000	1,860	5	80,000
ITALIAN SOMALILAND	5,400	300	—	1,194,000	300	—	1,200,000
TOTAL	2,198,075	229,750	7,954,500	52,462,500	7,239,570	566,005	70,650,000

[1] Included in Spanish Morocco.   [2] Un. = Uniate Catholics of Oriental Rites.

Statistics of the Religions of Africa (continued)

WEST AFRICA								
FRENCH WEST AFRICA and FRENCH TOGOLAND	630,410	116,154	2,380	8,588,249	8,972,144	32	18,309,369
SPANISH WEST AFRICA	4,000	—	—	78,000	—	—	82,000
PORTUGUESE GUINEA	8,000	—	—	57,000	455,000	—	520,000
SIERRA LEONE	16,033	48,700	—	470,000	2,240,267	—	2,775,000
GOLD COAST and BRITISH TOGOLAND	381,997 Un. 1,500	370,500	1,000	475,000	3,073,003	—	4,303,000
NIGERIA and BRITISH CAMEROONS	935,773 Un. 1,500	959,700	—	16,511,000	12,590,527	—	31,000,000
LIBERIA	13,500	33,700	—	340,000	1,312,800	—	1,700,000
GAMBIA	3,316	2,300	—	200,000	72,384	—	278,000
CAPE VERDE ISLAND	135,000	200	—	4,000	3,800	—	143,000
TOTAL	2,131,029	1,531,254	4,960	26,723,249	28,719,925	32	59,110,369

Statistics of the Religions of Africa (continued)

COUNTRY	CATHOLICS	PROTES-TANTS	EASTERN ORTHODOX	MOSLEM	ANIMISTS AND OTHERS	JEWS	TOTAL
CENTRAL AFRICA							
SAO TOME	36,000	200	—	24,000	—	—	60,200
SPANISH GUINEA	142,000	16,800	—	1,000	15,200	—	175,000
FRENCH CAMEROUN	528,978	212,900	700	577,200	1,929,540	71	3,249,390
FRENCH EQUATORIAL AFRICA	413,861	161,329	105	1,213,130	2,611,540	31	4,400,000
BELGIAN CONGO and RUANDA URUNDI	4,664,284	778,351	2,400	120,000	9,890,865	100	15,456,000
ANGOLA	1,100,000	127,800	—	—	2,902,200	—	4,130,000
CENTRAL AFRICA FEDERATION							
NORTHERN RHODESIA	309,369	107,800	—	5,000	1,693,247	—	2,115,416
SOUTHERN RHODESIA	101,457[1]	167,500	—	9,000	2,179,043	4,000	2,461,000
NYASALAND	326,147	223,700	—	195,000	1,511,131	—	2,255,978
TOTAL	7,622,096	1,796,380	3,205	2,144,330	22,732,766	4,202	34,302,984

[1] Includes Catholics of Bechuanaland, served by missioners of Southern Rhodesia.

Statistics of the Religions of Africa (continued)

SOUTH AFRICA							
SAINT HELENA	100	4,600	—	—	—	—	4,700
UNION OF SOUTH AFRICA	578,000 Un. 1,000	7,250,000	2,400	100,000	4,478,600[3]	110,000	12,520,000
SWAZILAND	15,340	—	—	—	184,660	—	200,000
BASUTOLAND	204,950	100,000	—	—	273,050	—	578,000
BECHUANALAND	—[1]	—[2]	—	—	275,000	—	300,000
SOUTH WEST AFRICA	37,870	96,600	—	4,000	245,530	—	384,000
MOZAMBIQUE	210,000	52,000	—	100,000	5,400,000[4]	—	5,762,000
TOTAL	1,047,260	7,503,200	2,400	204,000	10,856,840	110,000	19,748,700

[1] Included in Southern Rhodesia. [2] Included in Union of South Africa.
[3] Includes 50,000 Indian Hindus and 14,500 non-Christian Chinese, presumably Confucianists. [4] Includes 3,000 Indian Hindus.

Statistics of the Religions of Africa (continued)

COUNTRY	CATHOLICS	PROTES-TANTS	EASTERN ORTHODOX	MOSLEM	ANIMISTS AND OTHERS	JEWS	TOTAL
EAST AFRICA							
KENYA and ZANZIBAR	410,463	240,000	—	1,000,000	3,481,787[1]	1,000	5,133,250
UGANDA	1,229,014	489,800	—	1,000,000	2,159,646	—	4,878,460
TANGANYIKA	903,324	316,600	—	1,560,000	5,526,055	—	8,305,979
TOTAL	2,542,801	1,046,400	—	3,560,000	11,167,488	1,000	18,317,689

[1] Includes 100,000 Indian Hindus.

Statistics of the Religions of Africa (continued)

INSULAR EAST AFRICA							
MADAGASCAR	774,428	527,101	701	218,170	2,597,881	15	4,118,296
REUNION	239,500	500	—	6,000	15,000	—	261,000
MAURITIUS	164,436	4,200	—	60,000	271,364[1]	—	500,000
SEYCHELLES	32,502	4,000	—	1,000		—	37,502
TOTAL	1,210,866	535,801	701	285,170	2,884,245	15	4,916,798
TOTAL FOR AFRICA	16,752,127	12,642,785	7,965,766	85,379,249	83,600,834	681,254	207,046,540

[1] Includes 225,000 Indian Hindus and 14,500 non-Christian Chinese, presumably Confucianists.

SOURCES:

POPULATION:
United Nations Statistical Yearbook, 1951-1952.

CATHOLICS:
Annuario Pontifico, 1954.
Catholic Directory of South Africa, 1953.
Statistiques Annuelles des Missions Catholiques en Afrique Francaise, Dakar, 1951-1952.
Statistics of the Apostolic Delegation of British East and West Africa, Mombasa, 1952-1953.
Statistics of the Apostolic Delegation of the Belgian Congo, 1951-1952.

PROTESTANTS:
World Christian Handbook, 1949.
Official Annual Reports.

MOSLEMS:
Reports of Catholic Bishops.
Moslem Survey, *Grand Lacs*, 1952.

APPENDIX B

Personnel—Catholic Church in Africa

MISSIONARIES

COUNTRY	PRIESTS	BROTHERS	SISTERS	CATECHISTS
NORTH and NORTHEAST AFRICA				
TANGIERS and SPANISH MOROCCO	96	306	25	—
FRENCH MOROCCO	243	50	525	588
ALGERIA	56	5	135	7
TUNISIA	124	—	640	—
LIBYA	40	—	183	—
EGYPT	372	156	1,882	—
ANGLO-EGYPTIAN SUDAN	172	88	251	649
ETHIOPIA	87	2	72	—
ERYTREA	208	127	319	—
BRITISH SOMALILAND [1]	6	9	15	—
FRENCH SOMALILAND				
ITALIAN SOMALILAND	17	4	90	7
TOTAL	1,421	750	4,137	1,251

[1] Served from Aden, Arabia.

Personnel—Catholic Church in Africa (continued)

COUNTRY	MISSIONARIES			AFRICANS			
	PRIESTS	BROTHERS	SISTERS	PRIESTS	BROTHERS	SISTERS	CATECHISTS
WEST AFRICA							
FRENCH WEST AFRICA and FRENCH TOGOLAND	640	71	544	70	33	207	3,640
PORTUGUESE GUINEA	18	7	12	—	—	—	—
SIERRA LEONE	46	3	38	—	—	—	140
GOLD COAST and BRITISH TOGOLAND	207	19	123	27	—	30	742
NIGERIA and BRITISH CAMEROONS	529	17	245	33	—	57	6,073
LIBERIA	26	—	11	1	—	—	—
GAMBIA	10	—	11	—	—	—	53
CAPE VERDE	29	3	16	—	—	—	—
TOTAL	1,505	120	1,000	131	33	294	10,648

Personnel—Catholic Church in Africa (continued)

| COUNTRY | MISSIONARIES | | | AFRICANS | | | |
	PRIESTS	BROTHERS	SISTERS	PRIESTS	BROTHERS	SISTERS	CATECHISTS
CENTRAL AFRICA							
SPANISH GUINEA and SAO TOME	9	17	85	—	—	43	—
FRENCH CAMEROUN	255	67	155	75	27	87	4,103
FRENCH EQUATORIAL AFRICA	201	62	170	35	26	53	2,751
BELGIAN CONGO and RUANDA-URUNDI	1,884	741	2,130	316	360	589	—
ANGOLA	280	71	312	—	—	—	—
CENTRAL AFRICAN FEDERATION							
NORTHERN RHODESIA	226	50	152	23	—	21	611
SOUTHERN RHODESIA [1]	152	62	465	—	—	150	711
NYASALAND	148	27	116	35	—	104	1,776
TOTAL	3,155	1,097	3,585	485	418	1,047	9,952

[1] Statistics include Bechuanaland, which is served from Southern Rhodesia.

Personnel—Catholic Church in Africa (continued)

SOUTH AFRICA	MISSIONARIES				AFRICANS		
UNION OF SOUTH AFRICA	828	453	3,642		442		219
SWAZILAND	19	19	50		32		31
BASUTOLAND	125	62	204		284		786
BECHUANALAND [2]	73	35	215	[1]	20	[1]	102
SOUTHWEST AFRICA	256	67	440		—		102
MOZAMBIQUE					—		—
TOTAL	1,301	636	4,551		778		1,138

[1] African Priests and Brothers included in statistics for Missionaries.
[2] Statistics included in Southern Rhodesia, Central Africa.

Personnel–Catholic Church in Africa (continued)

| COUNTRY | MISSIONARIES | | | AFRICANS | | | |
	PRIESTS	BROTHERS	SISTERS	PRIESTS	BROTHERS	SISTERS	CATECHISTS
EAST AFRICA							
KENYA and ZANZIBAR	258	39	371	21		165	1,443
UGANDA	347	119	267	151		762	3,812
TANGANYIKA	730	261	508	161		497	5,157
TOTAL	1,335	419	1,146	333		1,424	10,412

Personnel—Catholic Church in Africa (continued)

	MISSIONARIES			AFRICANS			
INSULAR EAST AFRICA							
MADAGASCAR	357	150	418	103	178	240	4,786
REUNION	54	11	58	27	21	294	280
MAURITIUS	44	18	29	22		259	32
SEYCHELLES	20	14	44	1		14	
TOTAL	475	193	549	153	199	607	5,098
TOTAL FOR AFRICA	9,192[1]	3,212[1]	14,968	1,102	645	4,150	38,499

1 Statistics include African Priests and Brothers for South Africa.

SOURCES:

Annuario Pontificio, 1954.
Statistics of the Apostolic Delegation of British East and West Africa—Mombasa—1952, 1953.
Statistiques Annuelles des Missions Catholiques en Afrique Francaise—Dakar—1951, 1952.
Statistics of the Apostolic Delegation of the Belgian Congo, 1951-1952.
Catholic Directory of South Africa, 1953.

APPENDIX C

U.S. Catholic Missionary Personnel In Africa

It is an interesting commentary on American Catholic participation in the Christian movement in Africa that, as of December 31, 1953, only 245 priests and Brothers and 134 Sisters of United States citizenship labored in Africa. On the basis of the data supplied in Appendix B the total of Catholic missionary priests, Brothers and Sisters on the continent (excluding 5,897 African priests, Brothers and Sisters) is 27,372. Thus the 379 Catholic missionaries from the United States in Africa represent but 1.4% of the whole. The contributing societies and the number of their United States members in Africa are listed below.

COUNTRY	INSTITUTES OF MEN NAME, U.S. CENTER	U.S. MEMBERS IN AFRICA	INSTITUTES OF WOMEN NAME, U.S. CENTER	U.S. MEMBERS IN AFRICA	TOTAL
NORTH and NORTHEAST AFRICA					
ALGERIA	—		White Sisters, Metuchen, N. J.	8	8
ANGLO-EGYPTIAN SUDAN	Sacred Heart Brothers, S.C. New Orleans, La.	3	—		
	Verona Fathers, F.S.C.J. Cincinnati, Ohio	2 / 5			
EGYPT	—		Franciscan Missionary Sisters of Immaculate Conception, Chestnut Hill, Mass.	5	5
TUNISIA	—		White Sisters, Metuchen, N. J.	1	1
SUMMARY FOR NORTH AND NORTHEAST AFRICA		MEN			5
		WOMEN			14 / 19

U.S. Catholic Missionary Personnel In Africa *(continued)*

WEST AFRICA

	Men	Women	Total
GOLD COAST			
Divine Word Fathers, S.V.D., Techny, Ill.	33		
White Fathers, W.F. Washington, D.C.	3		
Holy Child Jesus, Society of the, Rosemont, Pa.		3	
Holy Ghost, Missionary Sisters, Servants of, Techny, Ill.		13	
Medical Mission Sisters Philadelphia, Pa.		4	
	36	20	56
LIBERIA			
African Mission Fathers, S.M.A., Washington, D.C.	3		
Franciscan Missionaries of Mary, North Providence, R.I.		3	
			6
NIGERIA			
Dominicans, O.P. Chicago, Ill.	4		
Holy Child Jesus, Society of the, Rosemont, Pa.		18	
			22
SUMMARY FOR WEST AFRICA	MEN		43
	WOMEN		41
			84

U.S. Catholic Missionary Personnel In Africa (continued)

COUNTRY	INSTITUTES OF MEN NAME, U.S. CENTER	U.S. MEMBERS IN AFRICA	INSTITUTES OF WOMEN NAME, U.S. CENTER	U.S. MEMBERS IN AFRICA	TOTAL
CENTRAL AFRICA					
BELGIAN CONGO			Franciscan Missionaries of Mary, North Providence, R.I.	1	2
	Divine Word Fathers, S.V.D., Techny, Ill.	1			
CENTRAL AFRICA FEDERATION					
NYASALAND			White Sisters, Metuchen, N.J.	2	11
	White Fathers, W.F. Washington, D.C.	3	Wisdom, Daughters of Ozone Park, Long Island, N.Y.	6	
				8	
RHODESIA, NORTHERN	Franciscans, O.F.M. Conv. Mt. St. Francis, Ind.	4	White Sisters, Metuchen, N. J.	1	10
	Franciscans, O.F.M. Conv. Syracuse, N.Y.	2			
	White Fathers, W.F. Washington, D.C.	3			
		9		1	
RHODESIA, SOUTHERN	Mariannhill Fathers, C.M.M. Dearborn, Michigan	1	—		2
	Marist Brothers, F.M.S. Poughkeepsie, N.Y.	1			
		2			

FRENCH CAMEROUN

	MEN	WOMEN
Holy Ghost, Daughters of the, Putnam, Conn.		1
Sacred Hearts, Religious of the Holy Union, Fall River, Mass.		1
Sacred Hearts, Religious of the Holy Union, Groton, Mass.		5
		7
SUMMARY FOR CENTRAL AFRICA	7	15
		17
		32

U.S. Catholic Missionary Personnel In Africa (continued)

COUNTRY	INSTITUTES OF MEN NAME, U.S. CENTER	U.S. MEMBERS IN AFRICA	INSTITUTES OF WOMEN NAME, U.S. CENTER	U.S. MEMBERS IN AFRICA	TOTAL
SOUTH AFRICA					
BASUTOLAND	Oblates of Mary Immaculate O.M.I., Lowell, Mass.	1	Good Shepherd Sisters of Quebec, Saco, Maine	9	
	Sacred Heart Brothers, S.C. Sharon, Mass.	10	Grail, The, Grailville, Loveland, Ohio		
			Holy Names of Jesus & Mary, New York, Oregon, Calif.	2	
		11		7 / 18	29
MOZAMBIQUE	—		Franciscan Missionaries of Mary, N. Providence, R.I.	1	1
SOUTH WEST AFRICA	Oblates of St. Francis de Sales, O.S.F.S., Philadelphia, Pa.	2	—	1	2
SWAZILAND	Servite Fathers, O.S.M. Chicago, Ill.	6	—		6

UNION OF SOUTH AFRICA

Organization	Men
Benedictine Fathers, O.S.B. Newton, N.J.	3
Irish Christian Brothers F.S.C.H., New Rochelle, N.Y.	5
Mariannhill Fathers, C.M.M. Dearborn, Michigan	1
Oblates of Mary Immaculate O.M.I., Buffalo, N.Y.	11
Oblates of St. Francis de Sales, O.S.F.S., Philadelphia, Pa.	6
Paulist Fathers, C.S.P. New York, N.Y.	5
Sacred Heart Fathers, S.C.J., Hales Corners, Wisconsin	6
Servite Fathers, O.S.M. Chicago, Illinois	2
	39

Organization	Women
Franciscan Missionaries of Mary, N. Providence, R.I.	1
Grail, The, Grailville, Loveland, Ohio	5
Precious Blood, Missionary Sisters, Shillington, Pa.	5
Ursuline Nuns (Roman Union), Kirkwood, Mo.	2
Ursuline Nuns (Roman Union), New York, N.Y.	1
	14

		53
SUMMARY FOR SOUTH AFRICA	MEN	58
	WOMEN	33
		91

U.S. Catholic Missionary Personnel In Africa (continued)

COUNTRY	INSTITUTES OF MEN NAME, U.S. CENTER	U.S. MEMBERS IN AFRICA	INSTITUTES OF WOMEN NAME, U.S. CENTER	U.S. MEMBERS IN AFRICA	TOTAL
EAST AFRICA					
KENYA	Sacred Heart Brothers, S.C. New Orleans, La.	5	White Sisters, Metuchen, N.J.	4	
	Maryknoll Fathers, M.M. Maryknoll, N.Y.	1			
		6		4	10
TANGANYIKA	Benedictine Fathers, O.S.B. Newton, N.J.	5	Maryknoll Sisters, Maryknoll, N.Y.	9	
	Holy Ghost Fathers, C.S.P. Washington, D.C.	47	White Sisters, Metuchen, N.J.	2	
	Maryknoll Fathers, M.M. Maryknoll, N.Y.	29			
	White Fathers, W.F. Washington, D.C.	4			
		85		11	96
UGANDA	La Mennais Brothers, F.I.C. Alfred, Maine	8	Franciscan Missionary Sisters of Africa, Brighton, Mass.	2	
	Sacred Heart Brothers, S.C. New Orleans, La.	11	Grail, The, Grailville, Loveland, Ohio	4	
	White Fathers, W.F. Washington, D.C.	3	White Sisters, Metuchen, N.J.	4	
	Xaverian Brothers, C.F.X. Baltimore, Md.	5			
		27		10	37
	SUMMARY FOR EAST AFRICA			MEN	118
				WOMEN	25

U.S. Catholic Missionary Personnel In Africa (continued)

INSULAR EAST AFRICA				
MADAGASCAR	La Salette Missionaries, MS., Bloomfield, Conn.	3		
	La Salette Missioners, M.S. East Brewster, Mass.	1		
		4		4
MAURITIUS	Maryknoll Sisters, Maryknoll, N.Y.		4	4
SEYCHELLES	La Mennais Brothers Alfred, Maine	2		2
SUMMARY FOR INSULAR EAST AFRICA			MEN	6
			WOMEN	4
				10
SUMMARY FOR AFRICA			MEN	245
			WOMEN	134
				379

SOURCE:

U. S. Catholic Missionary Personnel Overseas, December 31, 1953. Mission Secretariat, Washington, D. C.

FOOTNOTES

Section 1—WEST AFRICA

CHAPTER 1

1. Delavignette, *Freedom and Authority in French West Africa,* Oxford, 1950, p. 115.
2. *Africa Is Here,* Report of the North American Assembly on African Affairs, National Council of the Churches of Christ in the U.S.A., 1952, p. 65.
3. Delavignette, *op. cit.,* p. 51.

CHAPTER 2

1. Hardy, *Un Apotre d'Aujourd'hui, Le Reverend Pere Aupiais,* Larousse, Paris, 1949.
2. For a biography of Bishop Steinmetz, see Hazoume, *Cinquante Ans d'Apostolat,* Lyon, Procure des Miss. Africaines, 1950.
3. Martin J. Bane, S.M.A., *The Catholic Story of Liberia,* McMullen, 1950.
4. Homan, *Star of Jacob,* McKay, New York, 1953.
5. Donald Atwater, *The White Fathers in Africa,* Burns, Oates & Washbourne, London, 1937.
6. *Afrique Nouvelle,* Dakar, November 11, 1953.

CHAPTER 3

1. Toynbee, *Civilization on Trial,* Oxford University Press, New York, 1948, p. 85.
2. Delavignette, *Freedom and Authority in French West Africa,* London, Oxford, 1950, p. 102.
3. Delavignette, *op. cit.,* p. 105.
4. Emory Ross, *African Heritage,* Friendship Press, New York, 1952, p. 13.
5. *Comite d'etudes historiques et scientifiques de l'A.O.F.,* Bulletin 3, 1937.

373

CHAPTER 4

1. *Most of the World,* Columbia University Press, New York, 1949, p. 342.
2. Bourret, *The Gold Coast,* Stanford University Press, 1949, p. 81.

CHAPTER 6

1. Lugard, *The Dual Mandate in British Tropical Africa,* Edinburgh, Blackwood, 1922.
2. G. Parrinder in *African Ideas of God,* London, Edinburgh House, 1950.
3. Williams, *Africa's God,* Boston College Press, Chestnut Hill, Mass., 1936-38.
4. Parrinder, *Religion in an African City,* London, Oxford University, 1953.
5. *World Christian Handbook,* World Dominion Press, London, 1949, p. 192.
6. Jordan, *Bishop Shanahan of Southern Nigeria,* Clonmore & Reynolds, Ltd., Dublin, 1949.

CHAPTER 7

1. *Transactions of the Royal Society of Tropical Medicine and Hygiene,* Vol. 44, pp. 271-290, 1950-1951.

Section 2—CENTRAL AFRICA

CHAPTER 1

1. De Vaulx, *Histoire des Missions Catholiques Francaises,* Fayard, Paris, 1951, p. 436.
2. De Vaulx, *op. cit.,* p. 437.
3. For more detail, see Briault, *Sur les Pistes de l'A.E.F.,* Paris, Editions Alsatia, 1945.
4. De Vaulx, *op. cit.,* p. 464.

CHAPTER 2

1. Soeur Marie-Andre, *La Femme Noire en Afrique Occidentale,* Paris, 1935. Soeur Marie-Andre, "Woman's Indignity in Africa," *Worldmission,* Fall 1953. Soeur Marie-Andre, *La Condition Humaine en Afrique Noire,* Paris, Bernard Grosset, 1952.
2. Paternot, "Polygamy, West African Plague," *Worldmission,* Winter 1952, p. 487.

3. *Encyclopedie de l'Afrique Francaise,* 1950, p. 101.
4. Trowell, *The Passing of Polygamy, Oxford University Press,* 1940.

CHAPTER 3

1. *L'Eglise au Congo et au Ruanda-Urundi,* Editions Grand Lacs, Brussels, 1950. de Schaetzen, C.I.C.M., *Origine des Missions Belges au Congo,* Brussels, Missions de Scheut, 1937, p. 11.
2. Comhaire, *Aspects of Urban Administration in Tropical and Southern Africa,* University of Cape Town, 1953.

CHAPTER 5

1. For an interesting sociological study of native life in Leopoldville, see Comhaire-Sylvain, *Food and Leisure Among the African Youth of Leopoldville,* University of Cape Town, 1950.

CHAPTER 6

1. *La Mission Sacree de Civilization,* Belgian Government Information Center, New York, 1953.
2. Wigny, *A Ten-Year Plan for the Economic and Social Development of the Belgian Congo,* Belgian Government Information Center, New York, 1950, p. 29.

CHAPTER 7

1. *Problemes d'Afrique Centrale,* Belgian Colonial University, Brussels, 1953, No. 19.
2. Tempels, *La Philosophie Bantoue,* Presence Africaine, Paris, 1949.
3. Tempels, *op. cit.,* p. 25.
4. Tempels, *op. cit.,* p. 111.
5. Hardy, *L'Art Negre,* Laurens, Paris, 1927, p. 159.
6. Kochnitzky, *Negro Art in Belgian Congo,* Belgian Government Information Center, New York, 1952, p. 11.
7. Menjaud, "Art indigene et Liturgie," in *Le Monde Colonial Illustre,* No. 162, 1937.
8. Costantini, *L'Arte Cristiana nelle Missioni,* Vatican Press, Rome, 1940; French edition, Desclee, Paris, 1949.
9. *The Arts in Belgian Congo and Ruanda-Urundi,* Belgian Information and Documentation Center, Brussels, 1950, p. 81.
10. *L'Artizan et les Arts Liturgiques,* St. Andre-lez-Bruges, Belgium, No. 4, 1949, p. 383.

11. Kochnitzky, *op. cit.,* p. 43.
12. Smith, *African Ideas of God,* p. 240.

CHAPTER 8

1. Delmas, *Genealogies de la Noblesse de Ruanda,* Mission Press, Kabgaye, 1951, p. 149.

CHAPTER 9

1. Schimlek, C.M.M., "Rhodesia," *Umafrika,* Mariannhill, June 6, 1953, *et seq.*

Section 3—SOUTH AFRICA

CHAPTER 1

1. Millin, *The People of South Africa,* Central News Agency, Johannesburg, 1951, p. 13.
2. *World Christian Handbook,* World Dominion Press, London, 1949, p. 210.
3. Brady, "History of the Church in South Africa," pp. 114-122 in *The Catholic Church and Southern Africa,* Cape Town, 1951.
4. Marquard, *The Peoples and Policies of South Africa,* Oxford University Press, London, 1952, p. 209.

CHAPTER 2

1. For a Biography of Father Huss, see Schimlek, *Against the Stream,* Mariannhill Press, 1949.
2. Millin, *op. cit.,* p. 261.

CHAPTER 4

1. The pound is worth $2.80 U.S.
2. For a study on this, see the article, "Urban Areas," by Ellen Hellmann, Chairman, Johannesburg Joint Council of Europeans and Africans, in *Handbook on Race Relations in South Africa,* Oxford University Press, 1949, p. 229.

CHAPTER 6

1. Wells, *South Africa,* Dent, London, 1939, p. 230.

*Section 4—*EAST AFRICA

CHAPTER 1

1. Huxley, *The Sorcerer's Apprentice,* Chatto and Windus, London, 1951, p. 285.

CHAPTER 2

1. Oliver, *The Missionary Factor in East Africa,* Longmans, London, 1952, p. 41.
2. Thoonen, *Black Martyrs,* Burns, Oates and Washbourne, London, 1941.
3. Bazin, "Monseigneur Henri Streicher," *Grand Lacs,* April, 1953.

CHAPTER 3

1. *World Distribution of Leprosy,* American Geographic Society, New York, 1953.
2. Cochrane, "Leprosy a New Era and a Fresh Challenge," *International Review of Missions,* Oct. 1953, p. 430.
3. Follereau, *Tour du Monde chez les Lepreux,* Paris, Flammarion, 1953, 250 pp.
4. Brown, *A World Survey of Catholic Leprosy Work,* Mission Press, Techny, Ill., 1953.

CHAPTER 6

1. Leakey, *Mau Mau and the Kikuyu,* Methuen, London, 1952.
2. Rev. Sestero Ottavio, "The Story Behind the Mau Mau," *Worldmission,* Spring 1954, page 38.
3. Llewellyn, "The Mau Mau Death in the Dark," *Saturday Evening Post,* May 23, 1953.
4. De la Bedoyere, "From My Window in Fleet Street," *The Catholic World,* January, 1953.

CHAPTER 7

1. *Africans and the Christian Way of Life,* Tanganyika Mission Press, Kipalapala, Tabora P.O., 1953, p. 35.
2. *African Education,* Oxford University Press, 1953.
3. *African Education,* p. 63.

INDEX